Horror Film
Aesthetics

Horror Film Aesthetics

*Creating the Visual
Language of Fear*

THOMAS M. SIPOS

McFarland & Company, Inc., Publishers
Jefferson, North Carolina, and London

LIBRARY OF CONGRESS CATALOGUING-IN-PUBLICATION DATA

Sipos, Thomas M.
Horror film aesthetics : creating the visual
language of fear / Thomas M. Sipos.
p.   cm.
Includes bibliographical references and index.

ISBN 978-0-7864-4972-9
softcover : 50# alkaline paper ∞

1. Horror films — Production and direction.   I. Title.
PN1995.9.H6S485   2010   791.43'6164 — dc22   2010013729

British Library cataloguing data are available

On the cover: Advertising art for the 1978 version of
Invasion of the Body Snatchers (United Artists/Photofest)

Manufactured in the United States of America

*McFarland & Company, Inc., Publishers
Box 611, Jefferson, North Carolina 28640
www.mcfarlandpub.com*

Acknowledgments

I thank these filmmakers for allowing me to interview them about their works in general, and in some cases, answering my technical questions specifically for this book: Christopher Alan Broadstone, Jose Zambrano Cassella, Joe Fontano, Miguel Gallego, C.J. Johnson, Damon Packard, Erasmo P. Romero III, Bill Whirity, Andrew Wiest, and Daniel Zubiate. An additional special thanks to C.J. Johnson for reviewing Chapter 3 on Photography for technical errors; I bear the blame for any that remain. Thanks also to Shriekfest Film Festival founder Denise Gossett for sharing her ideas on the appeal of horror. And thanks to those professionals who've read my online film reviews, and responded by sharing their insights into the making of their films: screenwriters Ed Neumeier (*Starship Troopers*) and Stanford Whitmore (*The Dark*), actor Gary Wallace (*The Jar*), and director Norman J. Warren (*Terror*).

Table of Contents

Preface

The subject of this book, horror film aesthetics, sounds abstract and theoretical, but my intention is to present it from a practical point of view. The text provides analyses of how various cinematic tools — acting, makeup, costuming, set décor, framing, photography, lighting, editing, and sound — have been used in films to effectively (or in some cases, ineffectively) create horror on screen.

Understanding these tools and techniques expands one's understanding of the horror genre — its nature and appeal to viewers — and enhances an appreciation for the full creative potential of film and video equipment. Aspiring filmmakers will often read technical manuals to learn *what* the buttons on their cameras do, without learning how to use those buttons *creatively*. I know this from being a horror film fan, critic, and journalist, and also from screening entries to the Tabloid Witch Awards horror film contest and festival, which I founded in 2004 and continue to manage.

Student and independent filmmakers should find this book useful, but it is also intended for fans of the horror genre. I hope it will enable fans to "see things" in horror films they may have previously missed, and thus gain a deeper appreciation for the genre that leads to greater viewing pleasures. For aspiring horror filmmakers, this book may serve as a kind of guide to using film and video gear *effectively, creatively, aesthetically* in a way that conveys the story and themes in a clear, entertaining, and frightening manner.

The idea for *Horror Film Aesthetics* germinated while I was attending NYU's film school in the early 1980s. I was assigned several books on film aesthetics, but the ones that impressed me most were *Film Art: An Introduction*, by David Bordwell and Kristin Thompson, and *The Cinema as Art*, by Ralph Stephenson and Jean R. Debrix. These books analyzed cinema by its components: framing, photography, sound, etc.

The early 1980s were a Golden Age in horror cinema. When I wasn't watching French films in class, I was watching slashers and Italian zombies in local theaters. Film school cultivated in me a taste for magazines like *American Film* and *Film Comment*, but I also read *Cinemagic* and *Fangoria*. Unfortunately, few *books* on horror films existed back then. The film/TV sections in bookstores were tiny. I suspect it was because most authors couldn't easily obtain films to study, at a time when VCRs were just getting off the ground.

Since the 1980s, there's been an explosion in film books. Even so, aesthetics — especially its practical applications to genre filmmaking — remains a largely unexplored niche. Horror film books written for fans often focus on *history*. The history of a subgenre or cycle, or a national cinema (e.g., J-horror), or some actor or category of actors (e.g., "scream queens"). These books usually emphasize story and theme — what this or that film was about, what it meant, and was it any good. Production histories are also commonplace — what happened "behind the scenes" and how the film was financially or critically received. Academic books likewise concentrate on story and theme (or a film's "narrative" and "reading" as academics prefer to call it). Aesthetics are demoted in favor of "socio-political discourse" and "cultural deconstruction."

This book brings aesthetics to the forefront. I don't much care *what* a horror film is trying to say—politically or thematically—but rather, whether it conveys its message *effectively*. More importantly, does the filmmaker's use of cinematic tools unnerve, frighten, shock, or entertain audiences. We are talking about *horror* aesthetics, after all.

In 1982, I took a class in "The Horror Film" taught by William K. Everson. All we did was listen to his lectures and watch horror movies. There were no tests, just one paper on a related topic of our choosing. My paper, entitled "Horror Film Aesthetics," analyzed the unique ways in which cinematic tools were used in horror films. The paper got an A-. Two or three years later it was published as a three-part article in *The Journal of Horror Cinema*, a photocopied fanzine out of Utah, which lasted eight issues. That paper may be considered the seed from which this book grew.

Since then I continued to watch horror films, take notes, write online reviews, cover horror film festivals other than my own, and write for publications like *Filmfax, Midnight Marquee, Horror, Indie Slate, Sci-Fi Universe*, and *Mondo Cult*. I've worked on the sets of dozens of film and TV productions, from big studio features and sitcoms, to student projects—often as an extra, sometimes as an actor. Yes, like half of Los Angeles, I have a SAG card.

Throughout the text I refer to films by their title and year of release. That's not as simple and straightforward as it sounds. Many horror films are low-budget, independent works, the sort of films that undergo myriad title changes as they pass through different distributors, nations, and media (theatrical, broadcast TV, cable TV, VHS, DVD) with every release and re-release.

How to choose among a film's titles? I first saw *Night of the Zombies* in a theater under that name, and that's its name on my Beta cassette. (I'm talking about the 1980 Italian cannibal zombie film, not the 1981 Nazi zombie film of the same name.) But my DVD copy is called *Hell of the Living Dead*. The Internet Movie Database (www.imdb.com), which some people regard as a standard movie reference guide, lists it as *Virus* (not to be confused with a 1999 film of the same name).

I've used the IMDb as my default standard for titles, making exceptions when it seemed appropriate. Despite the IMDb's preference for *Virus*, I refer to the film as *Hell of the Living Dead* because I assume that most readers will know the film by its currently most prevalent DVD title. Most DVD editions on Amazon.com (another sort of standard) call this film *Hell of the Living Dead*, though some editions call it *Night of the Zombies* or *Zombie Creeping Flesh* (on VHS).

Because many horror films have multiple titles, I sometimes include an "aka." For example, *Hell of the Living Dead* (aka *Apocalipsis caníbal, Inferno dei morti viventi, Virus,* Italian-Spanish 1980). But do you see another problem? Four titles for one film, foreign and domestic. And the IMDb lists *13 titles* for it, not four. Listing every title in such cases strikes me as overkill, so I list only what I consider the more important titles for each film in the text. Some lesser titles are included in the index as cross-references, however, for the convenience of readers who know a film by one of its obscure titles. For example, the index entry for *Toxic Spawn* will direct you to *Contamination*. You won't find *Toxic Spawn* in the text, not even as an "aka." *Contamination*'s section mentions only *Alien Contamination* as an alternative title. Just know that if the index directs you from *Toxic Spawn* to *Contamination*, it's because the former is also known as the latter. There is method to my madness. The text calls the film *Contamination* because that's what its most recent DVD release and the IMDb call it. The text notes that it is also known as *Alien Contamination* because that's what my DVD, purchased a year earlier, calls it. The index includes *Toxic Spawn* because that's what my VHS box calls it, and some readers may still own it under that title.

Determining a film's year of release is another judgment call. It's not uncommon for a low-budget indie film to be released years after completion. Its print may list one year, the VHS and DVD boxes may list other years, Amazon.com may list yet another year, and the IMDb yet another. Every DVD and VHS edition on Amazon says *Hell of the Living Dead* is a 1984 film. Yet the IMDb has it as 1980. Likewise, Amazon twice lists *Contamination* as a 1982 film, and once as 1980. The IMDb says 1980.

Again, I used the IMDb as my default standard, but the IMDb is hardly infallible. I know a director/producer who completed shooting and editing his film in 2006. He registered his film's year of release on IMDb as 2007 because he wanted his film to look as new as possible. Distributors like new stuff. The film played some festivals but failed to find distribution. So this producer changed his IMDb listing to 2008. His rationale was that he'd recut the film, so it was really a different film. In 2009, he "recut" it again but was unable to change his listing to 2009. All he could do was insert "(2009 cut)" next to the "Runtime." It was his attempt to signal to any distributor who might be checking the IMDb that his film's failure to find distribution up to now should not be held against it because with this "2009 cut," it was a totally new and different film.

I only list a film's alternative title(s) and year of release once per chapter. After that I call that film by one name, whichever I have chosen. But if I refer to that film again in another chapter, I repeat the alternative title(s) and year of release, recognizing that some readers may choose to read chapters out of sequence or individually.

CHAPTER 1

Defining the Genre

Horror is an elusive genre to define. Horror television shows like *The X-Files* are mistaken for science fiction, while suspense and fantasy films are marketed as horror. Publishers categorize books according to the latest popular trend, so that a horror novel may be sold as dark fantasy, urban fantasy, suspense, or whatever sells best. Non-fans perceive horror to be its latest heavily promoted cycle. After a spate of slashers and chainsaw massacres, viewers who hate such fare condemn all of horror, forgetting 1950s bug-eyed monsters and 1930s Universal classics. But remind them of *Dracula* and *Frankenstein*, and they remember that they like horror too.

Genre Is Not Style

Film *genres* are usually defined by a set of *story conventions*, which may include plot, character, period, and/or setting. Story conventions spawn a genre's *icons*, such as vampires or spaceships. Genre should not be confused with *style*: the *techniques and manner* whereby the story is told.

Film noir is not a genre, but a filmmaking style characterized by rain-drenched streets, night-for-night photography, low-key lighting, claustrophobic framing and art décor, grimy sets, saxophones in the background music, and artificially heightened dialog. Although noir is usually associated with mystery's hard-boiled subgenre, the noir style has been applied to science fiction (*Blade Runner*, 1982), to horror (*Werewolf*, Fox TV, 1987-88), and even to "a rock & roll fable" (*Streets of Fire*, 1984; a rock and roll story with saxophones).

Noir's only story convention is a fatalism that informs the themes and events in its tales, permeating the characters' attitudes and choices. Yet fatalism can inform many genres and does not by itself qualify noir as a true stand-alone genre.

Horror as an Emotive Genre

Horror is a difficult genre to define and delineate because its parameters are established by different criteria than those of most other genres. Although horror has its own story conventions, horror is an emotive genre, defined by its intent to scare.

Horror presupposes a *threat*, building tension with its promise that something hideous will occur, and there is no escape. *Sleepaway Camp* (1983) opens on an idyllic lakeside setting. It looks to be a family film, but its audience knows better. By their own *genre awareness*, viewers collaborate with the filmmaker to create tension as the speeding motorboat approaches the exposed swimmers. Horror audiences stick their hands into a black box, knowing something will bite, only uncertain as to how and when.

5

Other genres strive to emotionally stir audiences, but only horror and comedy solicit audiences primarily by promising a specific and consistent emotional effect: fear and mirth, respectively. And while other genres depict frightening incidents, only horror spotlights the fearsome, making fear its *raison d'être*.

Horror is difficult to peg because it's an emotive genre, a terrifying blob that absorbs new story conventions from every historical/societal shift. Horror always finds a new scary mask to resonate current concerns, finding the dark side to every wish, whether in outer space or in suburbia.

Horror as an Unnatural Threat

Because fear is a fundamental emotion evoked by many stories, genre and mainstream, one cannot classify as horror any and every tale that frightens an audience or depicts horrific imagery. Such a definition is overly broad. If every film depicting the fearsome or the horrific is of the horror *genre,* then everything from *The Godfather* to *Titanic* is horror. In which case the term loses all meaning, and horror ceases to be a distinct genre.

To differentiate itself, the *horror genre* must dramatize horrific events other than the commonplace, realistic, or historical. It must posit an *unnatural threat* that is outside the realm of normalcy, reality, or history. Defining the "weirdly horrible tale," H.P. Lovecraft wrote: "A certain atmosphere of breathless and unexplainable dread of outer, unknown forces must be present; there must be a hint ... of that most terrible conception of the human brain — a malign and particular *suspension or defeat of the fixed laws of Nature* which are our only safeguard against the assaults of chaos and the daemons of unplumbed space."[1]

Noël Carroll distinguishes the horror genre from horrific reality. The genre "is different from the sort that one expresses in saying 'I am horrified by the prospect of ecological disaster,' or 'Brinksmanship in the age of nuclear arms is horrifying,' or 'What the Nazis did was horrible.'"[2] Carroll terms the latter *natural horror,* and the genre as *art-horror.*

War films evoke fear and horror. Yet war films that naturalistically depict horrifying war images (e.g., *All Quiet on the Western Front,* 1930) are no more horror films than are films about the horrors of poverty, domestic violence, urban crime, or genocide. Only unnatural soldiers qualify for horror, such as the revenant Confederate corpses in *The Super-naturals* (1986), the vampiric Vietnam grunt in *Deathdream* (aka *Dead of Night* 1974), and Nazi zombies (e.g., *Shock Waves,* 1977; *Oasis of the Zombies,* aka *L'Abîme des morts vivants,* 1981; *Night of the Zombies,* 1981; *Zombie Lake,* aka *Le Lac des morts vivants,* 1981).

However, an unnatural threat can only exist in the context of a natural universe. As the bounty hunter Rogan observes in *Werewolf,* a talking flower is terrifying in a world in which flowers do not talk. His remark well defines horror: "When the world isn't the same as our minds believe, then we are in a nightmare."[3] A story in which talking flowers are the accepted norm may make for fantasy, even dark fantasy, but not horror, because such flowers do not *suspend the fixed laws of nature* as understood by any character within that universe. This is why Rogan scoffs at *Alice in Wonderland,* disbelieving that Alice would regard a talking flower with surprise rather than terror.

A horror story requires an unnatural threat, which is to say, in addition to being unnatural, the threat must be a *threat.*

But what of *sympathetic monsters*? What if a fantastical "threat" is sympathetic or desirable? Is it horror if the monster is hero rather than villain?

Carroll writes: "[T]he monsters we find in horror stories are uniformly dangerous or at least appear to be so; when they cease to be threatening, they cease to be horrifying."[4] But increasingly, formerly threatening horror icons are depicted sympathetically. David J. Skal writes: "By the mid–1980s, more people were reading about vampires than at any time in history, and for the first time, they were identifying with them positively."[5]

Is it still horror if the vampire is a hero? Sometimes.

There is no horror story if the unnatural "threat" is *wholly* sympathetic, positive, and desirable, and only mortals and mortal forces are villains. But an unnatural threat may threaten either mortals *or* the creature embodying it. A vampire who despises his condition may make for a horror story, even if he is sympathetic. In TV's *Dark Shadows*, vampirism is horrific, even if Barnabas is not.

Conversely, *Nightbreed* (1990) has no unnatural threats. The fantastical creatures were initially forbidding, yet they were later revealed to be moral and decent, once you got past their "differences." Nor was their condition unnatural or undesirable to themselves; they did not seek a cure. The only threat came from mortals using mortal weapons. Thus *Nightbreed* is dark fantasy rather than horror.

The Craft (1996) also features sympathetic "monsters." Four outcast girls form a coven to take vengeance on the popular crowd in high school. So long as every villain is mortal, and every witch a heroine who enjoys the occult, *The Craft* is not horror. Only when the Craft turns against the heroines, and they turn on each other, does *The Craft* tread (barely) into horror.

The Initiation of Sarah (TVM 1978) depicts a nerdy girl who unleashes unnatural powers upon her campus tormentors. Although Sarah is more sympathetic than *The Craft*'s high school witches, *Sarah* is more assuredly horror because (1) Sarah faces a moral struggle, fearing and rejecting her own unnatural powers early on (and is thus herself threatened by them), (2) a villainous sorority den mother enlists unnatural forces for evil ends, and (3) sympathetic and vulnerable characters are threatened by Sarah's unnatural powers.

A horror story requires *sympathetic* and *vulnerable* potential victims. For a threat to *threaten,* audiences must sense that sympathetic characters (preferably the principals) are at genuine risk of serious harm. Had the audience for *Sleepaway Camp* not sensed that the swimmers were vulnerable to the speeding motorboat, they would have felt no tension as the boat drew near.

A major weakness of many big studio horror films (rarely a fault in low-budget indie or foreign language horror fare) is that audiences correctly sense that the stars are safe from harm (a presumption Hitchcock betrayed to great effect in *Psycho*). An audience's perception of a protagonist's *invulnerability* (he cannot be seriously injured) and *invincibility* (he cannot lose) weakens the horror. *The Frighteners* (1996) is well structured with surprises, yet the audience just *knows* that stars Trini Alvarado and Michael J. Fox will enjoy a happy ending, even if they don't exactly know how. (I had mistakenly guessed that Fox would end up a happy ghost, as in *Ghost.*)

The Invasion (2007) is an especially weak version of Jack Finney's 1954 novel *The Body Snatchers* because (1) It stars Nicole Kidman, a Hollywood A-lister. Hollywood hates harming A-listers. (2) Kidman's character is a successful career woman with an adorable son.

Hollywood loathes injuring such a pair. Thus, when mom and moppet are threatened, it's a weak threat. We correctly sense that Kidman has all the moxie, spunk, smarts, sass, pluck, and strength needed to save her son and the planet. No matter how dire their situation, mom and moppet will triumph.

By contrast, the far superior *Invasion of the Body Snatchers* (1978) stars B-lister Brooke Adams. Alien spores prefer bullying B-listers. Furthermore, Adams's character is childless. She can't make viewers feel all warm and fuzzy with gooey displays of maternal love. Kidman does. So does JoBeth Williams in *Poltergeist* (1982), and Naomi Watts in *The Ring* (2002), and Julianne Moore in *The Forgotten* (2004). But Adams has no moppet to tug our heartstrings.

No fuzzy feeling for us? Off with her head!

To be precise, Kidman is not empowered by her son. She is empowered by her ability to make audiences feel warm and fuzzy through her son. Minor characters can breed all they want, it won't save them. Audiences don't care, so big studios don't care.

Some may argue that *Invasion of the Body Snatcher*'s real star was Donald Sutherland, and he was A-list. True. But he's a guy, and his character was childless. An A-list childless man is far more vulnerable than an A-list mother.

The Craft fails as horror partially because its heroine witches are ever strong, confident, and sassy. Even when the Craft turns against them, audiences *know* the heroines will triumph. Conversely, throughout *Carrie* (1976) and *The Initiation of Sarah,* Carrie and Sarah remain insecure, threatened, and vulnerable. Both seem unable to handle either the school bullies, or their own unnatural powers. This heightens the horror.

Over the past decade, studio horror films have been somewhat more willing to threaten their protagonists. This may partially be because modern studio directors were raised on 1970s and 1980s low-budget indie horror, inspiring such films as Universal's *House of 1000 Corpses* (2003). Even so, the rule stands: the more famous the actor (at the time of filming), the less likely he is to die. Especially if that actor is an actress. Or a child. Winona Ryder survived *Lost Souls* (2000), though Ben Chaplin did not. Naomi Watts and her son survived *The Ring*, unlike Martin Henderson. Both Halle Berry and Robert Downey Jr. survived *Gothika* (2003). Both Richard Gere and Laura Linney survived *The Mothman Prophecies* (2002). Conversely, the lesser known faces in the *Final Destination, Jeepers Creepers*, and *Saw* series provided for generous and quickly-mounting body counts.

Hollywood studios are ever tempted to dilute the horror. Compare the Hong Kong version of *The Eye* (aka *Gin gwai*, 2002) with the 2008 American remake. In both films a young woman, blind from early childhood, regains her sight. She then sees ghosts, "grim reapers," and flashbacks. Both films end with the woman stuck in a traffic jam, whereupon she sees dozens of "grim reapers" passing amid the cars, signaling that a catastrophe is soon to occur. She rushes out amid the vehicles, banging on windows, trying desperately to warn people to abandon their cars and escape.

Here the similarities end. In the Hong Kong version, everyone ignores Mun, thinking she's crazy. An overturned tanker truck explodes, its flames engulfing dozens of vehicles, killing perhaps a hundred people. Even babies. No one is rescued. No, not a one. Only Mun and her boyfriend survive, and that through some quirk of fate.

Compare this to the American version, wherein everyone heeds Sydney. She not only convinces everyone to head for the hills, but upon seeing a little girl trapped in a trailer,

Sydney breaks open the window and rescues the shrieking moppet. The tanker explodes, its flames engulfing all cars, but no one dies. No, not a one.

The American *The Eye* demonstrates two of Hollywood's weaknesses when it comes to horror: (1) an aversion to killing cute moppets, especially in gruesome fashion, and (2) a desire to elevate its stars to hero status. There is no way Hollywood would allow star Jessica Alba to be defeated. She not only succeeds in warning everyone, she even saves a moppet in heroic, 9/11 firefighter fashion. By contrast, star Sarah Michelle Gellar was defeated in the American remake of *The Grudge* (2004), perhaps because it was directed by the series's original Japanese director, Takashi Shimizu.

Both the Hong Kong and American versions of *The Eye* end with a mix of sadness and joy. In both films, the fire reclaims the woman's sight. Yet in both films, she also finds true love. However, Sydney's blindness is not in vain. Her sacrifice saved dozens of lives. Mun's gains are more modest. By failing to save lives, she gains insight into the nature of life, and understanding for her cornea donor. In Buddhist fashion, Mun learns to accept her fate. In the American way, Sydney makes her own fate. The Hong Kong film is more fatalistic. The American film more "feel good."

Hollywood loves "feel good." Horror prefers fatalism. Low-budget indie films are more likely to deliver. In *Superstition* (1982), a young boy (a major character), dies midway into the film. Mom opens the door, and her son's body drops down, arms dangling—a traditional way for people to stumble across stiffs in 1980s horror fare. In *Mimic* (1997), giant insects masticate two young boys, both well-established characters. These deaths heighten the horror. If a director will slaughter personable children, are *any* of the characters safe?

Horror Is a Fictive Genre

Because horror requires an *unnatural* threat, it follows that there is no such thing as "nonfiction horror" (unless one means critical reviews of horror fiction, films, artwork, etc.). Horror is a fictive genre, like fantasy and science *fiction*.

Yet some writers of supernatural books (those purporting to investigate "true" hauntings, UFO sightings, lake monsters, etc.), sometimes call their books "nonfiction horror." This may be an advantageous marketing label, or necessary to qualify for a "nonfiction horror" book award. Nevertheless, while these books may qualify as supernatural, occult, New Age, or whatever else, they are not horror.

Moral Avengers as Threats in Horror Anthologies

While Britain's *Dead of Night* (1945) pioneered the horror anthology film, many of those that followed also drew inspiration from EC Comic's *Tales from the Crypt*, whose aesthetic criteria included brevity, gore, black humor, and moral irony. This moral irony derives from the unnatural threat acting as moral avenger: a monster setting the world right. In a typical storyline, a corpse arises to kill his murderer.

Despite the corpse's "moral" mission, these EC-inspired horror anthology films may be regarded as horror because (1) the corpse is often as unsympathetic as his victim, (2) unlike some romantic vampires or feminist witches, these corpses suffer an undesirable existence due to their unnaturalness, and (3) audiences identify with the victim; they cringe at his gory demise, even if they enjoy his comeuppance. Audiences empathize, even if they do not sympathize.

In *Creepshow*'s "Father's Day" (1982), the revenant corpse was a domineering tyrant in life, as unsympathetic as his worthless heirs and victims. Plus, he's putrefying, and audiences rarely sympathize with ugly, rancid creatures. Likewise, though audiences may enjoy Wilma's comeuppance in "The Crate," the avenging monster is not pure of heart—he kills good folk too.

However, because horror anthologies have long functioned as morality plays, they are ever in danger of sympathizing too much with the unnatural, thus weakening its threat to a point of non-horror. In *Grim Prairie Tales* (1990), an irascible old white man desecrates an Indian burial ground by riding through it, mocking a dying old Indian in passing. As his comeuppance, he is buried alive. The tale ends with Indian children playing on his grave. But because these Indians are not evil or repugnant (unlike the monsters in *Creepshow*), this tale is less horror than a "revenge film" such as *Death Wish* or *Billy Jack* (revenge fantasies of the political Right and Left, respectively). Indeed, the sublime spirituality of the Indians' retribution evokes Yahweh's vengeance on the Egyptians in *The Ten Commandments*.

Horror's Three Subgenres

While a genre may be subdivided by various criteria, it's practical to partition horror by its threats. This is appropriate because every horror film requires a threat.

All of horror's unnatural threats fall under one of three categories: the supernatural, the monsters of nature and science (horror/Sci-Fi), and the human psyche's dark side (horror psycho). Skal writes: "With *Dracula, Frankenstein,* and *Dr. Jekyll and Mr. Hyde,* the psychic landscapes of castle, crypt, and laboratory were definitively mapped."[6] Skal doesn't label his threats, yet they are supernatural, horror/sci-fi, and the horror psycho. Yes, Jekyll uses science to transmute into Hyde, so he is monster rather than psycho. But Hyde remains a human, albeit purely evil. He can pass for a psycho in a pinch.

Supernatural Horror and Dark Fantasy

In *supernatural horror* the threat is mystical, lacking a rational, materialist explanation. Traditionally this has included vampires, ghosts, werewolves, witches, and demons.

Supernatural horror is often confused with *fantasy*. To distinguish, recall that in horror the fantastical element must be (1) unnatural to its universe, and (2) threatening. Is it a good ghost, or a bloodcurdling ghost? *Ghost Story* (1981) is supernatural horror. From its opening it promises to frighten. It has romance, but a romance secondary to horror. Conversely, *Ghost* (1990), while occasionally jolting its audience, is a romantic fantasy. *The Frighteners* is more problematic. Its storyline and playful supernatural milieu resemble that of *Ghost,* yet its more threatening supernatural villain pushes *Frighteners* toward horror.

Causing further confusion is the term *dark fantasy*. Dark fantasy is not a genre, but a subgenre of fantasy, being fantasy that's ... dark. Some horror writers inaccurately use the term to distinguish their works from slasher stories. Yet what they're usually writing is not dark fantasy, but supernatural horror. This is because regardless of how unnatural the threat, if the setting is an identifiable naturalistic universe, the story is horror.

The creatures in *Nightbreed* first appeared to be monsters threatening our natural world. But they were later revealed to be "nice monsters," inhabiting an alternate world that was natural to them, and non-threatening, even hospitable, to mortal visitors. Hence, *Nightbreed* is dark fantasy, not horror.

Horror Witch vs. Wiccan Witch

Wiccans have complained over the years that horror misrepresents witches. Wiccans insist that "real witches" are cute and cuddly, not evil or threatening. Wiccans want horror to portray witches as nice people.

These Wiccans miss the point. Horror is a fictive genre, one that recasts natural or historical elements into unnatural and threatening forms. It is silly and inappropriate to expect horror to depict the world with documentary accuracy. To complain that horror misrepresents witches is like complaining that Victor Frankenstein misrepresents the scientists at NASA's Jet Propulsion Laboratory. It may be true, but so what?

Warm and friendly witches more properly belong to fantasy than to horror (though even *The Wizard of Oz*, a fantasy, had some bad witches). Real life has many kinds of self-styled witches. Wiccan witches, and Satanic witches, and witches of every pagan subculture.[7]

The Horror Witch is none of these. She belongs to the genre, not to the real world. The Horror Witch and Mad Scientist are horror icons. They exist only in fiction, she with her black peaked hat, bubbling cauldron, and wicked cackle; he with his unkempt hair, bubbling test tubes, and megalomaniacal outbursts. And if they distort the images of their real-life counterparts, well, that is their job.

Horror/Sci-Fi

Horror stories about the monsters of nature and science, I term *horror/sci-fi* (a subgenre of horror, and not of science fiction). I use the term "monster" broadly, encompassing space aliens, Frankenstein's monster, mad computers, plagues, swamp creatures, any unnatural threat begat by nature or science. Note that a creature may be born of nature, yet still be contrary to Nature (i.e., the natural order), hence unnatural. Mutants and monsters are often referred to as "crimes against Nature."

Horror/sci-fi monsters have a materialist nature and a scientific rationale. Yet these monsters are an unnatural threat because, despite the rationale explaining their existence, they are either newly discovered or newly created. They are unnatural to our previous understanding of the universe. As with Rogan's talking flower, they reveal that the world is not as our minds believe.

Horror/Sci-Fi vs. Science Fiction

Science fiction is an intellectual genre, speculating about future technologies and their societal effect. Horror is an emotive genre, merely using sf icons for its own ends. Rather than speculate about the societal effect of space travel, horror drools over exploding astronaut heads.

Horror/sci-fi films include *Alien* (1979), *Galaxy of Terror* (1981), *Inseminoid* (aka *Horror Planet*, British 1981), *Forbidden World* (1982), and *Creature* (1985). All these films depict futurist space travel, as do *2001: A Space Odyssey* (1968) and *Star Wars* (1977). But their aesthetic goals and emphases differ.

2001's HAL 9000 computer is scary, but *2001*'s emphasis is on examining technology's influence on human history and human nature, and on our place in the cosmos. HAL's dramatic purpose is to stimulate such speculation, thus *2001* is science fiction. Conversely, while the drooling aliens in the above horror/sci-fi films may inspire speculation about human greed, hubris, or whatever else motivates astronauts in space (where no one can hear you scream), their dramatic purpose is to shock and frighten audiences by butchering hapless astronauts in darkened corridors or caverns.

Darth Vader's genocidal destruction of an entire planet may qualify *Star Wars* as one of the most violent films ever made. Yet despite its violence, *Star Wars* is a science fantasy/space opera (science fantasy being a subgenre of fantasy that uses sf icons without any serious attempt at scientific plausibility, as in Ray Bradbury's poetic *The Martian Chronicles*). *Star Wars* is not horror because (1) the Death Star's threat is a *natural* phenomenon in that galaxy's escalating arms race, (2) the violence is fantasy violence; death is distant and quick, not graphic and gory, and (3) audiences empathize with the pretty princess rather than with her extinct people. Horror must threaten, but audiences know that Princess Leia is safe, just as they knew the swimmers in *Sleepaway Camp* were not.

Most *Frankenstein* films are horror/sci-fi, but Mary Shelley's novel is more problematic. Its serious speculations on the ethics of science are endemic to science fiction. Yet Shelley's answer — some things Man was not meant to know — is anathema to classic sf. Her answer is horror's answer. Furthermore, her cursory description of Frankenstein's technology, the references to Paracelsus's alchemy, the monster's spiritual turmoil, and Frankenstein's physical, psychological, and spiritual anguish, all suggest *Frankenstein* is horror rather than sf.[8]

Science Fiction's False Claim to Horror Monsters

Some scholars claim horror monsters for science fiction. Per Schelde justifies this by first divorcing sf literature from sf film — abandoning speculation to literature and redefining sf film as what sounds suspiciously like horror.

Schelde writes: "[D]espite appearances, sf movies and sf literature have little in common and appeal to very different audiences. Science fiction literature is, at its best, not afraid of experiments, of intellectual speculation.... Sf movies are a very different kettle of fish: the closest relatives of the genre are the horror movie and the action/suspense movie.... Sf movies assiduously (with a few exceptions) avoid being intellectual and speculative. The focus is not the 'what if's' of science, technology, and the future. The sf film focus is on the *effects* of science, on the junction where what science has created (usually a monster) meets people going about living their lives. Sf science does not have to be logical. All that is required is a scary monster. How the monster came to be or where it came from is, if not irrelevant, peripheral."[9]

But if you redefine a film genre's sole requirement as having a scary monster, then you're describing horror. Especially if the science doesn't need to be logical so long as the monster is scary. So why not just call it horror?

Patrick Lucanio argues that 1950s "alien invasion" films are science fiction rather than horror, because sf seeks to instill in audiences a *sense of wonder*. He writes: "This connection between the notion of wonder and mystery and the science fiction film is most pronounced in films that take their audiences to other worlds."[10] He cites *2001* and *Star Wars* as examples, but then continues: "Although such matters as aspiration and wonder may be obscure when exploring the alien invasion film, this type of film nevertheless is rich with similar insights into the human condition.... The alien invasion film depicts humanity at the mercy of either malevolent or benign rational (albeit alien) forces."[11]

Lucanio is correct in that a *sense of wonder* is an aesthetic goal of sf, but he is wrong to claim it exclusively for sf. Horror too has its *sense of wonder* stories. So long as God and death and afterlife remain mysteries, we mortals will wonder, hope, and fear. In *Contact* (1997), Eleanor asked the aliens: "How did you survive your nuclear age?"—a trivial, but typically sf question. Horror's mad scientists think bigger. They ask: "Is there a God and what happens when we die?" Asked this in an *Outer Limits* TV episode, the dying alien replied: "Unknown." (Yes, the original *Outer Limits* is horror, not sf.) Additionally, if aliens are sufficiently malevolent, as in Lucanio's examples, they are horror aliens.

Lucanio further errs in focusing on the monster's origin instead of its intent. (Does it come in peace, or to steal our women?) Any monster with a rational explanation for its existence, Lucanio claims for science fiction. His broad criterion of having a "rational explanation" sweeps many monsters into his "alien invasion" sf subgenre. Lucanio writes that "James Whale's *Frankenstein*, Rouben Mamoulian's *Dr. Jekyll and Mr. Hyde*, and Ernest B. Schoedsack's *Dr. Cyclops*—all ... are best seen as alien invasion films."[12] So too giant insects, such as *Tarantula* (1955).[13]

Lucanio offers "proof" that *Invasion of the Body Snatchers, Attack of the Fifty Foot Woman, Killers from Space,* and *Tarantula* are sf by citing trailers: "Science Fiction Reaches A New High In Terror!" and "Science Fiction's Most Terrifying Thrill!"[14] Yes, the trailers say "Science Fiction," but their promise of "Terror" suggests the films are really horror. Furthermore, a poster for three of Lucanio's "science fiction" films — *The Spider, Beast with a Million Eyes,* and *Night of the Blood Beast*—explicitly screams: "3 HORROR HITS!"[15]

After such broad claims for science fiction, Lucanio necessarily defines horror narrowly, limiting it to the exotic: "The most important characteristic of the horror film is its emphasis on an alternate state of the actual world.... [I]ts exotic settings and characters ... the use of one without the other does not produce the horror film. Transylvania is perhaps the quintessential setting of the horror film."[16]

That excludes much, and Lucanio knows it. He robs horror of all non-supernatural films. "By the term *horror film* I mean *Gothic film*. This term distinguishes those films that have historically been molded out of supernatural stories ... from films dealing with slaughter and gore, the so-called 'mad-slasher' films. To my thinking such films as Hitchcock's *Psycho* and John Carpenter's *Halloween* are 'thrillers' and not horror movies in the traditional sense."[17]

But the proper question is not *Is it horror in the traditional sense?* but *Is it horror?* To Lucanio's way of thinking, horror is a very narrow and static genre.

But there's still less. Lucanio then excludes all supernatural films set in contemporary time and space. "A vampire prowling the streets of contemporary Los Angeles, as in Bob Kelljan's *Count Yorga—Vampire* (1970), or Dracula himself stalking London's 'miniskirt girls' in Alan Gibson's Hammer production, *Dracula A.D. 1972,* strains to the point of farce or satire the willing suspension of disbelief so crucial to the traditional horror tale."[18] By such stringent criteria *Rosemary's Baby* is not horror, though inexplicably, Lucanio cedes *The Exorcist* to horror.[19]

Generally, what Lucanio labels as "alien invasion" films, I term horror/sci-fi. But do these monsters belong to science fiction or horror?

Lucanio disputes critics who categorize films by their intent to frighten: "[T]he tradition of horror and science fiction criticism, a tradition that ignores the difference between them, is based on a Freudian dogma concerning the depiction of our repressed fears and desires. When the alien invasion film is discussed ... it is discussed in terms of the horror genre."[20]

Well, that's because malevolent aliens, being both unnatural and threatening, are indeed horrifying. Lucanio mistakenly ignores both genres' intended audience reaction: science fiction being an intellectual genre aiming to provoke speculation; horror being an emotive genre aiming to evoke fear. Both genres occasionally evoke a sense of wonder, so that's not determinative.

Cinematic Horror vs. Literary Science Fiction

Schelde, Lucanio, and the critics Lucanio disputes, all of them, implicitly or explicitly, judge sf literature and sf films by different criteria. Sf literature is settled, but as a film genre, sf must be tortuously redefined, lest many "sf films" be exposed as horror.

This highlights a key point: *Horror is primarily a cinematic genre, whereas science fiction is primarily literary.*

As a genre of ideas, sf is best expressed in print, a medium favorable to analyzing complex scientific or sociological concepts. But scripts do not permit lectures. TV writer Carleton Eastlake observes: "[I]n the majority of feature films, science fiction is largely used to provide a little flavor for the icing on what is basically your same old action-adventure, guy-with-a-very-big-gun cake."[21]

True, but then Eastlake continues: "Television, oddly enough, often does better: *Babylon 5* has miraculously risen to the level of good science fiction, and depending on your taste, the many faces of *Star Trek* are often creditable, as is *The X-Files.*"[22]

Here I disagree. My point isn't that authentic science fiction rarely makes it to the screen, but that when it does, it isn't very good. Horror *works* onscreen (big or small), whereas science fiction does not. The best "science fiction" TV shows are all horror, whereas true science fiction shows are usually dreary. Disregard horror shows like *The X-Files,* and science fiction is left with *Star Trek*'s somnolent pontificating.

This is not to say that horror is incapable of meaningful intellectual speculation in print form (e.g., Mary Shelley and William Peter Blatty's spiritual ruminations). But being an emotive genre, horror doesn't require long speeches. As in *The X-Files,* dark suggestions suffice.

Horror not only suffices on sparse suggestions, it thrives. Lovecraft recognized the power of implicit threats,[23] and cinema's sound-bite dialog is enough talk for horror. Lighting, special effects, acting, and music can create an eerie atmosphere in a way that words alone cannot. And if a horror artist elects shocks over suggestion, as some splatter stylists prefer, cinema delivers a bigger punch than text.

Supernatural Horror vs. Horror/Sci-Fi

At times it's difficult to distinguish supernatural horror from horror/sci-fi. The characters in *The Haunting* (1963) rationalize Hill House's malevolent influence, prattling off architectural and psychological explanations. But they are whistling in the dark. In the end, they discard their scientific rationales, and accept that the hauntings are supernatural (thereby confirming that the film is supernatural horror).

In *Bram Stoker's Dracula* (1992), a prince becomes a vampire by affirming Satan, so he is a supernatural vampire. But germs create the vampires in Richard Matheson's novel, *I Am Legend,* thus they are horror/sci-fi monsters. Likewise, a scientific rationale is retained by films based on, or inspired by, the novel (e.g., *The Last Man on Earth,* 1964; *The Omega Man,* 1971; *Night of the Living Dead,* 1968).

Some vampires straddle these two horror subgenres. In TV's *Dark Shadows,* Angelique, a Satanic witch, cursed Barnabas Collins into becoming a vampire. But Barnabas's vampirism was treatable through the scientific efforts of Drs. Julia Hoffman and Eric Lang.

TV's *The X-Files* often grafts scientific explanations onto supernatural threats, but not so plausibly as to always convince us a threat was material rather than mystical. Never before have horror's seams between science and the supernatural been so hard to discern. *Dark Shadows*'s Timothy Stokes raised Angelique from the dead through a blend of science and sorcery, yet we saw the test tubes apart from the pentacles. Not so in *The X-Files,* which is the show's appeal.

But while an occasional episode's subgenre may be difficult to peg, *The X-Files* is always horror, never science fiction. This is because an *X-Files* without science is conceivable, but an *X-Files* without scares is not. The vampire in the episode "3" had no scientific rationale. Nor the psycho in "Irresistible." Yet though "Irresistible" had neither supernatural nor sf elements, *X-Files* creator Chris Carter says of it: "I think it's one of our scarier shows."[24]

Carter cites many influences, such as horror's *Kolchak: The Night Stalker* and spydom's *The Avengers,* but he adds, "I was never what you would call a science fiction devotee ... I've never read the classic science fiction novels, except maybe one of each by Ursula Le Guin and Robert Heinlein a long time ago, and I've never watched an episode of *Star Trek.*"[25]

I offer this general principle: *Whenever a story combines science with the supernatural, allowing for the existence of both, the result may be horror or fantasy, but never science fiction.* Horror can feed on science; science fiction cannot stomach the supernatural. Science fiction either invalidates the supernatural with a plausible and rational explanation, or is subverted by it.

The Problem of Zombies

Zombies, too, blur the line between science and supernatural. The earliest film zombies were products of science seen through native superstition. Narcotics and hypnosis produced Legendre's zombie slaves in *White Zombie* (1932), yet this horror/sci-fi film's photography created an eerie ghostly atmosphere, a tradition continued in *I Walked with a Zombie* (1943).

Later zombies shed all ethereal pretense for cannibal appetites in films that rooted them firmly in science. A meteor created the zombies in *Night of the Living Dead.* Chemical warfare gas did so in *Hell of the Living Dead* (aka *Apocalipsis caníbal, Inferno dei morti viventi, Virus*, Italian-Spanish 1980). Even supernatural zombies embraced this new ravenous lifestyle. Satanically empowered zombies displayed an appetite for flesh in *Burial Ground* (aka *Le notti del terrore*, Italian 1981) and *Children Shouldn't Play with Dead Things* (1972).

Children highlights another zombie classification problem: How to delineate between zombies and revenant corpses? Are the risen corpses in *Children* zombies simply because of their cannibalism? The earliest film zombies had scientific rationales for their condition, while revenant corpses are rooted in the supernatural, finding modern expression in EC Comics and horror anthology films. Unlike most modern zombies (voodoo or flesh-eating), revenant corpses possess mental clarity and intent (usually vengeance or Satanic evil, as in Amando de Ossorio's *Blind Dead* film series). Revenant corpses eat no flesh; the supernatural reserves that role for ghouls. Yet the corpses in *Children* want it all: to consume flesh, but with a vengeful and evil mind. A conundrum.

Another classification conundrum: zombies overlap with vampires, as in *Nightmare City* (aka *Incubo sulla città contaminata, City of the Walking Dead*, Italian-Spanish 1980). *City's* zombies, created by a radiation leak, seek not flesh, but blood. Are they blood-drinking zombies? Yet the film's characters refer to them as monsters, superhuman, and *vampires* (at least in the English-language dub). Like vampires, these creatures run rather than shamble, and can think well enough to cut phone lines. Yet, like zombies, they travel in feral packs, seem unconcerned with their survival, and are unaffected by sunlight or other traditional vampire retardants. If they are zombies, then *Nightmare City* brings non-supernatural zombies full circle, returning them to their blood-sucking roots in *I Am Legend*.

Zombies continue to evolve. Initially a creature of Haitian voodoo. Then a shambling, mute, instinctual flesh-eater. But now they think. Talk. Run. Drink blood. They even have love lives. S.G. Browne's satirical novel, *Breathers: A Zombie's Lament*, is told in the first person by a morose, self-deprecating zombie who lives at home with his parents after arising from the grave. The term "revenant corpse" is becoming archaic. Increasingly, all risen corpses are called zombies.

The Horror Psycho as Uberpsycho

In horror's third subgenre the threat is a human, often mentally warped, but unenhanced by science or the supernatural. (Otherwise this human would be a monster of some sort.) But because other genres too have psychos (as does reality), the *horror psycho* must offer *something extra* to distinguish itself from the psychos of mystery, suspense, and the real world.

The classic horror psycho I call the *uberpsycho*, because, though unaided by science or the supernatural, he is an *unnatural* threat. He has a superhuman durability and tenaciousness that sets him beyond mortal control. Indisputably insane (not always true of serial killers in mystery and suspense), the uberpsycho's madness often originates from a physical or emotional trauma resulting in a severe psychic detachment. He feels neither empathy nor pain. He is oblivious to wounds inflicted upon him. What does not kill him makes him strong. He efficiently executes his victims with a skill beyond that of naturalistic psychos.

The uberpsycho (who debuted as Michael Myers in *Halloween*, 1978), is an impersonal force of nature, sometimes evil, sometimes dark avenging angel. In both *The Burn-*

ing (1981) and *Slaughter High* (1986), an innocent suffers extensive burns due to a botched prank, yet despite painful and crippling disfigurement, he leaves the hospital to wreak vengeance upon his former tormentors.

Conversely, the *suspense psycho* of mysteries and suspense stories is dangerous, but no superman. Prick him and he bleeds. Spook him and he runs. And though some people think that the mundane man-next-door is more terrifying because he is next door, his is a different kind of terror. A naturalistic terror that lacks Lovecraft's "suspension or defeat of the fixed laws of Nature." The suspense psychos in *Frenzy* (1972) and *Silence of the Lambs* (1991) are all-too-human. Their neighbors probably described them as friendly, polite, but quiet.

A second unnatural trait shared by many uberpsychos is their enigmatic persona. We rarely learn why they are indestructible. In *Halloween*, Dr. Loomis first explains Myers as "pure evil," ultimately allowing that Myers is the bogeyman. And that is explanation enough.

As with many of horror's threats, uberpsychos are scarier unexplained. Myers grew less interesting as the *Halloween* film series progressed, burdening him with inept and contradictory rationales (sometimes rooted in the supernatural) for his motives and strength. Likewise, *Friday the 13th*'s Jason Voorhees was initially enigmatic, but that film series too progressively layered Jason with ludicrous explanations, such as a lightning bolt sparking his corpse to life. Such irreconcilable rationales pushed the Jason mythos into self-parody.

Horror vs. Mystery vs. Suspense

Because psychos stalk all three genres, the line can blur between horror, mystery, and suspense. Horror psychos can be unnatural, or naturalistic (more on those later). Psychos in mystery and suspense are always naturalistic, and I collectively call them *suspense psychos*.

Apart from their psychos, another way to distinguish these three genres is my *timeline test,* an inexact but useful method. Suspense films often concentrate on events *preceding* a murder (e.g., *Strangers on a Train,* 1951). Horror on the *commission* of the murder. Mystery on events *following* a murder. Suspense films ask: Will X kill Y? Horror audiences already know; they came to watch it happen. Mysteries begin with the corpse, asking: Whodunit?

Suspense probes the minds of cat and mouse. Mystery probes for clues. Horror probes the corpse.

Suspense films reveal their psychos early on, to examine their warped minds.[26] Mysteries conceal their psychos for the sleuth to unmask. Horror too conceals its psychos, but for another reason: to empower them. Hidden, horror psychos remain a dark and enigmatic force of nature.

Horror's attempts at genuine mystery are usually half-hearted and lame. Either the "unseen" killer is obvious to audiences early on (such that they wonder why everyone in the film is so stupid), or the killer is revealed to be someone so unexpected, the choice appears arbitrary. Mystery audiences would feel cheated by such "surprise twist ending" killers. Not so horror fans, who seek a different thrill from horror. They wonder less about the killer's identity, than about *Who will survive and what will be left of them?*

Film distributors often misrepresent films according to the current hot genre. In the early 1980s, horror psychos were hot, so "bait and switch" marketers sold shoddy suspense and thriller films as horror. The skull poster for *Visiting Hours* (Canadian 1982) promised horror, but the film is a feminist revenge thriller in the vein of *Death Wish* and *Dirty Harry* [Figure 1.1].

Compare *Visiting Hours*'s killer, Hawker, with *Halloween*'s Myers. Myers is fearless, potent, enigmatic. Hawker is revealed to audiences early on, his life and lifestyle stripped to all its pathetic boredom, himself exposed as cowardly and weak, fearful of confronting his female victims. Myers is a dark force inspiring awe and terror. Hawker is a craven pervert, inspiring disgust and contempt.

As in *The Frighteners* and *The Craft, Visiting Hours*'s potential horror is diluted by its heroine's invulnerability and invincibility (especially up against a vulnerable naturalistic psycho). When the film opens with TV journalist Deborah Ballin broadcasting her feminist crusade against violent misogynists, audiences correctly sense that Hawker has more to fear than does Ballin. No tension derives from worrying over Ballin's fate, no more than we would fret over Dirty Harry. Rather than evoking fear or suspense, *Visiting Hours* offers thrills derived from its heroine's vigilante vengeance.

Regarding my timeline test, *Visiting Hours* again fails as horror because it concentrates on Ballin's sleuthing rather than on the killings. Yet the film is not a mystery because we know the murderer's identity, even if Ballin does not.

Eyes of a Stranger (1981) is another feminist revenge thriller falsely marketed as horror. TV journalist Jane Harris launches a crusade against a psycho, a weak and craven pervert.

Some feminist revenge films do lean closer to horror than to suspense or thriller, though naturally, they handle the revenge theme differently.[27] In *Demented* (1980), Linda, a rape victim, *becomes* the horror psycho, fearlessly torturing, castrating, and killing her tormentors with easy efficiency, even licking their blood from her knife. She is no uberpsycho (neither enigmatic nor indestructible), yet, like many horror psychos, she is a dark avenging angel, empowered by her pain.

This horror-oriented feminist revenge formula also emerges in *Last House on the Left* (1972) and *I Spit on Your Grave* (aka *Day of the Woman*, 1978). Both were marketed as horror, though neither have psychos, much less horror psychos. *I Spit on Your Grave*'s Jennifer nearly cracks, but only *Demented*'s Linda goes insane.

The Horror Psycho as Apparent Uberpsycho

Some horror psychos are vulnerable rather than indestructible, but because their identity remains hidden, their murders surprising and unpredictable, they create the illusion of being an undying dark force. They resemble uberpsychos because, unseen and enigmatic, neither victims nor viewers are certain of these psychos' strengths or weaknesses.

I term these horror psychos *apparent uberpsychos* because, though they are lucid and articulate (unlike Myers and Jason), their murders resemble the handiwork of an uberpsycho. Apparent uberpsychos appear in *Night School* (1981), *Curtains* (Canadian 1983), *My Bloody Valentine* (1981), *Happy Birthday to Me* (1981), *Splatter University* (1984), and *Pieces* (aka *Mil gritos tiene la noche*, Spanish 1982).

Whereas suspense films reveal their psychos early on, the above horror films depict the killings without revealing the killer. Yet despite the secrecy over the psycho's identity and motives, these films are not mysteries because little screen time is spent seeking the killer. Emphasis is on slaughter, not sleuthing. Victims are either unaware of any nearby slayings,

Figure 1.1—*Visiting Hours*. Looks like horror. But it's not.

or they trust the authorities to handle it. If authorities are investigating, they do most of it offscreen, only dropping by occasionally to interrogate or warn people. To the extent the authorities are involved, they do a poor job. In typical horror film fashion, the psycho's identity is revealed rather than solved.

Horror psychos are empowered by masks. Their faces hidden, every horror psycho is potentially a disfigured uberpsycho.

In *Night School*, Eleanor is a graduate student of anthropology, inspired by her study of primitive tribes to decapitate competing lovers while wearing a black leather motorcycle outfit, complete with helmet and tinted visor. Thus hidden from the audience, Eleanor becomes an unknown dark force, just as easily male or female, attractive or disfigured.

Eleanor's murders make her a serial killer. Her motivation qualifies her as psycho. But it is her dark, masked persona that qualifies her as a horror psycho. When she finally removes her helmet and reveals herself to us, she loses her uberpsycho persona. Even after all her butchery, she appears vulnerable, even sympathetic.

Curtains, too, depicts a series of murders committed by an unseen killer who occasionally wears a mask. But unlike *Night School,* in which an irrelevant police investigation finally corners the wrong suspect, the characters in *Curtains* aren't even aware that a killer is picking them off. There is no investigation, only a final revelation.

Ignorant victims (unaware of a killer among them) are common in horror psycho films. Although anathema to mysteries (because you can't solve a murder unless you're aware of it), this story convention is appropriate to horror. Horror seeks to evoke fear, and psychos are more fearsome if they stalk victims who are too ignorant to even attempt self-protection.

Another story convention in many horror psycho films is that of the police apprehending the wrong suspect *at the film's end*, with no time left for remedy (*Night School*; *Stage Fright*, aka *Nightmares*, Australian 1980; *Intruder*, 1989). Or they mistakenly determine the psycho is dead (*Friday the 13th Part VIII: Jason Takes Manhattan*, 1989), or cured (*Psycho II*, 1983),[28] or gone elsewhere (*Halloween*). More so than in mystery or suspense, authority figures in horror can't be too competent because that would dilute the horror. Authority figures are not only incompetent, but as vulnerable as anyone else. Entire police stations are attacked and defeated in *Jeepers Creepers* (2001) and *Darkness Falls* (2003).[29]

Pieces's horror psycho is even loonier than those in *Night School* and *Curtains*. He's stitching together his own handcrafted girlfriend, using other women's body pieces.[30] Even so, he has charm and status. And though he wears no mask, he is similarly empowered by secrecy; his identity is concealed from audiences, his deeds seen only through POV (point of view) shots.

Horror vs. Splatter

Horror is often confused with *splatter*, especially by non-fans.

John McCarty defines splatter movies as those striving "to astonish us with the perfection of their violent illusions, and, at their most extreme, mortify us with the gleefully presented realism of these often disgusting film tricks. Mutilation, or other forms of graphic mayhem designed to evoke in us a feeling of revulsion, is usually the theme; in the lesser of these films, often the only one.... Their plots are often openly derivative of other films, and usually dispense with logic or plausibility of any kind. Why? Because plot serves mainly as a springboard from one violent/splattery/FX-laden set piece to the next."[31]

McCarty mistakenly defines splatter and noir as genres,[32] but both are styles rather than genres because they have no story conventions of their own. A style may color a genre film's theme or atmosphere, but its story remains rooted in the genre and subgenre, be it hard-boiled mystery, horror psycho, or horror/sci-fi. McCarty acknowledges this even as he denies it, writing that splatter is "a genre unto itself which has survived over the years by feeding voraciously off virtually every other filmic form, especially the horror film, a genre which it has all but consumed."[33] What McCarty fails to recognize is the reason splatter feeds voraciously off other film forms is because it has no story conventions of its own. Only a true stand-alone genre can make that claim.

But McCarty is correct in that horror has made especial use of splatter. This is unsurprising because (1) splatter can heighten both the unnatural and the threatening (e.g., the gory plasticity of the shape-shifting alien in *The Thing*, 1982), and (2) splatter and horror share synchronous goals. McCarty says splatter intends "to evoke in us a feeling of revulsion."[34] So too, often enough, horror. Carroll considers impurity necessary for horror, adding that "nausea, shuddering, *revulsion*, disgust ... are characteristically the product of perceiving something to be noxious or impure."[35] The unnatural is often revolting.

But horror is more diverse and resilient than splatter. Gut-busting gore energizes 1982's *The Thing* with a delightfully revolting slam-bang punch. But 1951's *The Thing* relates the same horror/sci-fi story equally effectively with quietly atmospheric sets and lighting. No bloodied bodies or elastic aliens required. Horror does fine with or without splatter.

The feeling is mutual. Splatter does not require horror. McCarty cites *Indiana Jones and the Last Crusade* and *Wild at Heart* as examples of non-horror splatter.[36]

Horror and splatter are synchronous, not synonymous.

Horror as a Naturalistic Psycho Gorefest

Lovecraft, Carroll, and Rogan all suggest that horror *requires* an unnatural threat. Uberpsychos are unnatural. Apparent uberpsychos appear unnatural. But can an obviously mortal psycho ever be a *horror* psycho?

Blood Feast (1963), *Don't Look in the Basement* (aka *The Forgotten*, 1973), *The Texas Chainsaw Massacre* (1974), *Mother's Day* (1980),[37] *Demented, House of 1000 Corpses, Saw* (2004), and *Hostel* (2005) are widely regarded and marketed as horror. They pass my timeline test: their stories highlight the violence. Brutality is their *raison d'être*. Greater themes may color some of them, but audiences came for the gore. No cat-and-mouse maybes. No whodunits. These films ask: *Who will survive and what will be left of them?*

But their psychos are vulnerable, however deviant or sadistic. *Saw*'s Jigsaw is arguably empowered by his cancer (like an uberpsycho empowered by a botched prank), yet despite his formidable willpower and sharp mind, he is clearly dying. And once *Hostel*'s Paxton (the hero) escapes, he turns tables and racks up a respectable body count, dispatching villains in prolific *Death Wish* fashion. So, too, the escaped heroines in *Mother's Day*.

What qualifies these *naturalistic psycho gorefests* (for lack of a better term) as horror? What distinguishes their psychos from suspense psychos? Can some mix of *insanity, sadism, perversion, and bizarreness* transform a killer into something unnatural, though he remains vulnerable? Jigsaw and Captain Spaulding are colorfully psychotic, but does that make them unnatural? Charles Manson is colorful, more so than *Hostel*'s banally sadistic torturers, yet *Helter Skelter* is no horror film.

No, a bizarre psycho is not enough for horror.

Is it that the victims in *Texas Chainsaw Massacre*, *Saw*, and *Hostel* are unexpectedly trapped in a *bizarre and frightening situation*, such that, to paraphrase Rogan, the world is no longer as their minds believe? Have they, like *Dracula*'s Jonathan Harker, entered an unnatural realm? Or an *apparently* unnatural realm? If not Transylvania, then a cannibal's torture chamber in Texas? But *Blue Velvet* (1986) and *Pulp Fiction* (1994) also depict bizarre and frightening situations, yet these are crime thrillers, not horror.

No, a bizarre and frightening situation is not enough for horror.

Is it *emotional perspective*? Horror is an emotive genre in which audiences are meant to empathize with, and fear for, the victims. Carroll defines horror as "one of those genres in which the emotive responses of the audience, ideally, run parallel to the emotions of characters."[38] To be unexpectedly caught in a modern-day torture chamber *feels* unnatural to *Hostel*'s backpacking students, but less so to *Pulp Fiction*'s gangsters, who are better inured to perverse sadism. Yet while psychos and torture chambers may *feel* unnatural to newcomers, so do trench warfare and prison violence. But we do not regard *All Quiet on the Western Front* or *Penitentiary* (1979) as horror.

No, merely *feeling* that something is unnatural (when it's not) is not enough for horror.

Is it *different attitudes* toward violence that separate *Texas Chainsaw Massacre* from *Saving Private Ryan*? Is the violence in the former more gratuitous, sadistic, or nihilistic? But *Pulp Fiction* and its copycats have been similarly accused, yet they are not horror films.[39] And horror can be hopeful and spiritual (e.g., *Jacob's Ladder*, 1990; *The Sixth Sense*, 1999). Horror has many attitudes.

No, there is no specific attitude that creates horror.

So what qualifies the *naturalistic psycho gorefest*— these splattery films with bizarre and sadistic (yet vulnerable) psychos — as horror?

Some people shrug and say, "Horror is whatever I say it is," dismissing their inability to formulate a consistent definition as unimportant. Yet this anti-intellectual attitude disrespects horror by treating it as a subject unworthy of study because it is pointless to study something that does not possess discoverable objective truths, whose criteria bend to any whim or opinion. Serious criticism, unlike mere opining, requires objective aesthetic criteria, which critics must deduce and justify and defend, modifying them as necessary.

To require an unnatural threat for horror is logical and defensible. This suggests that the naturalistic psycho gorefest is not horror. And yet, there it is. I can't justify calling it horror. But neither can I easily dismiss it as something else.

Maybe there are *two* horror genres: the *unnatural threat*, a metaphysically transcendent dark force that subverts the laws of nature and our understanding of reality, and the *naturalistic psycho gorefest* with its colorfully sadistic lunatics, an unsatisfyingly vague and broad criterion because non-horror films also have colorfully sadistic lunatics (e.g., *The Dark Knight*'s Joker). Yet like obscenity, you (usually) know it when you see it. *Blood Feast* is horror in a sense that *The Dark Knight* (2008) is not.

Two distinct horror genres — because the quality of fear each elicits, the psychological nerves they strike, feel different, just as the fears evoked by *The Ring* and *Saving Private Ryan* feel different. This would explain why some fans love certain horror subgenres, but hate others — because the story conventions are sufficiently different that they're not two *subgenres*, but two distinct horror *genres*.

"Scary Movie" Is Not a Genre

Although horror is an emotive genre defined by its intent to scare, horror fans and critics should avoid the term "scary movie" when they mean horror. This is because "scary movie" was born in confusion and has continued to muddy genre terminology ever since.

The phrase was popularized by *Scream* (1996), in which the teenagers say "scary movie" whenever they mean horror. But they only discuss slasher films, so it seems that "scary movie" means not horror, but slasher. It's as if these teens live in an alternate universe without *Alien, Frankenstein,* or *The Haunting.* "Scary movie" means horror, and horror means slasher. Except that *Saving Private Ryan* is also a scary movie, though not a "scary movie."

Scream spawned the mercifully brief *neo-slasher* cycle (e.g., *I Know What You Did Last Summer*, 1997; *Valentine*, 2001), rather than a cycle of "scary movies" featuring a broad range of threats. I say "mercifully brief" because neo-slashers pale beside *Halloween*-inspired 1980s slashers. Neo-slashers are weaker, more prone to running and stumbling, rather than striding in that resolute, self-assured manner of an unstoppable force of nature.

Furthermore, *Scream*'s self-referential and smart-alecky, tongue-in-cheek attitude ("We're too smart and hip to take this seriously!") diluted its own horror, and that of the cycle it spawned. It's no wonder that *Scream* inspired the parodic *Scary Movie* series.

That series did expand the term "scary movie" to include threats other than slashers. But whatever the merits of these parodies, and of the neo-slasher cycle, "scary movie" is a confusing term, and not a genre.

Horror vs. Snuff

Horror is not *snuff.* Horror is fiction. Snuff is real. Horror entices its audience with illusory threats. Snuff promises reality, its fans encouraged to believe (however falsely) that the onscreen splatter is authentic, which is snuff's chief "appeal."

When horror films depict splatter, it's usually achieved by special effects. I say usually, because real gore images can also be gotten from stock film footage of crime scenes, wartime combat, executions, slaughterhouses, surgeries, and autopsies. But when a horror film contains documentary footage, it's to support the fiction, not to subvert it. Stock footage can be cheaper than filming an event or special effect, so low-budget horror filmmakers sometimes edit stock footage into the fiction, hoping it will go unnoticed.

In *Hell of the Living Dead*, actress Margit Evelyn Newton was body-painted to resemble the tribesmen in some anthropological film footage. This stock footage was edited into the film to create the illusion of Newton interacting with the tribesmen. Thus, real tribesmen were used fictively, as characters in a story.

Horror does not entice fans with reality. *Hell of the Living Dead*'s aesthetic intent was to hide (not highlight) its documentary footage's authenticity. But gory reality footage is enough for snuff fans. The *Faces of Death* snuff video series is just compilation of real death scenes (though McCarty reports that various scenes in it have been proven fake[40]).

Aside from legally obtained footage, snuff may also be had by injuring or killing real-life "actors." Such films are periodically rumored to emanate from the Third World. Urban legend or not, this is snuff, not horror.

Snuff falls under what Carroll terms "natural horror," lacking Lovecraft's "suspension or defeat of the fixed laws of Nature." Even horror's naturalistic psycho gorefests are fiction. Snuff is functionally closer to reality shows like *Cops* and TV newscasts ("If it bleeds, it leads!") than to horror. Horror is a scary rollercoaster promising a safe return. Snuff appeals to lookiloos and rubber-neckers ogling a freeway pileup.

Humorous Horror vs. Comedy

Is *comedy* a genre or style? A set of story conventions, or a manner of presenting them? Both, really. Comedy is *sui generis*. Some comedic formats, such as TV sitcoms, have their own conventions. But other comedic forms, such as parodies, borrow conventions and icons from other genres. Yet because comedy *can* function alone (unlike splatter or noir), comedy is more genre than style.

Horror shares a special bond with comedy. These two emotive genres play off one another. Tension builds into fear. Fear is released through screams or laughs, often both in quick succession.

Yet through this interplay, horror and comedy fight a tug-of-war. This is because whenever comedy borrows another genre's icons, it subverts that genre in the process. Horror can employ splatter or noir stylistics and remain horror. But nothing horrifying remains of Dracula in *Love at First Bite* (1979). *Too much* humor subverts horror, though horror can survive, even benefit from, *some* humor. This is their tug-of-war. So we must distinguish *humorous horror* from *comedies borrowing horror icons*. The first is horror, the latter comedy.

Here is a test: *Does the fear survive the laughter?* If so, it's horror. If not, a comedy.

These films all have black comedy and dark social satire, but because fear prevails over laughs, they are horror: *Andy Warhol's Frankenstein* (aka *Flesh for Frankenstein*, 1973), *Motel Hell* (1980), *Mother's Day, An American Werewolf in London* (1981), *Re-Animator* (1985), and TV's *Tales from the Crypt*. In these other films, laughter overwhelms fear, so they are comedies: *Abbott and Costello Meet Frankenstein* (1948), *Young Frankenstein* (1974), *Love at First Bite,* and *Teen Wolf* (1985). And some films, such as *Braindead* (aka *Dead Alive*, New Zealand 1992), are a close call. The very young may feel fear, but older or more jaded viewers will likely laugh throughout.

Sometimes the laughs are unintentional. Comedy is the most subjective of genres. Senses of humor differ widely. *Extra Terrestrial Visitors* (aka *Los nuevos extraterrestres*, Spain-France 1983) was apparently intended as serious horror. Yet its conflicting moods and inept execution made it a favorite satirical target of TV's *Mystery Science Theater 3000*.

Another way to distinguish between humorous horror and comedy is *emotional synchronicity*. Unlike comedy, horror synchronizes our emotions with the threatened character. Carroll defines horror as "one of those genres in which the emotive responses of the audience, ideally, run parallel to the emotions of characters."[41] In horror, we fear *with* them or *for* them. In comedy, we laugh *at* them. We fear for Nurse Price in *An American Were-wolf in London*, but laugh at any hapless newcomer who espies Herman Munster.

Character vulnerability, so important to horror, is another distinction. In *Andy Warhol's Frankenstein* we dread what will befall the servant at the mercy of the two evil children. In comedies, we know the heroes are safe. Lou Costello can fall from a skyscraper, yet remains indestructible. A far cry from *Motel Hell*'s gory chainsaw realism.

Yet comedy works *with* horror as it does with no other genre. Humorous horror is abundant. The same cannot be said for other genres. TV's *The Hitchhiker's Guide to the Galaxy* is hilarious social satire, but contains no serious scientific speculation, whereas there's much horror in *Tales from the Crypt*.

Horror is bound to comedy by a human impulse to relieve fear with laughs. Fear is a fertile womb for laughter. Other genres use humor, but only horror carries an innate potential for humor. For better and worse. No other genre so risks unintentional laughs. Nothing is inherently funny about detectives or astronauts, but a zombie or swamp monster is always at risk of shattering its delicate tension at the wrong moment. This is why many 1950s "bug-eyed monster" horror/sci-fi films are today viewed for laughs.

William Paul sees another common thread tying horror to comedy, one similar to splatter. And like McCarty, Paul hopes to coin a new genre, calling it the *gross-out movie*, of which he writes: "A gleeful uninhibitiveness is certainly the most striking feature of these films — of both the comedies *and* the horror films — and it also represents their greatest appeal. At their best, these films offer a real sense of exhilaration, not without its disturbing quality, in testing how far they can go, how much they can show without making us turn away, how far they can push the boundaries to provoke a cry of 'Oh, gross!' as a sign of approval, an expression of disgust that is pleasurable to call out."[42]

Yet while the "gross-out" scenes in *Animal House* (1978) and *Carrie* (two of Paul's examples) may constitute a style, they do not a genre make. This is because, though a film's themes and atmosphere may be altered when filtered through a gross-out prism, the story remains rooted in its original genre. *Animal House* is funny. *Carrie* is scary. Thus the "gross-out movie" is not a true stand-alone genre.

The bonds between horror and comedy are strong and unique, yet the two remain distinct genres. A film may be one or the other, but never both. The test is whether the laughs have stifled the fear; whether the horror is subverted by its own innate potential for humor.

Horror vs. Action

Action films, particularly those based on comic books and video games, are increasingly borrowing horror icons. These films are often mistaken for horror because they feature vampires or zombies, ghosts or demons (e.g., *Ghost Rider*, 2007; and the *Blade*, *Underworld*, *Resident Evil*, and *Hellboy* series). Yet these films' protagonists lack the vulnerability necessary to be threatened by an unnatural threat. As with Superman, they may suffer from a token weakness to Kryptonite, or love for a Lois Lane figure, but this Achilles heal won't stop them from kicking werewolf butt and zombie ass.

These films are not so much fearsome as fun. Theirs are the emotional pleasures of the action film: the excitement (not the fear) of cars crashing, buildings exploding, and baddies blown away in large numbers. Horror offers different pleasures: that awestruck fear upon realizing that the world is not as we believe; those creepy moments that permeate *The Ring*, *The Mothman Prophecies*, and so many *X-Files* episodes.

Despite its zombies and mad scientists, *Resident Evil* (2002), and even more so its sequels, are laden with action film conventions. Alice is less a threatened protagonist than a female Rambo. She fights with casual élan, displaying no awestruck dread of the unnatural. She shoots with both hands, even while running, firing pistols big enough to give Dirty Harry penis envy. She blasts away at cartoon baddies who happen to be zombies, but could as easily be cartoon Nazis, Commies, or terrorists. Like Jackie Chan, she can walk on walls. So indestructible and invincible is Alice, she appears in sequels. In *Resident Evil: Apocalypse* (2004), she is flung full-force against a concrete wall, then gets up, shaken but not stirred. Like James Bond, she will return.

Were Jason Voorhees to fling some teenager into a concrete wall, that teen would burst into bloody pulp. Ash survives some hard falls in *Evil Dead 2* (1987), but even he loses a hand. Horror protagonists are vulnerable. Action heroes are not. Alice is a genetically enhanced, super-warrior. Her corporate and zombie enemies have more to fear than she. Nor is she threatened by her own unnatural abilities. Alice calls herself "a freak," but unlike Barnabas Collins, or Karen White in *The Howling* (so revolted by her own lycanthropy that she commits suicide), Alice feels no compulsion to harm innocents or herself. Unlike Seth Brundle in *The Fly* (1986), Alice's fashion model good looks remain unblemished. Viewers may not wish to be Brundle, but they'd love to be a "freak" like Alice. Or perhaps date her.

Erotic Horror vs. Splatterporn

Horror also shares bed with erotica and pornography. This is not surprising because though horror is an emotive genre, it is also a visceral genre. Paul's gross-out, McCarty's splatter, and Carroll's notion of horror as "terror plus impurity" all ascribe a visceral quality to horror.

Consider the bonds between horror and erotica/porn. Both seek to physically stimulate the nerves; erotica/porn to excite the flesh, horror to shudder it. Yet they send opposing signals. Erotica/porn encourages viewers to take it off. Horror warns teenagers to keep it on.[43] David Cronenberg has been described as "the king of venereal horror"[44] (*venereal* being an unlikely qualifying adjective for most other genres). Cronenberg's early film themes may be summarized as the revolt of the flesh.[45] Clive Barker's *Hellraiser* film series threatens characters with S&M imagery, depicting flesh as simultaneously seductive and repulsive. Porn stars regard horror as their nearest rung up toward legitimacy. Porn actress Marilyn Chambers made her "legit" debut in *Rabid* (Canadian 1977). Traci Lords's first non–XXX film was *Not of This Earth* (1988).

Some critics see a link between fear of sex and fear of death. "The bulk of academic research on the horror film has looked to Freud and his heirs for direction,"[46] writes Jonathan Lake Crane. He elaborates: "The uncanny may ... arise when infantile complexes, once banished from consciousness, are revitalized. When fears of castration, 'womb phantasies,' or 'animistic beliefs' are rekindled we are frightened."[47]

What distinguishes porn from erotica, and how does either connect to horror?

Pornography may be defined as a straightforward depiction of graphic sex, with little concern for story or character. This resembles McCarty's concept of splatter as a straightforward depiction of graphic violence, with little concern for story or character. Not surprisingly, porn and splatter function easily together, creating what I term *splatterporn*.

Erotica pays greater heed to story and character, combining with horror to create *erotic horror*.

Erotic horror is always horror. Splatterporn sometimes is, sometimes isn't.

Erotic horror cinema originated in Europe. "During the 1960s and 70s, the European horror film went totally crazy. It began to go kinky — creating a new type of cinema that blended eroticism and terror. This heady fusion was highly successful, causing a tidal wave of celluloid weirdness that was destined to look even more shocking and irrational when it hit countries like England and the U.S.A."[48]

Vampyres (British 1974) is representative of this erotic horror cycle. A lesbian vampire couple entice motorists and hitchhikers into their Gothic mansion just off a highway. The older vampress falls for a man and, instead of killing him, bleeds him a little every night. Weakened and imprisoned, the man witnesses the vampire couple's nightly sexual blood revelries.

Vampyres succeeds as both erotica and horror, properly balancing its sex, splatter, story, characters, and atmosphere. Lyrical shots of the vampires traversing a misty cemetery in dark robes accentuate their supernatural ethereality. They are alluring and not without sympathy; yet they remain unnatural threats. "In the blink of an eye Miriam's bloodlust changes her from provocative plaything to raging psychopath."[49] This careful balance between the sensuous, the surreal, and the savage, expressed with distinct characters, raises *Vampyres*'s sex and violence above gratuitous splatterporn.

Don't Go in the House (1980) is a naturalistic psycho gorefest that exemplifies *horror splatterporn*. When Donald was a child, his religious zealot mother (shades of *Carrie*?) burned his arms to drive out the demons. After Mom dies, Donald still hears her voice, so he keeps her corpse in her bedroom (shades of *Psycho*?). But because he partially realizes that Mom is dead, he's free to take revenge on other women, while simultaneously punishing the "sluts." He lures victims home, and ties them naked inside a fireproof steel room.

Here is where the splatterporn kicks in. The film "treats" viewers to lingering close-ups of a bound naked woman, the camera moving slowly from head to toe, front to back. When we've seen all of her, Donald enters the room, wearing a welder's suit. He wordlessly pours kerosene over his victim while she begs for mercy. He torches her. The camera lingers over her burning, naked, screaming body.

This is one of the most mean-spirited and misogynistic scenes in horror. *Don't Go in the House* also has some effective traditional scares, such as when Donald imagines his victims' charred corpses attacking him. But the clinically photographed and gratuitous use of nudity and gore edge this film toward *horror splatterporn*, despite having a story, characters, and themes. So too the welder's mask. Donald's mask does not transform him into an enigmatic uberpsycho, because we know it's him. Rather than empower Donald, the mask merely depersonalizes him during his "sex scene," in the tradition of porn.

Ilsa: She-Wolf of the SS (1974) is *non-horror splatterporn*. Its story structure is standard for porn. Ilsa is an SS officer who tortures naked men and women, in S&M fashion, in order to prove her "scientific theories" about female supremacy. She castrates men who fail to perform, until she finds a POW with a unique talent: He can stay hard for as long as he likes. Pleased by his ability to avoid premature ejaculation, the well-endowed Ilsa forces him to perform nightly. His sexual prowess buys him time to escape.

Unlike *Don't Go in the House, Ilsa* is a film that's mostly interested in sex, the intent of its S&M violence being to titillate rather than to frighten. *Don't Go in the House* wants to scare audiences (hence, a horror film), but its execution feels suspiciously like it's inviting some of the sicker viewers to enjoy its "nude burning" scene (hence, the film has splatterporn elements). The film does have a story, characters, and themes (e.g., child abuse creates a cycle of abuse), but despite these, the burning is presented in a coldly clinical and depersonalized fashion (hence, splatterporn rather than erotic horror).

As *Ilsa* demonstrates, not all splatterporn is horror. But because many people wrongly equate horror with splatter, they now also equate horror with splatterporn. The *Threat Theatre* video catalog (claiming to specialize in "horror & sleaze," as though they were similar) confirms this genre confusion. *Threat Theatre* lumps *Vampyres*, and films by Fulci and Argento, into offerings that it variously terms "erotic horror, sex, gore, shocks, sadism, sleaze, S&M, sex-n-gore, gore-nography, anime, and Hong Kong action/fantasy/sci-fi." Sex and violence, not horror, appear to be the common themes.

Here is a representative sampling from the catalog: "*Daughter of Rape* (Hong Kong, 1992) Hysterical rape-comedy-gorefest may be incoherent as hell, never making up its mind whether it is a comedy, a sex film, or a horror film, but damn does it deliver on all three! The movie opens with multiple gory murders which lead to a police 'investigation' ... Pervert cop shows up, grabs corpse's tits, insults grieving family members ('Does everyone in your family have big tits?'), and sniffs dead girl's crotches to 'tell if they've been raped'! It turns out that the daughter was being incestuously raped and blackmailed by her dad (who takes her up the ass in one scene happily singing, 'Row, Row, Row Your Boat!'), and no one in her family would help her, so she killed them all in a fit of rage. Quality sleaze that's a laff riot!"[50]

Well, I suppose it's some people's idea of a "laff riot." But whatever it is — sleaze, porn, splatter — it is not horror.

CHAPTER 2

Pragmatic Aesthetics

By the term *pragmatic aesthetics* I mean when a filmmaker *puts technical and budgetary compromises to artistic effect*. Practical choices are put to aesthetic service. Others may use the term differently.

Pragmatic aesthetics is a recurring theme in this book. I first discussed the subject in a 1999 *Midnight Marquee* article, "Art of the Low-Budget Horror Film." In this chapter, I'll just summarize the concept.

Some of the best horror films are low-budget efforts in which budgetary and technical compromises are made to work aesthetically.

What does that mean, to work aesthetically? Or when someone says that a film's lighting "works" for them? Or that an actor's performance choices don't "work" for the film? Sounds pretentious, no? It is — if the speaker hopes to impress by being intentionally obscure. But the concept is simple.

If a technical element in a film (say, the lighting, acting, script, set décor, etc.) *serves the story, characters, or themes, then that technical aspect works aesthetically.*

Story, characters, and themes make up most dramatic films. Technical elements (what I sometimes call "cinematic tools") create the images and sounds, which then construct the story, characters, and themes.

If a scene is meant to be dramatic, and the lighting intensifies the drama, then the lighting works aesthetically. But if the lighting "mellows out" the scene, or over-intensifies the scene so that it becomes satirical, then the lighting doesn't work. The story was meant to be dramatic, but the lighting sabotaged it.

If the filmmaker can't afford lighting equipment, but uses natural daylight or street lamps (which are free) in a dramatic manner, then the lighting setup works *pragmatically* (it didn't cost money) and *aesthetically* (it serves the story). Hence, *pragmatic aesthetics.*

Fancy words, but it's that simple.

Horror abounds with pragmatic aesthetics. In *Night of the Living Dead* (1968), an urgent "you are there" documentary sensibility is evoked by the film's grainy, high-contrast, black and white photography, its harshly reverberant soundtrack, and its rough, handheld camera work. These elements were praised for aesthetically evoking the feel of Vietnam War combat footage, yet director George Romero's technical choices were dictated by budget. He couldn't afford a meticulously lit color film, with slick sound and set design. Film stock, gore, even the genre itself (a zombie horror film), were determined by financial considerations.

Paul R. Gagne writes: "[T]he decision to use black and white was always a budgetary rather than an aesthetic consideration.... The decision to do a horror film was made purely for commercial reasons.... Similarly, the decision to take a direct, visceral approach to the gore was purely an attempt to make the film noticeable, to make it the kind of film that kids would tell their friends they *had* to see; it wasn't a political or artistic statement or anything else that critics have read into it."[1]

Yet *Night of the Living Dead* emerged as a horror classic precisely because many of its pragmatically motivated technical compromises serve aesthetic functions, whether intentional on Romero's part, or being "one of the film's many critical appeals that they stumbled into for simple lack of money."[2]

Pragmatic aesthetics is discussed throughout this book. Nevertheless, I gave the concept its own chapter (however short), to underscore its importance — especially to low-budget filmmakers.

CHAPTER 3

Mise-en-Scène

Cinema abounds with words and phrases that are either French or rooted in French. For instance, *cinema* and *cinematography*. And *montage*. And *aesthetics* (rooted in the French *esthétique*). Why so much French? Partially because of the influence of *Cahiers du cinéma* (translated as *Notebooks on Cinema*), a French journal founded in 1951 that helped legitimize serious film criticism, as opposed to movie reviews written for a mass audience.

Mise-en-scène is another French film term (borrowed from French theater), which has been translated as "putting on stage" or "putting into the scene." The term refers to everything "on stage," i.e., before the camera: location, props, actors, set décor (from the French *décor*), costumes, and makeup. Lighting is another *mise-en-scène* element, though it also relates to cinematography. This book gives lighting its own chapter. Finally, all *mise-en-scène* elements (including light and shadows) can now be created or enhanced digitally, and thus CGI effects may also be classified under *mise-en-scène*.[1]

Low-budget filmmakers often use whatever locations they can easily access, and cast any friends or family members who are willing to perform, and use whatever wardrobe may be found in these actors' closets. Yet this approach is less pragmatic than lazy. To ignore the creative potential of *mise-en-scène* is a mistake, because, to a large extent, the *mise-en-scène is* the film. It's what audiences see onscreen. An exciting and literate screenplay about the Trojan War is a good foundation, but the film will fail if your Greek warriors look like high school students waving cardboard swords in a municipal park. (Unless you're filming a camp or parody.)

Creating a Character

Characters are established by what they *say* and *do* in a script. But though the script is important —*If it's not on the page, it's not on the stage*—it's still only a blueprint. *Mise-en-scène* "fleshes out" that blueprint into a finished film. Actors bring alive the script's characters, assisted by props, costumes, makeup, etc.

Clothing, makeup, and props all inform us about a character's personality and inner life. Films often introduce characters by exploring their rooms' contents. Early in *Lost Souls* (2000), Maya is huddled over a desk, deciphering a possessed man's Satanic code. As the camera moves over her desk, we see reams of worksheets with tiny, neat handwriting (block letters), a cigarette lighter bearing a peace symbol, spent cigarette butts, and Maya, who is still smoking, her eyes fixated on her work.

We may infer from the worksheets, and actress Winona Ryder's body posture, that Maya is determined, dedicated, perhaps even a bit of a fanatic. (As is later implied by Peter Kelson's conversation with the police detective.) The peace symbol may suggest either a shallow, trendy fashionista, or a strongly committed idealist. Seeing Maya diligently at work, we may infer the latter. Films have associated cigarettes with glamour, power, and sophistication — but also with boozed up hags and dirty old men. However, Maya is neither sophisticate nor lush. In the scene's context, the cigarettes suggest Maya's mortality; she is vulnerable and has weaknesses. (She was once demonically possessed, and later tells Peter that she's "not strong enough for this.") The cigarettes also imply that she is focused on her work, and hence, indicates her commitment. (Many smokers claim that cigarettes aid their concentration.) The cigarettes further imply that Maya is less concerned with long life than with doing right.[2]

Maya's clothing and makeup render a contradictory picture. Throughout the film, her clothes are modest. Long dresses and dark colors. Nothing flashy or tight. Yet she wears heavy, goth girl eye makeup. Although seemingly in conflict, her clothing and makeup effectively support her character as written in the script. Maya has a sordid past: a teenage runaway who engaged in petty theft, drugs, and vandalism; we may also infer that she prostituted herself. All this opened her up to demonic possession. Her demons have since been exorcised and she now works as a Catholic school teacher. Thus, her clothes reflect her present religious conservatism; her heavy eye makeup, a remnant habit from her wild youth [Figure 3.1].

The only time the present-day Maya breaks her "look" is when she first contacts Peter. She pretties herself up before approaching him, putting on lipstick and a shorter skirt. She apparently remembers from her wild days that if a woman wants something from a man, it helps to look her best.

In *Lost Souls*, Maya's clothing informs us about her *actual* personality and background. But clothes can also render a character *symbolically*. In explaining her aesthetic intent for *Bram Stoker's Dracula* (1992), costume designer Eiko Ishioka says: "Throughout the film, red is highly significant as the color that symbolizes blood. Therefore I decided to use red only for Dracula. The only exception was for the dress that Mina wears when she dances with Dracula on their 'first date.' This was a dress Dracula had made especially for her, the object of his passionate love, so for this dress he chose his theme color — suggesting that Mina soon will become a vampire."[3] By contrast, "Mina's clothes are mainly green,

Figure 3.1—*Lost Souls*. Maya's (Winona Ryder) modest, conservative clothes conflict with her heavy eye makeup, reflecting her contradictory past and present lifestyles.

reflecting her youth, simplicity, and naiveté. Lucy and Mina wear similar green dresses in a party scene, but the embroidery — Mina's of leaves and Lucy's of snakes — differs significantly."[4]

The Garden of Eden provides the metaphors for these embroideries. Mina is a good girl who is shocked by Lucy's openly flirting with three men. Lucy is more "horny," an easy sexual conquest for Dracula. Mina is ashamed of her nakedness, and covers herself with leaves. Lucy is a fallen woman who listens to the serpent.

Mina's dress also resembles that of Elizabeta, Dracula's 15th century wife. Both women wear green dresses embroidered with leaves. Green leaves for Mina. Gold leaves for Elizabeta. (The gold suggests Elizabeta's royal rank, and that she is no longer a virgin and thus no longer completely "green.") The two women are linked by their similar dresses, which is appropriate, because Mina is the reincarnation of Elizabeta. The characters are further linked in that both parts are played by Winona Ryder.

Dracula's clothing informs not only through its color, but through its variety. Ishioka says: "Every costume was designed to be totally unique and never seen before, to cause a fresh sensation each time Dracula appeared."[5] Some of his costumes are unexpectedly bizarre, drawing inspiration not only from medieval or eastern Europe, but from the Far East. Regarding her overall aesthetic philosophy, Ishioka says: "Costumes should be more than just items that explain the role of the actors who wear them.... Costumes must have enough force to challenge the actors, the cinematographer, scenic designer, and director. And at times, the costumes should challenge the audience and make them think about why the actor is wearing that costume."[6]

Perhaps most challenging to audiences is Dracula's bizarro "muscle armor." Unlike every other costume in the film, this one looks entirely unreal. It does not resemble a suit of armor; it looks like exposed muscle tissue, less appropriate to horror than to fantasy. It seems particularly inappropriate in a film that director Francis Ford Coppola claims to have roots in history. Yet Ishioka justifies her fantasy armor: "He has the power to control all beasts. So his armor had to be quite extraordinary. I wanted to depict him in his armor as a cross between man and beast, and came up with the stylized muscle armor, like that in anatomy books. The helmet is also stylized muscles, but the effect here is a mixture of a wolf's head and a human skull."[7]

Ishioka goes too far here, sacrificing the overall film to her creative baby. The red muscle armor does not work aesthetically because it contradicts the story. Dracula is not yet a vampire when he dons the armor; he is not part beast. Ishioka may argue that the armor foreshadows what Dracula *will* become, or perhaps that, being a great warrior, he is *already* part beast. Yet these arguments fail because, though *Bram Stoker's Dracula* is a highly stylized film, it also strives for historical accuracy, and the muscle armor is too ahistorical even in the context of the other stylized costumes. The film crew jokingly referred to Dracula's muscle armor as "the beetle suit"[8] [Figure 3.2].

Color lends itself to easy (at times obvious) symbolism, and is thus a quick shorthand tool (hopefully, never a crutch) in rendering characters. In *The Velvet Vampire* (1971), the changing colors and patterns on the characters' clothing effectively support the film's shifting events and themes.

Reflecting its hippie counterculture era, *The Velvet Vampire* is about a bisexual vampire artist, Diane, who invites a groovy young couple to her desert home for a weekend

Figure 3.2 — *Bram Stoker's Dracula*. Dracula (Gary Oldman) in his "beetle suit" bids goodbye to Elizabeta (Winona Ryder).

getaway. The three of them engage in free love, dune buggy rides, free love, a ghost town visit, free love, some neck-biting and blood-sucking, and free love. When Diane isn't participating, she lurks behind a two-way mirror, watching Susan and Lee make love.

However much everyone in *The Velvet Vampire* enjoys taking off their clothes, it's also interesting to see them wearing them. As with Ishioka's Dracula, only Diane wears red. She wears passionate reds and dark red-oranges when seducing men, but stiff yellow or white dresses when approaching women. Morally pure Susan (who is initially troubled by Diane's lasciviousness), wears bright yellows, whites, and pinks. In these soft colors, she is helpless against Diane. Only after Susan puts on a rough, earth-toned jacket does she destroy Diane. Wayward husband Lee initially wears "blue for boys," but switches to a morally ambiguous striped shirt after he commits adultery. Juan (Diane's emasculated Indian housemate) wears a pink top. After Diane kills a mechanic, his girlfriend (who is spunkier than Susan) wears a pumpkin orange top when confronting Diane, but this strong orange is no match for Diane's red top. Diane defeats the girlfriend.

Were these costumes intentional or serendipity? No matter. They are in the film and they work aesthetically because they support the characters, story events, and themes. Regardless of director Stephanie Rothman's intentions, *The Velvet Vampire*'s color scheme makes for a stronger film.

Vampyres (British 1974) sports a similar color scheme. The two lady vampires' capes and dresses emphasize Satanic reds and blacks, and a deep (almost black) velvet blue. In contrast, the housewife wears browns and beiges. She is dowdy and "of this earth," whereas the vampires are vibrant, alluring, and otherworldly; their colors that of blood, evil, and the night.

In *Creepshow* (1982), Wilma is a faculty wife who attends a party in a bright and showy red dress. More importantly, she is the *only* character in red. Other guests wear beige or gray, or muted pastel colors. This color scheme not only establishes Wilma as loud and abrasive, but that she "sticks out like a sore thumb" at this college, offending everyone, and embarrassing Henry, her henpecked husband.

Happily, this color scheme supports the characters, story, and themes. Wilma's red dress accurately represents her rude manners and pushy personality. The guests' muted colors correctly reflect their genteel manners, hushed voices, and taste for the sedate, classical music that plays at their party. We needn't even follow the dialog, or hear Wilma's incessant insults. A quick glance at the color scheme provides an immediate shorthand visual explanation as to why Henry would want to murder Wilma.

Of course, a filmmaker can achieve powerful results by "playing against expectations" or "casting against type," but that's not *Creepshow*'s aesthetic goal. The 1950s EC horror comics from which *Creepshow* draws inspiration were not subtle. Even their "surprise twists" were formulaic and morally heavy-handed.

The hair styles and demeanors of mad scientists have traditionally been both formulaic and sex-specific. Menfolk, such as Drs. Frankenstein, Pretorius (*Bride of Frankenstein*, 1935), and Rotwang (*Metropolis*, German 1927), favor unkempt hair and megalomaniacal outbursts, unable to contain their enthusiasms when their big experiments come to fruition. Lady doctors, conversely, rarely display any emotion at all. Their lips are as tight as their hair buns. Examples include *Dark Shadows*'s Dr. Hoffmam[9]; Dr. Parkinson in *Strange Behavior* (Australian 1981); and Dr. Carter in the "And Now the News" episode of TV's *Friday the 13th: The Series*.

Clothes, makeup, and accessories (e.g., Maya's peace symbol lighter) are highly personal items, and thus carry much potential in creating a character. Yet *location* and *set décor* can also contribute. Where a person lives and works, how that place is furnished, provide clues as to a person's wealth, neatness, religious or political beliefs, cultural sophistication or crudeness of taste. But apart from clues to concrete personal traits, location may also mirror or symbolize a character's psychology.

In *White Noise* (2005), Jonathan's young wife, Anna, is apparently killed in an accident. The film begins at their house, while Anna is still alive. Inside, warm earth tones predominate. Outside, it is sunny and bucolic. Much greenery beside a nearby river. Neighbors leisurely ride bikes and walk dogs.

Anna dies ten minutes into the film. Jonathan moves so as to begin a new life. Gone is the warm house. He now lives in a modern condo or townhouse complex. It looks like an office building. Steel and glass and concrete. Gray and gleaming and sterile. Instead of a life-giving river, surrounded by greenery, outside is a concrete fountain, its waters nurturing nothing.

This change of location reflects the change in Jonathan. With Anna now dead, Jonathan feels dead inside — as dead and empty as his new home. He sits on his bed crying to himself, rain spattering the glass walls that reveal a cold, urban landscape.

He later tries to contact his dead wife through EVP (electronic voice phenomenon), but his inner emptiness (reflected in his home) leaves him open to the influence of hostile spirits. He grows obsessed with EVP, to the exclusion of everything else. He ignores his son. He fills his home with TVs and computers and electronic gear — props that reinforce his home's cold décor. His sterile home has nothing to anchor Jonathan to the world of the living, further increasing his dangerous obsession with the afterlife.

White Noise's locations and set décor support the main character, his relationship to the shifting story events, and the theme (that the emotional emptiness following the loss of a loved one can lead to a dangerous withdrawal from the world of the living). But the film's use of props is noteworthy in another respect. EVP is an audio phenomenon. Practitioners claim to record the *voices* of ghosts and spirit entities. But cinema is a primarily visual medium. And so, perhaps worried that characters staring at audio recorders might be boring, *White Noise* changes the rules. Not only does Jonathan *listen* to ghostly recordings, he *sees* ghosts on his TV screen, as recorded by his video gear.

White Noise uses *mise-en-scène* to make the story more visual and exciting, exchanging "electronic *voice* phenomenon" for "electronic *face* phenomenon." Curiously, it's still called EVP throughout the film. And none of the characters ask: "Why do they call this 'electronic voice phenomenon' when we can see faces too?"

In *The Unseen* (1981), three TV newsgals visit Solvang, California, to report on the town's annual Dutch festival. Unable to find a vacant hotel room, they board at the home of Ernest and Virginia Keller. The Kellers live as a married couple, but are also brother and sister. Hidden in the basement, crawling "unseen" through the air ducts, is Junior, their born-of-incest mutant spawn. Junior sees the newsgals walking nekkid past his air ducts ... and the body count mounts!

The film's *mise-en-scène* supports the shifting dramatic events and character revelations. The newsgals arrive in Solvang on a cheerful, sunny morning. After Junior kills two newsgals, and the audience learns the Kellers' dark secrets, and Ernest decides that the final newsgal must also die, a thunderstorm erupts.

A dark thunderstorm to underscore a darkening in the tale? A cliché, no? Thunderstorms have been used in horror films and literature, and in oral ghost tales before that, for like, forever. Of course it's a cliché. It's a cliché because it works.

Acting

An actor's performance helps to create a character, and to influence the overall tone and atmosphere of a film. Acting styles should also support the film's story and themes.

In *Anaconda* (1997), an expedition of anthropologists and documentary filmmakers ride a boat down the Amazon river, seeking a lost tribe. Along the way, they take aboard Paul Sarone (played by Jon Voight), a villainous snake poacher who later commandeers the boat. Voight's performance is not only creepy, but *appropriately* creepy. He eyes his boatmates, never blinking, never shifting his gaze. Squinting through slit eyes, scowling, hair slicked-back, he *resembles* a snake.[10] This resemblance is achieved mostly through facial expression and demeanor, unassisted by makeup or CGI effects. Only hard lighting lends occasional aid, accentuating his face's snake-like features, and his villainy, by casting shadows so that Voight's slit eyes becomes black slits, like two dark holes. Very creepy [Figure 3.3].

The performances in *Bram Stoker's Dracula* are a sort of "stylized realism." Assisted by Method acting, actor Gary Oldman's Dracula shed real tears over the corpse of his dead bride, Elizabeta.[11] In his desire to accurately recreate the film's 1897 period, director Coppola had flyers distributed to the 400 extras in the London street scene, instructing them on the proper demeanor and mannerisms of Englishmen and women according to their class rank in society. But the cast's realistic performances are leavened with hints of a stylized theatricality (more than a hint in actor Tom Waits's scenery-chewing Renfield) that is more

Figure 3.3 —*Anaconda.* Actor Jon Voight's performance imbues his snake poacher character, Paul Sarone, with a snake-like visage.

common to 19th century stage actors. As with the cinematography's use of pixilation, this older acting style helped ground the film in its 1897 milieu.

Different periods and cultures have differing views on what is realistic behavior. Or even acceptable behavior. In *Contamination* (aka *Alien Contamination*, Italian 1980), a New York City cop is assigned to work with a U.S. Air Force colonel to track down deadly alien eggs. The cop is a man. The colonel a woman. She's in charge. Then she gets mouthy. So he slaps her. She gloats at him, as if being hit by a man were perfectly normal.

If a respectable man were to strike a female co-worker on a contemporary American TV drama, one aiming for "realism," the incident would not be glossed over. Her lawsuit and sexual harassment charges, his need for counseling and possible jail time, would become key storylines. But men hitting women is common in 1970s French and Italian films. In *Street Law* (aka *Il cittadino si ribella*; Italian 1974), the hero slaps his journalist wife when she gets mouthy — and it's clear that neither she, nor the audience, are expected to think any less of him.

Hitting women may have been even more acceptable in 1890s Victorian England, yet it's not something Coppola's Dracula would do to Mina. He'll murder people — he almost bites Mina — but he'd never punch her. The "realism" in *Bram Stoker's Dracula*, despite its attempts at 1890s verisimilitude, nevertheless reflects 1990s American values.

Low-budget filmmakers often can't afford quality actors.[12] Or they live far from urban areas where many trained actors live. Fortunately, amateurish acting styles are appropriate for certain scripts.

Children Shouldn't Play with Dead Things (1972) is about a low-talent acting troupe who trespasses onto an island cemetery to steal a corpse. At one point, some of the members perform in the graveyard, challenging each other to see who's the better actor. The actors portraying these actors are themselves bad actors. Their performances are hammy and overplayed. But because they are playing bad actors, their poor performances "work" for this film, aesthetically supporting the story and its characters. *Children* demonstrates that if a filmmaker only has bad actors available, it's a good idea to cast them as bad actors.

It's also a good idea to cast bad actors *according to type.* (Good actors can always break out of type.) If your script has creepy characters, cast creepy actors. In *Kiss Daddy Goodbye* (aka *Revenge of the Zombie*, 1981), a single dad raises two psychic children. Then some bikers murder dad. So the children paint occult symbols on daddy's corpse, reanimate it, and send it to take revenge on the bikers.

These kids are *weird*— as characters and as actors. In the film, brother and sister look out a window, see their father killed, and barely react. They bring daddy's corpse into the house and leaf through a magazine for ideas on how to paint his face. "Oh look, those colors are real pretty," says sister. *Huh? Her father was just killed!*

The actors are real-life brother and sister, Patrick Regan III and Nell Regan. They look creepy. They have that blond *Village of the Damned* look. Vacant eyes. Cold expressions. Eyes and mouths like sinister slits. Monotonal voices. Nell's curled lips look like she's been sucking on a lemon. Her lisp is an additional eerie touch.

If these two young actors entered my casting office, I'd run away screaming.

Were they directed to play their characters so emotionless? Are they bad actors? Are they truly weird? I'm not sure. One might say this is good casting for a horror film. But *Kiss Daddy Goodbye* was directed and co-written by the kids' real-life daddy, Patrick Regan. That's right. Daddy wrote a script about two kids who reanimate daddy's corpse, to be performed by daddy's real-life kids. One wonders what Freudian family demons inspired this film. *Brrrrrr!*

Freaky Farley (2007) is about a small town Peeping Tom who turns serial killer and is later released from prison to rid the forest of evil trogs. It's an outlandish throwback to 1950s monster movies, unique, quirky, and satirical. Part of its strange charm lies in its intentionally amateurish acting style. Freaky Farley and his peers are (apparently) young adults, yet they still live at home and display mannerisms that are both hyper-childlike and anachronistic. Their sighs and shrugs are exaggerated, as those of a sulking child. Their cultural references are Nancy Drew. When she is disappointed, Scarlett exclaims, "Aw shucks!" (Not your typical adult cuss word.) Delivery of the dialog is often both exaggerated and stilted, like from a bad 1950s era TV show. Likewise, the trog monsters look like something from a bad 1950s horror/sci-fi film. *Robot Monster* (1953) comes to mind.

Aesthetically, this unusual "childlike adult" acting style supports the film's satire and its anachronistic innocence. *Pragmatically*, the cast includes many untrained actors, and this acting style (with its exaggerated mannerisms and wooden dialog) is something they can handle. The older adult characters (such as Farley's father) are not played childlike, just wooden. But since *Freaky Farley* is not their film, their amateurish acting impairs but does not destroy the film.

Satirical horror films (hopefully, intentionally satirical) often do well with broad, hammy performances, which support the satire, leavening the gore with humor (e.g., *Blood Feast* 1963; *Motel Hell*, 1980). Because the acting is over-the-top and unrealistic, audiences have a harder time believing the reality of the gore and can thus stomach more of it. Despite his obvious lack of Method training, horror writer Stephen King gave an appropriately hammy performance as Jordy Verrill in the darkly humorous *Creepshow*.

Even so, while audiences find some poorly acted horror films to be "so bad it's good," they are more likely to find them "so bad it's unwatchable." It's easier to create crap than to create good crap.

Star Crystal (1986) strives to be a genuinely frightening *Alien* ripoff, yet it falls short on many levels, including the acting. The film's astronauts should be serious, yet the men engage in silly frat boy banter. One woman is a crybaby, and another woman is a snarling bulldog. All of them contribute to a discordant, unprofessional atmosphere that destroys any suspension of disbelief. We expect inanity from *Children Shouldn't Play with Dead Things*'s acting troupe, but we expect *gravitas* from these astronauts. Unfortunately, neither their dialog, nor their delivery of that dialog, conveys any serious professionalism.

Sleepaway Camp (1983) is unusual in being a summer camp slasher film that appears to have cast adolescent actors to portray adolescent characters. Usually, adults in their twenties are cast to play high schoolers. Hardcore slasher fans may thus sense something different about this film, without quite knowing what.

Sleepaway Camp also feels odd due to its contrasting acting styles. Most of the cast performs in a naturalistic manner, whereas Desiree Gould's performance as Aunt Martha is strikingly stylistic: broadly overplayed to the point of caricature. Her bright, colorful clothing further segregates her from the film's naturalism. She only appears near the film's start and end, forming bizarre bookends to the seemingly ordinary murders. Her first scene signals that weird undercurrents will flow through the following events, and warns us not to trust in their apparent normalcy. Her last scene explains the origins of that weirdness, before the final scene with Angela reveals the fruits of Aunt Martha's madness.

Acting styles cannot simply be divided between the naturalistic or stylized, theatrical or hammy. The actor's art is subtle, with potential for many styles, and gradations within those styles. Imaginative directors and actors should be able to find new ones. With *The Unbelievable Truth* (1989), director Hal Hartley developed a "deadpan style" for his actors that has become his unique trademark. Some critics theorize that this deadpan delivery is meant to strip away all falseness and pretense, exposing the raw truths conveyed in the dialog and relationships. Does it? I found Hartley's deadpan performers initially intriguing, but eventually off-putting. More interesting than engaging. Even so, *Henry Fool* (1997) is one of my favorite films of the 1990s, and Hartley demonstrates that there remain new acting styles yet to be discovered.

Motif vs. Cliché

A *motif* is something that recurs in a film, hopefully with an aesthetic intent or effect. Anything can function as a motif: a POV (point of view) shot, a lens's focal length, a particular sound, or an editing transition. But a motif is usually most noticeable when it's an element of the *mise-en-scène*.

In *Bram Stoker's Dracula*, the color red is a motif for Dracula. Its aesthetic intent is to visually connect Dracula to vampirism through the color of blood.

Birds are a motif in *The Visitor* (aka *Stridulum*, Italian 1979), an *Omen*-inspired tale about a demonic space child. Although *The Visitor* isn't about birds, they recur throughout the film. Falcons protect Katy, the evil child, and attack her enemies. Her mother, Barbara, buys Katy a decorative artificial bird for her birthday, which leads to Barbara's paralysis. The caregiver (who sees the evil in Katy) collects "artificial birds" because they make her feel "less lonely." Katy is defeated by a flock of white doves, whose feathers blacken as they "pull the sin" out of Katy, cleansing her of evil.[13] The doves also save Barbara's life, biting off the cord (or fishing wire?) that's strangling her.

What *meaning* does this bird motif convey? *The Visitor* borrows from so many films and subgenres (demonic horror, science fiction, global conspiracy thriller, New Age mysticism), that the film is a mishmash of plausible symbols and interpretations. But let's try to find an objective and defensible interpretation for these birds.

The falcon is a predator, so it's appropriate that they protect the evil Katy. The CEO of the world conspiracy cabal that's supporting Katy says that she was born with "the power of Sateen." (As in Satan? — very subtle, no?) Doves have historically been a symbol for both peace and the Holy Spirit. This sort of makes sense when we see the final scene, set on a distant planet. (Or in another dimension?) A blond Jesus smiles in a room full of happy, bald children, including a sinless and bald Katy. Their bald heads evoke a New Agey Buddhism, as did the young bald men who assisted the "space visitor" who defeated the "evil Katy" back on Earth (before she became the "good Katy" on this other planet/dimension). As for Barbara's and the caregiver's artificial birds, I suppose one interpretation is that their lifeless birds were no match for Katy's evil falcons, and that only the Holy Spirit's doves can defeat the evil space child.

Is this an accurate interpretation of the bird motif? Or am I imposing a meaning onto the *mise-en-scène*? It's fun to read symbols into a film, and discuss them in class or at coffee shops. But serious film criticism (as opposed to mere opining) requires objective and defensible aesthetic criteria, applied to what's actually onscreen.

Apart from the bird motif, how does one interpret *The Visitor*'s *mise-en-scène* mishmash onscreen? A God-like voice on another planet (or other dimension?); a disciplined squad of sweatsuit-uniformed, bald, young men, resembling Buddhists or Hare Krishnas; a world conspiracy type conference room, with international businessmen around an immense table under a huge chandelier; their elderly black butler; a blond Jesus amid bald children in New Age robes; a tractor trailer truck that resembles a UFO (due to its colored lights), and from which radiation-suited figures emerge, amid smoke, to abduct Barbara and implant her with another space child; a funhouse mirror maze through which the evil Katy chases the space visitor.

None of these iconographic people or objects are explained. Audiences are expected to find meaning in the images' clichéd familiarity. Bald heads can suggest strength or villainy, but in this context they imply a morally positive spirituality. Wealthy businessmen often symbolize evil. The elderly black butler, a force for good. Elderly blacks are often associated with sagelike wisdom and goodness (e.g., *The Matrix* series, or any Morgan Freeman role). Sure enough, the butler survives the cataclysm that befalls his masters at film's end. He peeks into the conference room, sees the deceased businessmen, and nods his sagelike approval.

The Visitor is an enjoyable but weird exploitation film, as only the Italians can produce. Full of icons, motifs, and clichés, your interpretation may be as good as mine.

Cars are a motif in *Terror* (British 1978), a film about witchcraft in modern London. Susie's car stalls near Buttercup Lodge. A policeman is attacked and killed by his driverless squad car. Ann is safe riding the tube (subway), but once on foot to Buttercup Lodge, she is harassed by gusts from an approaching storm. So she breaks into a deserted car on the road. The car levitates, spins, then drops to the ground.

Is there a unifying theme to all these unruly cars? Or is it just that European cars are so lightweight, they make for easy props?

Ultimately, a film must be judged by what's *onscreen*, rather than by the filmmaker's *intent*. This is because, once a work of art is finished, it exists on its own merits, much like an adult must be judged by his actual life, and not by his parents' intentions while raising him. Even so, while film critics and viewers will determine what a film *does* mean, a filmmaker's intent can provide clues as to what a film *might* mean.

Terror director Norman J. Warren says he just wanted to make a fun film. Whatever meaning or motifs may be found in *Terror* are entirely accidental. Warren writes: "There is no real storyline and very [little], if any, logic."[14]

Shapes can be a motif. A circular motif pervades *Hardware* (1990), a post-apocalyptic horror/sci-fi film about a killer droid. Some of the film's circles are likely accidental and inevitable; a shape inherent in the prop, such as the zone tripper's round compass and goggles. We should hesitate before reading meaning into these. But other circles are more emphatic, either made for the film, or underscored by camera or editing.

Hardware begins and ends with an electronic flash of bluish-white circular light. This *electronic circle* sets the theme that machines (i.e., hardware) are expanding their territory, permeating human existence, and then concludes the film by noting that machines remain undefeated. A telephoto lens magnifies the *round, burning sun*, emphasizing that nature is also hostile to humanity.[15] These circles symbolically link machines and sun; the source of pollution, and a polluted nature's blowback.

Throughout *Hardware*, circles link related elements. We dissolve from the droid's round red eyes in the living room, to a round showerhead pouring water on the humans. *Dramatically*, this linking of circles (through a *graphic match* in the editing) foreshadows the droid's death in that shower stall. *Thematically*, it supports the film's anti-hardware outlook. Water is life-giving to humans, but destructive to droids. Humanity can have clean water, or industry, but not both.

Another scene depicts the droid's POV as it watches Jill and Mo making love, and then Linc's POV as he watches the love-making from across the street. Both POVs are seen through electronic lenses (Linc uses a camera's telephoto lens), with a circle demarcating the lens's glass. *Dramatically*, these electronic POVs link the droid's and Linc's perversities. *Thematically*, this linking (with "Linc") supports the conceit of machines run rampant, encroaching upon humanity. Jill and Mo can't get any privacy with all those machines about.

Linc introduces himself to Jill through a perverse circle. After cutting a hole in a pinup girl's paper asshole, Linc calls Jill on the video phone, his round eye staring at Jill through this pornographic "hole within a hole."

After the droid injects Mo with drugs, we enter Mo's mind through a closeup of his eye's (round) iris. He is hallucinating fractal circles. Thus is Mo linked to the machine world. He was already partly machine, having a bionic right hand. His electronic voice recordings, made during his hallucinatory death, later help save Jill.

Hardware's set décor reinforces its circular motif's political message. Jill paints American stars and stripes on the discarded military droid's head. She says her art means nothing, just how she feels, but arguably, she's commenting on the American military machine. Stars and stripes on nontraditional or inappropriate objects is a 1960s art cliché, so Jill's art links her to the rebellious politics of that period's antiwar era.

Hardware also borrows 1940s noir set décor. While lamenting the wretched state of the planet, Mo glances through the Venetian blinds in Jill's apartment. Critics have interpreted the noir style's Venetian blinds as evoking prison bars, and suggesting that characters are trapped by a malevolent universe. Mo and Jill are indeed trapped by hostile circumstances: unemployment, pollution, high taxes, radiation, wars and rumors of wars, and an uncertain future. Jill sums it up by saying: "I just think it's stupid and suicidal and sadistic to have children right now."

Which is the sort of attitude you'd expect from people who live behind Venetian blinds. The characters in *Blade Runner* (1982) weren't a cheerful bunch either.

Circular images are also a motif in *The Ring* (2002). These include a shower drain, the sun, closeups on Rachel's eye, a horse's eye, and an eclipse (that turns out to be a closing well cover). All these recurring circles foreshadow the well in which Samara died, the closing cover being the last thing she saw.

Spike imagery abounds in *Blood and Roses* (aka *Et mourir de plaisir*, French-Italian 1960), an appropriate motif for a vampire tale. Inspired by Joseph Sheridan Le Fanu's novella, *Carmilla*, the film is about a young, 20th century countess, Carmilla, who is possessed by her 18th century vampire ancestress, Millarca. Both of them love Leopoldo, soon to marry Georgia.

Despite moments of horror, *Blood and Roses* is heavy on romance. Its story plays out on Leopoldo's estate. The set décor follows Gothic romance tradition, in that while the family lives in a modern mansion, the estate also has an old family crypt, a cemetery, and castle ruins, which allow for plenty of spike imagery. Grecian white pillars are scattered about the grounds, broken to various lengths. Crumbling towers loom over jagged stone walls. Tall, pointy trees shoot upward. Posts are staked about the ranch area. Carmilla shatters a mirror into sharp pieces. Her metal bed frame features multiple decorative spikes pointing down at her. One shot is composed with Carmilla lying on bed, with a spiked bedpost in the foreground visually (if not actually) decapitating her. When Carmilla enters the cemetery, another shot is composed so that a wooden post looms in the foreground, presaging her fate.

As in *Bram Stoker's Dracula*, red is a motif in *Blood and Roses*. White too. The mansion has only red or white candles. Millarca is associated with a white dress and a red rose. Carmilla is drawn to that white dress shortly before she is possessed by Millarca, and continues to favor that dress through much of the film. Despite being possessed by a vampire, Carmilla sees herself reflected in a mirror, a growing red blood stain spreading over her white dress.[16] No one else sees this blood. (The film coyly asks: *Is Carmilla possessed, or is it her imagination?*) In an especially striking scene, Carmilla/Millarca attempt to possess Georgia as she sleeps. Color drains from the film image, as though Georgia's life spirit were draining, leaving only black and white — and red. In Georgia's following dream sequence, a red blood stain (once again) spreads over Carmilla's dress. Georgia enters a surgical room, everything in black and white, apart from the surgical team's red rubber gloves.

Why the red gloves? What do they symbolize? Perhaps that surgeons hold life and death in their hands. ("The blood is the life," as Dracula might put it.)

Blood and Roses ends with Georgia holding a red rose, its color draining, implying that now she is possessed by Millarca. Is she? Or has Georgia merely assumed Carmilla's psychosis, perhaps out of guilt over Carmilla's death?

Evidence exists for both interpretations: (1) Georgia apparently feels the stake piercing Carmilla's heart, suggesting that Georgia is possessed by Millarca. But how can Georgia be *already possessed*, if Carmilla is *still alive and possessed*, wandering the cemetery? Or if Millarca had passed from Carmilla to Georgia *at the moment* of Carmilla's death, why was Millarca/Carmilla crying over losing Leopoldo to Georgia, since she'd know that Georgia's body would soon be hers? Perhaps Georgia doesn't feel the stake, but is only reacting to the sound of the explosion in the cemetery, her vivid imagination supplying the rest? (2) Carmilla knows much about 18th century history and dance after she is "possessed." But even before any possession, she knew much about her ancestors. (3) The red color drains from roses, twice. Once when Carmilla touches a rose, once when Georgia touches a rose. Yet no one but the woman holding the rose notices. Just as only Carmilla saw the blood stains on her dress, reflected in the mirror. Do these "possessed" women only imagine their roses' discolorations? (4) Carmilla apparently kills Lisa. But is it through a neck bite, or scaring/pushing Lisa off a cliff? Dr. Verari finds rational explanations for both Lisa's and Carmilla's deaths. No explanation of vampirism or possession required.

Clichés differ from motifs. Motifs recur throughout the same film or film series (water is a motif in the *Alien* series). Clichés recur across different films. Motifs recur to convey and underscore meaning. Clichés recur either due to lack of imagination, or because of their proven entertainment value; what worked before will work again. The uberpsycho's indestructibility originated as an innovative character trait in *Halloween* (1978), but because this was a crowd-pleaser, later films turned this trait into a cliché.

Clichés can be tiresome, but also enjoyable. Like most genres, horror abounds in clichés. The decapitated head found inside a toilet (*Curtains* 1983; *Night School*, 1981), or in a bucket (*Anthropophagus: The Grim Reaper*, Italian 1980), or in a microwave oven (*Superstition*, 1982). The uberpsycho who lifts a victim off his feet, then pins him to the wall with a knife. The corpse that drops from a ceiling or rafter, dangling and bobbing, just as the next screaming victim rushes past.

Apart from their entertainment value, clichés are a form of symbolic language, providing a shorthand tool by which films communicate with audiences. Glowing red eyes indicate that a character is either demonic or demonically possessed, or, less often, a vampire or a witch. Horror fans know to beware of characters with glowing red eyes, just as they know that a golden glow often signals angelic powers. In *Child of Darkness, Child of Light* (TVM 1991), a young boy's eyes glow red, whereas a blond girl emits a golden halo. Yes, you guessed it. The boy is a son of Satan. The girl is a daughter of God.

This Rule of the Golden Glow is nearly universal. In *The Hidden* film series, good aliens *are* a golden glow.[17] This glow is visible whenever they transfer from one human host to another. The evil aliens are slimy, tentacled, slug-like creatures, invading human hosts through the throat — a time-honored method for evil creatures invading humans (e.g., *Shivers*, Canadian 1975).

Imaginative filmmakers can turn around clichés, to strong effect. In *The Visitor*, the evil Katy's eyes glow not red, but golden. This is a nice and original touch. Katy's golden eyes are both unexpected, and effectively creepy. And because there's something sci-fi about her golden eyes, they support the conceit that Katy is an evil *space* child.

However, as discussed above, *The Visitor* also uses clichés for their traditional meanings, to quickly and wordlessly "explain" its inexplicable story. We know one side is evil because it's managed by wealthy international businessmen. Another side is good because it has bald young men helping a sagelike elderly man. We never learn what they're doing, but they're bald, so they must be spiritual.[18]

Demonically possessed or empowered people have also sported glowing green eyes (e.g., *Mausoleum*, 1983; *Shock 'Em Dead*, 1991). A lesser punch than golden eyes. Horror associates green with slimy things, so we're not *that* surprised when demonic eyes glow green rather than red.

Because of their familiarity, clichés are easy satirical targets. In *Horror Hospital* (British 1973), Jason, a rock singer, checks into a country health spa for some rest and recuperation. The spa is run by Dr. Storm, a mad scientist who captures Jason and his girlfriend Judy. As Dr. Storm recounts his tragic life story and fiendish future plans (and what mad scientist doesn't?), lightning and thunderclaps punctuate his story's portentous points.[19]

Yes, that's right. A storm assists Dr. Storm in telling his stormy tale. It's not subtle, but satire often isn't. More satire comes from mixing mad scientist clichés (an uptight female doctor, a mansion with castle-like turrets, victims of experimental surgery, a deformed assistant [a dwarf rather than a hunchback], thunder and lightning) together with contemporary pop culture icons (hippie victims, leather-clad biker henchmen).

Finally, let us note that *motif* too is a French word. As is *cliché*.

Creating a World

Through *mise-en-scène*, filmmakers create entire worlds. Fantasy and far future worlds may involve imaginative costumes and set décor. Dramas and comedies often depict fictional worlds that resemble a more mundane reality. Even so, an office comedy like *Clockwatchers* (1997) must still strive to create a *suitably* mundane office environment, one that *specifically* supports the film's characters, story events, and themes.

Horror inhabits many worlds, from the naturalistic summer camps of slasher films, to the stylized past of *Bram Stoker's Dracula*, to the future worlds of *Alien* (1979). *The Cabinet of Dr. Caligari* (aka *Das Cabinet des Dr. Caligari*, German 1920), employs German expressionist set design to create a world as seen by a lunatic.[20]

In *Caligari*, an evil psychiatrist compels a young man, through hypnosis, to kill people. However, the murders are later revealed to be the paranoid delusions of a mental patient. ("It was all a dream!") His skewed perspective is depicted visually in the skewed and surreal set design: crooked houses, windows, and roads; outdoor scenes that are obviously shot indoors; misshapen and disproportionately-sized furniture that looks to be designed by Dr. Seuss. Painted shadows. This expressionism extends to the acting. The murderer's angular body posture and arm stances reinforce the angular set pieces.

Caligari's expressionist *mise-en-scène* supports both story and theme. Dramatically, the set décor and acting help render a tale told from a lunatic's perspective. But these elements also work thematically. *Caligari* has been interpreted as a metaphor for the then recently concluded First World War, when older and respected authority figures (be it Dr. Caligari or politicians) convinced millions of young men to become mindlessly marching, murder machines.[21]

Caligari uses the common horror conceit of a world turned frighteningly unnatural; a world in which ordinary, rational men suddenly become mindless killers, be they zombies, or pod people, or hypnotized madmen. Its expressionist sets later inspired those in *Mur-*

ders in the Rue Morgue (1932) and *The Bride of Frankenstein* (1935), the latter complementing its slanted sets with canted frames and the mad scientists' angular stances. *Caligari's* expressionism extends to modern times, influencing the set design in *Bram Stoker's Dracula*.

Hospital Massacre (1982) is a slasher film that draws much of its terror from a *mise-en-scène* that magnifies all our paranoid fears about doctors and hospitals. Just before Susan enters the building, her boyfriend sets the tone by asking, "Isn't this the hospital where they had all that trouble last year? Some patient ran amok or something." Soon thereafter, Susan confronts every viewer's nightmare when her "routine" tests indicate a potentially serious illness (a psycho has switched the results) and she must stay for several days of "observation."

Although *Hospital Massacre's* psycho kills doctors and nurses and visitors with gusto, the greater threat is the hospital itself. Its *mise-en-scène* creates a house of medical horrors, where no single incident is outrageously wrong, but the creepy drops accumulate in Chinese water torture fashion. Gruesome medical photos cover the walls, casting ominous shadows. The abandoned 9th floor is filthy and hazy (it's "being fumigated"), suggesting Dickensian dirt and disease. Doctors finger their scary scalpels, saws, and needles. They assure Susan that nothing is wrong with her, then whisper ominously to each other *in front of Susan*, treating her as an object rather than a partner in her own treatment. They scowl over her X-rays, but won't show them to her. (We've seen them — they're terrifying!) Their incompetence is astounding. Test results are switched under their noses. They're paged to the empty 9th floor, and go without suspicion.

Dr. Saxon's cold, slow examination of the near naked Susan suggests a bedside manner that is part lecher, part sadist. A creepy janitor leers at Susan. While Susan waits on a pay phone, a creepy doctor with a thick, black beard lurks behind her. When her ex-husband doesn't answer the phone, Susan is further isolated in the hospital.

Nurses are stern and unresponsive, robotically obeying doctors and behaving like prison guards. When Susan's boyfriend tries to free her, Dr. Saxon orders the nurses to drag Susan back to her room. The boyfriend meekly acquiesces to this authority figure.

Patients are scary; old, crazy, or ghastly ill. In an elevator, Susan is trapped with a patient who appears unconscious and bleeding. He later turns out to be a lecherous slob. Another patient has seizures as he's wheeled past Susan. Susan's hostile roommates, three crones, discuss Susan's "rancid organs." After witnessing a murder, Susan runs for help into a room, finding three patients covered in casts, helplessly waving their limbs. When Susan screams that she's seen Dr. Saxon murdered, she is strapped down and adjudged insane. "This whole hospital is nuts!" she screams. "What is wrong with everybody in this hospital?" A doctor announces that unless she calms, he'll have to operate. (A lobotomy, perhaps?)

Hospital Massacre concertizes and exploits audience fears of a medical authority that has all the knowledge and all the power. This conceit is supported by props (scary medical photos, X-rays, surgical instruments, body casts), set décor (the filthy, smoky, fumigated 9th floor), and acting (the taciturn, authoritarian doctors and nurses who rule our fate; and the hostile, freakish patients we fear we might become). Also impressive is the backlit screen, creating silhouettes of (1) the undressing, hence vulnerable, Susan, and (2) the "speaking doctor" who turns out to be a corpse, and (3) the psycho pushing the screen down the hall toward his next victim.

Mise-en-scène can be challenging, in both resources and imagination, when creating a far future world. Filmmakers have a poor track record in imagining futurist clothes or set décor with accuracy. In 1930s *Flash Gordon* serials, "the future" meant gleaming chrome, neatly groomed astronauts, and aliens in Grecian helmets and glittering underwear. Many early sf films depict an antiseptic world, free of dirt. (Maybe it's all been paved over by those moving sidewalks?) To this day, futurist *mise-en-scène* continues to be either ludicrous (pills or blue paste for food, or impossible-to-sit-upon chairs) or stuck in the filmmaker's present. Sf TV shows from the 1960s, such as *Star Trek* and *UFO*, feature miniskirts and Nehru jackets. Characters in 1980s *Star Trek* episodes discuss their feelings as if they were on *Oprah*. Their 24th century "communicators" are more primitive than 21st century cell phones. The astronauts in *Alien* use green phosphor computer monitors that look like they run on DOS or even CP/M. The hefty "laptops" in *Aliens* (1986) have technologically advanced to amber phosphor.

Ironically, horror is often more accurate about the future than is sf. Horror recognizes that the future will still have grit and dirt. In *Alien*, the crew of the spaceship *Nostromo* includes grimy, unkempt astronauts, working amid broken, hissing steam pipes. *Alien* exchanges the bright, antiseptic gleam from *Forbidden Planet* (1956) and *2001: A Space Odyssey* (1968) for a mostly darker, uglier set décor. Horror always has been less optimistic than sf about our future in space.

Storywise, *Alien*'s gritty set décor supports its tale of a stingy corporation, unconcerned with crew safety.[22] This heightens the horror, because when astronauts are ill-equipped due to a bottom-line corporate mentality, they are more vulnerable. *Aliens* brought heavily-armed troops into the picture, but still, they were easily slaughtered. This is why *Aliens* is a horror film, despite borrowing action film icons (e.g., some really big guns). *Alien³* (1992) was set on a prison planet. Inmates aren't allowed to have guns, making them, once again, more vulnerable—and the alien threat more threatening.

Alien has been described as "a haunted house on a spaceship," a conceit that is supported by the *mise-en-scène*. Much of *Nostromo* is dark and lonely, its passageways filled with hissing, fog-like steam (or is it smoke?). At one point, Brett enters what might be a cargo hold, but looks like a torture dungeon. Chains dangle from the ceiling. Water showers down, like a spooky rainstorm.

Why is it raining inside a spaceship? While that ship is out in deep space? Where is that water coming from? Brett seems not at all bothered by this. Is not water, like air, a precious commodity in deep space?

And speaking of a downpour, what about the *Nostromo*'s artificial gravity? We know the *Nostromo* is not a cylindrical ship, as in *2001: A Space Odyssey*, where centrifugal force creates a semblance of gravity. So how is the *Nostromo*'s artificial gravity created? As in most film/TV sf (which is mostly bad), *Alien* assumes artificial gravity and leaves it at that. However, because *Alien* is horror, not sf, we can overlook the story and set design's ignoring the laws of physics.

Whatever causes that rain shower (a broken cooling system?), whatever kind of "gravity" pulls down that water, the aesthetic effect of the *Nostromo*'s set décor is to create the appearance and atmosphere of a leaky torture dungeon, in some castle basement, on a stormy night. Poor science fiction—but great horror/sci-fi.

Later, Ripley activates the *Nostromo*'s self-destruct sequence, filling the halls with hissing steam (or is it smoke?), flashing strobe lights, and ringing sirens. Flames belch across a corridor. Again, *why?* The light show and sirens are to warn the crew, but why all that smoke or steam? Is it that damnable cooling system again? And why the flames? Surely, a spaceship could self-destruct in a less showy manner. *Nostromo* is quite the drama queen.

Although much of this set décor is dramatically illogical, aesthetically, the loud and flashy *mise-en-scène* heightens tension as Ripley escapes the alien, with scant minutes left before the ship self-destructs. This demonstrates a fundamental rule: *The more entertaining the story or special effects, the less likely the audience will notice the logical flaws.* With all that excitement, how many viewers wondered about the hissing steam, or showering rain, or belching flames?

Ripley returns to the alien planet in *Aliens*, a film with its own logical flaws. Alien blood is corrosive, and burns through even metal. Yet when a land rover drives over an alien, crushing its head and spattering its yellow blood onto the vehicle, neither the wheels nor hull appear damaged. Even had the rain washed off this alien blood, some damage should remain. But again, in all the excitement, most viewers miss this logical inconsistency.

Water is a motif throughout the *Alien* series. In *Aliens*, it rains on the planet. (At least it isn't raining inside the spaceship.) This rain drizzles into the ruined colony building. In *Alien³*, water is always dripping in the prison basement. In *Alien: Resurrection* (1997), the characters must swim underwater from one area of the space station (out in deep space) to the next.

Why is the *mise-en-scène* so wet? Academics like to impose highbrow interpretations onto films, perhaps because otherwise they'd feel like they were slumming.[23] But while reading symbols into a film can be fun, if one respects horror, one should let the film *speak for itself.* Explicit interpretations overrule the implicit. Aesthetic effect (how cinematic tools support character, story, and themes) overrules tenuous, socio-political symbolism. Absent strong contrary evidence, water must always be taken to symbolize water. That may not impress colleagues, but it is common sense.

In the *Alien* series, the water's primary aesthetic (rather than symbolic) effect is that it looks cool. That's not highbrow, but it is so. In *Alien*, the water contributes to the film's scary, haunted house atmosphere. The set décor in *Aliens* and *Alien³* include whirling fan blades, which, together with the drizzling water, lend the spooky atmosphere a rainy *noir* quality.

Water in the *Alien* series also serves dramatic functions. In *Alien³*, cold water from the sprinkler system causes the alien, who'd been dipped in molten lead, to explode. In *Alien: Resurrection*, water heightens the threat: (1) The astronauts may drown, because they must swim a long time underwater while holding their breath, and (2) Aliens are even scarier underwater than on dry land, because they swim fast, whereas humans (especially without scuba gear) are slower and more vulnerable.

Water also functions to create characters, and humorous effect. In *Aliens*, while working under muggy conditions, one space marine complains, "It's hot as hell in here." To which another replies, "Yeah man, but it's a dry heat." Apart from the humor, this dialog, together with the *mise-en-scène*, establishes the discomfort of the marines, and their cynical personalities. Their joking cynicism during a tough situation further suggests that they are battle-hardened. This in turn makes the aliens appear that much more threatening when these tough marines are so easily massacred.

Alien is not unique in featuring an indoor rain shower. In *White Noise*, evil spirits lure Jonathan to a warehouse near the piers. It's dry outside when Jonathan arrives. Bone dry. Yet once he enters the warehouse (which again, has a torture chamber ambiance), water showers in what appears to be a courtyard area. *Why* is it raining inside a building? Where did that water come from? Broken pipes along the ceiling? Or maybe there's no roof over the "courtyard" (if that's what it is) and a downpour started *the instant* Jonathan entered the warehouse. Quite a coincidence. A "mystery shower" also appears at the end of *Jeepers Creepers* (2001). Outside, bone dry. Inside the abandoned factory, water drips from the ceiling. *Why?*

I assume the sole aesthetic intent of all these indoor rain showers is to build a creepy atmosphere. It's illogical, but it does look really cool.

A similar emotional effect (a sense of ruin and decay, with a hint of "Gothic cool") is achieved with merely a "leak noise" in the deserted barroom of New Orleans's dilapidated Joy Theater, in *Frankenstein* (TVM 2004). Same emotional effect, yet a leaky pipe in a barroom is logical. (What's not logical — and remains unanswered — is how detective Harker managed to squeeze so many refrigerators — or even one — up through that narrow crawlspace to the forgotten attic.)

Creating Low-Budget Worlds

Happily for low-budget filmmakers, the *mise-en-scène* for a far future world need not be expensive — especially if it's a post-apocalyptic near future, such as inspired by *Mad Max* (1979). Most post-apocalyptic films are science fiction,[24] but some are horror/sci-fi, such as *Hardware* and *Parasite* (1982).

Parasite is about a scientist seeking a cure for ... a parasite. A big, slimy thing that jumps out at you (because *Parasite* was filmed in 3-D), clings to your body, and sucks you dead. Although the story occurs in the future, the actors wear contemporary clothes. No "futuristic" sparkly turtlenecks. The desert locations include a garage, motel, bar, and gas station, all of it dilapidated. Only a few props indicate that we are in the future. The villain wields a laser gun that resembles a cheap glow stick, and drives a "futuristic" sports car.[25] Store signs are meant to indicate that prices are shockingly high. (Alas, gas prices in this "future" are not so shocking by today's standards). People pay in silver, because money has lost its value. A biker sports a labor camp tattoo.

Parasite demonstrates that if you're going to shoot a horror/sci-fi film set in the future, a post-apocalyptic milieu is a pragmatic choice. It's no problem if the filmmaker can't afford a gleaming, high-tech set, because the story doesn't require it.

Nevertheless, shooting a horror/sci-fi film set in deep space need not be a budget-buster. *Star Crystal* uses imagination (both in story and *mise-en-scène*) to compensate for its low budget. Storywise, *Star Crystal* is an *Alien* ripoff that bizarrely morphs into an *E.T.* ripoff. After slaughtering several astronauts, the slimy, tentacled alien reads the New Testament, finds Christ, and turns warm and cuddly. (No, *Star Crystal* is not intentionally funny.)

The film's set décor is a marvel of cheapness. As in *Alien*, some astronauts find an alien egg on another planet. (In this case, Mars). But rather than an intricately veined and pulsating egg, *Star Crystal*'s alien egg resembles a lifeless lump of copper-tinted aluminum foil. One critic called it "a baked potato." Instead of *Alien*'s elaborately designed passageways (with grated iron floors and ceilings, hissing steam pipes, cables, flashing lights, video monitors, computer consoles — even doors!) the astronauts in *Star Crystal* crawl about inside featureless tubes. Tubes that look to be constructed from aluminum sheets, or possibly cardboard. The space station does have "futuristic" escalators, in that they look clean and modern — like those found in a shopping mall.

This is a common low-budget film technique. If your story is set in the far future, find a location with modern architecture. Lots of glass, aluminum, and sparkling concrete. Maybe at a state college campus. Because, as we all know, the future won't have any wooden frame houses.

Star Crystal demonstrates why low-budget sf or horror/sci-fi films often present greater location hurdles than do psycho or supernatural horror films. If a script has a graveyard scene, real graveyards are easy to find. But to film in a space station, one must rent a soundstage and construct a space station's interior, or rent an existing space station set, assuming one lives near a film production center where such a set may be available. If not, one is reduced to shooting in a shopping mall that can hopefully pass for a space station's interior. Or maybe fill up the director's parents' basement with steam, smoke, and flickering colored lights, and hope that it will pass for a low-budget *Nostromo*.

Of course, despite sf film clichés, the future need not be all gleaming glass and steel. *Contamination* is an *Alien* ripoff that morphs into a James Bond thriller. An astronaut returns from the first Mars mission with an alien egg, intending to use it for world domination. Despite the futurist setting, the film's characters drive 1970s cars, dress in 1970s clothing, and live in red brick houses. Some police officers wear brown, storm trooper style uniforms (though they're the good guys), but that's one of the few visual cues that we're in "the future." Apparently, the *mise-en-scène* is whatever the producer had on hand.

Anyway, *Contamination* is horror/sci-fi, not sf. Horror is less concerned with predicting the future than with the gory handiwork of futuristic threats. And *Contamination*'s alien eggs create much gore. The eggs themselves are less intricate than the eggs in *Alien*, though they do pulsate and glow. They're certainly several notches above *Star Crystal*'s baked potato egg.

Understandably, low-budget filmmakers can't easily portray great wealth. The fabulous homes of the rich and famous never look quite so fabulous in direct-to-video exploitation films. In *Shock 'Em Dead*, Angel, an aspiring rock guitarist, sells his soul to Satan in return for rock stardom "and everything that goes with it."[26] After the occult ceremony, Angel awakens in a cheap middle class house that's supposedly the luxurious home of a wealthy celebrity. The walls are thin. The furnishings are drab. The decorations are tacky. The "extravagant wardrobe" in the closet resembles thrift store crap. Sure, Angel is impressed by these "great treasures" that Satan has bestowed upon him. He has to be. It's in the script.

Shock 'Em Dead director Mark Freed cleverly mitigates the house's drabness by setting Angel in a crappy trailer before selling his soul. The cheap house is a marked improvement over Angel's previous digs, and may therefore seem fabulously wealthy to viewers who don't pause to analyze such things.

The mob boss in *Possessed by the Night* (1994) has a nicer Los Angeles house, but it's still middle class. Upper middle class, but no *Godfather* mansion. Fortunately, the wide angle lens help. If you want to upgrade a house from nice to sumptuous, photograph it with a wide angle lens.

Outdoor venues are equally impressive regardless of budget, hence their popularity with campsite slasher films. *The Final Terror* (1983) and *The Prey* (1984) are practically travelogues. Low-budget master Roger Corman also notes the advantage: "My theory, as I began studying some of my own films that were shot in studios, was that if I continued to shoot primarily in studios, my films would always look cheap. Budgets were so low and the sets we could afford were so small that we'd wind up giving the picture away as a low-budget film from the very first shot. You just knew it was going to be a little picture. If I filmed on natural locations, I wouldn't have such a low budget look."[27]

The Jar (1984) is a surrealistic horror art film about an unassuming young man, Paul, who chances upon a jar containing a pickled demon-thing. This demon torments Paul with surreal visions, while Paul struggles to understand and overcome the demon's creeping psychic encroachment. The film's outdoor locations are impressive: children ride a merry-go-round; a youth kills a boy in a foggy urban park and escapes with Paul; black-robed monks trudge toward a crucifixion in the desert; during a hairy Vietnam War battle, a tuxedoed yuppie sipping wine observes Paul's neighbor landing in a helicopter to rescue him.

These bizarre and visually impressive locations aesthetically serve the story, in that Paul is going mad. Furthermore, director Bruce Tuscano fully exploits his outdoor locations. He pans across the widely-spaced monks in the desert, and tracks the American platoon's trek along a river. He reverts to a tight frame when he must hide his less impressive (or nonexistent) locations in offscreen space.

Apart from exploiting the inexpensive majesty of nature, low-budget filmmakers often shoot outdoors because it's generally easier to obtain permission to film (or avoid getting caught filming) at a public outdoor location than inside a mall, office building, or other private property. Easier still when filming at night because there will be fewer cops or pesky passersby.

Filming without permits or insurance is called *guerrilla filmmaking*. About *Carnival of Souls* (1962), Jeff Hillegass writes: "A small crew allowed the filmmakers to sneak in and out of settings in order to grab a few shots, without having to bother to obtain permits and close streets for shooting."[28] This inexpensive but risky option is why some low-budget films are shot in barren urban areas during early hours, or on remote beaches, or in secluded forests.

An *empty set* is always an option for creative low-budget filmmakers. With the right few pieces of set décor, in the right dramatic context, an empty set can look stylish rather than cheap.

In *Bram Stoker's Dracula*, Dracula takes Mina dancing. Perhaps they're in a grand ballroom, yet we see no ballroom, furnishings, or other dancers. There is only Dracula and Mina, and dozens of lit white candles. The room appears vast, yet aside from the candles, it is empty and dark. Apart from saving money, this scene works aesthetically because it supports the characters and story. Dracula and Mina are in love, thus they "only have eyes for each other." Dancing together, the world beyond them does not exist. Thus, they (and the audience) do not see it.

In *Creepshow*, actors are often set against blank "comic book panels" of bright, primary colors. Some panels contain a simple graphic image (e.g., a spiral or lightning bolt) [Figure 3.4]. Actors and furnishings sometimes morph into cartoon images, either to emphasize an emotional or dramatic peak in the story, or to begin or conclude a story. *Aesthetically*, these shots support *Creepshow*'s conceit of a filmed comic book. *Pragmatically*, these

Figure 3.4 — *Creepshow*. Red and black, cartoon lighting bolts emanate from Cass's (Elizabeth Regan) head, signifying her shock upon seeing a walking corpse.

shots are *not* pragmatic. No money was saved, because these empty "comic panel" sets supplement, rather than replace, the furnished sets. Sometimes, art alone justifies an empty set.

Actors similarly blend into comic book panels in the "Tales of the Undead" episode of TV's *Friday the 13th: The Series*. However, whereas the *Creepshow* comic book is mostly a stylistic device, the *Tales of the Undead* comic book, and its protagonist, Ferrus the Invincible, are active participants in the story and its *mise-en-scène*. Satan has cursed a particular *Tales of the Undead* comic book, allowing its owner to transform into Ferrus and (seemingly) draw his victims into the comic book's pages, where their struggle continues across the panels.

I say "seemingly," because though Ferrus exits the comic book, and lives and kills in the real world, it's unclear whether he drags his victims into the comic book, or if their depictions in the panels are merely *Creepshow* type stylistics. Although Micki and Ryan's defeat of Ferrus is depicted in the comic panels, they make no mention of having lived inside a comic book.

For a slasher film, *Sleepaway Camp* has some unusual subtext and stylish flair. As so often, the killer is motivated by an early childhood trauma. And, as so often, that trauma includes seeing one or both parents having sex. In *Stage Fright* (aka *Nightmares,* Australian 1980) and *The Initiation* (1984), the killer saw mommy sleeping with an illicit lover. In *Sleepaway Camp*, Angela sees her "two daddies" having sex.[29]

These daddies were filmed on a sparse set, containing only a brass bed and the two men. The rest of the set is hidden in darkness. In the next shot, Angela and her sibling share a bed in a similarly darkened set, presumably playing doctor. *Pragmatically*, these empty sets may save a little money. *Aesthetically*, they underscore that these are Angela's memories. Since memories are selective, it's natural that Angela only remembers those events that upset her. To her, the room's furnishings are unimportant [Figure 3.5].

Figure 3.5 —*Sleepaway Camp*. This lighting setup saves money on set décor and props, while surrealistically suggesting a child's selective memory.

"The Obsolete Man" episode of TV's *The Twilight Zone* uses sparse, expressionistic set décor for the State's courtroom, in stark contrast to the prisoner's cluttered room. The courtroom's barrenness may (or may not) have saved money. Nevertheless, it aesthetically supports the story and theme of a humorless, Spartan society that prizes efficiency and obliterates "non-essentials" (e.g., books, ideas, art, and useless, "obsolete" human beings) that do not serve the State.

In *Star Crystal*, a space station's conference room reveals only a table, and a few actors on chairs, bathed in light. The rest of the room is hidden in darkness, aside from some blinking lights, suggesting a computer or a map against the wall. *Aesthetically*, this darkness focuses our attention on the brightly lit actors, and heightens a tense dramatic situation. *Pragmatically*, the room is likely dark because the filmmaker could not afford to construct an elaborate, "futuristic" conference room (see Figure 6.14).

In *Bram Stoker's Dracula*, *Sleepaway Camp*, and *Star Crystal*, the lighting (or rather, the *lack* of lighting) supports the aesthetic function of these films' sparse sets. Empty darkness can be stylish, even surrealistic, inviting viewers to fill in that black canvas. We imagine an opulent ballroom, or furnished bedroom, or space station command center within that dark void.

Ed Wood used sparse sets, but then brightly lit them for all to see. *Plan 9 from Outer Space* (1959) depicts an airplane cockpit with just two actors sitting in chairs, holding steering wheels, with a shower curtain behind them. In such a shabby cockpit, pilots should only fly at night. With the instrument panel lights dimmed.

Tip for low-budgeters: *If your set looks crappy, consider hiding it in the dark.*

Disguising Locations

By *location*, I mean where a film is shot. By *locale*, I mean where the story occurs. The trick is to make the location resemble the locale.

A low-budget filmmaker may use his mom's garage as the *location* for a scene set in a NASA space station *locale*. Bigger-budgeted films often use *foreign locations* to substitute for *American locales*, because while it can be cheaper to film outside the U.S., producers believe that American audiences prefer stories about American characters, set in America.[30]

This means that foreign cities must be disguised to resemble U.S. cities.[31] This disguise can be *active*, as in placing familiar American store or traffic signs at the location, or covering foreign signs, or dressing foreign extras in American clothes. Or the disguise can be *passive*, as in being careful not to film foreign signs or telltale landmarks. When filming "New York City" in Vancouver, you don't want to see the Rocky Mountains looming in the background (e.g., *Rumble in the Bronx*, aka *Hung fan au*, 1995).

Disguising locations can create aesthetic problems: (1) A blooper may reveal the locale's true location, thus lessening the "suspension of disbelief" for discerning viewers, or (2) the location is so aggressively disguised that it looks nondescript and devoid of personality. If Toronto is disguised to resemble New York, the film fails to benefit from New York's unique landmarks (because it wasn't shot in New York), but neither can it benefit from Toronto's landmarks (because then we'd know the characters are not in New York).

Canada is the most popular foreign country to substitute for the U.S., but Eastern Europe is gaining ground. Yet despite set designers' best efforts at disguise, European locations are usually detectable, because, to quote Vincent in *Pulp Fiction*: "Everything is a little different." Buses are bigger, boxier, and cleaner. Buildings are older, with big stone walls. Cobblestone streets and poster kiosks abound.

Thr3e (2006) is a serial killer film shot in Poland.[32] We're supposed to assume that we're in some American city, but the ambiance feels oddly foreign. This arguably contributes a weird sensibility to the film's brooding atmosphere, because we feel that something's "not right." If so, it's serendipity. *Thr3e* does not highlight any Cracow landmarks, but instead tries to conceal its foreignness. (Who wants to see a film about a *Polish* serial killer? assume the producers.)

Opening shots establish *Mimic 3*'s (2003) locale as some New Jersey city overlooking Manhattan. Yet there remains an odd feeling that something's not right. No, it's not the Judas Bugs. It's that *Mimic 3* was shot in Romania, and we can *feel* it. At least, those of us familiar with the New York/New Jersey area can feel it. A Nebraskan may not notice.

Extra Terrestrial Visitors (aka *Los nuevos extraterrestres*, Spain-France 1983) was shot in Spain (the actors speaking their dialog in both French and Spanish), yet the story concerns an American family living in a cabin in the woods. We see their boxes of Corn Flakes and Sugar Frosted Flakes. We see a little American flag set inside a glass on the bar. A portrait of George Washington hangs in their living room. No subtlety there. Maybe Europeans hang portraits of their national and historical leaders in their homes, so they figure Americans do so too. A picture of President Reagan hangs in the forest ranger's cabin, but that makes sense, being a government office. This clumsy and excessive *faux* Americanness contributes to the film's overall weirdness and curious charm.

Canadian locations often substitute for American locales, without convincing. Toronto, Montreal, and Vancouver can't fool a native New Yorker. Their streets, buildings, subways, and parks look different. *Bless the Child* (2000) has what looks to be a CGI insert of the Manhattan skyline, as seen from Satanist, Eric Stark's, Brooklyn roof. Yet the film's streets do not resemble Brooklyn (too suburban), its upstate highway does not resemble upstate New York highways (too narrow and rural), and the park at film's end is not Central Park.

The park was the giveaway for me. *Bless the Child* was filmed in and around Toronto. It is a fine occult thriller, with unexpected twists and an excellent cast.

Island of the Dead (2000) is a creepy, supernatural horror film about evil flies. The flies are possessed by the homeless dead, swarming over people and infecting them with a fatal pus-spewing rash. Early on, we see an establishing shot of the lower Manhattan skyline as seen from Brooklyn. The Twin Towers are still prominent. We cut to a series of low angle shots of the skyscrapers. *Aesthetically*, the low angles emphasize the social insignificance and vulnerability of the "lesser" people who walk beneath these looming buildings. This is reinforced by NYPD detective O'Keefe's voiceover, which soon muses over the missing people whom no one but she seems to care about. *Pragmatically*, this camera angle avoids showing us the actual streets at this location, which is not lower Manhattan, but Montreal. The less seen, the less likely that New Yorkers will "catch on."

Later, a ferry boat takes O'Keefe to Hart's Island, where New York has its potter's field. The boat collects its passengers at what is supposed to be The Bronx, but which resembles a hick town. As the ferry crosses the water, we see an oddly unpopulated shoreline. The real Bronx or Nassau should be more populous.

Island of the Dead's locations, in and around Montreal, do not resemble New York. They don't *feel* like New York. Yet ironically, Canada's barren shores and gloomy, gray skies enhance *Island of the Dead*'s eerie atmosphere — much like Vancouver's gray skies contributed to *The X-Files*'s creepy atmosphere. Horror can happen under glaring sunlight (e.g., *The Devil's Rejects*, 2005), but gray skies are the preferred canopy.

Just as *Island of the Dead*'s low angle shots hide Montreal's streets, *They* (2002) achieves a similar effect by using overhead camera shots to look *directly down upon* (rather than *from an angle* at) city buildings. *Aesthetically*, seeing the building roofs and city streets passing below us creates (1) an emotionally unsettling geometric pattern, because an ordinary city suddenly looks "alien" to us, and (2) a sense of some evil looming overhead. *Pragmatically*, this camera angle establishes that the locale is a city, without showing any telltale landmarks or building skylines. For all we know, the locale could be Manhattan. *They*'s Vancouver location is thus effectively disguised [Figure 3.6].

The giveaway is when Julia rushes into the Victory Square subway station. No such station in New York. Maybe another U.S. city? Yet "Victory Square" sounds so British. I immediately suspected Canada, a nation with British monarchs on its currency.

As in *Island of the Dead*, *They*'s sets are underpopulated. Its low budget didn't allow for many background actors (i.e., extras). O'Keefe finds only one attendant at work in the morgue. Wherever she or Julia go, there are fewer people than one would expect. Yet in both films, these unusually barren sets enhance the atmosphere. Directors generally like to fill their sets with a "realistic" number of extras.[33] But while horror can work with crowds (e.g., *Invasion of the Body Snatchers*, 1978), desolate sets are the preferred backdrop.

They's story is surprisingly similar to that of *Darkness Falls* (2003), shot in Australia. Both films feature strikingly attractive young adults who suffer from "night terrors" because, when they were children, monsters marked them. (Extra-dimensional demons, and an evil tooth fairy, respectively.) Now these monsters want to claim them. But these monsters can only act in the dark. So these young adults carry lots of flashlights and batteries, and try to

Figure 3.6 — *They.* This passing overhead view of city streets is both unsettling and an effective way to hide a city's identity.

avoid darkness and shadows. Neither film is explicitly set in the U.S., yet American audiences are encouraged to assume this. (Unless a film has *obviously* foreign characters, set in an *explicitly* foreign locale, Americans always assume the story is about Americans in America.)

The Rats (2002) is explicitly set in Manhattan, though the streets aren't recognizably New York. How can they be? *The Rats* was filmed in Toronto. And as with *They*, the giveaway is the subway. Jack rushes into the 39th Street subway station and, as experienced New Yorkers know, there is no 39th Street station in Manhattan.

The Rats is an enjoyable, albeit a bloodless and laughably silly film about genetically enhanced killer rats. The loopiest scene is when thousands of rats spout "geyser like" from the drainage openings in an empty swimming pool, filling up the pool like furry water. Whereupon Susan falls into, and is engulfed by, this "ocean of rats." Minor characters had previously been savagely and quickly killed by far fewer rats, yet Susan is pulled out a minute later, with nary a nick. No gore, just some red streaks on her face. Tame makeup for a horror film, but director John Lafia likely didn't want to mar his beautiful heroine.[34] Especially since *The Rats* is a TV movie, and hence, is gore-phobic.

Because the locales in *They* and *Darkness Falls* remain unknown, with no recognizable landmarks or spoken references to ground the viewer in a familiar locale, these films convey a vaguely insubstantial sensation. Their stories *feel* rootless and incorporeal, as if we're inside a nightmare. Where exactly *is* this town of Darkness Falls? On a coast, but in which state? Surely, somewhere in the United States. Apparently, it's near a city with a gambling industry, but which city?

This "ungrounded, nightmare quality" is lacking in *The Rats*, *Island of the Dead*, and *Bless the Child*, which are set in New York, but in an anemic and nondescript New York. These films share a "sense of place" that is not incorporeal, but bland. Contrast these films with *Lost Souls*, which has many scenes actually filmed in Manhattan and New Jersey. *Lost Souls*'s streets and tunnels and bridges are recognizably New York. Awaiting Peter, Maya sits on the familiar steps of the Main Branch of the New York Public Library on 42nd Street. These Manhattan locations ground *Lost Souls* in the story's Manhattan locale.

The Sentinel (1977) is another extraordinary occult film whose ambiance benefits from being shot on location in Brooklyn Heights and Manhattan. Seeing Alison live and work amid recognizably New York locations, we more easily believe that she is a New York high fashion model, and more easily suspend disbelief for the supernatural story elements.

Despite one week shooting in Manhattan, *Inferno* (Italian 1980) evokes an unsettling sensation of being *not* grounded in Manhattan. Assistant director Lamberto Bava explains: "There is the scene of New York City, which was actually shot in Italy, and he [director Dario Argento] used the real buildings of New York to superimpose on those scenes. It was kind of surrealistic, the way Dario Argento liked it."[35]

By imposing a Manhattan skyline over an Italian set, *Inferno* uses recognizably New York buildings and landmarks in a way that renders them alien. The result is, as Bava asserts, eerily surreal. It doesn't *look* like New York. Yet it clearly *is* New York.

Aesthetically, this surrealism works, because it supports the characters and story. The "New York" apartment building is home to a witch. We're told that, should you seek her, the "first key" to knowing that you've found the right building is the area's foul odor. Thus, we know that her presence affects the environs. It's to be expected then that, since the air smells strange in her building's proximity, the New York skyline should look strange. It's as if her building has warped the space-time continuum; natural physical laws are suspended. Certainly, little inside the building makes sense (e.g., the flooded room beneath the basement, the garish colors, the holes and pipes that transmit sounds, the secret space under the floorboards).

By contrast, *Bless the Child*'s CGI Manhattan skyline, as seen from Stark's roof, may look surreal to New Yorkers. But this surrealism is unintentional, less pronounced, and less supportive of the characters and story. Nothing explicitly indicates that Stark, though possessing Satanic powers, warps his environs.[36]

Highlighting Canadian Locations

Many horror films are shot in Canada. Few will admit it. Yet Canada need not hide. It too has contributed to horror, on its own merits.

Rather than disguising his Canadian locations, director David Cronenberg instead uses them to enhance his stories and themes. *Shivers* (Canadian 1975) is set in the Starliner Tower luxury apartment building. The film opens with a promotional slide show, during which a building manager brags that Starliner Tower is only twelve and a half minutes away "from downtown Montreal." Blatant and upfront: We are in Canada.

Shivers is about a mad scientist who creates a parasite, hoping it will help modern man regain his "primal urges."[37] This parasite is a slimy, slug-like creature, resembling the one in *Parasite*. But rather than attaching itself to the victim's body, *Shivers*'s parasites enter people's throats or vaginas, nestling inside them, and transforming them into mindless nymphomaniacs. As these parasites spread throughout Starliner Tower, all taboos are broken. All sexual acts are practiced by the tenants. Orgies. Rape. Gang rape. Adultery. Seniors with youth. Interracial sex (still eyebrow-raising in 1975). Incest. Pedophile sex (still shocking today). Sex-crazed children led around on dog leashes.

All elements of *mise-en-scène* support *Shivers*'s story and theme of an emotionally and sexually repressed society, hiding behind a civilized facade, finally releasing its pent-up desires with destructive force. Regarding *location*, Starliner Tower sits isolated on an island, providing "all the modern amenities" to residents: laundry, grocery, health clinic, etc. These residents have severed themselves from humanity, just as they are severed from their own humanity.

Regarding *set décor*, the building's modern architecture is bland, featureless, and sterile; lacking personality, or individuality, or creativity. Its furnishings are modern, immaculate, and antiseptic. Apartments do not looked "lived in." They provide housing, but not homes.

Regarding *acting* and *clothing*, the characters ride silently in elevators; they do not converse. They conceal their desires. Nicholas leaves his apartment in a conservative suit, as if going to work, then sneaks up to his nineteen-year-old mistress's apartment. His wife struggles to emotionally reach out to Nicholas, with difficulty. They don't connect. She herself is very proper, avoiding sex with him. She wears beige. When the manager learns of the mistress's bizarre death, he marvels, because she was a "very civilized young lady. Never complained about anything." One senses that this building is full of civilized people.

Ironically (but not inappropriately), the happily sexual doctor and nurse are the last to be "converted" into sex fiends by the parasites. They are the least in need of it.

In *Rabid* (Canadian 1977), Cronenberg returns to his theme of medical science gone bad. A new graft technique allows skin taken from one part of the human body to replicate skin found on another part. Well, that's the plan. When a doctor grafts skin from Rose's thigh onto her arm, she unexpectedly grows a penis-like, blood-sucking fang under that arm. With it, she drinks blood from people, whereupon they turn rabid.

As with *Shivers*, *Rabid* is explicitly Canadian. Characters mention Montreal. Signs refer to the Provincial Health Bureau. (No provinces in the U.S.) Canada's bleak, snowy landscapes emotionally support *Rabid*'s fatalistic story and ending. As do those gray skies.

In *The Brood* (Canadian 1979), Cronenberg rehashes his medicine-gone-bad theme for a third time. A psychiatrist develops a therapy by which patients manifest their emotional rage in physical form. One patient, Nola, births mutant midgets, grown in sacs hanging from her body. These midgets terrorize or kill anyone who upsets Nola. Which is often. Nola suspects that her husband, Frank, wants to dump her and take away Candy, their daughter.

Apart from indicting modern psychiatry, *The Brood*'s core theme is the trauma of divorce and its resultant child custody battles. Cronenberg has said that his then recent divorce inspired *The Brood*. His depressing story and themes are (once again) effectively supported by Canada's bleak, snowy landscape, its gray skies, and its sterile, modern architecture. And once more, we *know* we're in Canada: We see the Toronto Police, and hear people mention Vancouver.

The Canadian Film Development Corporation subsidized all three of these films, so some token "Canadian content" may have been mandatory. Even so, these films form a thematic trilogy that remain Cronenberg's greatest work — partially *because* of their Canadian content.

Also, I'm a sucker for wintry horror. *The Changeling* (1980), *The Shining* (1980), *Ghost Story* (1981), and *Curtains* (1983) — another "dead marriage" horror film shot in Canada and starring Samantha Eggar — all derive part of their emotional power from snowy landscapes.

Hidden or Unseen Threats

A threat frightens. If a threat is hidden, and then sprung upon audiences, that threat also shocks. *Shock* and *fear* are not the same, but they are related. A shock unnerves viewers, fraying their emotional defenses and making them more susceptible to fear. The reverse is also true. A suspenseful story or creepy atmosphere instills fear into audiences, setting them "on edge" as they nervously await potential shocks.

Not only genuine threats shock. Horror filmmakers often shock audiences, only to reveal the source of the shock to be harmless. Characters in a film may hear a strange noise. Audience tension rises. Then a cat leaps out of a cupboard.

Some horror filmmakers forgo atmosphere, suspense, story, and character — and instead rely solely on shocks, because it's easier to jolt audiences than to frighten them. Especially when an audience consists of hardcore horror fans who have become inured to the usual monsters and clichés. Even so, a talented filmmaker should balance shocks with fear, much like a skilled music composer balances high and low notes, and fast and slow movements.

To shock, it helps first to hide. Cinema offers many ways to hide a threat. A monster may lurk beyond the film's frame line in *offscreen space*. Or it might remain hidden in darkness, or in blinding bright light. Or the camera lens may throw the monster out of focus, blurring it.

Or the threat may be hidden by the *mise-en-scène*.

Hiding a threat inside a closet, or under a bed, will work, but props and set décor can be used in more imaginative ways. In *Resident Evil* (2002), soldiers enter an underground complex that is overrun with zombies. They stop to plan their next move. Behind one man (taken prisoner by the soldiers) is a glass wall to a room that is flooded with a murky, orange liquid. We can't see into this room. We only see the orange liquid.

As the soldiers converse, a corpse floats up against the glass wall, emerging into view. This corpse is no threat, yet its sudden appearance shocks us. We never expected anything to emerge from that orange murk. Our attention was on the soldiers' conversation. The scene has effectively surprised the audience.

Extra Terrestrial Visitors hides a threat with steam. After showering, a young woman wipes the steam off the bathroom mirror. Whereupon she sees an evil alien, behind her, reflected in the mirror.

While threats can hide *behind* the set décor and props, a more imaginative use of *mise-en-scène* is to *camouflage* the threat. In *Alien*, Ripley escapes to the space shuttle, thinking that she's left the alien behind on the *Nostromo* and is finally safe. She calmly begins working near some tubes (or are they pipes?), whereupon ... the alien's hand pops out! Ripley is shocked (as is the audience) and backs away. The alien moves its head.

We then realize that its long, smooth head was always visible. But its head resembles, in shape and color, the nearby tubes (or pipes?), and was thus effectively camouflaged. Ripley had worked right alongside the alien, without realizing it. Making it all the more shocking when the alien finally moves [Figures 3.7, 3.8].

This camouflage trick recurs in *Aliens*. (Curiously, the aliens' heads are now corrugated, rather than baby smooth.) Space marines enter the cavernous rooms of a destroyed human colony and find the walls and ceilings covered with a baroquely styled "secreted resin."

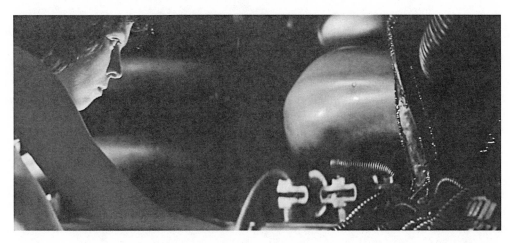

Figure 3.7 —*Alien.* Ripley (Sigourney Weaver) is practically staring at the alien's head, yet doesn't notice...

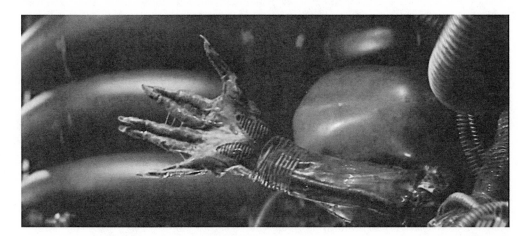

Figure 3.8 —...until the alien's hand pops out, scaring Ripley away. Note how similar the alien's head is to the surrounding space shuttle tubes.

They see no aliens, though their computer sensors insist that aliens surround them. Then the walls and ceiling "begin to move."

It's the aliens, of course. But until they began moving, they were indiscernible, because their grooved heads and bodies fit the pattern and color of the walls and ceiling.

This motif is put to reverse effect in *Alien³*. Ripley is searching the prison basement, when she spots an alien's head, hunkered down amid the pipes. She sneaks up and slams a pipe against the alien's head—which turns out to also be a pipe. This pipe is so corroded that Ripley has broken a hole into it. Bugs spill out, adding a gross and creepy touch to the scene.

Ripley (and the audience) breathes relief. Then the real alien, *effectively* camouflaged, emerges from the ceiling behind her.

In *Mimic* (1997), camouflaging a threat isn't merely a device to shock; it's the basic story concept. In this horror/sci-fi film, genetically modified bugs have evolved to resemble their chief predator and prey: humans. These people-sized bugs wander the subways and poorer sections of New York City, looking like perverts in tightly wrapped raincoats. Nobody notices anything strange from afar. (This *is* New York.) But get close enough to notice that the "face" is not quite human, and the Judas Bug (as it's called) spreads its "raincoat" into wings and pursues the now screaming human.

Mise-en-scène can camouflage heroes as well as threats. In the "Poison Pen" episode of TV's *Friday the 13th: The Series*, Micki breaks into a monastery office and substitutes a Satanic pen with a counterfeit. She hears someone approaching from outside. We cut outside and see the pen's evil owner (an impostor monk) ascending some stairs, then entering the empty office.

Where's Micki? She's nowhere in sight.

The impostor leaves with the counterfeit pen. Micki then emerges from a coat rack. She'd hidden herself by standing up against the coats. From behind, her hooded monk's robe blended into all the other robes hanging from the rack.

Mise-en-scène's ability to conceal not only has *aesthetic* applications (hiding a threat, so as to shock), but *pragmatic*, money-saving uses. Low-budget filmmakers often use props and set décor to imply unseen (and expensive) horrors. Such as the ever-popular *blood splatter from offscreen space*.

In *Aliens*, a pilot flies a shuttle to retrieve some space marines. She hears a door open. She turns. Sees the alien. She reaches for her gun. The alien lunges. Blood splatters the shuttle's windshield. We see the pilot's hand, still on her gun in its holster. We see it through the blood-stained windshield. We never saw her gory death, but the blood is a giveaway.

Mise-en-scène (the blood and windshield), framing (hiding the gory death in offscreen space), and editing here cooperate in creating this relatively inexpensive death.

Some critics argue that horrors are more horrific if unseen and left to the imagination. A cynic may counter that it's cheaper to toss fake blood against a wall than to invest in the special effects required to dismember an actor. However, in this case, we've already seen these aliens' handiwork, so nothing is left for our imagination. So why not kill the pilot in offscreen space? Even big studio films watch their pennies.

Tossing blood onto a wall or windshield, rather than showing the full gore, is a horror film cliché. Of course it's a cliché. It works. It arguably works aesthetically. It certainly works pragmatically.

Set décor and props can not only *hide* threats, but suggest the presence of *unseen* threats. Such as ghosts. In *Black Sunday* (aka *La maschera del demonio*, Italian 1960), the camera travels through a vast living room as various furnishings and props are knocked over by some unseen force, suggesting that a spirit has returned from the dead.

In *Evil Dead 2* (1987), an unseen demon's presence is suggested by demonic *sounds*, a POV shot rushing through the woods (*framing*), and the POV shot breaking through a car's rear window (*mise-en-scène*). Unseen demons are also suggested by furniture moving about the room, and by smoke effects.

Misleading or Suggested Threats

In *Alien³*, Ripley thought she saw an alien lurking amid some pipes, but it was only another pipe. Such "false alarms" or "red herrings" mislead an audience, unnerving them by defying their expectations, thus setting them "on edge" and making them more emotionally vulnerable to the next horrific happening.

In *Superstition*, two teenage boys trespass into an abandoned house at night, then split up. One boy enters the kitchen. He sees a knife, prominently *stuck into a wall*. He pauses to look at this knife, touches it, then walks on. (Can the director be any less subtle?)

The audience, knowing this is a horror film, naturally expects this knife to be used, and soon. Framing and editing heighten this expectation: after the boy continues into the kitchen, leaving the knife behind, the editing cuts to a shot from the hallway (rather than from inside the kitchen). We see the boy from the hallway. The frame shakes, implying that this is a POV shot. The POV of someone who is following the boy. Someone dangerous, who is approaching the kitchen, and thus, the knife.

But instead, supernatural forces kill the boy. The knife is never used. If anyone were following him (it's never made clear), it may have been the witch's spirit, or her mortal servant who lives on the property. Or maybe the shaky camera frame, like the knife, was a red herring, used to mislead audiences into thinking that somebody was following the boy.

After this first boy dies, the second boy enters the kitchen, seeking his friend. He too notices the knife, thus reminding us of its presence. Yet this boy is soon severed by an ascending window frame. Again, the knife is not used.

Yet this knife does serve an aesthetic purpose. By drawing the viewer's attention to this prop, the director heightens audience tension, because we expect to soon see someone stabbed. When the knife is ignored, audiences realize, perhaps only subconsciously, that they are unable to identify forthcoming dangers. They'd assumed that they'd spotted a risk, but the boys died in unexpected ways.

In *The Funhouse* (1981), Amy and her friends are trapped in a carnival funhouse, stalked by a mutant slasher. Amy peers past some whirling fan blades. She sees her parents outside. She screams, but her parents can't hear her due to the fan's noise. Tension rises. Amy is "so close, yet so far" from safety. But apart from supporting this dramatic tension — *those blades are begging for human flesh*. I expected those blades to slice *someone* before film's end.

We cut to another funhouse area. Liz is trapped behind another set of whirling fan blades. The mutant appears at the end of the corridor. I was sure that Liz would be pushed through those blades. But no. She distracts the mutant with sex — then finds a knife and stabs him. Whereupon the mutant murders Liz with his bare hands.

Like *Superstition*'s knife, *The Funhouse*'s fan raises audience expectations of a specific form of death, then unnerve us when those expectations are denied.

Unnerving audiences by misleading them, by raising and then denying their expectations, is an old trick. In *Psycho* (1960), Hitchcock establishes Marion's character and storyline, so that viewers expect her to survive. Then he denies those expectations by killing her off midway into the film.

But in order to mislead, *most* items in a film must be what they appear to be. In *Aliens*, a pilot enters a shuttle and notices a bit of slime dripping from the cargo bay. He doesn't know what this means. The audience does. The slime indicates that an alien is on board. And this time the audience is right. Soon after the pilot enters the shuttle, he and the other pilot are both dead.

Strange Behavior uses a simple door to imply a threat and create fear. Mrs. Haskell, a housekeeper, discovers her employers' son, Timothy, dead in the bathroom. She rushes into

Figure 3.9—*Strange Behavior*. Mrs. Haskell (Beryl Te Wiata) doesn't notice the closet door, quietly opening behind her.

a bedroom to phone for help. While she is on the phone, a closet door behind her slowly opens. She doesn't notice. She walks away a few feet, the frame following her, and leaving the door in offscreen space. When she returns, still on the phone, we see the door is now wide open. The closet appears empty, but it's dark, so we can't be sure. She doesn't notice the wide open door. She hangs up the phone, and lies down on bed [Figure 3.9].

The killer has presumably exited the closet and is nearby. Where? In the bedroom? Or maybe the killer is still in the closet? Of course, Mrs. Haskell doesn't even know that someone was (is?) in the closet. This ignorance makes her all the more vulnerable, thus heightening the horror.

Then Mrs. Haskell hears strange noises coming from the bathroom. She enters and finds the killer, eating Timothy. A gruesome scene, made all the scarier by the previous scene, which unnerved viewers and set them "on edge."

Scary Props and Masks

Some props are inherently unnerving. Sharp utensils and power tools are scarier than guns, the uglier the better. Slashers understand this. Guns kill people, quick and clean. Chainsaws and hacksaws dismember limbs, leaving the victim aware while it's happening. The boy in *The Gates of Hell* (aka *Paura nella città dei morti viventi*, Italian 1980) knew that the whirling power drill was nearing his head, director Lucio Fulci savoring the moment, the boy still conscious and screaming as the drill bore into his skull.

Medical instruments are inherently unsettling. Mad scientists understand this. In *Strange Behavior*, Dr. Parkinson wields a ridiculously long hypodermic needle. Its very sight terrifies Pete. Medical instruments are perhaps even more frightening when someone is under anesthesia in surgery because such scenes exploit the audience's fears of what may happen to *them* during surgery. In *Rabid*, we know that Dr. Keloid is ready to go berserk, just as he's about to perform surgery. We fear for the patient under anesthesia. Dr. Keloid surprises us by attacking *another physician*.

A mask is a prop that also functions as a costume. Masks empower slashers by rendering them anonymous, at times inhuman. This "inhuman effect" is especially pronounced when audiences can't see a slasher's eyes. Jason's hockey mask and Michael Myers's "shape" mask are empowering partially because the masks' eye sockets often appear empty. This eyeless effect is created by lighting, and the distance of the mask from the wearer's face. A slasher with visible eyes will typically appear more naturalistic, mortal, and vulnerable than an "eyeless slasher." An eyeless slasher is more likely to be an *uberpsycho* (i.e., a dark force of nature). Thus, masks not only anonymize and depersonalize, they also dehumanize.

Satanic hoods function similarly, hiding not only the wearer's face, but eyes. Eyes are the "windows into the soul." If you don't see a threat's eyes, that threat will appear more mysterious, soulless, inhuman, and threatening. Some threats don't even have eyes to look into, such as the demonic "physician" in *Jacob's Ladder* (1990), who had only skin where his eyes should have been. He was, of course, wielding a hypodermic needle.

Masks have personalities. The hideousness of a mask can heighten its horror, and empower its wearer, as with the ugly Tor Johnson mask in *Strange Behavior*. That mask had its own, bulging eyes. However, hideous comes in many flavors. A grotesquely innocent mask can be frightening in the right context. Clown masks unnerve many people. Of course, some clowns forgo a mask and just go with the makeup, as does Captain Spaulding in *House of 1000 Corpses* (2003).

The crone mask in *Curtains* is not only hideous, but aesthetically appropriate, because it supports the story, characters, and themes. In the film, several actresses are invited to director Jonathan Stryker's house (and casting couch) to audition for his upcoming film. Thematically, *Curtains* is about people so desperate to "make it" in Hollywood that they are always "in character," their personal identities as contrived as the characters they portray, their real selves hidden behind curtains (or masks) of their own making. Stryker forces actress Samantha Sherwood to audition a love scene while wearing the crone mask. "Seduce me with your eyes alone," he orders. When she fails, he yanks off the mask, forces Samantha to face a mirror, and barks, "This is a mask too."

This crone mask, being ugly, empowers the slasher and heightens the horror. But it also augurs the fate of these pretty young actresses. Just as Stryker discarded his first actress wife, so too will these actresses grow old and be discarded by Hollywood. The mask supports *Curtains*'s dual themes of (1) aging in Hollywood, and (2) wearing a false front in Hollywood.

Less impressive is the Munch-inspired mask in *Scream* (1996). Rather than support the story, characters, or themes, this mask seems calculated for merchandising revenue. Yes, the film is called *Scream* and the mask is of someone screaming. But the film is not about screaming. The mask supports the film's title, not the film itself. This is clever marketing, not creative aesthetics.

The *Scream* mask is popular not on its or the film's merits, but due to Miramax's heavily bankrolled, Halloween merchandising machine, trying to do by design what *Halloween*'s "shape" mask did by serendipity. The "shape" was merely a William Shatner mask, spray-painted and the eyeholes enlarged.

Sight Gags

Creepshow uses set décor for *humorous* sight gags. "Space moss" from a meteor covers Jordy's fingers. Jordy considers going to a doctor. But then he imagines a creepy doctor saying that he must amputate Jordy's fingers. A medical model of a skeleton slides across the examining room behind a fearful Jordy. Of course, he fears the doctor, not the skeleton. The skeleton moves for comedic effect, expressing Jordy's comical (for the audience) fears about doctors and surgery.

Deathdream (aka *Dead of Night*, 1974) offers a *satirical* sight gag. Andy's domineering father stands before a pair of bull's horns that hang in Andy's bedroom. The camera is angled so that the horns appear to be growing from dad's head. Is it serendipity? Or is director Bob Clark commenting on the father's "bull-headed" nature? Certainly, dad appears bull-headed to Andy and his mother [Figure 3.10].

Intruder (1989) features a *creepy* sight gag. A psycho hunts a young checkout clerk in a grocery store. Late at night, when the store is empty. The clerk hides inside a popcorn display case. The psycho stops before some water bottles. Seen through the bottles, his face is distorted, as in a funhouse mirror. He pauses, slowly turning his head from side to side, emphasizing the bottles' visual distortion. His head looks as twisted as is his mind. (This sight gag would have been more unnerving were the clerk hiding behind those bottles, rather than behind the popcorn, because then the distortion shot would have been her POV.)

Apart from being funny or creepy, these three sight gags also comment on the characters. Jordy is spooked. The father is bull-headed. The psycho has a twisted mind.

Blood is a popular sight gag in horror films. In *Terror* (British 1978), Viv spots *blood dripping through a ceiling*. Apparently, much blood was shed upstairs. Audience tension rises. Susie goes upstairs to investigate and discovers a can of *spilled red paint*. Audience tension relaxes. Whereupon Viv, who's waiting downstairs, is stabbed by an unseen killer.[38]

This gag unnerves viewers by first misleading them into fearing a threat. Then misleading them again into thinking they are safe. And then after fraying their nerves, striking for real.

Figure 3.10—*Deathdream*. **Intentional or serendipity? Either way, the father (John Marley) appears to have sprouted bull's horns.**

Sleepaway Camp 2: Unhappy Campers (1988) features a similar gag. Someone is killed, unnerving the audience. A new scene opens on a *floor covered by blood*. A camper's sneakers and legs are *sprinkled with blood*. Somebody *screams*. Another killing? The camera moves up to a table in an arts and crafts room, covered with *spilled red paint*. A camper screams and whines that she hates camp and wants to go home. Both the "blood" and scream are innocuous. Again, audiences were unnerved with a gag.

Sleepaway Camp 2 later plays the same gag in reverse. Two boys at Camp Rolling Hills wear Freddy and Jason costumes to scare Angela, their camp counselor. Being psychotic, Angela not only wears what appears to be a Michael Myers outfit to scare the boys back, but she actually kills them. When she returns to the camp grounds, Ally, another counselor, sees Angela covered in blood. Ally remarks: "Cute. But the blood looks like ketchup."

The audience knows the blood is real. We are "in" on the joke with Angela. This gag is not unnerving, but funny. *Sleepaway Camp 2* and *3* are satirical to the point of being comedies. This is why the physically weak Angela successfully kills stronger people, even when she loses the element of surprise. Because comedic killings require even less logic than do horror killings.

Hospital Massacre twice plays the old "fake blood" sight gag. After entering a hospital elevator, Susan sees a man leaning against the wall, apparently unconscious, *blood smearing his mouth*. Susan looks unsettled, but doesn't scream or try to help. We cut to a closeup of her white shoe. *Blood drips* onto it. We cut back to Susan and the man. The "unconscious" man becomes alert, then raises a partly eaten hamburger to his mouth. The "blood" *was only ketchup*.

Unlike in *Sleepaway Camp 2*, the character, Susan, was "in" on the joke. She saw the hamburger in offscreen space. But the hamburger was hidden from the audience, so we were fooled and unnerved.

Later, Dr. Jacobs is paged to the hospital's abandoned 9th floor. She searches a cluttered room, wondering why she was called up there. She sees what resembles a body lying on a table, under a sheet. Tension mounts. She nervously pulls up the sheet. It's only a dummy![39] (There's one gag.) Tension eases. Then she hears a noise. Coming from a metal cabinet? She approaches it. Tension mounts. She opens the cabinet. We see her from inside the cabinet, past the tops of *paint cans*. (Do you see the second gag coming?) Tension eases. Then the psycho attacks Dr. Jacobs from behind, stabbing and killing her.

Soon thereafter, a janitor searches the room and sees what resembles a body lying on a table, under a sheet. *Blood stains the sheet*, dripping onto the floor. Is that Dr. Jacobs under the sheet? Tension mounts. The janitor pulls off the sheet. No, it's only the dummy! But now there's a can of *spilled red paint* beside it. (Fooled you again!)

Why did the killer put the paint can under the sheet, beside the dummy? Apart from wanting to give us a good gag, it was to make room for Dr. Jacob's body. For when the janitor opens the cabinet, there's Dr. Jacobs, hanging upside down where the paint cans had been!

In *The Legacy* (1978), Maggie and five others are invited to a mansion to inherit Satanic powers. But only one shall survive to inherit anything. Late in the film, Maggie waits downstairs for Barbara, so they can escape. Maggie stands in the background. She hears water dripping. In the foreground is a blurry image, its upper part darkening from saffron to crimson. Maggie turns at the sound of the droplets. She gasps. A *rack focus* sharpens the blur, revealing a wine glass, red drops staining its clear liquid contents.[40] Maggie looks up. We zoom in on her POV of red liquid soaking through the ceiling. Another sight gag, as in *Terror*?

No, we *know* it's blood. Only moments earlier, we saw Barbara in her bedroom upstairs, stabbed by a broken mirror's shards. Red-soaked ceilings can't always be a sight gag, otherwise the gag wouldn't work.

Interacting with the Camera

Filmmakers normally avoid shots that remind audiences that they're watching a film, so as to encourage suspension of disbelief. Actors know never to look directly into the camera lens unless specifically requested (which is usually for a POV shot). This is less true in comedy than in horror because comedy is a more self-conscious genre. Actors in comedies are more likely to point at, or talk to, the camera. *Mise-en-scène* is more likely to interact with the camera.

In *The Evil Dead* (1981), blood drips *onto the camera lens*. This shot depicts a dying demon's POV, but it also makes us aware of the lens's presence. In the context of the film's satirical story and gore, the aesthetic effect is to remind audiences that it's only a movie, so "join in" on the fun.

Highlighting the filmmaking process's artificiality can invite audiences in as collaborators rather than mere spectators. In *The Undertaker and His Pals* (1966), during the end credits roll, every actor who had "died" in the film, hero and villain alike, rises up in their respective death scenes, and smiles and waves at the camera. "See, I'm all right! I had fun! Hope you did too!"

In the humorless vampire/goth film, *Nadja* (1994), raindrops *strike the camera lens*. Arguably, the aesthetic *effect* is to emphasize the gloominess of the weather. Goths love gloom. However, the aesthetic *intent* is often unclear in *Nadja*, an artsy film that overvalues style at the expense of substance and clarity.

Composition

Pictorial composition is the art of arranging *mise-en-scène* inside the borders of the film frame. In composing a shot, a director guides the viewer's attention to certain areas within the frame, and away from other areas. Viewer attention may be guided by balance, contrast, focus, and movement.

Regarding *balance*, viewers are attuned to symmetry. Placing people or objects off-center within the frame creates an *unbalanced shot*, which may pull viewer attention, or create strong emotional or aesthetic effects. A shot may be unbalanced not only through the staging of actors or props, but through *contrast*. A bright patch within a dark setting, such as a lit window in an otherwise dark house, attracts our attention.

In *Suspiria* (Italian 1977), Pat, a ballet student, escapes a coven of witches and runs to her friend's apartment for safety. Soon thereafter, Pat looks nervously out of the bathroom window. One shot is composed from outside the building. The window is a small pool of light, surrounded by nighttime darkness. This composition has two aesthetic effects: (1) it draws our attention to the brightly lit woman in the window, and (2) because the bright area is small, Pat seems threatened by the vast, surrounding darkness.

Director Dario Argento repeats this composition in *Suspiria*, to the point of creating a motif. Pat's friend hears Pat under attack in the locked bathroom. The friend rushes into the hall, banging on doors, shouting for help. One shot is composed from the building's interior courtyard (for lack of a better term). An open arch reveals the friend in a tiny pool of bright light, banging on a neighbor's door. The vast walls of the surrounding courtyard are dark. The aesthetic effect is the same as before.

Depicting a tiny, brightly lit, solitary figure surrounded by darkness is a popular horror film composition. In *Darkness Falls*, it is night and the house is dark. The tooth fairy attacks a young boy, Kyle. He escapes to the brightly lit bathroom because the tooth fairy can't enter the light. (Why doesn't Kyle just turn on the other lights in the house?) One shot is composed from *outside* the bathroom. Its doorway occupies only a small portion of the film frame, so that it's a small patch of bright white light, surrounded by the hallway's darkness. The indistinct shape of the tooth fairy undulates above the doorway, in darkness, avoiding the light [Figure 3.11].

Powerful compositions can also be created when the balance between light and dark are reversed. In the above scene, another shot is composed from *inside* the bathroom. Huddled in the bathtub, a terrified Kyle watches the doorway into the hall. The doorway is dark and empty, surrounded by the bathroom's vast brightness. Because (1) the doorway is centered in the frame, (2) the mostly bright surroundings make the doorway's darkness stand out, (3) the doorway is dramatically important, because the tooth fairy is lurking out there, and (4) the unseen tooth fairy's creepy noises emanate from the hallway, the aesthetic effects are to (1) direct viewers' attention to the doorway, and (2) create an emotionally unsettling sense of an ominous and threatening dark hole. [Figure 3.12]

Contrast not only concerns brightness or darkness, but colors. In *The Brood*, two mutant midgets kidnap Candy from her school, and lead her across a snowy landscape. Candy wears a bright red parka. The mutants wear bright orange and blue. The three are framed in a *long shot*, so they appear as small figures against a vast snowy landscape. Aesthetically, this composition disempowers Candy. She appears weak and vulnerable amid the barren snow. Yet the bright red parka directs our attention to her. Without subverting the composition's disempowering effect, the red color "corrects" for the possibility that the audience may not notice the tiny Candy.

Candy is further disempowered by the staging. A mutant walks on either side of her to keep her captive. Normally, the center position is the "power position" (i.e., the leader's position), but in this dramatic context, Candy is weakened rather than strengthened by being in the center. As with the red parka, this staging also directs audience attention to Candy, as the human eye naturally seeks the center in a group [Figure 3.13].

The colorful parkas serve another aesthetic function. They remind us that these are children. (Even the mutants are children, however unnatural.) These bright, playful, children's colors create a dramatic contrast with the mutants' brutal murder of Candy's schoolteacher, just moments earlier. Thus, the *color contrast* within the composition reinforces a *dramatic contrast* within the story.

A red truck drives up the road alongside Candy and the mutants, then passes them by. Because the truck is (1) red, and (2) in the center of the frame, and (3) the fastest *moving* object in the frame, our attention is drawn to it. The truck promises to become a dramatic

Figure 3.11 — *Darkness Falls*. The young Kyle (Joshua Anderson), mostly hidden behind the shower curtain, huddles in the bathroom's tiny brightness, while the evil tooth fairy lurks in the dark hallway. This composition...

Figure 3.12 — ...is graphically similar, despite a reversal of light and dark areas, to this view from inside the bathroom. Now a dark patch is centered amid brightness.

element. We expect it to stop, and for something to happen. Perhaps someone will rescue Candy? Or maybe the truck is from the psychiatric institute that shelters the mutants?

But as with *Superstition*'s knife in the wall, and *The Funhouse*'s whirling fan blades, *The Brood*'s red truck is a red herring. It serves two aesthetic functions: (1) it emotionally unnerves the audience by raising, and then denying their expectations, however subconsciously, and (2) it makes Candy's situation feel all the more hopeless. Three apparent children are alone on a barren road, and regular people don't even bother to stop and check if anything is amiss.

Unlike in painting or still photography, cinematic composition also involves *movement*. When a person or object moves amid surrounding stillness, or moves at a different rate of speed than everything else, it draws the audience's attention. In the above example, the red truck is the fastest moving object in the frame. All else is still, apart from the three children, who trudge slowly. Thus, the red truck attracts our attention. The reverse is also true:

Figure 3.13 — *The Brood.* Candy (Cindy Hinds) walks between two mutants. That distant red truck catches our attention, raising our expectations as it nears the children (and the frame's center), only to drive on past.

if a person or object is motionless amid surrounding animation, viewers will notice the solitary still figure.

Filmmakers should beware of *inadvertently* directing audience attention. If the lead characters wear gray suits in a dull gray office, it's a mistake for a dramatically insignificant character to wear red. Red draws attention. This is why background actors are usually instructed to avoid red or yellow clothing. Of course, if everyone in a crowd scene wears red, except for a solitary character in gray, the latter will attract the attention.

Composition may also support a film's story, characters, and themes. In *Blood and Roses*, many outdoor shots are composed to resemble an impressionist landscape painting. The aesthetic effect is to evoke the romantic past of Carmilla's vampire ancestor, Millarca. Because Carmilla is possessed by Millarca, it's appropriate that she (and audiences) see the world as Millarca sees it.

Early in *Lost Souls*, all aspects of *mise-en-scène* unite to create a beautiful and visually striking composition, which in turn is supported by all other cinematic tools. In this shot, two priests, a deacon, and Maya enter an asylum to perform an exorcism. The four of them stride in single file. They step in unison. Their long coats evoke the superheroes from *The Matrix*.[41] This impression is further supported by them being photographed in silhouette, which strips away nonessential details, leaving only the outlines of their *Matrix*-like coats. Sound effects support this staging, their every step thundering and reverberating. Their steps are further exaggerated and made ponderous through (1) slow motion photography, and (2) a wide angle lens, which expands space. Lens and staging create a comfortable amount of room between the four people, giving each their "own space." They appear not as unruly rabble, but as strong individuals. This "tough guy" image is further reinforced by location and set décor. They stride through a room of concrete, exposed pipes dripping water, prison grills on the doors and windows [Figure 3.14].

Figure 3.14 —*Lost Souls*. This beautifully silhouetted composition momentarily transforms four frail mortals into kick-ass superheroes.

All these elements are supported by the composition's low-angle frame, which further empowers them.

In the story's context, these are three physically unimpressive clergymen, and one slight, frazzled woman. Yet for one brief moment, in this one shot, *mise-en-scène*, composition, sound, and photography (the wide angle lens, and slow motion speed) transform these four mortals into futuristic superheroes, or Old West gunslingers, come to battle Satan in a portentous duel.

That is the power of *mise-en-scène* and composition. But to fully appreciate composition, one must understand the aesthetic potential of the film frame.

CHAPTER 4

Framing the Image

A camera can frame an image from many vantage points. A film frame creates a visual perspective that "comments" on the images inside its borders, and conveys an emotional impact. To frame an image is to make an aesthetic choice.

Level or Canted

A *level* frame is parallel to the horizon. *Non-level* frames are also called *canted, oblique, slanted, sloped,* or *inclined* (but not *tilted,* which is a camera move, discussed below).

Most frames are level because that's how we see, and expect to see, our world. Audiences find level frames to be less obtrusive, enabling them to concentrate more easily on a film's story. Canted frames are more noticeable, more likely to remind viewers that they're watching a film, and are sometimes regarded as self-conscious or "artsy-fartsy."

American films have traditionally emphasized story over style, and thus framed non-obtrusively, careful not to draw audience attention away from substance to form. Continental European cinema has been more experimental, stylistic, and self-conscious. Of Roger Vadim's *Blood and Roses* (aka *Et mourir de plaisir*, French-Italian 1960), David Hogan writes: "Like many other European directors who have worked in the [horror] genre, Vadim sacrificed logic and narrative at the altar of imagery."[1]

It's a cliché to say that level frames depict a stable world as seen by "level-headed" people, and canted frames suggest either a character's *subjective* fear, madness, desperation, or hysteria, or an *objective* collapse of normalcy, society, or reality. It's a cliché because that's often how canted frames are used.

In *Night of the Living Dead* (1968), the opening scene in the cemetery uses level frames — until a zombie attacks Barbara. This dramatic shift is supported by a sudden switch to canted frames. Barbara's normal reality has been overturned. The framing reflects both this objective upending of reality, and Barbara's subjective fear when it happens.

In *Don't Go in the House* (1980), the opening shots of Donald at work have level frames. But when Donald returns home, the first shot upon his entering the house is canted. We have left normalcy outside and entered a house (1) with a history of physical and psychological abuse, (2) on the night that Donald's mother dies, (3) which causes Donald to finally "snap" into full blown madness.

Horror often depicts an unbalanced world, and has been a leader among American film genres in embracing European style artistry.[2] The expressionistic *mise-en-scène* in *The Cabinet of Dr. Caligari* (aka *Das Cabinet des Dr. Caligari,* German 1920) inspired *The Bride of Frankenstein* (1935), which reinforces its skewed set décor with frames that cant ever more steeply as story events grow more desperate. Initially, *Bride* uses mildly sloping cants to frame the drawbridge as townsfolk return the Baron Frankenstein to his castle. By the final lab scene, the mad scientists are framed steeply, suggesting (1) their madness, and (2) their experiment's overturning of God's natural order. The actors' angular stances reinforce the canted frames; the actors, set décor, and cants creating a pattern of sharply sloping lines.

The Evil Dead (1981) uses ever steeper cants as the demonic attack advances, and Ash's fear and desperation increase. At one point, a canted frame shifts in seesaw fashion, creating a sense of vertigo which further unnerves the audience. Ash is standing on the left side of a frame that's canted down to the left. As he moves rightward, the frame cants rightward, as if Ash's weight were pulling down the frame's right end [Figures 4.1, 4.2].

Figure 4.1—*The Evil Dead*. This frame cants down leftward. Yet as Ash (Bruce Campbell) walks right...

Figure 4.2 —...the frame seesaws, dipping right, as if pulled by Ash's shifting weight.

A clock's pendulum stops swinging shortly before another demonic assault, *freezing at a slant*, eerily defying gravity. Thus *mise-en-scène* and cants reinforce each other, both supporting the chaotic story events and characters' emotional turmoil.

In *Creepshow* (1982), canted frames support characters and story. The characters have an emotionally unbalanced "frame of mind." Storywise, they commit crimes that "overturn" societal rules.[3] But *Creepshow* has a third aesthetic intent for its cants: to evoke the old 1950s EC horror comics' canted panels.[4]

Canted frames can buttress an eerie, ominous atmosphere. In *Vampyres* (British 1974), two lady vampires entice two unsuspecting men to their mansion lair. The mansion is darkly silhouetted and framed obliquely, intimating the unnatural threats lurking inside. *The Haunting* (1963) similarly uses canted frames to suggest the evil, supernatural presence within Hill House [Figure 4.3].

Fay Grim (2006) is shot almost entirely canted, creating a metaphor for the topsy-turvy world of international espionage, with all its secrets, lies, aliases, conspiracies, uncertainties, betrayals, and revelations. While not a horror film, *Fay Grim* is an intriguing example of canted frames taken to an extreme. Horror contrasts the natural and unnatural, and generally saves cants for when the unnatural intrudes upon normalcy. But there is no normalcy in Fay's life among spies; her entire world is canted [Figure 4.4].

Canted frames can help depict story events, especially when the cant moves. The 1960s *Star Trek* TV series is infamous for seesawing its frame whenever the starship *Enterprise* is attacked. And in *She Creature* (2001), a gently canting frame recreates the swaying motion aboard a 1905 sailing ship.

Similarly in *Thirst* (Australian 1979), a vampire cult locks Kate, a prospective recruit, inside a room, hoping to brainwash her into joining their ranks. The frame cants over slowly to suggest the room tipping over. And just like *Star Trek*'s actors would sway back and forth to dramatically support the seesawing frame, *Thirst* actress Chantal Contouri gawks at the tipping room, the shattering walls, and the furniture sliding across the floor. Actually, one heavy table "slides" in fits and starts, as if a stagehand offscreen were tugging at it with a cord. Which also demonstrates that a canted frame is a *pragmatic* tool for low-

Figure 4.3 — *The Haunting.* Theo's bedroom door, canted, and also distorted by a slightly wide angle lens.

Figure 4.4 — An almost entirely canted spy film. Actors Parker Posey and Jeff Goldblum in *Fay Grim.*

budget filmmakers. It's cheaper to seesaw the camera, and pull furniture with a cord, than to tip over the entire set.

Distance

A frame is also characterized by the camera's perceived *distance* from the subject. If the subject is a person, an *extreme long shot* means the person is a tiny dot on screen. A *long shot* is when the person's entire body is discernible. A *medium long shot* is from the knees up. *Medium shot* is waist up. *Medium closeup* is chest up. A *closeup* is just the face. An *extreme closeup* is part of the face, or some other body part, such as a hand. These terms, like distance itself, are relative. One can't precisely say when an extreme long shot becomes a long shot.

Extreme closeups (ECUs) can function as exclamation points; by magnifying an actor's features, they intensify his emotions. The ECU of actor Bela Lugosi's glaring eyes in *White Zombie* (1932) emphasizes his evil heart, and intimates his mesmeric powers over zombies. In *Ice Cream Man* (1994), ECUs of the parents screaming mouths suggest the stress their constant bickering places on their son. An ECU of the demon queen's red lips in *Seizure* (Canadian 1974) punctuates her sinister sexuality.

Horror director Lucio Fulci favored ECUs, especially of eyes. In *House by the Cemetery* (aka *Quella villa accanto al cimitero*, Italian 1981), a babysitter exchanges coy glances with her employer. The wife notices, and glances suspiciously at them. They glance away. The scene is brief and wordless. Just three pairs of eyes, framed in ECUs, glancing about or turning away. It's enough to convey a mutual attraction, suspicious uncertainty, and deceitful guilt. No story event or dialog has so far indicated that the babysitter is slutty, the husband unfaithful, or the wife distrustful. Yet these brief ECUs inject a wholly new emotional subtext into the film [Figures 4.5 — 4.8].

Left: Figure 4.5 —*House by the Cemetery.* The babysitter (Ania Pieroni) and wife (Catriona MacColl) in an innocent conversation. *Right:* Figure 4.6 — After announcing that he's found the keys, the husband (Paolo Malco), who is beside his wife, glances at the babysitter. An ECU of his eyes conveys his lust, while forming an *eyeline match* to...

 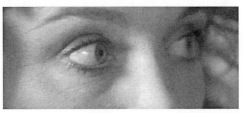

Left: Figure 4.7 —...the babysitter. This ECU of her eyes dramatically reciprocates his lust, while editorially creating an *eyeline match* to him. Cut to... *Right:* Figure 4.8 —...an ECU of the wife's eyes, suspiciously scrutinizing her husband and forming an *eyeline match* to him. (Eyeline matches are discussed in the chapter on Editing.)

ECUs can also heighten warmth and gentleness. In *The Evil Dead*, two lovers toy over a gift. ECUs of their eyes stress Linda's impatience to snatch and open the gift, and Ash's playfulness in holding it back. Later ECUs will underscore the characters' fear and desperation.

Closeups can also intensify the significance of objects. In *Tales from the Crypt* (British 1972), the Major must traverse a narrow corridor, the walls embedded with razor blades. As he creeps forward, moving POV (point of view) closeups of the razors underscore their danger. And because they are POV shots, audiences are even more likely to *feel* the Major's fear.

Apart from intensifying what is already present, ECUs can transform the mundane into something bizarre or unsettling. Director David Lynch has used ECUs to achieve disturbing, transformative effects in such surreal, quasi-horror works as *Eraserhead* (1977), TV's *Twin Peaks* (1990-91), and *Mulholland Drive* (2001).

An old rule says: *Tragedy is a closeup, comedy is a long shot.* By this theory, a closeup of an actor's face draws in the audience, closer to the character, creating an intimacy that encourages viewers to identify and sympathize with the character. This is doubly true when a closeup is used with a *long take* (a shot lasting for a long period time, as opposed to a *long shot*, which refers to camera distance). The longer we observe a character in closeup, uninterrupted, the more we sympathize. Conversely, a *long shot* distances viewers from actors. This apparent physical distance creates an emotional distance, making it easier for audiences to laugh at a character's misfortunes.

Because horror requires *audience identification and sympathy* with the victims, so they will fear for the victim's safety, closeups are helpful. A horror film with few or no closeups may risk becoming a very dark comedy, or a coldly nihilistic, grindhouse bloodbath. Which is fine, if that's the filmmaker's intent.

While long shots can emotionally distance an audience from the characters, *extreme long shots* can suggest a character's insignificance, impotence, or vulnerability, contrasting her tiny form amid awesome and menacing powers. In *The Final Terror* (1983), two campers are killed by an inbred family living amid California's redwoods. Borrowing from *Deliverance* (1972), the survivors flee on a raft. Extreme long shots emphasize these urbanites' vulnerability, lost amid the mighty forces of nature (e.g., their tiny raft floating on the river; a tiny camper clambering a giant redwood tree; another tiny camper trudging upon a fallen redwood "bridge").

Similarly, many horror/sci-fi films build tension by juxtaposing tiny astronauts against ominously huge starships or the vast emptiness of space (e.g., *Alien*, 1979; *Galaxy of Terror*, 1981; *Outland*, 1981; *Lifeforce*, 1985; *Nightflyers*, 1987; *Moontrap*, 1989).

In *Inferno* (Italian 1980), long shots suggest the powerful supernatural forces menacing vulnerable characters. Rose exits a Manhattan apartment building (owned by a witch) to mail a letter. The building is framed at a *straight-on angle*, so that it appears flat and two-dimensional. Blue and pink lights color its imposing facade. This unsettling angle and color scheme lend a hostile countenance to the building, intensified by an extreme long shot, so the building looms threateningly over the tiny Rose.

Later, Sara escapes an alchemist in Rome. An extreme long shot frames her running beneath a huge, ornate archway. A gargantuan chandelier hangs from its center, over Sara's head. This extreme long shot, together with the enormous set décor, emphasize Sara's tiny vulnerability, at the mercy of vast, menacing forces [Figure 4.9].

A frame's aesthetic effect is always influenced by other cinematic elements. A long shot will not always disempower a character. In *Blood and Roses*, long shots frame Carmilla's stately departure from the crypt after she is possessed by the vampire, Millarca. In her regal white

Figure 4.9—*Inferno*. Sara (Eleonora Giorgi) appears tiny and vulnerable under a huge archway and gargantuan chandelier, framed in an extreme long shot.

dress, carrying herself with a dignified posture, Carmilla walks against a backdrop of crumbling castles and autumnal colors. This *mise-en-scène*, together with the long shot, creates the appearance of an impressionist painting, drawing Carmilla into the Old World of her aristocratic ancestor. This long shot (in the context of story, acting, costuming, and art direction) helps to empower, rather than weaken, the character emerging from the crypt.

Angle

A frame's angle is its degree of tilt. A *high angle* shot looks down. A *low angle* shot looks up. This is because the camera is in a low position. However, this can get confusing. A *high* angle looks *low*. A *low* angle looks *high*.

Most shots in any film are *straight-on angle*, with perhaps a slight tilt for pragmatic rather than aesthetic reasons.

As with level framing, we normally prefer to see people eye-to-eye, straight-on, not staring up or down at them. Audiences are comfortable with a straight-on angle. As with level frames, a straight-on-angle is usually the least obtrusive choice. The more extreme the tilt, the more likely that audiences will remember that "it's only a movie."

A common theory holds that high angle shots (like extreme long shots) disempower or denigrate characters, while low angle shots empower or lionize them.

In *Jeepers Creepers 2* (2003), an *extreme high angle/extreme long shot* shows teenagers running in a field, without cover to hide under, fleeing a flying monster. The shot depicts the teens as tiny and exposed, disempowering them and emphasizing their vulnerability. The shot also suggests the monster's perspective, though it's not a POV shot, because the monster enters the frame, thus disorienting viewers who'd thought otherwise [Figure 4.10].

Near the end of *Warlock* (1989), the warlock finally attains the "Grand Grimoire," a book of black magic. He looks down at the book, lying on cemetery soil. An *extreme low angle* shot looks up at him. Aesthetically, this shot (1) empowers him, as he looms over the book, and (2) creates a sense that this evil book is alive, because we are seeing from its POV.

However, because a frame's aesthetic impact is influenced by its context, a low angle

Figure 4.10—An extreme high angle/extreme long shot disempowers these fleeing teenagers in *Jeepers Creepers 2.*

can mock or satirize, rather than lionize. In *The Twilight Zone* episode, "The Obsolete Man" (1961), *extreme low angle* shots of a totalitarian state's Chancellor imply his hubris, and simultaneously mock it. This effect is reinforced by the set décor (25 feet tall doors, and a ridiculously long conference table), by Fritz Weaver's pompous performance, and by the story and its theme.

As with distance, angle is relative. How low before a low angle becomes an extreme long angle?

Extreme low angles occasionally frame Ash near the end of *The Evil Dead*. Yet in the film's context, with frames alternating from every angle and level, the low angle shots do not lionize or satirize Ash. Rather, the cumulative aesthetic effect of the frames' alternating vantage points (done through camera movement, zooming, and editing) is to (1) convey Ash's fear and desperation, and (2) suggest the presence of unseen demonic spirits swirling around the room.

Similarly in *The Haunting*, as Theo and Eleanor huddle against the ghostly noises outside the bedroom, the women are framed from many angles and distances (at times we see only their reflections in a mirror), and shot with multiple focal lengths. In the scene's dramatic context, the cumulative effect is to convey these women's fear and desperation. However, these alternating vantage points don't *quite* indicate the presence of ghosts in the bedroom, because we assume the ghosts are outside in the hall, with the noises. (Although we really can't be sure...)

In the "He Who Kills" episode of *Trilogy of Terror 2* (TVM 1996), characters are often framed at low angles. Yet this fails to empower them because (1) storywise, they are vulnerable; frightened and easily injured or killed, (2) the threat is a demonic Zuni doll; the low angles suggest the doll's location, on the floor (though these are mostly not POV shots), rather than the characters' strength, and (3) the frames are often canted, suggesting the characters' lack of control over their situation (hence, their vulnerability).

In *Don't Go in the House*, the second shot upon Donald first entering his house is an extreme low angle. Rather than empower anyone, this angle reinforces the previous canted shot, and our growing sense that something is "not right" in this house.

A camera angle may be chosen simply because it's the best one from which to show an item (e.g., a high angle to film a desktop). Some shots are framed solely for pragmatic reasons, having no aesthetic intent other than to tell the story unobtrusively. That's fine too.

Height

Height refers to the degree to which the camera is above, below, or even with a subject. Height should not be confused with angle, which refers to tilt.

Low height shots can suggest the POVs, and thus the presence, of unnatural creatures. Sometimes we already know the creature is there, because we see it (e.g., the Zuni doll). But sometimes the threat is unseen, its presence implied solely by an unnaturally low (or high, or fast) POV. In *The Jar* (1984), a low height POV shot following Paul's feet intimates the presence of an unseen demon. In *The Evil Dead*, a POV shot rushing through the forest, low to the ground, combines an unnaturally fast speed, with a low height, to suggest a demon.

Figure 4.11—A low height/straight-on angle depicts events from a crab's eye view in *The House Where Evil Dwells.*

Shots often use high heights with high angles, and low heights with low angles, but this need not be so. In *The House Where Evil Dwells* (1982), possessed crabs invade a haunted house. We see events from a *low height*, near the floor, but from mostly *straight-on angles*, depicting events from a crab's eye view. Less often, from a low height, low angle. Apparently, crabs *are* capable of glancing upward [Figure 4.11].

Offscreen Space

Offscreen space is the unseen area outside the frame, be it just beyond the frame line, or behind the camera, or behind the set décor. Offscreen space is *aesthetically* useful for all film genres, but especially for horror. Threats can hide offscreen, waiting to attack victims and shock audiences. Offscreen space can also unnerve viewers by *hinting* at some threat lurking out there, just beyond the frame line. Possibly standing right beside the hero.

Offscreen space is also *pragmatically* useful for all filmmakers, but especially for low-budgeters. If you can't afford to create a monster or special effect, you can instead have your characters react to an unseen monster in offscreen space.

Aesthetically, offscreen space can be the cinematic version of the old horror storytelling technique of omitting details, on the theory that a listener's imagination will conjure something more frightening than anything the storyteller can invent. In *The Haunting*, we never see what's pressing the door inward; our fear derives from wondering what lurks offscreen and unseen.

One may conceal details for the opposite reason: good taste. In *Alien³* (1992), Clemens performs an autopsy on Newt, a 12-year-old girl. Ripley watches, hoping to learn whether an alien had impregnated Newt. Her autopsied body remains entirely offscreen, probably to spare audiences the gory details. Big studio films dislike carving up kids. Even dead kids.

Pragmatically, offscreen space saves money. In *Alien³*, money was saved on a latex body to autopsy. Offscreen space also shortens production time (thus saving more money), by making scenes easier to film. In the post-apocalyptic sf film, *Circuitry Man* (1990), Danner performs an amazing shot on a pool table, all balls (apparently) falling into the correct holes. During his shot, the table is offscreen. We know he succeeds from the astonished looks on the characters' faces as their eyes follow the sound of the balls.

Offscreen space can unease audiences by misleading them. The frame reveals one thing, implying a threat. Then the frame pans over to what was previously offscreen, and we now see that thing to be something else. The horrific shock the audience was expecting, and tensing for, turns out to be harmless.

In *Rosemary's Baby* (1968), Rosemary learns that her gynecologist is yet another member of a Satanic coven with designs on her unborn child. In a scene of mounting paranoia, Rosemary enters a phone booth to call Dr. Hill, perhaps the last person she can trust, even as every friend and stranger appear increasingly suspicious. As Rosemary awaits Dr. Hill's return call, a tall man enters the frame, his back looming darkly against the phone booth's door, the rest of him hidden offscreen. Rosemary doesn't see him (her back is to him), but we do. The ominous framing is reinforced by sinister music. Audience tension mounts. But the man turns out to be a harmless stranger, just waiting to use the phone.

Although this "threat" was a false alarm, audiences remain unnerved and increasingly uncertain about future threats. Indeed, this technique is later reversed. After Rosemary locks herself in her apartment, she fails to see two people sneaking past a doorway behind her (entering from, and returning to, offscreen space). Audiences see these people and are again frightened for Rosemary — and this time, the threat is real.

Horror films often use offscreen space to spring outright shocks. In *Creature* (1985), an astronaut lies beside a spaceship's port window. He is startled (as are audiences) when a recently killed astronaut leaps up from below the window's edge, pouncing from offscreen. Later, another astronaut creeps toward a door's window, expecting an alien leap up from below the window's edge. Already, we are unnerved. When the alien leaps up — we are shocked again.

Fearful anticipation need not always be followed by a shock. A horror film may toy with viewers' emotions, sometimes paying off a scary buildup, sometimes not. This unnerves viewers because they can't anticipate the next attack.

Shocks are one of the easier types of cinematic tricks to evoke (as opposed to, say, slowly building up a tense atmosphere of ghostly dread), and rely heavily on offscreen space. This is why slasher films (which, in turn, rely heavily on shocks), often use offscreen space. Consider all those gory corpses tumbling out from cupboards, and closets, and air ducts while young women run screaming through a summer camp, sorority house, or campus.

Dropping corpses from cupboards or ceiling rafters is a favorite low-budget shock, but films which can afford it have used offscreen space for arms smashing through walls (*Terror*, British 1978), corpses reaching up from graves (*A Day of Judgment*, 1981; *Creepshow*, 1982; *The Crypt Club*, Canadian 2004), monsters emerging from beneath the sea (*Shock Waves*, 1977) and from under the sand (*Blood Beach*, 1980).

Monsters may also emerge *slowly* from offscreen, creating tension rather than shocks. Drooling aliens often arise from below the frame line, or drop from above the frame line (e.g., *Alien* and its progeny). The alien then looms behind its unaware victim, as audiences gaze and gasp. Fear increases, and the alien's enormity emphasized, if the alien requires some length of time — rising, rising, rising from offscreen — before emerging fully into view.

Subjective Framing, aka POV Framing

A frame can be objective or subjective. A *subjective* frame sees events from a character's point of view. The character is offscreen, behind the camera.

POV shots can build tension or fear in many ways. They can suggest the presence of a threat. This is a common slasher film technique. A killer lurks outside a house and peeks into windows, or skulks about a summer camp and spies from behind bushes. We don't see the killer, but because of the frame's perspective (shaky, moving, of low height, ducking behind set décor), we assume we're seeing from someone's POV, so someone must be *there*.

In *The Unseen* (1981), three TV newsgals can't find a vacant room in town because all hotels are booked for an upcoming festival. Driving farther out, they come across a dilapidated hotel. They stop and Jennifer exits the car. We cut to a POV shot looking out from an upstairs window, through a screen, watching Jennifer approach the front door [Figure 4.12]. Having seen enough, the voyeur drops a curtain across the window.

We don't see this voyeur, but the POV implies someone threatening. This is because (1) the voyeur is unseen, so we must imagine the details, (2) this is a horror film, so we imagine the worst, and (3) peeking from behind a curtain suggests stealth, secrecy, even hostility, confirming our dark imaginings. Audience tension increases.

But our fearful expectations are defied when we return to Jennifer outside the hotel, knocking on the door, peeking in the window, seeking service. She gives up and begins to leave, when the door suddenly opens. It's Ernest Keller, a bubbly, smiling, giddy man. Odd, but not threatening. Audience tension eases.

Figure 4.12 — **A high angle POV, looking out of a screened upstairs window, watches Jennifer (Barbara Bach) approach the hotel in *The Unseen*.**

Ernest explains that the hotel is now a museum. He makes some phone calls, but can't find a hotel for the newsgals. He invites the ladies to stay with him and his wife at their house. Soon thereafter, we cut to Ernest, alone on the phone, talking ominously to his wife. We were right to be suspicious of that POV shot! Audience tension again rises.

POV shots can empower a threat by hiding it. Threats are usually more frightening when unseen or unknown. If we don't know the nature or appearance of a monster (its full abilities and hideousness), we imagine the worst. If we don't know the identity of a killer, it could be anyone, even loved ones. This is why characters in horror films shout for the killer to "show yourself." (To disempower the threat by seeing it.) It's also why, after locating the monster, characters are so timid about opening that cupboard, and finally seeing it. (Having imagined the worst, we now fear the worst.)

POV shots can unnerve audiences by subverting their expectations. When viewers see a POV shot in a horror film, they often assume that some dreadful threat is present. In Fox TV's *Werewolf*, Eric enters the apartment he shares with his roommate, Ted. We already know that a werewolf is loose, killing people. Most recently at a nightclub that Ted patronizes. As Eric calls out to Ted (where is he?), we cut to a POV shot, moving at low height through the apartment. Earlier, we'd seen a low height POV that belonged to a werewolf. The two POVs are also similar in that both see *solarized* images.[5] This second POV now runs toward Eric and pounces. Scaring the audience.

But when we cut to an objective shot, this "werewolf" turns out to be Heathcliff, a gentle pet dog. The low height POV, aided by the solarization and story (we know a werewolf is loose, and Ted is suspect), first frightened the audience by suggesting a threat in off-screen space, then unnerved the audience when the "threat" was revealed as harmless.

Horror films often unnerve audiences by defying their expectations for an ominous POV. In *Splatter University* (1984), a menacing POV clambering up a fire escape is later revealed to be a harmless prankster. In *The Funhouse* (1981), a POV stalks and stabs a teenage girl in a shower, only to be exposed as her kid brother wielding a plastic knife. In *Head-hunter* (1989), an ominous POV breaking into a house at night turns out to be a drunken but friendly cop.

POV shots are such a horror film cliché (especially among slashers) that they can impart fresh menace even to familiar characters. Late in *Splatter University*, someone's POV enters Julie's apartment, scaring her. Julie calls this person "Mark." Thus, the POV shot does not hide Mark's identity. Nor is there a reason to conceal his appearance; we already know what Mark looks like.

More tellingly, *this is the first time that we see events from Mark's POV.* Slasher films generally use a killer's POV *until* his identity is revealed. *Splatter University* does the opposite. Mark is framed objectively until the film's end —*then* we switch to his POV. The aesthetic effect is to *imbue him with menace.* Because we suddenly see events from his POV, we assume he must be evil.

This POV shot's portent is reinforced by the story. Julie had recently found some clues implicating Mark in several murders — clues that turn out to be red herrings. This POV shot sets up our expectations, only to subvert them. Marks turns out to be innocent.

In *Tales from the Crypt*, Maitland is *initially* framed objectively. *After* his car accident, we see events from his POV. People run from him, but he doesn't know why. In the end, he looks into a mirrored table and sees that he is now a revenant corpse. His earlier POV shots did not transform him into a threat, but conversely, concealed (from himself and viewers) that he had become a threat. His POV did not imbue menace, but postponed it.

Because subjective frames are thought to encourage audience identification with the character whose POV we share, critics have accused slasher films of misogyny. The theory is that audiences are invited to join the killer in his work, to enjoy it, to empathize with him as he spies on and slaughters scantily clad women. (Slashers are assumed to be men, unless and until revealed to be women; women slashers appear in e.g., *Friday the 13th*, 1980; *Night School*, 1981; *Deadly Blessing*, 1981; *Curtains*, 1983; and *Stage Fright*, 1980.)

But seeing events from a killer's POV may elicit emotions other than empathy. More likely, just as viewers' cinematic tastes differ, a killer's POV should elicit different emotions from different viewers. For some, a killer's POV might create the sensation of being inside an onrushing train and unable to stop it. We see the victim lying ahead on the tracks, we want desperately to yell a warning or to stop the train, but we are helpless and forced to experience the train tearing over the screaming victim.

A *victim's POV* can heighten tension and fear by increasing audience identification with that victim. Horror is more horrifying when it strikes someone we care about — or when it strikes *us*. Seeing someone's POV as he leans over an alien egg about to burst, or as she approaches that door to the forbidden room, puts us into the story. Like 3-D photography, a victim's POV helps audiences experience scary events firsthand.

In *Don't Go in the House*, Donald ties naked women inside a steel room, then burns them alive. The camera lingers on his first victim's struggling, nude body, as if inviting us to enjoy her vulnerable terror. Yet the film's misogyny is mitigated (if one accepts the "POV equals empathy" theory) in that we see the victim's death from *her POV* (Donald pours gasoline over "us" and then shoots his flame thrower at "us"), and from objective shots, but never from Donald's POV.

Another aesthetic effect results when we see these victims' POVs *after* they're dead. Donald seats the charred corpses in chairs, and imagines that they talk to him. When he berates and slaps a corpse, tipping over her head, her POV cants to one side, and sways in the rocking chair. These *dead victim POVs* do not create sympathy for the victims, but transform them into threats; monsters awaiting revenge.[6] As with *Tales from the Crypt*'s revenant corpse stories, the victim turns monster, the murderer turns victim. This effect is reinforced when *Donald's POV* sees the corpses rise up and attack him.

Are we meant to sympathize with both Donald and his victims? It seems so, because his insanity, sadism, and misogyny result from his mother physically abusing him as a child, burning his arms over a stove to "burn out the evil." In the film's final scene, we see *a child's POV* of his mother berating and slapping him, continuing the cycle of abuse. This beating ends with Michael, like Donald before him, hearing voices, indicating that he will grow up to repeat Donald's pattern.

Some frames unnerve because they are ambiguous. We are uncertain as to whether we are seeing events from someone's POV, or are witnessing them objectively. In *Blood and Roses*, Carmilla speculates to her guests about her ancestor's thoughts and feelings, while what appears to be a POV shot glides through the room, the guests gazing into it. This POV, in the context of Carmilla relating her ancestral tale amid the sumptuous art décor, costuming, and music, imbues the atmosphere with romantic mystery, and a hint of the supernatural. The offscreen "entity" behind the POV may be an ancestral vampire's spirit, or it may only be the romantic fantasies of the storyteller and her guests, as they vividly imagine someone from a more aristocratic past joining their company.

Pragmatically, a subjective frame (like offscreen space in general) can suggest the presence of monsters that are too pricey to show onscreen. *The Evil Dead* ends with a POV shot speeding through the forest, then through a cabin, then finally leaping at Ash. This POV depicts Ash's horrified expression, but never the demon behind the POV. Effective and inexpensive.

Wide or Tight Framing

A frame can be wide or tight. A *wide* frame leaves a comfortable amount of space between the subject and the frame lines. If Mary is widely framed, she'll have room above her head and around her body. A *tight* frame sets its borders close to the subject. The term can also refer to leaving much of the surrounding area in offscreen space. If a frame is tight on Bob, we don't see what's around Bob.

Film noir crime dramas are known for tight frames. Some critics think these tight frames symbolize noir's claustrophobic world and support its oppressive psychological atmosphere. The characters are hemmed in by a malevolent fate (i.e., the frame's borders). Unseen and unknown threats lurk offscreen, waiting to pounce upon the characters, and because they are close to the frame line, they're close to any threats lurking offscreen.

This theory should hold true in horror films, though in horror, the threat is actual as well as psychological. Femmes fatales do not pounce upon detectives with the frequency of slashers, who are always pouncing on everyone.

Cheerier film genres may frame more widely, leaving space ahead of a character, so that when she walks the frame line isn't directly ahead of her. If it were, audiences may feel that she's not looking where she's going, or will bump into the frame line. Sure, audiences *know* she won't bump into the frame line, but film also affects viewers subconsciously. They don't always know why they feel anxiety, only that they do.

Horror can use that anxiety, which increases if a character is fleeing a threat. A frame line directly *ahead* of a fleeing character may create a sense that (1) she is trapped, with no room for escape, or (2) she will collide into something offscreen because she can't see what's ahead of her, or (3) she will collide into the frame line itself. Conversely, a frame line directly *behind* a fleeing character may unnerve viewers as they wonder: How close behind is that threat?

In *The Dark* (1979), as a woman flees an alien, the frame line ahead of her keeps moving, creating and removing space for her to escape into. This may instill a feeling in audiences that she is running blind, but the shifting frame line also supports her panic. Every time she reaches the frame line, it pulls away. She flees a monster, yet makes no progress, as if trapped in a nightmare. This framing may be unintentional (perhaps the camera operator just couldn't keep the frame line steady ahead of the running actress), but the emotional effect is there nonetheless. Aesthetic serendipity.

In *Silent Scream* (1980), tight framing cooperates with story and set décor (a cliff and an ocean) to unnerve viewers. A young couple stroll along a beach. They are alone, blissfully drunk (hence, careless), and it is night. They are vulnerable. The beach is narrow. The cliff behind them blocks escape from the rising tide. They are framed with the cliff (rather than the ocean) behind them, increasing our sense of claustrophobia. These story and set elements heighten our anxiety that the rising tide may drown this trapped and drunken couple.

The couple arrive at a promontory extending from the cliff, blocking their path. Tension mounts as the woman circumvents the promontory, hurrying past the rising tide. She attains the other side and awaits her man. He does not appear. Tension rises as she calls his name. She goes back around the promontory, searching for him. He is gone. She circumvents the promontory yet a third time — and there he is, waiting to scare her (and us). How he got there is left unexplained. In any event, he is safe. Tension eases.

The woman is angry and departs. The man is tired, drunk, and falls asleep on the beach. Alone, unconscious, vulnerable. Time passes. He is aroused by tidewater, which has risen since he fell asleep. Our previous fears are aroused. Will he drown?

He pulls himself to higher ground and safety. Tension eases. The frame is tight, so we don't know what lurks near him in offscreen space. A high angle shot reinforces his vulnerable position, setting him low, at the mercy of any passerby.

He is startled to see someone looming over him, offscreen. Who is this unseen person? Tension rises. He good-naturedly greets this person, implying that it's a friend. The audience relaxes. A knife plummets, repeatedly stabbing him, shocking the audience.

Framing, location, and story all heighten this scene's tension. The tight frame (1) instills a sense of unease by creating (with the cliffs and tide) a narrow space offering no room for escape, (2) hides the full extent of the tide (and any escape routes), suggesting that the situation may be worse than we see, (3) hides all possible threats offscreen — how many threats? are they nearby? are they armed? do they look eager to kill?, and (4) hides the identity of the attacker.

These effects are reinforced by the scene's "cry wolf" story structure, which toys with our emotions, repeatedly unnerving us, then lulling us into security. Having mistakenly expected the worst after each setup, the audience's mental guard is down when the attack finally, unexpectedly strikes (especially since the man *seems* to recognize his attacker — he doesn't), thus shocking the audience all the more.

Low-Budget Framing

Creative framing can compensate for a low budget. *The Jar* opens with a car accident, one that director Bruce Tuscano couldn't afford to stage. His tight frame reveals closeups of car headlights, a car's door, the two drivers after the accident, but leaves most everything else — the wrecked car (is it wrecked?), other cars on the highway, the highway itself— in offscreen space. Murky lighting obscures what little we do see.

We see Paul "driving" on the road, but for all we know, the car is parked in Tuscano's driveway while a "special effects" garden hose sprinkles the windshield to fabricate rain. Later, we see Paul "running" in the rain. As before, surrounded by darkness and a tight frame, he looks to be running in place, possibly in Tuscano's backyard. Actor Gary Wallace (Paul) confirmed my initial suspicions: "The scene with the rain was filmed in a warehouse Tuscano rented for many scenes. Yup, I was in Bruce's car and hoses were splashing water on the windshield. Yup, I was running in place."[7]

Pragmatically, this tight framing saves money on special effects, set décor, and location shooting. *Aesthetically*, the resulting surrealistic visuals support the story's premise of demonic possession and insanity. Hence, pragmatic aesthetics.[8]

In *Stage Fright* (aka *Nightmares*, Australian 1980), a slasher is killing people during a live theatrical performance. We only see a few theater-goers, tightly-framed, but we hear loud applause. We're supposed to believe that hundreds of theater-goers are offscreen, beyond the frame line. Of course, the seats offscreen are empty. *Pragmatically*, this tight framing saves money on hiring hundreds of extras to fill those seats. *Aesthetically*, the tight frames foster a claustrophobic intimacy with the victims, so we're more likely to emphasize with and fear for them.

Camera angles also help hide *Stage Fright*'s low budget. The rising and falling curtain is shot from various stylized angles, *pragmatically* hiding the empty theater seats offscreen, while *aesthetically* symbolizing the erratic emotional undercurrents circulating among the theater's actors. When the play's director approaches the stage to thunderous applause, an *extreme low angle* frames him so that only the ceiling is visible above and behind his grinning face. This low angle *pragmatically* hides the empty theater, while *aesthetically* conveying his swelled ego and simultaneously mocking it.

In *Star Crystal* (1986), a killer alien aboard a spaceship is initially framed only in tight closeups and extreme closeups. This is unsettling. We see only orange fragments of this creature, and infer something huge and horrifying. But when we finally see the entire alien, framed in a wide, long shot, we discover that he's a small creature, more frail than fearsome [Figures 4.13, 4.14].

This change in framing is aesthetically appropriate because it supports a simultaneous dramatic shift: the alien's physical revelation coincides with his spiritual revelation. Finding a Bible in the ship's computer, he "finds Christ" and is born again, his soul morphing from *Alien* to *E.T.* Previously silent and ruthless when slaughtering astronauts, his newfound voice is halting and humble, resembling Caine in *Kung Fu*.

Star Crystal uses framing and story symbiotically to overcome its inability to finance a formidable alien; the kind that drools and looms and flexes massive musculature. Audiences expect to see the entire alien at some point. Director Lance Lindsay scares us for as long as he can, with what little he dare show us. When he can no longer hide his alien offscreen, Lindsay gives it a humble spirit to match its humble form.

Low-budget filmmakers use offscreen space to hide what would otherwise be expensive to film. In *The Final Terror,* a woman runs into a primitive trap that flings serrated tin cans into her face. We see only her POV of the tin cans; her butchered face remains offscreen. This POV shot, from the victim's perspective, has us flinching and imagining the worst, while also saving money on the makeup effects.

Director Ed Wood used offscreen space extensively during his career. In *Bride of the Monster* (1955), Wood depicts the interior of a diner with no more than a table, some utensils, and a phone on the wall. The nonexistent counter, cashier, kitchen — the entire diner — remain offscreen. If not for an establishing shot of a diner's exterior, the actors might be anywhere.

Wood is often criticized for using cinematic tricks to compensate for a low budget. He is justly criticized, but not because he used such tricks frequently, but because he used them lazily, unimaginatively, and sloppily. When actor Bela Lugosi's death necessitated "killing off" his character in *Plan 9 from Outer Space* (1959), Wood used a film clip of

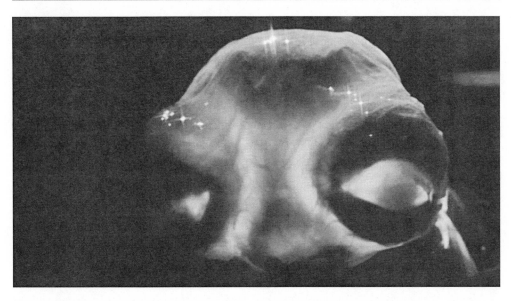

Figure 4.13 — *Star Crystal*. A tight frame leaves this alien's full appearance and size a mystery. We only see portions of him, and no objects (tables, chairs, etc.) beside him to impart a sense of scale. This suggests something large and ominous. But later...

Figure 4.14 —...it turns out this alien is rather small. And harmless, after he finds Christ and stops butchering astronauts.

Lugosi walking offscreen, followed by sounds of screeching tires and a scream. Leaving aside that the scream sounds ludicrous, other low-budgeters might have made the extra effort to film a pair of legs crossing a street, then a car bearing down, *then* the sounds of screeching tires and a scream. Some may have even filmed a stuntman's body hitting the car, or striking the pavement.

Wood only did the bare minimum, creating a scene so sloppy that it borders on parody. In François Truffaut's *Day for Night* (aka *La Nuit américaine*, French 1973), a car drives offscreen, followed by the sound of a collision, then a shot of the wrecked car. The accident is never seen. Yet with its story set in the world of cinema, this final scene is meant to satirize filmmaking's ersatz special effects, whereas Wood's efforts are unintentionally satirical.

Forced Perspective

Forced perspective is a cinematic trick to make objects appear farther or nearer, or larger or smaller, relative to other objects. The technique may be described as photographing the *mise-en-scène* in a way that the apparent framing misrepresents the actual framing.

All genres use forced perspective, though the technique is primarily associated with low-budget monster movies. A rat (or spider, lizard, etc.) is placed near the camera lens, so that it looks huge. An actor stands in the distance, so that he appears shrunken, beside a normal-sized rat. Or normal-sized, beside a giant rat. Or normal-sized, beside a giant bimbo (e.g., *Attack of the 60 Foot Centerfold*, 1995).

Thus, the shrunken item (human, animal, or object) is placed in the *background* plane of action, and the giant in the *foreground* plane of action. The trick is to frame and photograph in a way that they both appear to be on the *same* plane of action, face to face, so that one appears tiny relative to the other. When filming items on different planes of action, but so that they appear to be on the same plane, it's important that both items (1) are sharply focused (this requires a lens with a good depth of field), and (2) are lit at equal intensities. It won't work if your mad scientist and his shrunken victim are supposedly under the same laboratory lights, yet one is lit brightly and the other dimly.

The use of forced perspective is not always obvious. Nor is the intended illusion always that the objects share the same plane of action. Many films use forced perspective to create the illusion of normal-sized buildings (or landscapes, machinery, etc.) *behind* normal-sized actors, when in reality, those buildings are miniature models or paintings, not as far behind the actors as may appear.

In *Bram Stoker's Dracula*, the mansion, Hillingham Manor, was the size of "a very large dollhouse."[9] Yet it looked normal-sized when Dracula returned Mina to Hillingham's gates after their night on the town. In this instance, it was proper for the house to be blurry, while Dracula and Mina were sharply focused, because the intended illusion was not a tiny house on the same plane of action as Dracula and Mina, but that it was tiny because it lay in the distance.

Horror films are increasingly using digitalized, post-production special effects to create giant monsters (e.g., the spiders in *Eight Legged Freaks*, 2002). Yet forced perspective remains a cheaper alternative, with an aesthetic all its own. Francis Ford Coppola used many old cinematic tricks for *Bram Stoker's Dracula*, partially for financial reasons, but also because, since most of the story is set in 1897, he wanted to mimic the feel of older films. "'We didn't have the budget to compete with the big movies that use electronic and computer effects,' says Coppola. 'So we decided to use our own naive effects, and that would give the film almost a mythical soul.' He is referring to a whole range of within-the-camera and onstage, or 'floor,' effects that date back to the earliest days of moviemaking."[10]

Cheating

An actor sits at a desk. A lamp is on that desk. You want to frame both the actor and the lamp. You do so in some shots. Then you want a tighter frame on the actor. Only now, the lamp is outside the frame, offscreen. Which is no good. So you move the lamp closer to the actor, so that both are framed. You hope viewers won't notice the lamp has been moved. This is called *cheating*.

Cheating is when you move actors or props about a set, from shot to shot, while trying to maintain the appearance that they haven't been moved. Or when you place them in a spot, often relative to other items, that's meant to look like some other spot onscreen.

The infamous eye-gouging scene in *Zombi 2* (aka *Gli ultimi zombi*, Italian 1979) cheats the position of a wooden shard. A zombie breaks into Paola's house. She hides in a closet. The zombie smashes through the wooden door, grabs Paola's hair, then pulls her toward the smashed door and himself.

A broken wooden shard *points directly at Paola's eye* as she's pulled toward the zombie. She'll have her eye gouged out! But freeze the frame. Study it. You'll notice that the shard is a few inches to actress Olga Karlatos's right. Her eye does not directly face the shard. Because of the framing and staging, the eye and shard *appear* to share the same plane of action — yet the shard has been *cheated* to Karlatos's right, for her protection and comfort [Figure 4.15].

This shot is a cheat rather than forced perspective because there's no attempted illusion of the eye or shard being a different size than it really is relative to the other.

This illusion (of the shard pointing at Paola's eye) is strengthened by intercutting Paola's POV shots of the shard drawing nearer, with the cheated shots of her head being pulled toward the shard. Eventually, we cut to a closeup of the shard penetrating Paola's eye. No cheating here. But this is an obvious special effect. No eyes were harmed in this shot.

Cheating should not be confused with *moving*. Film students often say "cheat" when they mean "move." If they want a prop or actor moved, they'll say, "Cheat her over a bit to the left." I suspect this is not so much confusion, as a love for newly acquired jargon. Hope-

Figure 4.15 — *Zombi 2.* **Looks to me like that wooden shard is "cheated" to the right of Olga Karlatos's eye, rather than directly in front of it. (She still doesn't look too happy about it, though.)**

fully, most film students eventually get it out of their system and return to saying *move* when they mean *move* and saying *cheat* only when they mean *cheat*.

The Moving Frame

Film frames can move. A camera may roll along tracks (aka a *tracking* or *dolly* shot), or rise up (often on a crane, hence, a *crane shot*), or be carried by hand (for that "jittery" look) or on a Steadicam (for a smooth glide). A camera, while fixed to a tripod, can *tilt* up or down, or *pan* (short for panorama) left or right.

The frame also moves when a camera lens *zooms* in or out for a closer or wider look. If the camera is still, the objects within the frame enlarge or shrink but do not change perspective in relation to each other. Images may also be enlarged or shrunk or panned across (again, without changing perspective) during post-production.

A moving frame often *draws our attention* to some person or object by closing in on the item. We begin with a long shot of a table, then zoom in on the apple sitting on the table. Notice that apple? It's important!

A moving frame can also *energize* a story event. In *House by the Cemetery*, a decaying mad scientist drags a woman down some cellar stairs, her head banging upon every step. With every bang, the lens zooms in, then out, then in again on her next head-bang. These zooms reinforce the sound effects and story event (the woman's painful trip down the stairs), and thus aesthetically "work" by supporting the story's intent to unnerve viewers. (I say "zoom," though the effect was likely achieved in a post-production optical house; it'd be difficult to cue on-set lens zooming with the actress's head-bangs.)

In the short film, *Night of the Hell Hamsters* (England/New Zealand 2006), a babysitter locks herself in a bathroom while demon-possessed hamsters assault the door, trying to break it down. We only see events inside the bathroom: the babysitter leaning against the door, not the hamsters on the other side. Each hamster strike yields a loud bang on the door, punctuated by a quick zoom-in-and-out. This visual device reinforces the sounds and story. As the film frame "shudders," we feel what the babysitter feels, leaning against that shuddering door.

In *Lost Souls* (2000), a Catholic school teacher, Maya, helps two priests and a deacon thwart the Antichrist. She does so partially because she herself has suffered demonic possession. In a flashback to her own exorcism, we see Maya shuddering and bouncing on bed, while Father Lareaux prays over her. A moving frame further energizes events. Explains director Janusz Kaminski: "It's a brief scene that helps the audience understand where the character comes from and explains her intimate knowledge of the devil's existence. Photographically, it is a very experimental scene that employs handheld camerawork to evoke the kinetic pull of the moment."[11]

A moving frame can energize a *static* object. *Contamination* (aka *Alien Contamination*, Italian 1980) is part *Alien* ripoff, part James Bond thriller, in which deadly alien eggs are sent across Earth in a bid for world domination. In one scene, a federal agent, Stella, is locked in a bathroom with such an egg. The heat from her shower will soon cause the egg to explode, its toxic spray gorily killing her. (Victims explode, as in *Alien*, but without any alien bursting from their bodies; they simply explode, veins popping, organs spilling out, etc.) Stella could just go behind the shower curtain, or dunk the egg into cold water. But instead, she bangs on the bathroom door, screaming for help, while the egg pulsates near her.

That's all the egg does. It looks like a glowing, pulsating, bumpy eggplant. Pretty static. And it's taking its own sweet time before bursting, giving Stella plenty of time to scream for help, hopefully building tension as audiences wonder: *Will she or won't she escape?* But this is liable to get boring, watching Stella bang the door while the egg does nothing but pulsate. So director Luigi Cozzi energizes the egg with a moving frame. If his egg can't move, his frame can. The frame closes in on the egg, and cants, and spins, emotionally enlivening the scene.

This moving frame is supported by weird pulsating noises, presumably coming from the egg. Although, since no one in *Contamination* remarks on the noises, they may be a nondiegetic sound effect, to create atmosphere.

Moving frames can not only energize a scene, but an entire film. *The Evil Dead* and *Evil Dead 2* (1987) draw much dramatic energy from their incessantly mobile cameras that speed at ever-changing heights, cants, and angles. At times the moving frames imply the characters' rising hysteria, at other times the POV of unseen demons. Often we don't know which. We wonder: *Is that a demon circling Ash's head? He doesn't see anything, but the demon could be invisible.* Sometimes we think that we are seeing from a demon's moving POV, but it turns out to be nothing. Merely a moving camera. This *uncertainty* about what we are seeing increases our empathy for Ash's uncertainty, and our own anxiety.

A moving camera can impart *authenticity* to a film, making the threat more believable, and thus, scarier. *The Blair Witch Project* (1999) is a "mockumentary" about three filmmakers who get lost in the woods while filming a documentary about a witch. Because they're working on a low budget, and much of their equipment is stolen, most of their shots are naturally hand-held and jittery. These images are appropriate to the *Blair Witch*'s story of a "film within a film." But apart from being dramatically appropriate, these jittery images also create a "you are there" documentary sensibility, making the images *feel* more believable. And because we feel that we're watching reality unfold, we feel closer to the characters and their plight. *Aesthetically*, these jittery images support the story and bolster its horror. *Pragmatically*, it's cheaper to film hand-held (no need for a Steadicam, or even a tripod). Once again, pragmatic aesthetics.

As seen in the section on "Level or Canted," a moving cant can also support the story. In *She Creature* (2001), a gently canting frame recreates the pitch and keel of a 1905 sailing ship.

Smaller cameras with image stabilization technology make it easier and cheaper to record *steady* hand-held images. Yet some filmmakers (especially those producing "reality TV") prefer jittery images because they suggest "non-fiction." The most jittery images have historically been of dangerous situations (e.g., war and police shootouts) because the filmmaker was running or ducking for safety. Hence, jittery frames should have much horror potential, which *Blair Witch* broaches.

When Theo and Eleanor first huddle in the bedroom in *The Haunting*, terrified of the ghostly noises outside, the shots are mostly static. The scene is energized chiefly by editing; by intercutting shots of various focal lengths, framed at different distances and angles. Then we hear ominous scraping sounds and animalistic grunts outside the door, and the frame becomes vigorously mobile. It moves along the door frame, canting back and forth.

Together with the eerie sounds, this moving frame suggests an unseen supernatural entity on the door's other side, seeking a crack, a weak spot, a way in. This impression is strengthened by the moving frame's contrast with the scene's previous, static frames.

This is not a POV shot (the implied presence is on the door's other side). However, POV shots are an inexpensive way to suggest the presence of unseen creatures. The effect can be even creepier when a POV shot has an unnatural movement (e.g., the canting, above) or speed.

A fast-moving frame not only establishes a threat's unnaturalness (scary enough), but it heightens the audience's fear because humans cannot outrun something traveling so fast. In *Evil Dead 2*, a frenzied POV hurtles through the woods, breaks into the cabin, races down hallways, smashes down doors, snatches Ash off his feet, carries him screaming through the air, and smashes him into a tree. Other cinematic elements (the wide angle lens's distorted view and the sound of demonic shrieks) reinforce the implication of a hideous and powerful demon behind the POV. No demon is seen in this shot, yet these elements are enough to fuel our imaginations.

Moving POV shots not only imply an unseen entity, but the *nature of its movement* can suggest the nature and temperament of that entity. In *Bram Stoker's Dracula*, the unseen vampire Dracula flies off a ship as it approaches London, his frenetic POV (now racing along the ground, now swaying and swinging through the air) implying a frenzied passion and impatience. These emotions are reinforced by the *mise-en-scène* of the thunderstorm, and the intercutting of other characters' wild activities: Lucy running in the rain and kissing Mina, frantic wolves in the zoo, the lovesick Dr. Seward injecting himself with drugs while pining for Lucy.

By contrast, in *Blood and Roses*, the vampire Millarca's POV glides gracefully through the air, suggesting a refined and patient spirit, confident that her time will return. Again, her POV's emotions are supported by other cinematic elements, such as the serene characters in a calm drawing room setting.

The Evil Dead's demons were often invisible, yet frightening to behold when seen. But what if a horror filmmaker must make do with a threat that is not so threatening when seen? Happily, a fast-moving POV shot can instill menace into an otherwise unimpressive monster. In *Trilogy of Terror* (TVM 1975), Amelia smirks upon removing the Zuni doll from its box. The doll looks ugly, but harmless. But Amelia is no longer smiling when the knife-wielding doll's POV races across the floor toward her. Its POV shots help make *Trilogy of Terror* frightening rather than unintentionally funny — a serious risk considering the silly-looking doll.

Karen Black's performance also helps. How do you shake a doll so it appears as if *it* were moving, and not look ridiculous? Black manages it.

Advances in CGI technology enable modern horror filmmakers to more easily avoid unintentionally funny doll attacks. No more sending the doll along a track, or flinging it across the room. Even so, a moving POV shot, and little else, remains a viable option for low-budget filmmakers.

Ever smaller cameras have aided a trend toward greater frame mobility, creating a high-energy, post–MTV cinema that's been especially favored by action films. In turn, action genre aesthetics have increasingly influenced other genres. *The Matrix* series and *Underworld* (2003) are as much action films as they are science fiction and dark fantasy, respectively.

A moving frame can also condense story time, but that will be discussed in the section on "Constructing Time," in Chapter 7 (Editing the Image).

Masking the Image

Images can be masked, altering the frame's shape. This mask is often black, but need not be. Its contours sometimes move, further changing the frame line.

An image may be masked for stylistic reasons. In *Bram Stoker's Dracula*, some masked frames resemble an opening or closing (moving) iris, mimicking an early cinematic style. The aesthetic intent is to emotionally anchor the story in its 1897 setting.

In the early 1980s, director Russell Mulcahy masked the top and bottom portions of his music videos to evoke a widescreen, cinematic appearance. Widescreen TVs did not yet exist, so viewers were puzzled to see the top and bottom areas of their TV screens blacked out. Mulcahy's style made an impression.

Sometimes the masked area bears graphics (i.e., *mise-en-scène*). In *Creepshow*, masks are cut in a variety of shapes and illustrated with darkly whimsical, colorful graphics, the specifics depending on the scene's dramatic context. In the "Father's Day" story, Aunt Bedilia prepares a cake, which is masked inside an oval shape, trimmed with cartoonish orange and red cream. (Or is it orange cream and dripping red blood?) [Figure 4.16.] This same mask later frames Father as he screams for cake. When he is killed, another mask's edges are trimmed with dripping blood.

In the dark fantasy short film, *The Ancient Law* (2008), filmmaker Erasmo P. Romero III masks his entire film inside a baroque painting frame, as if the film *were* an old painting. The story has a Renaissance milieu, and Romero hopes his "frame within a frame" will evoke a more romantic, earlier era.[12]

Figure 4.16 — *Creepshow*. Aunt Bedilia trims the cake, framed inside a cake-shaped mask that is trimmed in a cartoon image of orange cream and dripping red blood.

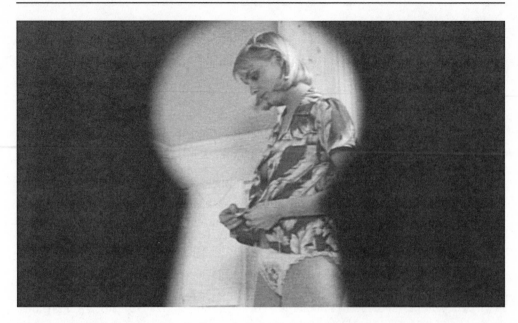

Figure 4.17 — The traditional keyhole mask. Ernest's POV of Vicki (Lois Young) undressing in the bathroom in *The Unseen.*

A mask can suggest a POV. In *The Unseen*, a *keyhole mask* depicts Ernest's POV as he spies through a bathroom keyhole at Vicki while she undresses. Now you know why he invited the newsgals to stay at his house when they couldn't find a vacant hotel room [Figure 4.17].

Horror films often use *eyehole masks* to suggest a masked slasher's POV. A POV is more unnerving when the POV's "owner" wears a mask, because a mask implies that the wearer seeks anonymity, and hence, intends evil. This assumption can be misleading, inspiring sighs of relief, or even comic effect, if the wearer is revealed to be harmless.

In *Halloween* (1978), when we first see Michael's POV, we assume he's a threat because he's skulking outside a house, which implies a burglar or worse. Then he puts on a *clown mask*, which is supported by an *eyehole mask* overlaying his POV. His skulking and clown mask tense the audience. Then his sister yanks off the mask, revealing Michael to be a little boy. Audience tension eases. But this dramatic turn is misleading, for then Michael kills his sister.

To avoid confusion, note that I use the term "mask" in two different ways. There is the mask worn by the slasher, which is a costume item or prop. And there is the mask that covers the film image, altering the shape of the frame.

Split Frames, aka Split Screens

A frame may be split to display several images simultaneously. In *Sisters* (1973) this is done to heighten suspense. A newspaper reporter sees a murder in a neighboring apartment. The frame then splits in half, to depict two simultaneously occurring events: (1) the reporter phoning the police to report the murder, then going to the neighboring building's lobby, then arguing with the police about when and if to investigate the apartment, and

(2) the murderess's husband frantically cleaning the apartment of blood evidence. This split frame creates a tight race between the police and the husband, with audiences anxiously wondering if the husband will destroy the evidence before the police arrive.

Split frames can increase energy. In *Dead Noon* (2007), Old West outlaws arise from the dead and compel Logan, a modern day sheriff, to return to town to defend it. The acting sheriff (his brother, Stewart) is unhappy to see Logan return. An argument ensues. The frame splits in *two*, alternating among *three* characters: Logan, Stewart, and Louise (Logan's bride). Their arguing and bouncing about the frame segments (three characters competing for two spots, in a sort of musical chairs) creates a visual energy, which in turn increases the emotional energy.[13]

A second aesthetic effect is that the cramped sheriff's office appears larger. Tip for low-budgeters: a split screen is an effective way of "expanding" a small set. Simultaneously showing different areas of a small room, from different vantage points, makes the room look larger. It's a viable alternative to using a wide angle lens (which can capture a larger portion of a small room, but which also distorts space), or cramming your actors together into a single frame.

Director Andrew Wiest's aesthetic *intent* for the split screen was to hide his office set with his actors. "I hated that set," Wiest explains.[14] The office looks fine to me.

Split frames can be used for stylistic effect. In *Creepshow*, the frame sometimes splits into multiple segments to create the appearance of comic book panels. Events inside these panels move successively (rather than simultaneously, as in *Sisters* and *Dead Noon*), as though we were reading a comic book, panel by panel. In the "Father's Day" story, Aunt Bedelia's car drives down the road in one panel, and as it disappears from view, enters another panel. As it drives off that panel, the lower panel (with Bedelia in the car) comes alive [Figure 4.18].

Figure 4.18 — *Creepshow.* As the car drives offscreen in the first panel, second row, it enters the second panel, second row. When it again drives offscreen, the fifth panel (the bottom one) rises, and we see Bedilia driving behind the wheel of the car.

A POV shot may be split to suggest something alien or unnatural. In *Phenomena* (aka *Creepers*, Italian 1985), the frame splits into multiple images to suggest the POV of insects. This lends an eerie and unnatural aspect to these natural creatures. Likewise, in *Invasion of the Bee Girls* (aka *Graveyard Tramps*, 1973), an objective shot of a woman cuts to an insect's split frame POV. The effect is startling, because until then, we didn't know the woman was part insect.

Aesthetic Justification

In any film, all cinematic elements should be *mutually supportive* (either reinforcing, or *intentionally* contradicting, one another) and *aesthetically motivated*. Critics often disagree about whether these criteria are met. *Variety*'s critic reproached *Inferno* for "using closeups and fancy camera angles gratuitously and with no relevance to the story."[15] Yet I disagree on both counts. *Inferno*'s camera angles aren't all that fancy, just mildly stylized. And relevant to the story: they suggest the dissolution of natural laws within the witch's unnatural sphere of influence.

Alison's Birthday (Australian 1979) uses framing, lighting, editing, set décor (the foliage), and sound effects in a mutually supportive and aesthetically motivated manner, reinforcing a dramatic and thematic shift in a scene's atmosphere from serenity to dread.

A modern day Druid cult intends for Alison's body to be possessed by Myrna, a Celtic demon. One scene begins with the unsuspecting Alison widely and comfortably framed in medium shots, sitting in the secure warmth of her aunt and uncle's sunny backyard. They had warned her not to go beyond a stone wall. Snakes, they said. Overtaken with curiosity and boredom, Alison transgresses the wall, entering an overgrown area, birds cawing, sunlight scarce. Beyond the dense growth, she discovers a Stonehenge replica in a sunny patch.

Alison's developing unease corresponds to the shifting bird caws, which slowly morph into what sounds like sinister human laughter. Alison flees the replica, reentering the growth, seeking the backyard's safety. Laughter intensifies as she staggers in the shady dark, unable to see past the tall grass and bushes, unaware if she's running in the right direction. Contrasting with her *entry* into the overgrowth, Alison's *flight* is framed in tight closeups and apparent POV shots. (*Whose* POV — hers or an unseen entity's? — ominous either way, but doubly so because we don't know.) Tight frames convey Alison's claustrophobic sense of impending entrapment in the overgrowth, whereas the closeups encourage audience identification and sympathy for her, intensifying our fears for Alison. Meanwhile, the pace of the editing quickens, a succession of brief shots matching Alison's frantic heart rate.

Rushing into her backyard, Alison drops to the ground, once again framed in a medium shot, with ample sunlit space between her and the frame lines. The sinister laughs cease. Shots last longer, leisurely depicting Alison as she arises and stares back into the overgrowth. Wide framing, leisurely editing, bright sunlight, and serene quiet all imply that Alison is safe again.

A fine example of a filmmaker, Ian Coughlan, employing all his cinematic tools in a manner that is mutually supportive and aesthetically motivated.

CHAPTER 5

Photographing the Image

The cinematic image has many elements (sharpness, exposure, contrast, graininess, focal length, motion), each of which can support, subvert, or comment upon a film's story, characters, or themes. Some critics also classify framing and lighting as aspects of the image. Others classify lighting under *mise-en-scène*. Contributing to these classification problems, the rise of video and computer digitalization means that many traditionally photographic issues are now resolved in post-production.

In truth, these elements all overlap and influence each other (e.g., lighting affects depth of field and sharpness), making it difficult to discuss any one element apart from the others. For the sake of organization, I've given framing and lighting their own chapters. Motion is covered here, but also in the chapters on framing and editing. And though I may mention it, I won't worry *too* much about how an image was created technologically (be it camera or computer) because my focus is on the image's aesthetic function.

Sharpness, aka Focus

An image may be sharp or blurry. In focus, or out of focus. Some people say *resolution* when they mean sharpness. Others say *resolution* to refer to an image's degree of graininess. Confusing, no?

The quick assumption may be that images should always be in focus, yet the blurry too has aesthetic value. Filmmakers commonly use *selective focus* to draw audience attention to key actors, props, or dramatic incidents. Joe in the middle of a crowd is sharply focused, while the foreground and background planes are blurry. Thus, audiences are not distracted by the extras walking before and behind Joe.

We'll explore the aesthetic uses of sharpness in greater detail in the sections on depth of field and focal length.

Exposure

An image may be overexposed, underexposed, or "properly exposed." By the latter term, I mean an exposure that best captures the most image detail, unlike over- or underexposure, which lose image detail. However, as with sharpness, it's not always aesthetically "proper" for an image to be "properly exposed." Over- and underexposure also offer artistic advantages. As with selective focus, a filmmaker may use *selective exposure* so that one area of an image is properly exposed, another area overexposed, and still another area underexposed.

In *The Redeemer* (aka *The Redeemer: Son of Satan, Class Reunion Massacre*, 1978), a priest is apparently assisted by an angel of death, in the form of a young boy, Chris, to punish sinners. The priest arranges for a bogus 10th anniversary class reunion at the sinners' now abandoned high school (foreshadowing *Slaughter High*, 1986). Naturally, the body count mounts.

The Redeemer is historically noteworthy in that its gory massacre of "sexual sinners" predates the *Halloween*-inspired slasher cycle. *The Redeemer* is aesthetically noteworthy for its admirable use of overexposure.

Unlike in typical slasher films, all of *The Redeemer*'s victims are killed before nightfall. Dead before dusk. This has *pragmatic* value: it's easier to light a scene with sunlight, at least if your primary goal is not a pretty image, but a discernible image. But the film also uses daylight *aesthetically*. Windows and sky are often overexposed, imparting a spiritual ambiance to many scenes, as if some angelic force fills the sky, bleeding brightly through the windows.

In one scene, the frightened victims huddle on the stairs, trapped inside the high school. Behind them, sunlight glares through a window, overexposed and diffuse, "bleeding" over the window frames, resembling an "angelic glow." Sunlight likewise "bleeds" through the church's windows. An overexposed sky looms over the high school as the priest approaches it. When he walks past an overexposed window in his dim bedroom, he almost disappears into the light, the sunny window nearly obliterating his head, so that it appears as a smudge within a bright haze. Aesthetically, this radiant glow affirms his holy victory and spiritual growth. It also imbues his barren room with a heavenly atmosphere. That the light is diffuse (i.e., *soft* light) heightens this spiritual sensibility[1] [Figures 5.1].

Figure 5.1— *The Redeemer.* As the priest (T.G. Finkbinder) walks past his bedroom window, he appears to disappear into a heavenly glow. The window is so overexposed, you can barely see its interior frames.

Director Constantine S. Gochis's overexposed windows and skies "work" aesthetically, because this angelic glow supports *The Redeemer*'s conceit of an avenging angel. But was there aesthetic *intent* behind this aesthetic *effect*, or was the effect serendipity? While the windows are overexposed, the actors (when indoors) are often underexposed. They are dimly lit. Sometimes almost in silhouette. Maybe they walk in darkness because they live in sin — but is that pushing the interpretation too far? Imposing a meaning that's not onscreen?

It may be that Gochis couldn't afford too many stage lights. So he wrote his story for daylight, with many scenes set near windows, using sunlight in lieu of stage lights. Properly exposing for the sunny windows would have meant throwing his actors into darkness, and so he overexposed the windows. Even so, the actors are often underexposed, but properly exposing for them (i.e., opening the lens aperture any wider) would have admitted so much light as to wash out much of the image. So Gochis picked some midway point, overexposing the windows and underexposing the actors.[2]

Intentional or serendipity, *The Redeemer*'s eerily beautiful, diffusely glowing windows lend a spiritual ambiance to this dark tale of an avenging angel.

I say "avenging angel" because Chris helps the priest smite sinners in merciless Old Testament fashion. We never see how Chris helps, yet some form of supernatural assistance is implied. Is Chris an angel of death? In his sermon, the priest refers to an "angel of the lord" and an "angel of redemption." Yet at film's end, Chris resubmerges himself into the lake from which he came. Superimposed words state: "From out of the darkness the hand of the Redeemer shall appear to punish those who have lived in sin ... and return to the watery depths of hell."[3] So is Chris a fallen angel come to claim sinners' souls for Satan?

Some critics suggest that *The Redeemer* condemns religion. Yet I suspect that the priest and Chris were originally meant to be regarded as fearsome but righteous "instruments of the Lord." Then changing public attitudes about gays caused distributors to retitle *The Redeemer* as *The Redeemer: Son of Satan*, so that Chris and the priest are more explicitly condemned.[4] I say this because one victim's "sin" is that she is a lesbian, whereas the other victims practice what many horror filmgoers still regard as evil (e.g., greed, lust, vanity, despoiling the environment). It makes no sense for the priest to be morally inconsistent. Either we are to regard all the victims as sinners, or all as innocents. I suspect Gochis intended the former.

Even if Chris is an emissary from hell, that does not mean his victims are innocent. *Tales from the Crypt* often has evil monsters punishing sinful mortals. Just because a monster is bad doesn't mean the victim is good. Satan and his "fallen angels" commonly come after sinners. Innocent souls are beyond their grasp.

Overexposure and underexposure can also *hide threats*, either in the glare of light or in the darkness of shadows. Of course, darkness is the more common hiding place in horror films. In *Anthropophagus: The Grim Reaper* (aka *Antropofago*, Italian 1980), a killer stalks an isolated Greek island. Knowing this, a young man carrying a lantern checks in on a blind girl. Seeing that she's all right, asleep in bed, he leaves, shutting the door to her bedroom. Now the bedroom is in darkness. Lightning flashes, revealing the killer by the door!

The killer had previously been *hidden by the door*. When the man leaves with his lantern, he closes the door, "exposing" the killer who'd been behind the door. But we still don't see him because now *darkness hides him*. Then suddenly and shockingly revealed by the lightning.

Underexposure is a topic that touches on darkness and shadows, and is covered in greater detail in Chapter 6 (Lighting the Image).

Contrast

Contrast refers to the degree of difference between an image's lightest and darkest areas. A *high-contrast* image has dark "true blacks" and bright "true whites," and relatively few shades of gray. A *low-contrast* image has lighter "blacks" and off-white "whites," and many subtle shades of gray. Colorwise, a high-contrast image is said to have *vivid, vibrant,* or *saturated* colors. A low-contrast image is *desaturated* of colors, so that its colors appear *washed-out* or *faded.*

In *Suspiria* (Italian 1977), an American dancer, Suzy, attends a ballet academy in modern Germany, which unknown to her, is run by a coven of evil witches. The film's fairy tale plot structure (an ingénue enters the forest and befalls upon witches) is supported by vivid, fairy tale colors. "Within individual shots, huge solid areas of single colours abound; the background will be dominated by strips of yellow, the middle ground cool deep blue, while in the foreground a character's face will glow red. Pure, intense red light pulsates behind the odd-shaped panes of glass in the academy's many doors; ... The consistency of *Suspiria*'s colour strategy, in which the riotous dayglo colours embody the hysterical, hypersensitive world of witchcraft and sorcery, is truly marvelous."[5]

Suspiria's colors threaten because they are unnatural. Too bright, too vivid, too many of them. They overload our senses. Their omnipresence escalates into an assault. Yet our conscious, rational minds don't understand why the colors are so unsettling. The wallpaper in one room has white doves against a pink background. What's so threatening about doves?

Suspiria's aggressive colors are assisted by the disorienting *mise-en-scène*. Not only the architecture, but creepy little touches. When Suzy exits the airport, the editing cuts to the sliding glass doors' electronic inner gears, then back to Suzy, outside the airport. Storywise, there is no need to see the sliding doors' electronic gears. This is not a film about machines gone haywire (e.g., *The Lift,* aka *De lift,* Netherlands 1983). Nevertheless, there is something strangely unsettling about those gears and their fast, impersonal slicing motion.

Finally, without Goblin's eerie music soundtrack to lend support, would *Suspiria*'s gaudy colors be so scary? Or merely ugly? Comedies often use vivid color palettes, without frightening the children.

On a technical note, *Suspiria*'s vivid primary colors were "emphasized by the use of imbibition Technicolor prints. The imbibition process, used for *The Wizard of Oz* and *Gone with the Wind,* is much more vivid in its color rendition than emulsion-based release prints, therefore enhancing the nightmarish quality of the film."[6]

Terror (British 1978) also uses saturated colors in a way that supports its confused tale of witchcraft and slashers in modern London. Director Norman J. Warren admits: "Your search for a story is in vain. There is no real storyline and very [little], if any, logic. With the success of *Satan's Slave,* I was able to team up with Les Young again to make another film. The Hammer style of horror was fading fast, and young audiences were looking for something new. After seeing *Suspiria,* which was a breath of fresh air and a great inspiration to me, we just sat down and made a list of all the scenes we would like to see in a horror film. We handed the list to writer David McGillivray, who incorporated the ideas into a 'sort of story.'"[7]

Confused though this "sort of story" is, *Terror* is so immensely enjoyable that I saw it several times before realizing just how disjointed it is, discovering new plot holes with every viewing. This high entertainment factor derives largely from the film's "style over substance" approach, and much of that style stems from the film's brightly colored, nondiegetic lights.

Whereas *Suspiria*'s colors saturate the *mise-en-scène* (buildings, clothes, props, etc.) and are merely reinforced by the lighting, *Terror* primarily gets its vivid colors from lighting. Warren seems to have settled for whatever sets and clothes were available on his budget. *Terror* is a poor man's *Suspiria*, demonstrating that a low-budget filmmaker who can't afford to dress a set, may yet afford a few colored gels or lens filters.

Aesthetically, *Terror*'s nondiegetic colored lights evoke a supernatural atmosphere, lending emotional credibility to the bizarre events onscreen. Yes, when you think about it, that scene in which the filmmaker is attacked by studio props, and empty film cans, and reels of film, is rather silly; but *Terror*'s stylistic lighting helps you to *not* think about it. Which assists the audience in that "suspension of disbelief" required to fear the unbelievable and the unnatural.

Pragmatically, *Terror*'s pretty colors help to draw audience attention away from the film's gaping plot holes. The lights are so pretty and bright, hopefully no one will notice that none of this makes any sense. For instance, that the witch has cursed her descendants, yet the descendents' *enemies* are also being killed. Or that there are slashers afoot, seemingly unrelated to anything. And just *why* did that driverless squad car kill the police officer?

Suspiria has influenced many horror films, yet was itself influenced by its predecessors. Mario Bava's *Black Sabbath* (aka *I tre volti della paura*, Italian 1963) also uses highly stylistic, nondiegetic colored lights to suggest malevolent supernatural forces. And Narciso Ibáñez Serrador's *The House That Screamed* (aka *La residencia*, Spanish 1969) is credited with establishing the conceit of a psychotic killer in a girl's boarding school.

Vivid colors can also suggest the handiwork of weird science. In *From Beyond* (1986), a mad scientist builds a "resonator" that opens portals from our world to a dimension filled with ravenous monsters. When his resonator is activated, brightly saturated lights (mostly of pinkish-violet and blue hues) depict this unnatural world. We know we've opened the doors of perception to another realm, because, as when using LSD, the colors are a giveaway. "Everything is *so beautiful!*" marvels the assistant mad scientist. *The colors! The colors!*

Vivid colors suggest alien planets in *The Visitor* (aka *Stridulum*, Italian 1979) and *Phantasm* (1979). And let's not forget Dr. Julia Hoffman's brightly colored, bubbling formulae in her beakers and test tubes on TV's *Dark Shadows*. Colorfully bubbling formulae are a staple of mad scientists everywhere.

Creepshow (1982) uses vivid, nondiegetic colors to evoke the visual style of a comic book. These vibrant colors are supported by the film's canted, comic book frames, providing another example of different cinematic tools reinforcing a single aesthetic effect.

But not all horror is saturated. Desaturated, faded colors also have threats to contribute. *The Signal* (2006) is a horror/sci-fi short film about an impending alien invasion. In this *X-Files* type thriller, while government "men in black" plan from offices that are lit in vivid red or stark white, the outside world is overexposed and desaturated.

In explaining his technique and aesthetic intent, filmmaker C.J. Johnson says: "I achieved the look of the desert scene by shooting with my ND [neutral density] filter on. I shot on digital video to create a 'cinematic-documentary' look. I washed out the colors by desaturating all of the scenes in post, then placing a 'bleach bypass' filter on everything, to give my footage an even 'colder' look. I wanted to create my own world of science fiction that you're not used to seeing. In most science fiction films, colors are vibrant, or there are a lot of blue tones to create this sort of new environment filled with technology. It's rare that you see a desaturated look in science fiction films.

"I wanted a dark, gritty look that brought to life this story of tragic heroes. Throughout the whole piece, the characters are facing inner and external conflicts which translate onscreen in this drab, colorless world. A world where hope seems bleak."[8]

The supernatural can also look gritty and bleak. There's more to occult malevolence than the kaleidoscopic witchcraft of *Suspiria* and *Terror*. Just like *The Signal*'s drab colors evoke the depressing prospect of a cataclysmic alien invasion, so too do *Lost Souls*'s somber hues support the depressing prospect of Armageddon.

Storywise and stylistically, *Lost Souls* (2000) reinvigorates the *Revelation of St. John*, retelling its End of Times prophecies from the perspective of a reluctant Antichrist. Peter, an atheist, is slowly convinced by Maya that on his 33rd birthday his body will be "taken over" by Satan to become the Antichrist, whereupon Peter will "cease to exist." The conceit is strikingly original yet faithfully Christian. God is all-good and all-powerful. Satan is evil, the Great Deceiver. Man (or Maya) can defeat Satan with sufficient Faith in Christ.

Director Janusz Kaminski's moody, murky colors lend the impression of a world under a cloud (it's often overcast), of an impending doom descending upon humanity. People and cars move in an occasionally jolting, jerky fashion (a visual effect achieved by an intentionally mistimed camera shutter), as if the world's moral and metaphysical foundations are already disintegrating.

Cinematographer Mauro Fiore says that he and Kaminski wanted "a gritty, realistic drama [rather] than a stylized Gothic thriller,"[9] and thus sought "a cool, grainy, slightly underexposed and desaturated look.... There are few warm tones, just a few specific pieces of wardrobe over the sets. We went more into cooler tones, like blues and greens. We also played a lot with glossy paint so that we could add texture to a wall by shining a light on it and getting glare off of it. Every set was aged with varnish over the paint to give it an older feel."[10]

Explaining his aesthetic intent, Kaminski says: "If the film was overly stylized, it wouldn't seem real; it would be a fable. Although *Lost Souls* is a stylized movie, it is still reality-based, which will help viewers more readily accept the story as something that could possibly happen.... By using Fuji [stock film] with the CCE process at Deluxe, we were able to get a very interesting, specific, gritty and desaturated look.... There was a little bit of shifting going on in underexposure that we found particularly interesting. When we got into the grittier, underexposed range, the film got very greenish and almost dirty-looking.... Everything is fairly played-down in terms of the rainy, overcast feel. It's a bit gritty without being overly stylized. I wanted the film to be very pale white and pale blue, without too much color, and I didn't want any hard light. I wanted soft light, but with some mood and contrast in the faces. There is very little direct sunlight in the movie."[11]

Fiore adds: "We were resisting hard, contrast sources.... Instead, we often worked with big soft sources that we underexposed, rather than putting hard light on people's faces."[12]

Lost Souls was a critical and box office flop. But so was *Blade Runner* (1982). Both films were accused of a "style over substance" approach. Yet *Blade Runner* has since enjoyed a favorable critical reappraisal. So should *Lost Souls*. *Lost Souls* is the *Blade Runner* of horror, deserving admiration both for its thematic substance and arresting style. *Suspiria* showcases the malevolent power of primary colors. *Lost Souls* demonstrates that beauty and terror also reside among murky and desaturated hues.

The right hues go far in making a horror film "work." Compare *The Ring* (2002) to the vastly inferior *The Ring Two* (2005). Almost every scene in *The Ring* has desaturated colors, tinted a murky bluish-green. This color scheme creates a gloomy atmosphere; a feeling that the story is caught in a depressing downpour, even when it's not raining (which is rare). This aqua palette reinforces both the story and *mise-en-scène*, both of which abound in water: the rain, the Seattle location, the ferry boat to the island, the sea into which Mrs. Morgan leaps, the well in which Samara drowned, her dripping body emerging from TV screens.

The Ring's desaturated hues also aesthetically support Samara. When she emerges from TV screens, she flickers toward her victims, disappearing, then reappearing at ever closer spots. Her flickering journey is not only ghostly, it evokes a TV image. Her pallid skin tones likewise resemble a ghostly, black and white TV image. This is appropriate, because Samara's sole joy in the barn was her TV set (despite its poor, flickering reception), she targets her victims through a videotape, and she begins her attacks by emerging from TV screens.

Because of *The Ring*'s dim lighting and desaturated colors, the visual contrast and its emotional impact are that much greater whenever the film unexpectedly shifts to overexposed, bright, saturated colors. Twice, the demon/ghost Samara grabs Rachel's arm, causing Rachel to see radiant flashbacks of Samara's past. These sudden intrusions (1) support the story's abrupt turn of events, and (2) jolt and unnerve audiences. These brightly saturated scenes would have been less forceful without their contrast to the dreary, dim hues elsewhere in the film.

The Ring Two is inferior in many ways, but let's focus on its color palette. It's boring and normal. Inappropriately normal, because Samara remains abnormal. True, in the possessed deer attack scene, the colors are so vivid, they look almost surreal. It's a bit creepy. But on the whole, *The Ring Two* discards the first film's gloomy, aqua atmosphere, without replacing it. *The Ring Two* has no atmosphere. Nor do its colors support the story or themes. *The Ring Two* severs all visual connections to the first film, so that we don't *feel* that it's a continuation of the first film's story.

This is sharply evident when Rachel visits the Morgan ranch. Whereas in *The Ring*, the Morgan ranch was drenched in a greenish-blue haze, in *The Ring Two* the ranch is brightly lit with dappled sunlight. Maybe the set designer did carefully match the two films' houses, but the second film's house (indeed, the whole ranch) looks different. It feels different. Benign and dull. Pay attention to the dialog, or you'll miss that Rachel is now at the Morgan ranch. You certainly won't recognize it by sight.

Why all this daylight? And cheerful, dappled sunlight! Rachel visits the Morgan ranch during daylight in both films, yet in *The Ring*, the house was suffused in gloomy aquagreens. All of Seattle was so drenched. Samara is still working her evil in *The Ring Two*, so why is everything bright all of a sudden? Because Rachel has moved to Portland? (Another mistake, substituting rainy Seattle for sunnier Portland, but still no excuse for the normal color scheme — *Lost Souls* was grittily desaturated, despite not raining in New York.)

The sole color connection between *The Ring* and *The Ring Two* is that the sequel continues to desaturate Samara into almost grayish hues. There is some emotional punch at the sequel's end, when Rachel leaves her normally hued world, and enters Samara's mostly gray realm. Yet by now we've grown so used to Samara's grayish hues that the surprise factor (and thus, the emotional impact) is mitigated.

Color and contrast are affected by many overlapping cinematic elements, such as film stock, video chips, lighting, *mise-en-scène*, and post-production processing. For instance, one might film actors wearing vivid colors, but then desaturate those colors in post-production. Thus, categorizing cinematic elements by chapters and subheadings is necessarily somewhat arbitrary. *Suspiria*'s and *Lost Souls*'s colors could as justifiably be discussed in Chapter 3 (*Mise-en-Scène*) as here. But no matter. Our primary concern is not how a certain "look" was achieved technologically, but rather, its aesthetic effect.

Graininess

An image may be *grainy* or *fine* (aka *high definition*). A grainy image looks like it was projected upon grains of sand, because fewer pixels record the image information. Naturally, there are degrees of graininess. You might notice the pixels in an extremely grainy image upon first glance. However, you may not notice the pixels in a moderately grainy image until you compare it to a higher resolution image.

Among other things, *speed* refers to a film stock or video chip's sensitivity to light. The *faster* the film, the more quickly it reacts to light, so the less light required to capture an image. Film speed is measured in ISO/ASA ratings. The higher the rating, the faster the film.

In general, faster film stocks have higher contrast, and more grain, than do slower stocks. Slower film stocks have lower contrast, and finer resolution. In terms of video, bigger sensor chips (or more of them) generally yield higher resolution and less grain.

Manufacturers are developing film stocks and video chips that are ever more sensitive to light, while simultaneously providing greater definition. They seek to minimize grain, believing that audiences prefer high definition images. Even so, grain has aesthetic benefits.

The aesthetic intent of *Lost Souls*'s moderate graininess is to evoke a gritty world, one grounded in reality rather than fantasy, so viewers will more readily believe its supernatural tale. Graininess serves a similar aesthetic effect (if not intent) in *Night of the Living Dead* (1968).[13] The film's grainy, high-contrast, black and white images lend authenticity to its zombie attacks, by creating a 1960s TV news "look" that is supported by the film's *mise-en-scène*.[14] Helicopters flying over an armed posse, trekking through a Pennsylvania field, evoke TV news footage of helicopters flying over soldiers patrolling Vietnamese rice paddies. Grainy newspaper photos of sheriffs and posse gunmen suppressing zombies with shotguns and meat hooks resemble the sheriffs and vigilantes brutally suppressing Civil Rights demonstrators of that era.

Night of the Living Dead differs from *Lost Souls* in that one is black and white, the other color. The former is high-contrast, the latter is desaturated. Yet the aesthetic effect in both films is authenticity. High-contrast, black and white images evoke TV news footage in one film. Low-contrast colors depict a drab world in the other.

Nadja (1994) applies grain to opposite effect, using it to invoke a sense of the surreal and the supernatural. This meandering horror art film relates the tale of Dracula, his daughter Nadja, her brother and his nurse, Van Helsing and Renfield, a boxer and his wife, and this, that, and the other. It's shot entirely in black and white, but contrast and grain vary throughout the film. Some scenes are low-contrast and fine. Others are high-contrast and grainy. Some scenes are shot on film. Others on video, a grainer medium than film. And not on standard video, either. Director Michael Almereyda shot *Nadja's* video scenes using PixelVision.

In 1988, Fisher-Price introduced the relatively inexpensive PXL 2000 video camera (aka PixelVision). This children's toy recorded extremely grainy images on standard audio cassette tapes. Never intended for serious videomakers, the PXL 2000 was discontinued in 1989. Soon thereafter, independent filmmakers fell in love with its "unprofessional" image quality.

"No matter how poor the light, the camera lends a distinctively hazy, dream-like quality to almost everything it shoots, accentuated by a ghostly optical shimmer when anything passes too quickly across the screen. Contrastingly, the simple fixed-focus lens lets one get uncannily close to people or objects, miraculously registering both detail and depth. Even more strikingly, the images produced reveal an extraordinary sense of intimacy and spontaneity, as well as with a desire to experiment that is no doubt encouraged by the ridiculously small-scale costs."[15]

Having seen *Nadja*, I'm less impressed by PixelVision's ability at "registering both detail and depth." Worse, Almereyda's use of PixelVision is inconsistent. He uses PixelVision both to depict a flashback during a vampire attack, and "present day" scenes involving sex and bathing. He switches from one recording medium to another, without motivation. Furthermore, *Nadja* abounds with unmotivated visual and audio tricks — and pretentious, vapid dialog — making it the stereotypical "artsy-fartsy" film. Occasionally interesting to observe, but more often boring and annoying. Still, *Nadja* does achieve a mondo bizarro, otherworldly sensibility, partially due to PixelVision's low-resolution grain.

Even as film and video technology offer higher resolutions, filmmakers continue to use grain for aesthetic reasons. In *The Grudge* (2004), Karen sees a flashback (actually, a haunting) of how two ghosts came to be ghosts. This is because, according to a police detective, whenever someone dies with great rage or sorrow, "the memory of what happened repeats itself there."

Actually, Karen witnesses two flashbacks, back-to-back. The first flashback shows Peter finding Kayako's corpse, and running away. This flashback is shot in same color tone as the rest of the film, so that Karen (and the audience) is initially unaware that it's a flashback.[16]

Karen then looks into the room that has Kayako's corpse, whereupon we switch to high-contrast, grainy, black and white. This signals the start of a new flashback, set further back in time. It's a more dramatically intense flashback: Kayako's husband murders her and their son, then commits suicide. The high-contrast and heavy grain (1) convey that this is a flashback, (2) reinforce the scene's emotional intensity, and (3) evoke the feel of gritty, "true crime" TV news footage.

A similar "true crime" effect is achieved by the "Electrocutioner" episode of TV's *Fri-*

day the 13th: The Series, with its grainy, high-contrast, black and white flashbacks of Eli's execution in the electric chair.

In *The Grudge*, the grain works aesthetically, yet looks "artificial," like a post-production effect rather than the "true grain" of film stock. (I'm less sure about "Electrocutioner.") Thus does modern technology compensate for itself. Recording technology captures images at ever higher resolutions, only to have post-production technology put the grain back in. Much like those fake "film scratches" you sometimes see on TV comedies or music videos, done to create the illusion that you're watching an old film.

Lens Speed

As with film stock, a lens's *speed* refers to its sensitivity to light, or rather, its maximum ability to admit light. Speed is determined by the quality of the lens's glass, any coatings on the glass, the quantity of glass in the lens (in general, zoom lenses have more glass elements than fixed focal lenses), and the lens *aperture*'s widest possible opening.

As a filmmaker opens or widens the aperture (measured in *f/stops* or *f-numbers*—the *f* stands for "focal"), more light enters and the *f-number* lowers. As one closes or shuts down the aperture, less light enters and the *f-number* rises.

Higher numbers, *less* light. *Lower* numbers, *more* light.

The more light a lens admits, the faster it is. The faster the lens (and the faster the film stock), the less lighting equipment and labor is required, and the quicker a scene can be set up and shot. A lens capable of a very low *f/stop* is a fast lens.

Focal Length

The *focal length* is the distance from the center of the lens to the *focal plane* (where light rays converge to a point of focus). In a human eye, the focal plane is the retina. In a camera, the focal plane is the film stock or video chip.

Fixed focus (aka *prime*) lenses are fixed to one focal length, whereas *zoom lenses* have a range of focal lengths, changing as the lens zooms in and out on the image. Zoom lenses are convenient; one zoom lens does the work of many fixed focus lenses. Zoom lenses also save time and money, because the cinematographer doesn't have to change lenses between shots.

So why use fixed focus lenses? Because they are sharper and faster than zoom lenses. However, this superiority may be slight, so many low-budget filmmakers prefer the one-lens-does-all convenience of the zoom.

Focal length affects, and often distorts, the image captured by a lens, including the image's size, its relative size to other images within the frame, and the size and depth of the empty space around and about the images. Generally, focal lengths can be divided into three categories: short, medium, and long.

Medium lenses are also called *normal lenses* because they most closely capture images as seen by the human eye, with minimal distortion.

Short focal length lenses are called *wide angle* lenses because they cast a "wide net," seeing images within a wide viewing angle. A normal focal length lens approximates the human eye, whereas a wide angle lens expands that eye's peripheral vision. It captures images on either side of your eyes, squeezing them into the picture.

To squeeze this additional visual information into the picture, a wide angle lens distorts images as we normally see them. Images near the edges of the frame become skewed, their lines slanting. Empty space within the image is expanded. Distances look greater than they would to a human eye. Images far from the lens appear small and distant; images near the lens loom large and close.

The shorter the focal length, the wider the angle. A 28mm lens has a wider angle of view than a 35mm lens. Lenses of extremely short focal lengths are called *fisheye* lenses, because they distort the world so it appears as it might from a fish's POV [Figure 5.6].

Long focal length lens are called *telephoto* lenses. Rather than expand the human eye's normal peripheral vision, telephoto lenses narrow peripheral vision (in a sort of tunnelvision effect), then magnify what's left. Whereas a wide angle lens expands space, a telephoto lens flattens space. Distances appear shorter than they would to a normal eye. Images are drawn closer together, sometimes to the point that they appear pressed flatly upon one another.

The longer the focal length, the greater the magnification. A focal length of 250mm provides greater magnification than one of 150mm. And greater image distortion.

Whether a lens qualifies as medium (or short, or long) depends on the focal plane's width. With 35mm gauge film (*gauge* refers to a film stock's width), a lens with a focal length of 50 to 55mm (distance from the lens's center to the film frame) is considered normal. A 25mm lens is normal for 16mm film. A 14mm lens for Super-8 film. A 12.5mm lens for 8mm film. For video cameras, the numbers may differ again, depending on the size of the chip.

Likewise, while a 25mm lens creates a normal image on 16mm film, it yields a wide angle image on 35mm film. Etcetera.

Do not confuse focal plane with gauge. Super-8 and 8mm film stock both have an 8mm *gauge*, but the *frame* (the area exposed to light) is larger in Super-8 than in 8mm. Thus, a 14mm lens yields a normal image on Super-8, and 12.5mm lens for 8mm film.

Finally, there is wiggle room. Some cinematographers consider any lens from 35mm to 75mm to be normal for 35mm gauge film.

Unless I say otherwise, I'll use 35mm film as my default reference point, because that's the standard gauge both for professional filmmakers and serious still photographers.

Depth of Field

The focal length of a lens affects its *depth of field* (DOF), which is the range of distance in front of the lens that is sharply focused. A lens with a *long* DOF might keep all objects from 10 to 1,000 feet (to make up some numbers) in focus. A long DOF allows filmmakers to capture *deep focus* shots (where many planes of action are simultaneously in focus).

Conversely, a lens with a *short* DOF might only have objects 15 to 16 feet before it in focus. To focus on something, say, 18 feet away, the lens must be refocused, thus blurring the previous plane of action.

The *shorter* the focal length, the *longer* the DOF. Wide angle lenses are thus very sharp. (Ever notice how sharp the fisheye lens in a door's peephole is?) Extreme wide angle lenses are impossible to shoot out of focus. By contrast, telephoto lenses have a short DOF and are difficult to focus; extreme telephotos especially so. Yet a shallow DOF and the ability to blur images is a valuable aesthetic option.

DOF is also affected by the lens aperture. The more light on a set, and the faster the film stock, the more the filmmaker can "close down" the aperture and still record an image. *Closing down* a lens's aperture *increases* its DOF. (Ever notice how squinting your eyes causes images to sharpen?)

Short Focal Length, aka Wide Angle Lens

Aesthetically, extreme wide angle lenses can suggest fear, panic, illness, drunkenness, a drugged stupor, or nausea. Because these conditions are subjective, the wide angle lens is often used together with POV framing.

In *Alison's Birthday* (Australian 1979), Alison is drugged so that she will acquiesce as a human sacrifice to the demon goddess Myrna. As Alison is led from her bedroom, a wide angle lens, together with a canted POV shot, suggest Alison's stupor. She is brought to a gathering of Druid cultists in another room, their faces warped into sinister visages by the wide angle lens.

This wide angle POV shot achieves three results: (1) It arouses audience fear for Alison's safety, because her POV indicates that she lacks the physical coordination and mental clarity required to defend herself; she is vulnerable, (2) The POV encourages the audience to identify with Alison, and thus fear for their own safety, and (3) The wide angle distorts the faces of the Druid cultists, making them appear more ominous.

A wide angle can evoke subjective conditions with or *without* a POV frame. In *Seizure* (Canadian 1974), three demons attack a house party. The guests resist, but their confusion turns fatal. Edmund inadvertently shoots and kills one of his own dinner guests. Ever wider angles (with ever increasing spatial distortions) depict the escalating carnage and panic. Most of this violence is shown *objectively*, not from anyone's POV, yet the wide angles convey the mounting panic that every guest *subjectively* feels.

After the demons subdue the survivors, we return to a more normal lens. But *Seizure* will return to extreme wide angles whenever the remaining characters face new threats.

In *Vampyres* (British 1974), Ted escapes the lesbian vampires' mansion lair in a stupor induced by blood loss. Initially, we see Ted staggering to his car. Although *not a POV shot*, the wide angle, combined with actor Murray Brown's stumbling, express Ted's *subjective* state of mind.

We *cut to* what *looks like Ted's POV* of his car, shot in the same wide angle. Ted then *enters the shot!* This is momentarily disorienting, because it looks as if Ted is entering his own POV. We were fooled. This new shot looked subjectively framed, but it was objective. Viewers now share Ted's disorientation. Thus do editing, framing, and photography unite behind a single aesthetic effect [Figures 5.2–5.4].

Wide angles lenses can make the normal appear sinister. In *Rosemary's Baby* (1968), Rosemary is disoriented by her baby's birth, by news of her miscarriage, by the drugs she had until recently been taking, and by her compounding fears. A wide angle follows Rosemary's walk through a dim hallway, into a living room where elderly Satanists are gathered, and toward a black shrouded crib containing Satan's son. *Pragmatically*, this wide angle better captures the narrow hallway, and the many Satanists within the large room.

Figure 5.2 — *Vampyres*. A wide angle lens's spatial distortion conveys Ted's (Murray Brown) disorientation as he stumbles to his car, in this *objective* shot. We then...

Left: Figure 5.3 — ...cut to Ted's car in an apparent *POV cut*. Same wide angle distortion. A shaky camera circles the car, further implying that this is Ted's *subjective* POV. But we are further disoriented when... *Right:* Figure 5.4 — ...Ted enters the frame, revealing this shot to have been *objective*. He opens the door and enters his car.

Aesthetically, the lens's spatial distortion suggests Rosemary's disorientation and mounting fears.

In *Silent Night, Deadly Night 4: Initiation* (1990), as Kim sickeningly realizes that her good fortune came at an evil price, a wide angle lens imparts a sinister aspect to her co-workers at an office Christmas party. All of them seem to be "in on it," demonstrating the wide angle's ability to convey a character's paranoia — and to instill that paranoia in audiences. Why do *we* suspect the co-workers? Because we trust Kim, and they look distorted to her.

The Christmas party, and Ted's trek to his car, are objectively framed. The scenes with Alison and Rosemary intercut POV and objective shots. In all cases, the wide angle is sufficient for a subjective perspective. Subjective framing is helpful, but not required.

A wide angle lens can heighten our sense of the occult or the supernatural. In the "Bottle of Dreams" episode of TV's *Friday the 13th: The Series*, a wide angle sets the mood when Jack and Rashid perform an alchemical ritual, huddled over a collection of smoking bottles, jars, and decanters. In *Evil Dead 2* (1987), a demonic presence is suggested by a wide angle, together with an unnaturally fast-moving frame, swinging from Ash on the floor, to a deer head on the wall, to books, to a laughing lamp, etc.

Much of *The Legend of Hell House* (1973) is filmed in wide angle. Aesthetically, the lens's spatial distortion (1) creates an eerie atmosphere, (2) suggests that a supernatural presence is watching the paranormal investigators, (3) imparts a supernatural aspect to normal subjects by speeding up their movements, such as the cat running atop a garden wall [Figure 5.5], (4) expands space so that Hell House looms larger and more menacingly, dwarfing the investigators in its vast rooms and amid its over-sized furniture. This immensity is also dramatically appropriate because Hell House is described as "the Mount Everest of haunted houses." Mount Everest is big, yes?

A *sudden shift* to wide angle can herald the supernatural. In *Pumpkinhead 2: Blood Wings* (1994), a sheriff, his wife, and their doctor friend are sitting around the dinner table. Each is framed in medium closeup, the background softly blurred, indicating a normal or slightly long focal length. When the sheriff begins to relate a childhood spook tale, we *cut to* him, now seen through a wide angle lens.

The change of perspective is jarring. The space behind him is vaster, the background in focus, and because of the wide angle peripheral view, more shelves and furniture are visible. I rewound the tape, comparing this shot to previous shots of him, to determine whether it was a blooper, because he now looked to be in a different room. The effect was that jarring.

No blooper. Same room, same background. But now more of it was visible, and all of it in focus.

This abrupt change in focal length supports a dramatic shift: a casual dinner conversation turns to the telling of a spook tale. This scene also demonstrates the power of focal length and editing, working together. The jarring effect of the wide angle was intensified because it was preceded by several shots of the same scene, including the sheriff, similarly staged, taken with a normal lens.

Figure 5.5 — A wide angle lens distorts, and quickens, a cat scurrying across a wall in *The Legend of Hell House*.

Wide angle lenses, together with a subjective frame, can suggest the unnatural vision of an unnatural being. In *Spiders* (2000), two college reporters climb an elevator shaft. This is shot with a relatively normal lens. The elevator doors open. Cut to a fisheye lens view of the students screaming in horror. The fisheye perspective signals that we are seeing the students from a giant spider's POV [Figure 5.6].

In *Eyes Behind the Stars* (aka *Occhi dalle stelle*, Italian 1978), a wide angle depicts the POV of aliens who've come to abduct or kill humans. We don't see the aliens as they enter the house, but their unnatural presence is intimated by the wide angle POVs (which see our world through bluish faceplates), the house lights dimming, muffled breathing, and a high pitched noise as they approach their victims. Horror/sci-fi on a low budget.

Eyes Behind the Stars is an unnerving film, *X-Files* before there was an *X-Files*, partially because characters can't find security in their own homes, or amid friends or police. When the aliens come, they'll get you. Unfortunately, our fear lessons when we *see* the aliens. Rather than classic (and expensive to create) gray aliens, these creatures look like humans in gray polyester body suits, with faceplate masks. Filmmaker Mario Gariazzo later resumes his wide angle POV shots, but our having seen the aliens has destroyed his atmosphere of mysterious, otherworldly menace. Low-budget filmmakers are sometimes wise *not* to show us what's lurking behind that wide angle POV.

Headhunter (1989) uses a wide angle lens in three related ways: (1) In two early scenes, an extreme wide angle POV shot depicts the *subjective vision* of an African demon; (2) Having established this as the demon's perspective, when we later see a wide angle POV approaching a house in Miami, we assume it's the demon. But it's only a harmless police detective's *drunken POV*. Director Francis Schaeffer has fooled us, defying our previously established expectations, thus unnerving us; (3) Nevertheless, as the film progresses, a wide angle POV becomes the demon's motif. When the detective chases a professor, we correctly

Figure 5.6 — A fisheye lens depicts a giant spider's POV of two college reporters opening an elevator door in *Spiders*.

sense the demon's presence, despite the absence of POV shots, because part of this scene is shot in wide angle.

Warlock (1989) effectively uses the wide angle lens's ability to expand space. A warlock has cursed Kassandra so that she ages 20 years every day. To break the curse, she must regain her bracelet. At a railroad yard, the warlock lies unconscious in a boxcar, his arm hanging from the door. Kassandra sees the bracelet on the warlock's wrist, just as the train leaves the yard. She chases the departing train.

One shot depicts the warlock's hand looming in the foreground, Kassandra running in the distance. At least, it *appears* to be a great distance. Although the warlock is in the middle of the boxcar, and Kassandra is just behind the boxcar, a wide angle lens expands space, making the distance appear great. Which is how it feels to Kassandra, now age 60, hobbling after the train. So close, yet so far.

That's the aesthetic *effect*, but was that the *intent* or serendipity? The wide angle may simply have been a *pragmatic* means of getting all elements into one frame.

Because wide angle lenses expand space, they create an impression of objects *moving faster* when crossing that space. This illusion was effectively used in *House of Death* (1982). A psycho suffocates Sara on a merry-go-round. After she is dead, her corpse rides the merry-go-round at an *eerily quick* glide due to a wide angle lens. This spooky speed, combined with the wide angle's spatial distortion, and a slightly canted frame, emphasizes the senseless, insane, and terrifying nature of Sara's death.

An unnaturally spooky speed can also be gotten by increasing a merry-go-round's actual speed, but low-budget filmmakers don't always have that option. Some low-budgeters may shoot a merry-go-round (or whatever else) "guerrilla style," without permission of the owner. In these situations, asking the owner to quicken the ride is not an option. So it's nice for low-budgeters to have other, less expensive means of achieving the same goal.

Wide angles lenses have pragmatic uses. Due to their wide peripheral vision, they're ideal for shooting in cramped spaces. This is useful for low-budget filmmakers who can't afford to rent a spacious studio, and must instead shoot in a friend's apartment. If the filmmaker can't pull back the camera far enough to capture the entire room with a normal lens, a wide angle may do so.

A wide angle lens is a pragmatic choice for low-budgeters in two other ways: (1) It's a *fast lens* (if it's fixed focus; zoom lenses have more glass elements even if set to wide angle), so fewer stage lights and stagehands are required, (2) Because of its *long depth of field*, shots are easier to focus. The lens can often record events without being refocused whenever the actors change position, thus saving worries, retakes, and labor costs.

In *Children Shouldn't Play with Dead Things* (1972), an extreme wide angle lens shows corpses emerging from their graves at night. *Pragmatically*, the lens optimally uses all available light. *Aesthetically*, its spatial distortion imparts an eerie sensibility to the cemetery. Up till now, *Children*'s production values are crude. Interior shots reverberate with a hard, hollow sound. (No sound blankets?) Lighting is harsh and high-contrast. This creates a rough verisimilitude, which is now interrupted by beautifully atmospheric, extreme wide angle/slow motion shots of arising corpses, reinforced by spooky music and creepy noises.

Besides distracting from the corpses' gruesome but amateurish makeup, this suddenly stylish photography parallels a shift in story: a surreal supernatural event intruding upon crass reality.

Long Focal Length, aka Telephoto Lens

The telephoto lens's most obvious *pragmatic* use is its ability to magnify images. This allows filmmakers to photograph events that are distant, dangerous, or difficult to access (e.g., behind a chain link fence).

However, the telephoto's spatial distortion (magnifying images while flattening the space around them) also has *aesthetic* potential. Telephoto lenses can capture arresting images of the sun or moon looming over the horizon. Huge glowering suns have suggested the oppressive and mysterious power of nature and its capricious gods (*Conan the Barbarian*, 1982), the discovery or birth of a wondrous new world (*THX 1138*, 1971), and the advent of Armageddon (*The Visitor*). Huge looming moons can suggest the dark forces that grip lycanthropes and serial killers (*Nightstalker*, 2002).

Because telephoto lenses "close in" on an image, some people confuse telephoto images with closeups. But telephotos can aesthetically work with any frame. In *The Ring*, Rachel comes to believe that she is doomed to die within a week because she has viewed Samara's cursed videotape. An extreme long shot frames Rachel stepping out onto her balcony, while a telephoto lens compresses the high-rise buildings around her. Because Rachel appears so tiny (the extreme long shot), against such cold, impersonal set décor (the *mise-en-scène*), we feel that she is weak and forlorn. Because the telephoto draws in the buildings upon Rachel, we sense her emotional suffocation. This oppressive atmosphere is further supported by *The Ring*'s oppressively rainy, aqua-blue hues. The cumulative aesthetic effect is to intensify Rachel's vulnerability [Figure 5.7].

Hardware (1990) is set in an over-populated and polluted post-apocalyptic city on the edge of a desert. Director Richard Stanley uses a telephoto lens to magnify and harshen the sun, emphasizing its unrelenting and oppressive heat. His telephoto also magnifies factory pipes and smokestacks, flattening the space between them so that these pipes and stacks

Figure 5.7 — *The Ring.* Rachel (Naomi Watts) is on the left side of the frame, the third balcony up. A telephoto lens's spatial distortion compresses the space (and buildings) around her.

appear pressed together, creating a sense of urban congestion and claustrophobia. One senses that these factories and machines are growing entities, vibrating with life, their growth squeezing humans out of the city. Which is thematically appropriate, given that *Hardware* is about a killer "droid."

These telephoto images of the city foreshadow what later occurs on a small scale in the story. Jill, a metal sculptor, tries to create "organic" images, but wryly complains that the metal is "fighting her." She incorporates a discarded droid's head into a sculpture, inadvertently enabling the droid to rebuild itself. The droid attacks Jill and other humans, in essence trying to squeeze them out of its machine world.

Rather than merely photographing the story, *Hardware*'s telephoto comments on it. Its early images suggest that there is no room in the future for humans, who've destroyed the planet with war and pollution; there is room only for the hardware they'd built for killing and polluting, for spreading radiation and depleting the ozone. Sun and desert drive humans into their urban refuge, from where they are squeezed out by urban decay.

Hardware also uses wide angle lenses where appropriate, such as when suggesting Mo's drugged-induced hallucinations.

Telephoto's compression of space creates the impression that crossing a distance to or from the camera should require *less* time than it actually does. This is because there is more space for the actor to traverse than appears onscreen. *The Graduate* (1967) is famous for Ben's "running in place" shot as he races to stop Elaine's wedding to another man. Ben runs, yet the telephoto *slows* his progress. This is the opposite effect of *House of Death*'s wide angle lens, which appears to *quicken* the merry-go-round.

The telephoto's *running in place* effect captures the sensation of being in a nightmare, where one feels as if running through molasses, making no progress. Naturally, the longer the focal length, the more pronounced this effect.

This effect has much fear-generating potential, whether a film's character is in an actual nightmare, or in a nightmarish situation where time is of the essence. In *Headhunter*, police detective Giulliani investigates an African demon who's been decapitating Nigerian immigrants in Miami. In one scene, Giulliani spots professor Juru strolling down a street. Giulliani had just interviewed Juru elsewhere in town. Something is amiss. Giulliani calls out to Juru. The professor glances back, yet ignores Giulliani and turns a corner. Giulliani begins running, chasing Juru. Over catwalks and through alleys. Juru isn't running, yet Giulliani can't catch up. Juru is always ahead, turning another corner or entering some building.

During this chase, Giulliani is twice photographed with a telephoto lens while "running in place" in an alley; the second time with a longer focal length, thus compounding the effect. He is running, running, running toward us, gasping and sweating, yet appears to make no progress.

This visual effect supports the scene's story event. Mysteriously, as in a nightmare, Juru is always just beyond reach. By compressing space, the telephoto conveys Giulliani's emotional and physical frustration. (Of course, there is no real mystery; Giulliani is chasing the African demon disguised as Juru.)

While low-budget filmmakers value the wide angle lens for its great depth of field, allowing easy focus in even dim lighting conditions, a telephoto's shallow DOF offers unique aesthetic advantages. The shallower the DOF, the more easily a filmmaker can focus on a specific, narrow plane of action, blurring the rest of the image. Such *selective focus* enables filmmakers to highlight key actors or incidents, guiding the audience's attention, and is thus a compositional tool.

In *Thirst* (Australian 1979), the vampires drug or hypnotize Kate (we don't know which), fooling her into believing that she is at a romantic lakeside picnic with her lover. Kate is sharply focused, the lake blurry behind her [Figure 5.8]. A romantic, shimmering blur. This selective focus serves two aesthetic functions: (1) it draws our attention to Kate, and (2) it mimics romance film aesthetics, hoping to lull viewers into feeling the same romantic security that Kate feels — so that the sudden transformation of Kate's lover into a vampire is all the more shocking.

Because of its shallow DOF, the telephoto can easily *rack focus* (aka *pull focus*), which means *shifting focus* from one plane of action to another *during* the shot.

A rack focus can shift our attention to a new story development. In *Deathdream* (aka *Dead of Night*, 1974), Andy behaves oddly after returning from Vietnam. (Well of course; he's now a vampire). He is invited on a double date. He considers the offer in the foreground, sharply focused. When he accepts, the focus shifts to his relieved mother and sister in the background. They're glad that Andy is behaving normally again.

Director Bob Clark could have instead cut to the relieved family as an edit, or moved his frame from Andy to the family. But pulling focus is a more fluid, less obtrusive choice; the family's relief flows more directly and naturally from Andy's consent if they share the frame.

In *Hack-Man* (2007), teenagers break into an amusement park at night for a party. The audience knows there's a killer roaming the park. The teens do not, and so they misbehave in carefree fashion. At one point, we see the teens in sharp focus, floating in a swimming pool in the background, while the foreground is blurred. Then the lens racks focus, blurring the teens, and bringing the foreground into sharp focus. We now see an empty beer bottle on a table.

This rack focus not only *informs* us (as in *Deathdream*), but *comments* on events. We already know the teens are drinking, so this additional information (the empty beer bot-

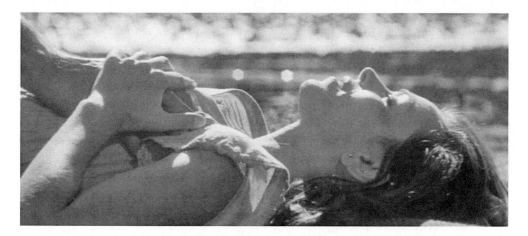

Figure 5.8 — *Thirst.* **The telephoto's shallow depth of field blurs the lake behind Kate (Chantal Contouri).**

tle) is not substantively new. But it is qualitatively new. The bottle emphasizes the growing inebriation (thus, the vulnerability) of these teenagers. This information is further emphasized by the rack focus, which functions as an exclamation point to the bottle. The bottle is not merely shown; it is highlighted.

It may be especially appropriate to place an exclamation point on a threat. In *City of the Living Dead* (aka *Paura nella città dei morti viventi*, *The Gates of Hell*, Italian 1980), an angry father catches his daughter with Bob, a local pervert. Dad overpowers Bob and shoves his head, slowly, toward a spinning power drill. Director Lucio Fulci intercuts between Bob's terrified face and his POV of the nearing drill, which is blurred. Then a rack focus sharply focuses just the *tip* of the drill. It's a nice effect, highlighting the oncoming threat.

The telephoto's shallow DOF allows a threat (or anything else) to *hide in plain sight*. In *The Initiation* (1984), three sorority pledges break into a mall at night, while a second group of college kids tries to scare them. Unknown to any of these kids, a psycho is stalking and killing everyone. In one scene, Megan is sharply focused, in the foreground. A blurry form enters the background. What is that, just behind Megan? The lens pulls focus, blurring Megan and sharpening the background. We now see a person carrying a bow and arrow. Another rack focus, and the psycho is blurred, Megan in sharp focus. Still blissfully unaware of the nearby psycho. But now the audience knows, and fears for Megan [Figures 5.9, 5.10].

In *Witchery* (aka *La casa 4*, *Witchcraft*, Italian 1988), a Boston family hires a boatman to take them to an island that has an abandoned building, reputedly haunted by a witch. The family hopes to turn the building into a hotel. Disembarking on the island, the family heads for the building, with their real estate broker and architect. The boatman, left behind, tends to his vessel in the foreground, sharply focused. The building is in the background, blurry. A rack focus then blurs the boatman and sharpens the building. We see a dark figure moving past an upstairs window. Another rack focus re-blurs the building and sharpens the boatman. As with Megan, the boatman is blissfully unaware of the threat behind him, but we are not.

In the short film *Larger Than Life* (New Zealand 1997), the audience already knows that Jo has spider problems, but it likely doesn't notice that dark patch on the bathroom wall behind Jo. Not until a rack focus reveals it to be yet another spider.

In these previous examples, the threats hide in the background blur. But a blur can also hide a threat in the foreground. Because these threats are "in our face," yet unseen, they can be that much more surprising (or shocking, or unsettling) when a rack focus finally reveals them.

In *Deadly Blessing* (1981), Lana is visiting her recently-widowed friend, Martha, in the country. Lana is a city girl, out of her element, and thus already vulnerable. She is searching for something inside the barn, when every door and window swings shut, locking her in darkness. Frightened, she runs upstairs to the barn's loft, stumbles through the darkness, running from she knows not what. Atop another set of stairs, she looks down and sees sunlight spreading across the downstairs floor, in the background plane, as if a door were opening. Seeing a means of escape, Lana approaches the stairs.

A rack focus blurs the background and sharpens the foreground — revealing a spiderweb, complete with nasty spider, blocking Lana's path. Spider and web had been so blurry as to be invisible, so it now appears like they materialize out of thin air. They did not, nor

Figure 5.9—*The Initiation*. What's that moving blur behind Megan (Frances Peterson)?

Figure 5.10—A *rack focus* reveals it to be a silhouetted person—carrying a bow and arrow!

does Lana imagine otherwise. But it's a neat visual trick, nevertheless. Surprising, shocking, and creepy.

Racking focus on spiders is a motif in *Deadly Blessing*. Prior to Lana's travails in the barn, she'd seen a spider crawling on her bedroom ceiling as she was trying to fall asleep. She later reveals her nightmare to Martha and Vicky, in which a man was trying to break into her bedroom. Lana dreamt that she shot the man with a cannon, whereupon he turned into a giant spider. Whispering her name, like a lover.

Sometime after the barn incident, Lana is asleep in bed. We see her from the ceiling, so that she is in the background plane. A rack focus then blurs Lana and sharpens the foreground, revealing another spider on a web, on her ceiling. Then an unseen figure holds Lana's mouth open while the spider drops into her mouth — and Lana awakes from another nightmare.

Deadly Blessing ends with Martha entering her house, believing the killer is dead. The room darkens unexpectedly. Her husband's ghost appears, and warns Martha to beware "the incubus." The ghost disappears. Then an incubus breaks through the floorboards and pulls Martha down with him. The room brightens. A rack focus blurs the background, and reveals a spider on its web in the foreground.

Deadly Blessing is a supernatural tale about an incubus's attack on a conservative, rural religious community and their modern neighbors, who don't believe in evil. Yet evil lurks everywhere, unseen, but ready to emerge at any moment. Like the incubus breaking up through the floorboards. Or like the "invisible" spiderwebs that are suddenly revealed by a rack focus, a motif that supports the film's story and themes.

In TV's *Werewolf*, Ted asks his roommate, Eric, to shoot him with a silver bullet after he transforms into a werewolf. Ted shows the red pentagram on the palm of his hand, to prove he is not insane. It appears before each transformation. Eric still doubts Ted's sanity, but he ties Ted in a chair and awaits midnight, when Ted says the transform will occur. The men talk. Ted explains how he became a werewolf. Both men doze off.

Eric awakes, sitting in a chair in the background, sharply focused. Ted is tied to a chair in the foreground, blurry. We see his blurry red palm. Eric checks the clock. The time is 12:20 A.M. "He made it," he says of Ted. Then the lens pulls focus, blurring Eric, and sharpening Ted's hand. We now see that the red pentagram is bleeding — signaling that the time of Ted's transformation into a werewolf is near. The rack focus has not only confirmed Ted's claim to be a threat, it has revealed Ted to be an *imminent* threat.

A shallow DOF allows filmmakers to place a threat *near* a potential victim, without the victim or audience being aware of the threat's proximity until the filmmaker reveals it. Nearby threats can also be hidden offscreen, or in the shadows, or inside a closet. Framing, lighting, and *mise-en-scène* all share the telephoto's ability to conceal a nearby threat. But the telephoto can most effectively hide a threat *in plain sight*, right before viewers' eyes, unnerving them all the more when a rack focus exposes the threat.

A shallow DOF can also achieve the opposite effect: *suggesting a threat where there is none*. In *Jeepers Creepers* (2001), an armored truck, looking like something a psycho redneck might drive, runs Trish and Darry off a country road. After the truck leaves, Trish and Darry return to an old church, where they'd seen the "redneck" dumping what looked like human bodies into a basement. Darry enters the basement (actually, he falls in) to see if anyone is alive and needs help. Trish waits by the road, on the lookout for the redneck's return.

A blurry vehicle approaches from the distance, coming up the road. Audiences notice the vehicle before Trish does. Compositionally, only the vehicle is moving in the scene, so it attracts our attention. But Trish is looking in another direction, so she does not see it. The vehicle draws nearer, tension rising [Figure 5.11]. When Trish finally sees it, ominous music swells, affirming our assumption that the blur is the redneck's returning truck. Trish rushes into her car, preparing to drive off, as Darry had instructed.

Figure 5.11—*Jeepers Creepers*. Note the blurry headlights beneath the foliage. Their bright movement catches our attention, but Trish (Gina Philips) is looking elsewhere.

The engine won't start! Trish keeps trying, but her car won't start. The blurry vehicle draws nearer. Music swelling. Tension rising. Trish panicking.

The vehicle comes into focus ... and we see it's another truck. Not the redneck's truck. It drives past Trish. Music dissipates. Trish sighs relief.

In *Alien* (1979), *mise-en-scène* camouflages the alien amid the space shuttle's pipes. The threat is hidden, so we mistakenly feel safe. In *Jeepers Creepers*, a shallow DOF camouflages the distant truck. Its harmlessness is hidden, so we mistakenly feel threatened. Both films hide the true nature of something, misleading us, toying with our emotions. *Alien* shocks us with a threat. *Jeepers Creepers* unnerves us by signaling a threat that doesn't materialize.

But *Jeepers Creepers* is not finished. After unnerving us with the truck, which we now know to be harmless, somebody bangs the car door. Music swells. A startled Trish draws away from the door. Whereupon we see it is only Darry outside.

Thus has *Jeepers Creepers* twice intimated a threat (the truck, and the car door bang) that twice failed to materialize. This incessant fraying of audience emotions helps soften them up for more threats (real and false alarms) to come.

Some of the uses for a shallow DOF are commonplace and even clichéd. A blurry image may represent a character's POV. In *Nadja*, a boxer is knocked out in the ring. His wife rushes to him. His POV sees her blurry face. Her face sharpens as he regains his senses.

In *Eight Legged Freaks* (2002), audiences know the moving blur on the cave's ceiling (seen from the POV of a near-sighted mall employee) is a giant spider, so the threat is not "hiding in plain sight." Yet the employee's ignorance makes him more vulnerable, so we worry for him even before he puts on his eyeglasses, bringing the spider into sharp focus.

Yet even so clichéd and mundane a function as showing a character's blurry POV can be used in gripping and memorable ways. In *The Twilight Zone* episode, "Time Enough at Last," Henry Bemis is the sole survivor of a nuclear war. He settles down to enjoy his remaining years reading books (his only joy), when he inadvertently breaks his eyeglasses.

His blurry POV is not only informative (showing us that he can no longer read), but in the story's context, emotionally powerful, eliciting deep audience sympathy.

Sometimes, a blurry image is aesthetically serendipitous. The occasionally blurry shots in *The Jar* (1984), such as when Crystal enters Paul's apartment and the camera tries desperately to bring her into focus, are probably unintentional. Most likely, director Bruce Tuscano couldn't afford a retake. Yet this particular blurry image supports the story. Because it is Paul's POV of Crystal that is unfocused, the shot suggests his weakening grip on reality. And all of *The Jar*'s blurry shots support the film's surreal sensibility.

Any lens with a shallow enough depth of field can perform selective focus, not just telephoto lenses. But the longer the focal length, the shorter the DOF. A normal lens may pull focus well enough, albeit less easily than a telephoto. An extreme wide angle lens, not at all.

Zoom Lenses

A zoom lens provides a range of focal lengths. However, we should distinguish optical zoom from digital zoom. Only an *optical zoom* changes a lens's focal length. An optical zoom is a "true zoom." A *digital zoom* merely enlarges the image, losing the outer areas. You can do the same with post-production software. A digital zoom does not change the focal length. If your zoom lens is set to a short focal length, then "zooming in" digitally will retain that wide angle spatial distortion.

A camera with a 3× optical zoom magnification, and a 10× digital zoom magnification, does not have a 30× total zoom magnification. It has a 3× total zoom magnification. A digital zoom is no "zoom" at all, and does nothing you can't replicate in post-production.

Many filmmakers reserve all digital zooms for post-production, because while you can always "zoom in" digitally in the editing room, you can never "zoom out" digitally because the visual information was never recorded in the first place.

Apart from offering a range of focal lengths, an aesthetic advantage of a zoom lens (over prime lenses) is its ability to *change focal lengths during the same shot*. A filmmaker can begin a shot with a medium lens's normal perspective, and then "zoom out" for a wide angle lens's spatial distortion.

Ideally, this visual effect is an intentional, aesthetic choice. In reality, many filmmakers zoom chiefly for pragmatic reasons: to get nearer to, or farther from, their subjects. Whether motivated by laziness or economic necessity, zooming is not always the best aesthetic choice. It might be better to move the camera, so as to follow the actors or explore the set.[17] Moving the camera provides a greater sense of three-dimensional space than does zooming, because when the camera moves, different objects within the frame shift perspective in relation to one another. Digital zooms create an especially static effect, even more so than optical zooms.

Filmmakers can move the camera while simultaneously zooming, combining these two forms of frame movement in various ways (different directions of movement or rates of speed), to achieve various effects.

One visually arresting effect is the *dolly counter-zoom* (aka *push/pull focus, contra zoom, compression shot,* among other terms). Alfred Hitchcock is credited with its invention in *Ver-*

tigo (1958), where he used a dolly counter-zoom to suggest John's disorientation. Hitchcock moved his camera in toward John, while simultaneously zooming out. The speeds of the "dolly in" and "zoom out" were synchronized so that John's size within the frame was unchanged. Only the space around him was distorted.

Vertigo's dolly counter-zoom was a *dolly in/zoom out*, which expands the space around the subject, because of the lens's shortening focal length. The *visual effect* is of the background moving away from the subject. The *emotional effect* can be of a character suddenly disconnected from reality. He feels as if he's "lost his moorings," the world no longer makes sense, he is adrift, faint and swooning.

One may also *dolly counter-zoom* in the opposite directions with a *dolly out/zoom in*, so that *visually* the empty space around a subject constricts, the background objects flattening and compressing against a character. The *emotional effect* can be that of events suddenly pressing in, the universe constricting and squeezing a character, eliminating breathing room and air, choking her.

The dolly counter-zoom is a favorite horror film cliché. In *The Howling* (1981), Karen is in a group therapy session, when she remembers being attacked by a werewolf in a porno booth, whereupon a *dolly in/zoom out* suggests her awakening fear. She is unmoored from reality, adrift and swooning [Figures 5.12, 5.13]. In *Hardware*, another *dolly in/zoom out* emphasizes Jill's swooning horror upon seeing the droid drilling through her neighbor's head. And in *Anaconda* (1997), a *dolly in/zoom out* expresses Terri's horror during a giant snake attack.

Conversely, in *Braindead* (aka *Dead Alive*, New Zealand 1992), a *dolly out/zoom in* suggests Timothy's shock upon seeing the zombies arise from his basement floor, a constricting universe trapping him, reducing his choices, making it harder for him to do good. Something he keeps trying to do.

In *The Eye* (2008), a shocked Sydney chases a girl's ghost in a hospital hallway while a *dolly out/zoom in* presses the back walls against Sydney. Although Sydney is running away from the walls, visually the walls appear to be drawing closer to her. As in a nightmare, she is running, yet makes no progress. Indeed, she appears to be falling behind. Thus *The Eye* combines the jarring effect of a dolly counter-zoom, with the telephoto's "running in place" effect.

Unless a filmmaker wants the subject in the frame's center to remain the same size, there is no need to synchronize the dolly and zoom speeds. Because Sydney runs *toward* the camera, she lessens the dolly *out*. She thus grows in size, appearing to run away from the wall, even as it draws nearer to her. These conflicting visuals are unsettling, much like an optical illusion, and reinforce this scene's nightmarish surrealism [Figures 5.14, 5.15].

Using different dolly and zoom speeds may achieve aesthetic results more appropriate to a story or theme. In *Warlock*, when Kassandra sees the warlock outside her house, holding two eyeballs in his hand, an *unsynchronized* dolly counter-zoom *enlarges* Kassandra in the frame's center while also distorting the space around her. The spatial distortion suggests both Kassandra's terror and the eyeballs' unnatural POV vision. Her enlargement is an exclamation point on her terror, and also emphasizes the eyeballs' interest in her.

Zooming can suggest the passage of time. In *Alien 3000* (aka *Unseen Evil 2*, 2004), three people flee an alien. They climb down a rocky desert hill, a truck in the foreground. "There's the truck," a woman says. "Let's get out of here," another replies. We zoom in and

Figure 5.12 — *The Howling*. A *dolly-in* maintains Karen's (Dee Wallace) size and position in the frame...

Figure 5.13 —...while a simultaneous *zoom-out* into wide angle expands space and causes the background to fall away from her.

out quickly, and the people are now in the truck. (Upon maximum zoom in, the film cuts to the new image, then zooms out.) The truck begins backing up, slowly. We zoom in and out quickly, again, and the truck is now on the road. The effect is similar to those spinning/zooming scene transitions in the 1960s *Batman* TV series.

    Passage of time may be indicated in many ways. Dissolving from shot to shot is popular. But dissolves are lyrical, suggesting a slow passage of time, whereas a quick zoom energizes a scene. It better conveys the panic that one feels when fleeing killer aliens.

Figure 5.14 — *The Eye.* Sydney (Jessica Alba) runs toward us...

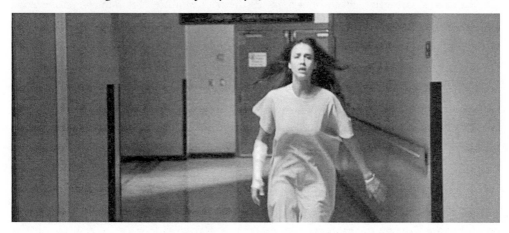

Figure 5.15 —...yet even as she advances, reaching the hall's archway, a *zoom-in* compresses space so that she appears to draw closer to the door behind her.

Speed of Motion

In the silent film era, cameras and projectors were hand-cranked. Because of this (1) film strips were exposed at varying speeds, though cinematographers tried to keep the film moving through the camera at an even pace, and (2) the projectionist's role was more creative than it is today. If an audience was bored or restless, a projectionist might speed up a film, or play it in reverse, for laughs. Sometimes they sped up a film for financial reasons. "Douglas Fairbanks' *Robin Hood*, for example, might have been shown in two hours and a half during slack periods of the day or in a little less than two hours during the evening, to squeeze in an extra show."[18]

The arrival of sound technology in the late 1920s required a consistent film speed. An audience might overlook a silent film that was cranked a little too fast or slow, but an actor's voice at the wrong speed sounds unbearably squeaky or deep. Film speed was standardized at 24 fps (frames per second), and electronic projectors replaced hand-cranking. Later, 8mm cameras introduced an 18 fps standard, to use less film stock and save money for consumers. Higher-end 8mm and super-8 cameras ran at both 18 and 24 fps, among other speeds; shooting at 24 fps was helpful if you wanted to "blow up" your 8mm film to 16mm or 35mm.

Fast and slow motion effects can be created "in camera," or at an optical house, or with computer software. If a movie is exposed (or recorded) at a *faster* rate than it is projected (or played back), images will move in *slow motion* onscreen. Actors filmed at 36 fps will move 50% slower when projected at 24 fps. (Do the math.) Likewise, when a film is exposed at a *slower* rate than projected, images will move *faster* onscreen. A 12 fps exposure rate will double an actor's speed when projected at 24 fps. A 6 fps exposure rate will quadruple his speed.

NTSC standard videotape normally records at 29.97 fps. That includes mini DV cameras. This difference in frame rate between film and video creates problems (or at least, issues) when transferring movies shot on video to film, or visa versa. A good technical manual will help you resolve these issues.

Fast and slow motion effects offer many aesthetic possibilities. From the Keystone Cops to Benny Hill, comedies have sped up characters for laughs. Horror has found other uses.

Jacob's Ladder (1990) introduced what has become a horror film cliché: head spasms. A head that shakes so quickly, it blurs, even as the body remains still. As with glowing red eyes, head spasms are an ominous sign in a horror film. In *Jacob's Ladder*, head spasms intimate a demonic presence or influence.

Director Adrian Lyne achieved his innovative effect "in camera" rather than in post-production. After instructing his actor to sit still and shake his head, Lyne filmed the actor at 4 fps.[19] When the scene is projected at 24 fps, the actor's head is a blur of demonic spasms. Other horror films have copied this effect, including *Lost Souls* and *Nightstalker*, though these later films may have created this effect in post-production.

Not only heads move rapidly in *Nightstalker*. Fast motion visuals permeate the film, symbolizing the Evil that permeates Los Angeles. Yes, that's Evil with a capital *E*. Although ostensibly dramatizing the murders and police hunt for true-life serial killer Richard "the Nightstalker" Ramirez, this is no true crime film. It plays too fast and loose with the facts. *Nightstalker* is history told as a horror film. As a Christian parable.

Satan (portrayed as an albino with head spasms), haunts Ramirez, goading him to kill. Ramirez orders his victims, "Say you love Satan!" He tells Satan, "I did it for you!" Ramirez snorts speed and lives in a "sped up" world. Cars and lights streak past him. Editing reinforces these fast motion effects with brief (hence, rapid) cutaway shots of demonic graffiti, the spastic Satan, and other violent visuals. As Ramirez approaches one victim's house, he flashes in and out (like *The Ring*'s Samara), appearing in multiple spots at once, emitting electrical halos. Demonic whispers and heavy metal music overwhelm the soundtrack. *Mise-en-scène* affirms this Evil world. Upturned pentagrams, written in blood, decorate Ramirez's apartment, and everyone is always watching or listening to news reports of the Beirut bombing, Iraqi violence, and Bhopal chemical plant leak.[20] *Nightstalker* even uses such traditional horror film clichés as a telephoto shot of a fast rising moon (albeit this moon rises jerkily).

Ramirez's nemesis is LAPD detective Martinez. She prays fervently every night, the camera hovering in extreme closeup over her quivering lips and tightly clutched rosary, racking focus on her aged crucifix. Martinez bears many crosses without complaint, including the care of two young brothers and a senile mother, compelling her to decline better job offers, to stay in East L.A.

A priest tells Martinez that the murders are the work of sickness, not some divine Evil. But *Nightstalker's* fast motion effects contradict this priest's modernist perspective. Martinez is surrounded by encroaching Evil. A black police lieutenant sexually harasses her. His head shakes rapidly, a sign of Evil. Martinez's Latino partner snorts coke in the squad car, his head shaking rapidly. Her white partner, Elliot, turns vigilante, his head shaking rapidly. A gal reporter breaks Martinez's confidence as a news source. This reporter too snorts coke, her head shaking rapidly.

The Evil is everywhere. In all races. In both sexes. None of these betrayals or lesser crimes are followed up, because the Evil is too widespread. Evil lurks beneath the surface of those Martinez might trust. Usually hidden, but always present. Its encroachment is suggested by the fast, jittery movements, and jump cut editing, implying that the moral fabric of the universe is unraveling. The devoutly Catholic Martinez is the moral core of this threatened universe. Her head never shakes.[21] Ramirez is a physical manifestation of the Evil, thus a vortex of fast motion. Yet even after he is captured, the gloomy *mise-en-scène* greeting Martinez's return home implies that Evil remains in the world.

The "Hellowe'en" episode of *Friday the 13th: The Series* uses fast motion to suggest strength. A demon chases Micki and Ryan through a mortuary. This demon is portrayed by dwarf actress Victoria Deslaurier. Demons are strong. Lady dwarfs less so. Yet when Micki shoves a gurney at the demon, she easily flings it aside. Discerning viewers will notice that this shot is *slightly* sped up. Slightly, so as to avoid an obvious fast motion effect. Probably, Deslaurier could not *forcefully* fling aside the gurney, but instead pushed it away with visible effort. Speeding up her *slow* push of the gurney, to what looks like *normal* speed onscreen, gives her demon character an illusion of strength.

Lost Souls appears to use *slightly* sped up motion to depict a shove while protecting an actress. When Maya tries to convince Peter that he will become the Antichrist, an enraged Peter shoves Maya against a wall. Later, just before he leaves, he shoves her away from himself. Both shoves appear slightly sped up, perhaps because director Janusz Kaminksi did not want actress Winona Ryder shoved so hard as to risk injury. The first shove also appears to have been shot with a *fast shutter speed* to create a jittery image, furthering the illusion of a quick (hence, a strong) shove.[22]

Slow motion effects can build suspense by extending the moments *before* an expected tragedy. Viewers anticipate a gruesome event and want to get it over with. Slow motion denies audiences a quick escape, increasing their anxiety as they await the coming terror. Much like a torturer displaying his cruel instruments before using them.

Slow motion can extend a horrific event *during* its occurrence, forcing viewers to keep looking. Some events happen too fast for the eye to see, or the brain to assimilate. Slow motion ensures that audiences will see, and notice, and suffer through every gory detail.

In *Contamination* (aka *Alien Contamination*, Italian 1980) an empty cargo ship enters New York harbor. The NYPD sends aboard a medical investigation team, wearing the usual white anti-contamination suits. They discover a cargo room filled with glowing, pulsating alien eggs. Much like the eggs in *Alien*. Despite admonitions to be careful, one team member picks up an egg.

The audience *knows* that's not a good idea. They anticipate the worst.

At this point, director Luigi Cozzi switches to slow motion. All we hear is the alien egg's unearthly pulsating. The man holding the egg arises ... sloooowly. The man across from him also arises ... sloooowly. (Well, they are in the same shot.) This slow motion effect, together with the soundtrack's emphasis on the egg's pulsating, heightens our anticipation of something horrible soon to happen, while simultaneously forcing us to wait for it.

When the team members are standing up, the egg bursts, spraying viral fluid on the men. In slow motion. The men scream. Their bodies pulsate, blood vessels throbbing and exploding. Editing emphasizes this horror by repeating the image (shot from a different angle) of the egg bursting and spewing its viral fluid. The men's bodies begin bursting, spilling organs upon the floor. (Yes, that happens when your skin touches viral alien egg fluid.)

Despite the slow motion visuals, sound remains at normal speed. Apparently, the actors' screams were dubbed over the slow motion images, so their screams wouldn't sound unnaturally deep.

Contamination uses slow motion both *before* the horrific event (to increase anxiety) and *during* the event (to emphasize the horror).

In *The Redeemer*, Jane runs from a killer in the woods. She runs and runs, down twisting paths, thinking she may have escaped. She clears past some brush ... and sees him standing before her. Slow motion ensues. Jane begins screaming, slowly, the killer lifts his shotgun, slowly, Jane is screaming, slowly, the killer aims his shotgun, slowly ... bang!

Storywise, Jane dies quickly. It takes an instant to shoot someone. The effect of the slow motion is to extend her (and the audience's) terrified awareness that she will soon die. The slow motion compensates for the shotgun. Guns are a poor weapon of choice for horror. While guns can maim, their handiwork is often quick and clean. Action films, even when they borrow horror icons (e.g., *Resident Evil*, 2002), enjoy working with guns — the bigger the better. But horror is more effective when death is up close and personal, drawn out and gruesome.[23]

The Redeemer's slow motion is supported by its editing, which intercuts between Jane and the killer, *repeating* the same shot of Jane running. Editing thus assists the show motion in extending the moment's horror.

The Visitor likewise uses slow motion to extend the horrific awareness of an impending, and then occurring, tragedy. Katy, a demonic space child, shoves her mother's wheelchair into a huge fish tank. Barbara sees the wall of glass drawing near. Or rather, we see her POV of the approaching fish tank. In slow motion. The editing then cuts to Barbara's terrified expression. Then to her POV again, this time of the glass shattering. Finally, to a shot of Barbara passing through the broken tank while shielding her face (conveniently hiding that this is likely a stunt double, and not actress Joanne Nail).

Crashing a wheelchair through a fish tank is gruesome, but relatively quick. Not wanting to cheat audiences of the scene's full grisly potential, *The Visitor* uses slow motion to extend the moment and heighten the horror.

The Omen (1976) has a similar scene.[24] Damien, the demonic Antichrist child, races his tricycle into a table, knocking off his mother. She falls over a balcony, and should plummet to the floor below. Instead, we see the fish bowl that Katherine had dropped, now falling in slow motion, falling, falling, falling ... then shattering upon the floor. This increases audience anxiety, as it conjures images of what *might* happen to Katherine if and when she falls. Right now, she's clinging to the balustrade.

She loses her grip, falling in slow motion, spinning through the air, in slow motion, then strikes the floor.[25] The film cuts to a closeup of her head against the floor, unconscious, blood trickling from between her lips.

Slow motion extends not only horrific gore, but the horrifically taboo. In *Shivers* (Canadian 1975), a parasite compels tenants in an apartment building on a sexual rampage. In one scene, a man and woman pin down a struggling security guard, while the woman's young daughter (a child) plants a blood-stained kiss on the guard's mouth, in slow motion. (Bloodstained, because the parasite is usually transmitted mouth-to-mouth.) The slow motion not only emphasizes the kiss, but creates tension. Audiences see the child's lips nearing the guard's lips, slowly, slowly, slowly, and have time to wonder if the filmmaker will dare allow them to kiss.

Another notable use of slow motion is at the end, when the tenants converge to gang rape the doctor. The slow motion begins when his nurse kisses him, transmitting the parasite into him, extending the subsequent orgy and our realization that the parasites have won.

Slow motion often suggests the supernatural. In *Black Sunday* (aka *La maschera del demonio*, Italian 1960), a horse-drawn carriage rushes down a forest path. We know the horses are running from the movement of their legs, yet the scene plays in slow motion, lending the horses and carriage an eerie, sinister quality. This is supported by the *mise-en-scène* (the fog effects, the black color of the horses and carriage), and the lighting (diffused by the fog into a ghostly glow). That the carriage looks supernatural is appropriate, as it is driven by a vampire.

In *Gargoyles* (TVM 1972), a professor and his adult daughter battle gargoyles in the American southwest. The gargoyles, a spawn of Satan, want to be fruitful and multiply, and supplant man on Earth. They are your typical rubber suit monsters.

That can look cheesy. But slow motion reduces the cheese factor. When the gargoyles overturn the professor's car and kidnap his daughter (rubber suit monsters *do* like our women), or when the gargoyle hatchlings break out of their eggs, slow motion lends a supernatural, ethereal quality to their rubber suits. It's a *slight* slow motion. Just enough for an otherworldly sensibility, without being too obvious. (Although, it is obvious.)

In the *Werewolf* TV series, werewolf transformations and battles are in slow motion, imparting an illusion of strength, and the supernatural, to the show's hairy monster suits. Note that both fast motion (e.g., "Hellowe'en") and slow motion can, in the right context, create an illusion of strength.

Among supernatural threats, ghosts are most likely to travel in slow motion. Slow motion ghosts, and eerie slow motion *dream sequences*, became such clichés in the 1970s (mostly on horror TV shows and movies on the ABC network) that avant-garde filmmaker, Damon Packard, parodied them in his short film, *The Early 70s Horror Trailer* (1999).

A *freeze frame* is when all motion stops. A single film frame is repeated, so the visual on screen appears as a still image. Motion doesn't get any slower than that. A freeze frame is not the same as slow motion, but some of the aesthetic effects are similar. Freeze frames emphasize a key dramatic incident, extending the moment, forcing audiences to emotionally absorb its full impact.

In *The House That Screamed* (aka *La residencia*, Spanish 1969), Theresa is trying to escape from a girl's boarding school. It's late at night. A thunderstorm rages outside. Sinister mood music builds suspense. While Theresa pries open a window, a killer sneaks into the room. He grabs Theresa's hair from behind, pulls —*freeze frame* on the image of Theresa's head pulled back. The image *enlarges*.[26] *Sudden silence.* No thunderstorm or music.

This silent freeze frame lasts two seconds. Then a knife slits Theresa's throat. We hear only the *knife slitting* and *Theresa gurgling*. No thunderstorm or music.

On a *thunderclap* we cut to Irene waiting for Theresa outside the building.

This freeze frame underscores the moment of Theresa's death. It's especially shocking because (as with Marion in *Psycho*, 1960), Theresa appeared to be the main character. A sympathetic good girl who was expected to survive. Instead, she dies 75 minutes into the film, with 22 minutes still to go. (Whereupon the dramatic focus, and audience sympathies, shift to Irene, up till now a villain.) This freeze frame's aesthetic effect is heightened by the image's enlargement, by the sudden silence (especially potent following the loud thunderstorm and music), and then, by the sounds of Theresa's death gurgle amid this silence.

Reverse Motion

Horror films often use reverse motion effects to suggest the supernatural. In *Deadly Blessing*, an incubus breaks through the floor, scattering floorboards, and pulls Martha down into hell. After they're gone, the floorboards reset themselves over the hole, fitting neatly into place. Not a mark or crack on them, thanks to reverse motion photography.

In *The Girl with the Hungry Eyes* (1995), the vampire Louise kills Johnny in a public restroom. She then places her blood-stained hands under a sink's faucet, as if to wash them. But, being a vampire, she decides against wasting food. She consumes the blood. Not by licking her hands clean, but by having the blood pour upward from her hands, into her mouth.

Clearly, actress Christina Fulton began the scene with fake blood in her mouth. She then spat out the blood. Reverse motion photography then created the illusion of the blood pouring up from her hands, into her mouth. This effect lends a supernatural air to Louise both by (1) having the blood flow upwards of its own accord, and (2) leaving her hands sparkling clean. Not a drop of blood left.

In *Gothika* (2003), a ghost possesses and forces Miranda to kill her husband. Initially, Miranda doesn't remember that night, but she later suffers flashbacks in a nightmare. She sees the murder, then dreams backward, in reverse motion, up to when the ghost first possessed her in the middle of a road on a rainy night. The eerie quality of the reverse motion is enhanced by (1) the *inconsistent speed* of the images; events flow backward at a herky-jerky pace, (2) the *incompleteness* of the images; we see only portions of events, creating a choppy sensibility, and (3) that *human voices are distorted*, playing backward at an uneven, jerky pace. These factors contribute to the scene's doubly unnatural nature: a *nightmare* of a *supernatural* event.

The raindrops "falling" upward are especially enthralling. When Miranda confronts the ghost in the road, the reverse motion slows to a stop. Raindrops are suspended in midair. One raindrop reflects Miranda, upside down, as if in a crystal ball [Figures 5.16]. Then the raindrops begin falling downward and the scene continues in forward motion.[27]

The raindrop/crystal ball effect indicates that *Gothika*'s reverse motion was enhanced

Figure 5.16—*Gothika.* A CGI *rack focus* sharpens foreground raindrops, one of them mirroring Miranda, upside down, as if in a crystal ball.

by CGI technology. But the low-budget *Girl with the Hungry Eyes* demonstrates that striking reverse motion effects may still be created by old-fashioned means: reverse filming "in camera," or reverse printing at an optical house.

In *Shadowzone* (1990), a chamber in an underground lab contains toxic fumes. It certainly looks smoky. Dr. Erhardt says that she will "clear the atmosphere." She presses a button and a vent sucks out the fumes. In a matter of seconds. We see smoke flowing into the vent, until the air is transparent, as clean air should be.

How is it that the vent targets toxic fumes, leaving behind the clean air? Shouldn't you vacuum the room, then replenish it with clean air? I dunno. The important thing, aesthetically, is that viewers *see* the smoke being sucked out. And so *quickly* and *completely*. Just like the blood from Louise's hand. Which suggests that the smoke was filmed *entering* the room, then reverse motion depicted the smoke being extracted.

In *Squirm* (1976), Mick must pass mounds of killer worms to rescue Geri. So he holds a lit candle before him (worms hate light) as he advances. Reverse motion depicts the mounds of worms flowing backward — and upward!— away from the candle.

In *Evil Dead 2*, reverse motion shows demonic smoke retreating into the forest as the sun rises. Later, torrents of blood spray Ash from a hole in the wall. Soon after which, the blood flies off of him, back into the wall, in reverse motion.

Reverse motion photography can also depict events moving *forward*, for a uniquely eerie effect. This should not be confused with *pixilation*, though it is discussed in that section.

Pixilation

Film speed can be altered in post-production by removing frames at random, for a jittery motion onscreen. Jittery images may also be created "in camera" through *pixilation*, a live action, stop-motion animation technique whereby an actor (or object) remains still, while a single frame (or a few) is exposed. Then the actor moves, stops, another frame is exposed, etc.

Pixilated actors and objects move in an eerie, unnatural fashion. In *Nosferatu* (aka *Nosferatu, eine Symphonie des Grauens*, German 1922), the vampire, Count Orlok, loads coffins filled with soil onto a wagon. He enters the top coffin, and the coffin lid floats up to cover him. Pixilated movements impart a creepy, supernatural ambiance to the scene. Pixilation is also indicated by the jittery fast motion in an earlier scene when Orlock drives a shrouded carriage though a forest. This scene is especially eerie when the horses turn the carriage, because, due to pixilation, what should be a smooth turn appears rigid and boxy.

It is partially because pixilation is an old — and "old fashioned" — special effects technique, predating CGI by over half a century, that director Francis Ford Coppola chose it for *Bram Stoker's Dracula*. In pixilating Dracula's POV, Coppola had two aesthetic intents: (1) to create an unusual POV for a vampire, and (2) to root the film in its 1897 period by evoking an old-fashioned style of filmmaking. As Coppola explains: "The predator's POV should always be scary, like it was in *Jaws*. I'd like to find something unique to represent that. Let's not just have an aerial view of some countryside; everyone has seen that shot of a vampire's point of view."[28]

Second unit director Roman Coppola, who filmed Dracula's POV shots, said of pixilation: "It's something like animation, and is produced by a device inside the camera that takes individual images. The trick is to click off frames erratically — single frames and then a burst of several per second — giving the effect of an animal-like sensory perception, something primordial."[29]

Because Coppola's camera was constantly moving over the landscape (rather than waiting for an actor to move, halt, expose a frame, etc.), Dracula's POV is not only erratic (because of the *randomly* missing frames) but fast motion (because of the *missing* frames).

In addition to their bluish-white skin tones, Japanese-inspired ghosts are known for their eerily erratic, creepy crawls. Samara in *The Ring* series, and Kayako in *The Grudge* series, both herky-jerk themselves across the floor, down the stairs, up the well, shuddering toward their intended victims.

Filmmaker Miguel Gallego (*The Crypt Club*, Canadian 2004) offers six suggestions on how filmmakers might achieve their creepy crawls: "(1) It could be editing, and the removal or repetition of frames within the motion. (2) In post-production you can also *selectively* speed up or slow down motion, and add *motion blur* to increase the sense of acceleration. (3) It can be the performers moving slowly or quickly, with the camera running slower or faster than 24 fps. (4) It can be live stop-motion animation. The actors move a fraction of an inch at a time, as the camera clicks one frame at a time. Even if the actor moves at half speed (possibly using a metronome as an on-set timing guide), and the camera is at half speed, when projected at full speed, the variance in the fluidity of the motion gives it an unsettling quality. (5) The actors may be moving in reverse motion. Then you process the film backward, to create an unreal/unsettling forward movement. They did this for the Lucy Westenra character in *Bram Stoker's Dracula*. The performer's hair, clothing, and gravity can give this trick away. (6) Or it could be a combination of all of these effects."[30]

Other filmmakers have their own preferred methods for achieving a Japanese "creepy crawl." Daniel Zubiate (*Hack-Man*) says: "It looks as if some frames were removed and other frames duplicated to give the unnatural motion. That's where I would start if trying to achieve that effect."[31] But filmmaker/animator Joe Fontano prefers the simpler, on-set solution: "You have your actors move really slowly. Then take the footage into post and speed it up. That's the effect I used for the vision in *Orange Bestiality*. Elaine moved like that when she grabbed the apple."[32]

Pixilation (with an *i*) should not be confused with pixelation (with an *e*). The latter is a visual effect in which the pixels on a video screen are visible to the naked eye. A pixelated image is grainy and low resolution. The sort of image created by Fisher-Price's Pixel-Vision camera.

Shutter Speed

Adjusting the camera's shutter speed allows the filmmaker to adjust for different lighting situations. The slower the shutter, the longer it stays open and the more light is admitted. A slow shutter is thus helpful when filming in a dim room. But apart from this pragmatic use, being able to control the shutter speed also has aesthetic potential.[33]

In *Zombie Island* (2005), three hunters visit an island to hunt zombies. The island is a tourist spot, known for its unusual game. The hunters pay a local boatman to transport them to the island, outfit them with weapons, and promise to return after their hunt. This short film has macho, Rambo-style swinging of weapons; gruesome zombie hunting; and eventually, running away *from* zombies. These action scenes are enhanced by a jerky, flickering motion, which filmmaker Bill Whirity achieved by experimenting with his camera's shutter speed.

"We shot on mini DV with the Panasonic dvx-100 in the 24p mode (not 24pa), so it was 29.97 fps but had the 24p look," said Whirity. "The jerkiness was achieved by changing the shutter speeds. I used it on scenes with fast actions, i.e. chase scenes, to give it a creepier feel. That, combined with handheld camerawork, builds the tension better than a smooth, wide, tripod shot. I'm not sure which shutter setting we used, but it wasn't complicated. Whenever adjusting the shutter speed, light always comes into play, as the speed of the shutter affects how much light reaches the camera's ccd chip. [Also,] when you shoot with the shutter like that, you have to remember that you can't remove that look in post, and will be locked into it."[34]

In another short film, *Mina* (2008), a young girl has difficulty adjusting at school because she is a werewolf—who can't control her hunger. She sells cookies door-to-door, and ends up eating her customer. The previously sweet child becomes a blood-smeared mess, tearing slabs of meat from her victim. The scene's grisliness is heightened by the blood droplets spraying from the victim's body in jittery spurts [Figure 5.17]. Explains director Jose Zambrano Cassella: "We shot in 720p HD DV. We used a shutter speed of 1/1000 second for the blood scenes, to achieve the 'jittery' look."[35]

In *Lost Souls*, the people and cars often move in a jerky, flickering manner. Whatever director Kaminski's aesthetic intent, this jerkiness supports the impression of a world whose moral and metaphysical seams are fraying. Which is appropriate, since *Lost Souls* is about the coming Antichrist.

This flickering look was achieved with a "mistimed shutter" that created "streaks" across the images. "Fiore and Kaminski shot *Lost Souls* in Super 35, using Panavision Platinums as their A- and B-cameras. The production also utilized a Millennium Panaflex specially modified with a mistimed shutter as the project's dedicated 'streaker' camera."[36]

Figure 5.17 —*Mina*. As Mina (Haley Boyle) devours her customer, a fast shutter speed captures the spurting blood as a contoured ripple, rather than as a smooth flow.

In explaining the aesthetic intent of the second exorcism scene, cinematographer Fiore says: "[W]e really didn't want to take it to the extreme visually.... This was the first time the audience was seeing these events in present time, so we employed setups that were a bit more classical. We didn't move the camera too much, although there was some handheld work. We dealt more with lighting things and then taking light away. In the second exorcism, we combined several different film stocks and formats. We made the images go much more astray with strobe lighting, 16mm, cross-processing and the use of a mistimed shutter on one of the cameras."[37]

What is a deliberately mistimed shutter? Normally, an unexposed film frame moves into position behind the camera gate, halts, the shutter opens and closes, the film advances another frame, halts, the shutter opens and closes, etc. But when a shutter is "mistimed," the film begins moving while the shutter is partly open, still closing over the gate. This causes bright highlights to vertically streak the frame, because only the brightest images have time in this brief instant to register, and because the frame passes the gate vertically.

These streaks create the impression of flickering, flashy, jerky movements. The specific "look" is determined by many factors, including the brightness of the object filmed, the amount of light admitted by the lens aperture, the film stock's sensitivity to light, and the amount of the shutter's "mistiming." This is why professional cinematographers take "test footage" prior to any shoot.

As in so many areas, work previously done on set is increasingly done in post-production. Some software programs, such as Magic Bullet Looks, have a "shutter streak" option that claims to emulate the "mistimed shutter" effect.

Superimposition and Dissolve

Superimposition is a photographic technique whereby a film strip is exposed two or more times, creating multiple translucent images atop one another. Superimpositions can be done at an optical house, with software, or in camera.

Horror films have traditionally used superimpositions for ghost effects. In *The House*

Where Evil Dwells (1982), an American couple rent a house in Japan. Unknown to them, the house is haunted by a samurai warrior who a century earlier had killed his young wife, her lover, and then himself. Their ghosts not only haunt the house, they possess the Americans, each ghost selecting a victim whose life parallels their own. The samurai possesses the American husband. The samurai's wife possesses the American wife. The lover possesses the couple's best friend, who starts an affair with the wife at the ghosts' instigation. Thus do these ghosts recreate the lovers' triangle that resulted in their own tragic deaths.

The ghosts are shown as superimposed images; a mostly translucent blueish-white, with traces of desaturated color. Each ghost approaches an American (who can't see the ghost), aligns with the American's body, and then "steps into" it. Then the ghost *dissolves* and vanishes. We no longer see the ghost, but we know it now possesses the American. When a possession is over, the ghost dissolves into view, and steps out [Figure 5.18].

In *The Curse of the Cat People* (1944), the enraged Barbara is set to kill Amy, a little girl. The frightened Amy calls out to "my friend" for help. Then Irena's ghost dissolves onto, and superimposes over, Barbara. Seeing Irena, Amy happily embraces Barbara. Barbara raises her hands, preparing to strangle Amy, but stops midway. Is it because Barbara was moved by Amy's embrace? Or because Irena possessed and influenced Barbara? Or a bit of both, in that Irena lured Amy to Barbara, knowing that Amy's embrace would melt Barbara's heart?

Possession by superimposition is an old ghost trick, but aliens do it too. In *I Married a Monster from Outer Space* (1958), aliens possess men's bodies so they can steal our women. Their possessions look pretty convincing too, except when lighting flashes. Then the alien's true form appears (superimposed) over the man he possesses.

CGI effects are replacing optically superimposed ghosts. In *Gothika*, a young girl's ghost, Rachel, possesses a psychiatrist, Miranda, to take revenge on the two men who killed

Figure 5.18 — *The House Where Evil Dwells.* **Superimposition creates translucent ghosts, one of whom enters Laura's (Susan George) body. Neither she, nor husband Ted (Edward Albert), see the ghosts.**

Rachel, one of them being Miranda's husband. At one point, Miranda walks through her home, trying to remember what happened while she was possessed. Rachel's ghost shows Miranda past images of herself killing her husband. Miranda sees herself in the bathtub, washing off her husband's blood. When this vision of Miranda looks into the mirror, Rachel's ghost surfaces, and the two females are superimposed (via CGI effects) on each other. Miranda suffers a seizure, her facial features *morphing* into that of Rachel, to greater and lesser degrees.

Compared to traditional optical superimposition, CGI offers more options and control. Miranda and Rachel not only morph into each other, but into creepy hybrids of various hues. Solid hues, not translucent. Sometimes Rachel is aflame, sometimes not. All these hybrid images stick together, staying superimposed atop one another, however frantically Miranda/Rachel twist and turn.

Old-fashioned, optically superimposed ghosts don't easily morph, because actors cannot be pulled and twisted, taffy-like. Not that all ghosts superimpose. Some ghosts look like regular folk. Flesh and blood. They do so to fool us mortals (e.g., *Haunted*, 1995). And sometimes they look flesh and blood only to themselves, and hence, are unaware that they are ghosts (e.g., *The Sixth Sense*, 1999; *The Others*, 2001).

Rachel doesn't superimpose much in *Gothika*. She is usually invisible, her presence evident through her control of *mise-en-scène* (writing on fogged glass, or tossing Miranda about her cell). When Rachel is visible, she might appear normal, or aflame. The girl likes to haunt in a variety of guises. Thanks to modern CGI technology, ghosts today have choices.

Closely related to superimposition is the *dissolve*, which may be described as a transitory superimposition. One translucent image appears atop another, the first image fading until it vanishes, while the second image solidifies until only it remains. Dissolves are usually done in post-production, but can be done in camera.[38]

A dissolve that transitions two shots may create a poetic effect, or signify a time lapse. Transitional dissolves are discussed in Chapter 7 (Editing). But dissolves also appear within shots. And just as ghosts favor superimpositions, werewolves like to dissolve.

Universal's 1940s *Wolf Man* film series is famous for Lon Chaney Jr. dissolving into a werewolf. It's not a very convincing effect. Yet as late as the 1960s, *Dark Shadows*'s werewolf, Chris Jennings, continued to suffer his share of bad dissolves. Advances in prosthetics makeup helped revitalize the werewolf subgenre in the 1980s, invigorating *The Howling*, *An American Werewolf in London* (1981), *The Company of Wolves* (1984), and TV's *Werewolf*. But just like prosthetics supplanted dissolves, CGI effects are pushing aside prosthetics.

Other monsters too dissolve. Early in *The Redeemer*, after Chris, the angel of death, emerges from the lake, his shadow flickers over the sleeping priest, and an extra thumb dissolves onto the priest's left hand. Then at film's end, when the priest has punished the sinners, and he is alone again in his room, his extra thumb dissolves off. We then cut to Chris outdoors, near the lake. He scratches his face — the extra thumb now on *his* left hand.

Storywise, this additional thumb links Chris to the priest. It may be that the thumb is meant to symbolize Chris's supernatural authority, or powers, which he delegates to the priest to smite the sinners. The specifics are unclear. However, such ambiguities enhance *The Redeemer*'s wonderfully oddball ambiance.

In *9 Lives of Mara* (2007), dissolves within the same shot suggest the tedious passage of time. As a boy, Robin killed his stepmother, believing her to be a witch. Now Robin is a young man, having spent the last fifteen years in an asylum. He sits before a psychiatric review board, the doctors trying to assess whether he is cured and ready to reenter society. Robin faces two psychiatrists and is asked such innocuous questions as "Robin, how are we feeling?" and "Do you feel you've been rehabilitated?" Robin offers safe, bland answers. The psychiatrists glance at each other. One of them dissolves and vanishes. Then the other one dissolves and vanishes. Then a third psychiatrist dissolves into view. And the cycle continues.

Robin is repeatedly asked the same tedious questions by psychiatrists. This repetitiveness suggests the many hurdles Robin must pass before he will be released. The multiple psychiatrists dissolving in and out emphasizes (1) the dreary, repetitive nature of the review process, and (2) the long passage of years. The acting supports this dramatic tedium. Everyone is calm and bland. Perhaps Robin is trying to give the doctors what they want, but his serenity also implies that he's been through many previous reviews, without release, and is by now merely going through the motions.

Similarly, in the "Tattoo" episode of TV's *Friday the 13th: The Series*, as Tommy awaits a phone call from a loan shark, he dissolves from one area of his living room to another. But in this story's context, these dissolves signify the tense (rather than tedious) passage of time.

Lens Filters

Filmmakers can modify an image by attaching one or more filters to a camera lens. A filter's presence is not always obvious. At times it's difficult to determine whether a particular scene's "look" was achieved with a lens filter, stage lighting, an optical house, or (increasingly) computer software. Sometimes it's a combination of these. But regardless of whether a scene was shot with a lens filter, or was modified in post-production by some software's "filter effect," the aesthetic impact is the same.

Entire manuals are devoted solely to lens filters. This is but a brief overview of some filters and their aesthetic effects.

Ultraviolet, polarizing, and *fluorescent light filters* are among the most popular, and are used to reduce glare or "color correct" for specific lighting conditions. Their primary function is to help capture as clean and pristine an image as possible. Like most filters, they are available in multiple gradations, depending on how much correction one desires.

Filters also serve a pragmatic function: they shield the camera lens from scratches. It's cheaper to buy a new filter than a new lens. Because ultraviolet filters only minimally affect the image, some filmmakers keep a UV filter on the lens at all times for protection. (Try doing *that* with a computer program's "filter effect.")

Diffusion filters soften images, such as an actor's facial lines and wrinkles, by diffusing light without blurring the image. The actor stays in focus, but looks younger! This is useful for romance films, but also for romantic scenes in horror films (e.g., *Thirst*).

Sepia filters add a warm, brownish hue to images. This can imply that a particular scene is set in the past, because *really* old photographs also have that brownish hue. In *Pumpkinhead 2: Blood Wings*, a teenager is murdered in 1958, because he is ugly and deformed. He returns from the dead, around 1993, as the pumpkinhead monster. Flashbacks to the 1950s are shown in sepia hues. In the end, Pumpkinhead is shot dead, and his childhood friend (now the adult sheriff) remembers the monster when it was still an innocent boy. His memories' sepia tones have two aesthetic effects: (1) they evoke a sense of the past, and (2) their soft brown hues romanticize this past, suggesting the boy's playful innocence, before murder transformed him into a vengeful demon.

Filters can deepen colors, lending an image greater power. In *Evil Dead 2*, Ash knows that when night returns, so will the demons. Yet he can't escape, because the bridge is ripped asunder. As he considers his fate, facing the torn bridge and the deep chasm beneath it, a huge sun sets behind him, sinking quickly into the clouds. A telephoto magnifies the sun. An orange filter deepens the sun's yellow, and casts the clouds in an orange glow.

This scene may be interpreted subjectively or objectively. Subjectively, the *mise-en-scène* of the torn bridge, and Ash's dejected face, convey Ash's hopeless situation. The telephoto lens, and orange filter, magnify and strengthen the sun, thus emphasizing its importance to Ash. Because he fears the onset of night, he perceives the sun as setting quickly.

Objectively, the unnaturally large and fast-moving sun, the orange clouds, the quick onslaught of night, all imply the fantastique. In the story's supernatural context, the sun may truly be setting abnormally fast, at least over that area of the forest. It may be a localized quantum time twist, caused by the *Necronomicon* (which later hurls Ash back in time to A.D. 1300).

In *Shock Waves* (1977), an orange filter effect is a story element in its own right. A small tourist boat in the Caribbean Sea enters the sort of "bad area" one associates with the Devil's Triangle. Radio and compass no longer work. Crew and tourists observe a strangely orange sky. "Jesus, look at the sun," exclaims one crewman. Everything — ocean, boat, people — is suffused in this bizarre, yellowish-orange glow. Why?

We never find out. Yes, Nazi zombies lie dormant in the sea, beneath the boat and soon to awaken. But why would that cause the radio and compass to fail? How would these zombies turn the sun orange?

Shock Waves's orange glow (whether achieved with a lens filter or in post-production) creates a "sense of weirdness," and that is all. There is no explanation for the glow. Nor is there a need. This is horror, after all, not science fiction. This unexplained phenomenon heightens our sense that these characters are entering a "nightmare zone" where the world is no longer as their rational minds believe.

Blue filters are helpful in *day-for-night* scenes.[39] *Red filters* are useful when shooting *Earth-for-Mars*. The low-budget *Star Crystal* opens with astronauts on the red planet, which looks to be shot in some California desert, with a red filter over the camera lens.

Horror filmmakers who set their story in a foggy forest, or on a misty moor, and find the weather uncooperatively clear, may opt for a *fog filter*. "A natural fog causes lights to glow and flare. Contrast is generally lower, and sharpness may be affected as well. Fog filters mimic this effect of atomized water droplets in the air. The soft glow can be used to make lighting more visible, make it better felt by the viewer. The effect of humidity in, say, a tropical scene can be created or enhanced."[40] Which is nice, since horror is not all foggy streets in Victorian London. Tropical, humid climates also suffer from monsters and mad scientists (e.g., *Shock Waves*; *The Flesh Eaters*, 1964; *Anaconda, Arachnid*, 2001).

A filmmaker can also rent a *fog machine* (aka *smoke machine*), and the Teamster to go with it, but fog filters are the cheaper, less cumbersome alternative. Also, fog machines rarely emit believable, natural fogs. A fog filter has an evenly spread, naturally hazy effect, whereas machine fog will waft across the set in an uneven, haphazard fashion.

However, an "unnatural" machine fog can be aesthetically appropriate. In *Horror Hotel* (aka *The City of the Dead*, 1960), a young coed, Nan, travels to the small New England town of Whitewood to research witchcraft. She finds a town that looks unnatural and surreal, largely due to the expressionistic *misé-en scene*: the town people's silent stares, outdoor scenes that were shot inside a studio, but especially the unnatural machine fog. Billows of white smoke (looking like clouds) snake across the ground, much like in the expressionistic Universal horror classics of the 1930s and 1940s. A fog filter would have created a more realistic-looking fog, but *Horror Hotel*'s undulating mist better suggests an evil town, located in a supernatural vortex. Black and white photography reinforces the unnatural fog, heightening the contrasts between the white fog and the dark night.

The Fog (1980) likewise uses fog machines (and real fog, I've been told). The film might have relied solely on fog filters, increasing the filter gradations as the fog neared and thickened, but that would have created practical difficulties. Ghosts travel and hide inside the fog, emerging suddenly to kill. Victims watch the fog approach, seeing only mist until a ghost emerges. Audiences are initially unnerved (because they never know if and when a ghost will emerge), then shocked when a ghost does emerge.

But for this to work, the ghosts must be *hidden*, and their victims *visible*. Viewers won't be shocked if they see the ghosts from a mile away. But a fog filter that's dense enough to hide ghosts would hide everything before the lens, including victims. Machine fog can hide ghosts, but allow victims to stand outside the fog, unobscured. Or it can enshroud the victims, creating tension as audiences wonder what's happening in that fog. Machine fog offers choices, because people can vanish deep inside it, or stand obscured on its edge, or visible outside it. Unlike fog filters, which obscure everything.

Practicalities aside, *The Fog*'s machine fog "works" better aesthetically, because a thick, surreal, moving fog appears sentient, like a character in its own right. That's not true storywise; the fog is merely a vehicle for the ghosts who travel within it. But it's emotionally true, in that a "living fog" is how it feels to audiences. Lighting reinforces this impression. The fog glows from within. Machine fog can do that, because it reflects light, whereas a filter fog does not.

A filmmaker can also combine a fog machine with a fog filter, should the result be aesthetically appropriate. Or one can take the modern approach, and work with digital fog.

A fog enshrouds the haunted mansion in *The Others* (2001). It is ever present. As in *The Fog*, this fog is almost a character in its own right. If not sentient, it still acts as a guardian. When Grace leaves the mansion and heads for town, Mr. Tuttle expresses concern because, unknown to Grace, she is not supposed to leave. "Don't worry," says Mrs. Mills. "The fog won't let her get very far." Mr. Tuttle smiles. "Ah yes. The fog."

The fog is hazy around the mansion, then thickens the farther away Grace walks. Soon she can barely see ahead of herself. We see her lost in a gray mist, with only the outlines of the nearest trees visible. This fog is not the motionless haze of a fog filter. Its misty tendrils waft through the air like real fog. However, it does not billow in puffy clouds, or undulate across the ground, as do machine fogs. This fog moves, but without obscuring the actors at inopportune moments. It thickens and thins on cue. It's a very well-behaved fog. Digital fogs take direction very well.[41]

Lens filters offer a vast array of visual distortions, for a vast array of bizarre POVs. It would be a boring universe indeed if every monster, alien, and supernatural entity all saw us humans with the same wide angle view.

Phantasm is famous for its silver sphere: a baseball-sized metal ball that flies through the air, chasing and killing all who invade the mausoleum. The sphere has no discernible eyes, yet it "sees." When it flies, we cut to its POV, which perceives our world in only red and black. These colors are aesthetically appropriate. While *Phantasm* is a horror/sci-fi film, it draws much of its menace from the traditionally supernatural setting of a mausoleum. That the sphere "sees" only in traditionally Satanic colors reinforces this supernatural sensibility. Furthermore, this mixing of sci-fi and supernatural icons supports *Phantasm*'s overall surrealism; the story is ultimately a nightmare.

Aesthetically, it's unimportant *how* the sphere's red and black POV was achieved, but a *red filter* over the camera lens is one possibility. Canadian filmmaker Miguel Gallego suggests: "It was produced in 1979, which is pre–CGI. From the look of it, they may have used a red filter on the camera, and played with the exposure to increase the contrast between the light and dark areas of the frame, so everything is either lit or in deep shadow. Whether or not they shot it with a filter on the lens, it looks like they took the footage and cranked up the red light, and dropped the blue and green lights, during the post-production color timing. That's why it has no trace of colors, other than the black and blood red. It helps that the mausoleum set is pretty monochromatic black and white, so the white is completely taken over by the red tones from the timing lights."[42]

If a monster or demon is going to see our world in only two colors, they'll likely see it in red and black. Pumpkinhead also saw our world in red and black, though his POV always saw things smearing and streaking. Don't ask me how that effect was achieved.

Both *Star Crystal* and *Eyes Behind the Stars* feature aliens with wide angle POVs. In

Figure 5.19 — A star filter depicts Karen's POV of TV studio lights before she blacks out in *The Howling*.

the former, the POV is blurry on the edges. In the latter, the POVs have a bluish tinge (because the aliens wear blue faceplates). As with *Phantasm*, I suspect these effects were created with filters, rather than in post-production or by on-set lighting. In any case, the aesthetic intent is the same: to suggest an unnatural creature by creating an unnatural POV.

I say it's likely these films achieved their POV effects with filters, because they are older films. Today, these effects would more likely be done with post-production software. Filmmaker Christopher Alan Broadstone advises: "You could put a red filter on the camera, but I wouldn't do that unless it was the only choice. Once you shoot it that way, you're pretty much stuck with it. I'd do it in post during the color correction process. It's best to shoot things as even and clean as possible. That way you have everything you need to work with visually in post."[43]

Which is why the foggy outdoor scenes in *The Others* were shot on a bright, sunny day, "as clean as possible," with the fog added later, digitally.

Filters can also depict the distorted POVs of people who are drunk, doped, delirious, or delusional. In *The Howling*, Karen, a TV anchorwoman, reports on her interview with a serial killer, having suppressed all memories of him being a werewolf. But her suppressed memories cause her to faint during her report. A *star filter* depicts her delirium just before she blacks out. Her POV looks up at the studio lights, which (due to the star filter) emit spikes of light [Figure 5.19].

CHAPTER 6

Lighting the Image

As with other cinematic tools, lighting comments on events in a film and conveys an emotional impact. Lighting can support characters, story, or themes, in which case the lighting "works" aesthetically. The aesthetic effect of any particular lighting setup can be supported or subverted by other cinematic tools. Lighting concerns both photography (which has been called "painting with light") and *mise-en-scène* (in that lighting affects the composition of the images within the frame, by directing the viewer's attention through highlights, shadows, and contrasts).

Lighting also has a pragmatic function. It lets us see things.

Quality and Intensity

The *quality* of a light can be hard or soft. *Hard light* creates shadows with sharp, hard outlines, and strong contrasts between light and dark areas. *Soft light* creates shadows with soft edges, and less contrast between light and dark areas. A clear, sunny day creates hard light. An overcast sky creates soft light. Examine your shadow on an overcast day, if you can find it.

Soft light is *diffuse*, in that light rays are diffused (i.e., scattered) in different directions. Clouds can do that. So can many of the tools used by lighting technicians. Naturally, there are degrees of diffusion, from pure hard light toward ever softer light.

Quality should not be confused with *intensity*. Light can be *bright* or *dim*, with many degrees in between. To reduce a light's intensity on a subject, you can either (1) use a less intense light source, i.e., change the bulb, (2) obscure the light with a *scrim*, a *barndoor*, or some other dimming tool,[1] or (3) move the light farther from the subject.

Motivated Lighting

A *motivated* stage light appears to shine from a source within the scene, such as a table lamp. This means that the stage light is shone from a direction, and with a brightness and color, that corresponds to that table lamp. If the table lamp is turned off, so is the stage light. Of course, some filmmakers use unmotivated lights for creative reasons. Others are just sloppy.

In *Satan's School for Girls* (TVM 1973), a young woman, Elizabeth, enrolls in the Salem Academy (hint, hint) to investigate her sister's suicide. One dark and stormy night, a power outage ensues. The perfect night for Elizabeth to search the campus for clues. She walks down a pitch black hallway, armed only with a kerosene lamp. We see *only* the lamp's orange glow in a sea of black. Elizabeth reaches the end of the hall, and though the lamp is now *farther from us*, the *end of the hall brightens* as Elizabeth turns a corner. Obviously, a stage light was positioned around that corner. It was lit when actress Pamela Franklin reached the end of the hall.

Then Elizabeth walks down some stairs. She begins in a *dark area* atop the stairs. The middle of the stairs *brightens* as she passes by, then *dims* when she reaches the bottom. Again, a stage light was positioned offscreen near the middle of the stairs. We're not supposed to notice that while Elizabeth's lamp "illuminated" the middle of the stairs, it did not similarly illuminate the top and bottom areas.

This lighting pattern repeats throughout Elizabeth's nocturnal sojourn. She leaves the dormitory, crosses the campus green in the middle of a thunderstorm,[2] enters the classroom building, removes a painting, returns to the dormitory, enters the basement, etc. Six minutes of screen time going up and down stairs, around corners, in and out of rooms — and always, the kerosene lamp continues its weird ways. Sometimes the lamp is a small bright spot in an ocean of black, and sometimes an entire room or hallway brightens as Elizabeth passes by. Obviously, stage lights are strategically located in offscreen areas along her journey, lighting and dimming as the kerosene lamp passes by.

These stage lights are *motivated* by Elizabeth's kerosene lamp. Naturally, the stage lights can't duplicate Elizabeth's journey, as they are in fixed positions, so their illumination does not precisely match Elizabeth's passage.[3] Nevertheless, *Satan's School for Girls* demonstrates one cinematographer's attempt to create a spooky atmosphere (a beautiful young woman wandering alone on a dark and stormy night, with only a kerosene lamp), while simultaneously attempting to motivate the stage lights along her journey.

And Tim Southcott succeeds. Elizabeth's six minute search is both spookily atmospheric and beautifully lit. Warm patches of light amid deep, rich blacks. The contrast is impressive. The bright flashes of lightning, with its cold hues, add a nice touch. The stage lights don't precisely correspond to the kerosene lamp, but you won't notice it unless you're looking for it. And even then, it needn't bother you.

Some lights lack motivation. In *Sleepaway Camp* (1983), Kenny and Leslie are riding in a canoe on a lake. It's night. Pitch dark. Kenny capsizes the canoe as a joke. Leslie swims off in anger. Kenny resubmerges and comes up again, under the capsized canoe.

We *see* Kenny under the canoe. He *glances around*, enthralled by his surroundings. He notices an echo. He calls out to Leslie, using a spooky voice. He begins to sing. Then someone pops up out of the water. We see only the back of the head. Kenny *glares* at the newcomer and says, "What the hell are you doing here? I bet the rest of the boys will be interested in seeing you." Apparently, Kenny *recognizes* this person — who then kills Kenny.

It's night. Pitch dark. Moonlight may motivate stage lights above the canoe, but there is no motivation for any light under the capsized canoe. The light exists for one pragmatic reason: so audiences can see what's happening. But even then, that's no logical reason for Kenny to see. He should be groping in the dark. Instead, he sees perfectly well beneath the capsized canoe.

Why? How so? Because director Robert Hiltzik wants Kenny to recognize his attacker. Lighting logic is sacrificed for the film's dramatic needs.

This is not a poorly motivated light. This is an unmotivated light, which audiences are not supposed to notice.[4] And to *Sleepaway Camp*'s credit, I didn't notice it the first few times I watched the film. That's the nice thing about horror films. You can watch the same film a dozen or more times, and you always discover new things.

Three-Point Lighting

Hollywood studios popularized the classic *three-point lighting* setup. In its basic form, a subject (say, an actor) is lit with three stage lights that are placed offscreen: a *key light*, a *fill light*, a *backlight*. Three-point lighting is not written in stone, but filmmakers should know it, if only because you must know the rules before you can creatively break them.

The *key light* is the main stage light shone on the actor. That's why it's the "key" light. It's usually (1) the brightest light shone on the actor, (2) shone from the actor's front, at an angle, and (3) the stage light most likely to be motivated.

The *fill light* usually (1) shines from the actor's side, from somewhere opposite the key light, and (2) is dimmer than the key. The fill light softens a subject's wrinkles and contours by "filling in" the shadows created by the key. But because a fill light is dimmer than the key, it lightens, but does not eliminate, shadows. *Attached shadows* remain, creating a sense of depth and three-dimensional volume.

Backlights are usually placed behind and above the subject. They too suggest depth and three-dimensional volume by *edge lighting* a subject, thereby "separating" the subject from the background. Without backlights, scenes look flat. Porno films often settle for such *flat lighting*. (Because, why bother?) So do some low-budget horror filmmakers, such as Herschell Gordon Lewis, who learned his craft on "nudie" flicks.[5]

In traditional three-point lighting, each actor gets three lights (not the extras — they don't count), and the setup is moved whenever the actors shift position.

There is wiggle room. The *same light source can simultaneously serve several functions*. In a scene with two actors, one actor's key can double as the other actor's backlight. Stage lights are not always necessary. A table lamp may double as both *mise-en-scène* and fill light. Natural sunlight can serve as an actor's key light or backlight, with a *reflector* (in offscreen space) used as a fill light. Nor is it holy writ that every actor must have three lights, no more, no less.

Apart from the key, fill, and backlight, *background lights* illuminate the set. Background lights should not be confused with backlights.

Hollywood developed three-point lighting to serve two aesthetic goals. (1) Lighting should be unobtrusive; it should not draw attention to itself. Emphasis is on story rather than technique. The theory is that unobtrusive lighting better enables audiences to suspend disbelief and enjoy the story, much as a magic show is more enjoyable if you aren't distracted by the strings. (2) Lighting should glamorize star actors. (While remaining unobtrusive — audiences should believe the actors are photographed as they appear in real life.)

Three-point lighting is time-consuming and expensive. Skilled (and pricey) union talent can speed things up, but even so, big studio producers are thrilled to shoot two or three pages of script a day. Low-budget filmmakers must work faster, with fewer resources. Regarding lighting setups, Roger Corman reputedly asked his DPs: "How long to get it perfect? How long to get it good? How long to get an image?" Then he opted for the image.

Because low-budget films can't afford elaborate lighting setups, hard shadows and contrasts are common. Fill lights are a rare luxury. At the end of *Children Shouldn't Play with Dead Things* (1972), Alan locks himself in an upstairs bedroom to escape the revenant corpses. But one corpse, Orville, is already in there. Orville arises from bed and approaches Alan, arms extended, preparing to grab and eat Alan.

Hard light shines on Alan from the front, off to the left. A sharp shadow is cast behind him, to the right. As Orville nears, his shadow "overshadows" Alan, looming larger than Alan. Yet Orville's shadow is more diffuse than Alan's shadow, because Orville is closer to the light source. *The closer an object is to a light source, the larger but more diffuse its shadow* [Figure 6.1].

A subject casts *attached shadows* on itself, and *cast shadows* onto other surfaces. Alan's jawline casts an attached shadow along his jaw. Orville casts a cast shadow onto Alan. Attached shadows suggest depth and volume, defining a subject's shape and texture. Cast shadows suggest a light's direction, and the subject's closeness to a surface. Film images are two-dimensional, yet shadows support the impression that we're viewing a three-dimensional world.

It seems director Bob Clark used only one light source in this scene: a hard key light. This was probably to save money, but the setup works aesthetically (i.e., pragmatic aesthetics). The hard light evokes Alan's desperation and hysteria; starkly lit, like a bug with nowhere to run. Orville's looming shadow is also appropriate, because he is a powerful threat, soon to devour Alan.

It's likely serendipity, but the hard lighting is aesthetically reinforced by the set décor's bare, whitewashed walls. Stripped of his petty power and irreverence, Alan is now in a naked struggle for life and death, his situation as stark as the walls and shadows.

Don't Look in the Basement (aka *The Forgotten*, 1973) is about a psychiatric nurse who accepts a job at an asylum, unaware that a murderous patient has taken over. This emotionally raw piece of Southern Gothic, with deranged and violent characters, is enhanced by its low-budget lighting. Director S.F. Brownrigg appears to have used a hard, bright key light in every scene, wholly avoiding fill and backlights. Nor are his lights motivated. The film looks as if he just plopped down his key light wherever he needed illumination. Hard,

Figure 6.1— **Hard lighting helps Orville's (Seth Sklarey) shadow loom over Alan (Alan Ormsby) in** *Children Shouldn't Play with Dead Things.*

high-contrast shadows cover the asylum's stark, white walls. So prevalent is this harsh lighting that it becomes *Basement*'s signature style; among its most memorable and endearing features.

Not that Brownrigg's lighting is entirely without thought. Near the film's end, after the nurse discovers that her boss is a murderous lunatic, Brownrigg shifts to *underhead lighting*, casting distorted shadows across the actors' faces. Again, this lighting is unmotivated. Why is light suddenly shining from below the characters? From where? [Figure 6.2.]

Aesthetically, Brownrigg's intense, irrational lighting setups support the story's intense, irrational situation. Furthermore, this crude lighting lends the film a raw, weirdly documentary verisimilitude. It creates a sense of intimacy with the characters that is common to low-budget films. The characters feel like "real people." By contrast, the glamorized characters in polished, big-budget films often feel "larger than life."

Basement's crude lighting is reinforced by crude sound recording. It seems no sound blankets or other noise dampening tools were used. Voices and footsteps reverberate harshly against the hard floors and walls. At times, you can hear the film camera whirring. As with the harsh lighting, the harsh sound recording enhances the film's *verité* sensibility. Perhaps not the best approach for a supernatural tale, but it works for this naturalistic psycho gorefest.

Figure 6.2 — *Don't Look in the Basement.* While Allyson (Betty Chandler) washes the blood off her hands, Nurse Beale (Rosie Holotik) stares in amazement at the underhead lighting on Allyson's face, apparently emanating from the sink.

High-Key vs. Low-Key Lighting

High-key lighting is a lighting style characterized by *low contrast* between the bright and dim areas. The lighting ratio between the key and fill light is low.

Lighting ratio can be measured in terms of *lux* or *footcandles*. If the key light is 200 footcandles in intensity, and the fill light is 100 footcandles, then the lighting ratio is 2:1. That's low. A 1:1 ratio is very low. It doesn't get any lower. A 1:1 ratio creates a "flat" look, because attached shadows are removed.

A low lighting ratio creates a uniform appearance, because everything is evenly lit. That can mean evenly dim, but usually it means evenly bright. Upbeat and peppy. Sitcoms and TV news shows generally favor low lighting ratios.

Low-key lighting is characterized by hard lighting, *high contrast* between light and dark areas, sharply defined shadows, and high lighting ratios; usually anywhere from 4:1 to 8:1. Low-key lighting is popular with film noir and horror films.

Here's a puzzle. *High*-key lighting means *low* contrast and *low* lighting ratios. *Low*-key lighting means *high* contrast and *high* lighting ratios. Go figure that one out.

Frontal and Sidelights

Light may shine on a subject from one direction, or simultaneously from many directions. *Frontal lighting* shines on a subject from the front. Frontal lighting often eliminates shadows and wrinkles on a contoured surface. An absence of shadows can create a "flat" appearance.

In classic three-point lighting, the key light is a mostly frontal light, but a bit off to one side, to create some shadows and avoid that "flat" look.

A *sidelight* (aka *crosslight*) can add shadows to a surface, making textures and contours visible. Or it can soften shadows. In classic three-point lighting, the fill light is a sidelight that softens the key light's shadows. But in some low-key lighting setups, the key light is a hard sidelight, creating a dramatic, high contrast image, unsoftened by a fill light.

Backlights: Halos and Silhouettes

Backlights suggest three-dimensionality, separating a subject from the background and creating an illusion of volume. Backlights do this by setting aglow a subject's edges (aka *edge lighting* or *rim lighting*), creating a kind of *halo effect*.

Hollywood developed three-point lighting partially to glamorize its stars. Fill lights remove unsightly wrinkles and harsh shadows. And, in the right context, halos infuse a scene with romance and beautify characters. Horror is not primarily concerned with romance, but it does want its "scream queens" to look nice.

Parasite (1982) is set in a gritty, post-apocalyptic future. People are grimy and sweaty. They live in the desert. After a biker gang brutalizes Dr. Paul Dean, he awakes to see Patricia nursing him, the most beautiful image in the film so far. Patricia's face and clothes are scrubbed clean. Curiously, the hot desert sun has not parched her skin. Dirty desert living has not mussed up her hair. Her skin is smooth. Fill lights further soften her face. Her clean hair is edge lit with a soft halo. This glamour lighting segregates Patricia from the film's other women (the aging lush and the biker girls), underscoring that she is the leading lady. Which is prescient, since Patricia is played by (then not yet a star) Demi Moore.

Some halos are more literal than others. In *Jacob's Ladder* (1990), Louis, a chiropractor, treats Jacob for back pain. After the treatment, Jacob lies on a medical table, gazing up at Louis. We see Louis from Jacob's POV, a low angle shot. Grateful, Jacob says, "You know, you look like an angel, Louis."

Louis's "angelic appearance" is enhanced by a backlight, which edge lights his hair, creating a minor halo effect. This backlight is motivated by sunlight entering a window, and by the examination light, both of which are behind him and to his left.[6] His angelic appearance is further reinforced by (1) the staging of the actors together with the POV shot's low angle, so that Louis looks down on Jacob from the perspective of a powerful "guardian angel," and by (2) the dramatic context, which has Louis acting as healer to Jacob [Figure 6.3].

Jacob's Ladder is a supernatural horror film (some have called it "metaphysical"), and this reference to Louis's angelic appearance will prove telling in the end.

When used without other lights, a backlight can create a *silhouette*. Like the masks worn by slashers, silhouettes can *empower a threat* by hiding it. Dark and featureless, a silhouette can be anyone or anything. Say a silhouette resembles a person wielding a hatchet. Who is it? Your best friend? Another silhouette might appear misshapen and grotesque. Is it human? Of course, when the lights are turned on, some grotesque silhouettes are revealed to be harmless. Just some furniture, or a prankster in a costume. Conversely, some human-shaped silhouettes are revealed to be monsters.

A common horror film technique is to *slowly reveal the threat*, ideally "upping the ante" with each new revelation. Showing the threat to be ever more formidable and frightening than previously believed. Silhouettes can assist in this "slow reveal."

Early in *Jeepers Creepers* (2001), a truck harasses Trish and Darry on a deserted coun-

Figure 6.3 — Backlighting imparts an angelic halo to Louis (Danny Aiello) in *Jacob's Ladder*.

try road. The siblings can't see the driver through the truck's dark windshield. They assume the truck is driven by some inbred, road rage redneck.

They later drive past the redneck, who is dumping what looks like human corpses down a pipe. They know it's him because of the truck parked out front. They only glimpse the redneck (1) for an instant, (2) from a moving car, (3) from afar, (4) with the redneck partly obscured by trees, and (5) partly obscured by his long coat and wide-brimmed hat. Thus, although Trish and Darry see the redneck for the first time, they get no good look at him.

Halfway into the film, Trish and Darry are leading a police car to the redneck's dwelling (an abandoned church). Darry wonders how the redneck moves around so fast. (This is the film's first intimation that the redneck has inhuman traits.) The redneck then drops onto the moving police car's roof. (How did he get there?) A police woman looks out of the car's passenger side window. She is yanked out by the redneck and killed. The redneck then pulls the driver's head up through the car's roof, and chops it off.

Both cars screech to a halt. Trish and Darry look back, and see the redneck sniffing the police officer's head, then eating the tongue.

We *still* don't have a clear view of this redneck. It's night. We see him only in silhouette. He no longer wears his wide-brimmed hat. We see from the silhouette that his head appears malformed. His long hair is in a ponytail. It shimmers white due to a backlight [Figure 6.4].

Who or what is this threat? We'd assumed he was an ordinary psycho. Now it seems that he's some sort of inbred mutant. An uberpsycho, like Jason Voorhees. But human, to the extent that uberpsychos may be regarded as human.

Ten minutes later, nearly an hour into the film, we get our first real look at this redneck's face. He carries an old woman by the neck out of her house. The redneck's face is partly hidden in shadows, but we see enough to know that he is, at the very least, an inbred mutant. Maybe even a monster. Maybe.

Figure 6.4 — Silhouettes hide the creature's (Jonathan Breck) true appearance and nature in *Jeepers Creepers.*

Soon thereafter, Trish tries to run over this mutant with her car. She drives at him several times. He prances over the moving car. At the very least, he has uberpsycho powers. He remains mostly in silhouette, yet we see more of his face, despite some shadows.

Trish's car finally hits him. She runs over him several times. He lies limp in the road. Darry asks if Trish thinks he's dead. "They never are," says Trish, implying that their adversary is an uberpsycho. She runs over him several more times. Finally, Darry convinces her to stop.

The mutant, or uberpsycho, lies still on the road. Then ... he sprouts a wing!

This wing is our first clear evidence that this creature is inhuman. Not an inbred mutant or uberpsycho. An authentic monster.

We're now an hour into the film. *Jeepers Creepers* has kept viewers on edge by slowly revealing its threat, its true nature hidden for two-thirds of the film by effectively using cinema's many tools. The monster was hidden by *mise-en-scène* (the truck's dark windshield, the monster's long coat and wide-brimmed hat, the trees), by framing (using a long shot when he was dumping bodies), and by lighting (both shadows and silhouettes).

Silhouettes can imbue even familiar characters with menace. In *Bless the Child* (2000), audiences have already seen Eric Stark, and know him to be a murderous Satanist. Over an hour into the film, Stark tries to teach Cody, a young girl, about Satan's cruel mercy. Through black magic, Stark convinces a suffering vagrant to drench himself with gasoline. But Cody stops the vagrant from setting himself on fire, whispering that God has not forgotten him. Stark is disappointed with Cody's intervention, and after she leaves, he flings a match at the vagrant, setting him ablaze.

Stark exits the alley, his body silhouetted by the firelight glowering behind him. In the story's context, this shot works as a visual metaphor, poetically evoking a demon emerging from hellfire. Although we already know what he looks like, this silhouette both empowers Stark and vilifies him [Figure 6.5].

Silhouettes can empower heroes. Recall the early shot in *Lost Souls* (2000), in which two priests, a deacon, and Maya enter an asylum to perform an exorcism, walking single file through a concrete room of exposed pipes, dripping water, and prison grills. *Mise-en-*

Figure 6.5 — A silhouette, backlit with an orange glow, empowers and vilifies Eric Stark (Rufus Sewell) in *Bless the Child.*

scène (the staging of the actors, clothing, set décor), sound, photography, framing, and lighting combine to empower these four physically unimpressive characters.[7] Lighting them as silhouettes (with their *Matrix*-like long coats billowing in slow motion) is especially empowering (see Figure 3.14).

Yet silhouettes do not automatically empower. In *Nightflyers* (1987), a team of scientists discover that their spaceship is piloted by Adara, a mad telepath whose mind has been uploaded into the ship's computer. Jon and Eliza are in a dim room, arguing over a plan to destroy Adara. The wall behind them bears a sort of arabesque pattern, emitting light. This wall backlights Jon and Eliza in silhouette. (Yes, their faces are sometimes discernible, *barely*.)

Jon and Eliza are vulnerable to Adara and emotionally desperate. In the story's context, their silhouettes do not empower them, but rather, strip the drama to its raw essence, exposing and intensifying these two characters' vulnerability and desperation.[8]

A "class ten" telepath, Jon takes a drug to boost his psychic powers so he can confront Adara's mind inside the ship's computer. He "awakes" in what looks like a hallway, but is really Adara's mind. She stands at the hall's end, before a bright light, in silhouette. Jon nears the light, not in silhouette, gazing at Adara's silhouette. *Dramatic context influences aesthetic effect.* We know Adara is powerful and dangerous, and Jon is vain and vulnerable. Thus, Adara's silhouette empowers her. Her empowerment is reinforced by the staging, in that Jon looks up at her, as if she were above him, standing on a pedestal.[9]

Adara turns to face Jon, suddenly. Her face is now visible. She is ugly, scarred, cackling with menace, electricity flashing across her face. She resembles certain images of Medusa. This unveiling of her horrific face is meant to shock. Unfortunately, we'd already glimpsed her ugly mug when she telepathically communicated with Royd. This previous exposure, however brief, diminishes her face's shock value when she now turns into the light, out of silhouette.

Nightflyers tries to *shock* by suddenly unveiling its villain. But you can't unveil what is already known. Not unless, as in *Jeepers Creepers*, you hold back some secrets, unveiling new horrific details with each revelation. Alas, *Nightflyers* has nothing new to reveal about Adara, so her silhouette, while empowering, is not shocking.

Silhouettes can *suggest nighttime*, if used with *day-for-night* photography.[10] In *Witchery* (aka *La casa 4*, *Witchcraft*, Italian 1988), Gary and Leslie are kissing in a dark room, silhouetted before a window. Outside it is night. Sort of. *Witchery* abounds with inept day-for-night shots, so that Gary and Leslie are actually silhouetted against a bright, bluish "night," rather than the pitch black of true night. Even so, despite the bright night, their silhouettes signal to audiences that it's night. *Witchery* is sufficiently entertaining that some viewers will say, "Okay, it's supposed to be night. I'll go along."

Silhouettes and *Mise-en-Scène*

Backlights can project silhouettes onto props and set décor. In *The Seventh Victim* (1943), Mary is searching for her sister, Jacqueline, a renegade Satanist. In one scene, Mary is showering when someone unexpectedly enters the bathroom. The silhouette of a person wearing a woman's hat appears on the shower curtain. Without pulling aside the curtain, the person identifies herself as Mrs. Redi. (We also recognize her voice, so we know it's her.)

Figure 6.6 — Mrs. Redi (Mary Newton), silhouetted against the shower curtain, warns Mary (Kim Hunter) to leave town in *The Seventh Victim*.

Mrs. Redi warns Mary to stop searching for Jacqueline. She says that Jacqueline is a murderer and it'd be better for everyone if Mary left town [Figure 6.6].

Although we already know what Mrs. Redi looks like, this "shower curtain silhouette" nonetheless empowers her. The curtain prevents Mary (and us) from seeing Mrs. Redi's facial expressions, or any weapons she might possess. This ignorance places Mary at a disadvantage. Mary is further disempowered by being naked, whereas Mrs. Redi is clothed. Storywise, Mrs. Redi has the advantage of surprise, having intruded unexpectedly. All these elements (Mary's nakedness, Mrs. Redi's silhouette, her unexpected entry, her shocking revelation of Jacqueline's crime) disadvantage Mary. And because audiences are "in the shower" with Mary, we share and identify with her vulnerable position.[11]

Yes, the scene does resemble *Psycho*'s shower scene of seventeen years later.

In *Suspiria* (Italian 1977), a maggot infestation at a ballet academy forces the students to sleep in the practice hall. Bedsheets are strung up to create privacy between the female students, the male students, and the teachers. When the lights are shut, the bedsheets glow red, as if from red lights on the teachers' side of the bedsheets.[12] Silhouettes of ladders, furniture, and teachers going to bed appear on the redly glowing bedsheets. One teacher's silhouette lays down on a bed and snores hideously.

On our side of the bedsheets, among the female students, Sara whispers to Suzy that she recognizes the snore as that of the academy's mysterious directress. Sara appears nervous being so close to the directress, separated by only a bedsheet. The audience shares Sara's trepidation [Figure 6.7].

Figure 6.7 —*Suspiria.* Susie (Jessica Harper) listens to Sara (Stefania Casini), while the snoring directress lies silhouetted behind the bedsheet.

What is so scary about a snoring old woman? There is no logical reason to fear her. No story events give cause for alarm. Yet lighting, *mise-en-scène,* camerawork, sound, and acting build the old woman into a threat. (1) After the lights are shut, black silhouettes appear on redly glowing bedsheets. Black and red. Satan's colors. Logically benign, but emotionally creepy. (2) The red glow is unmotivated. There is no logical explanation for red lights on the teacher's side of the bedsheets. The emotional and aesthetic impact is surreal and unsettling.[13] (3) Soon after the lights are shut, and the students settle down to sleep, we cut to the teachers' side of the bedsheets. From their side, the sheets are lit blue. We see no teachers, as the camera faces the sheets. The camera sweeps up and over the blue bedsheets, back into the female students' area (where the bedsheets glow red), and glides over the students, creating the sense of a probing POV shot. *Whose* POV? (4) Goblin's music soundtrack further unnerves us. (5) Creepy sound effects reinforce Goblin's creepy music. (6) The directress's snoring is so grotesque, it sounds almost inhuman. (7) Sara nervously whispers to Suzy about the directress's previous visit to the academy, when she slept next door to Sara's room. Sara is "creeped out" by the directress, and because we trust and identify with Sara, we feel that her trepidation must be justified.

All of the above factors — but especially Sara's trepidation and the directress's horrid snoring — help our imaginations to "fill in" that blank silhouette. We envision some ghastly crone. Her silhouette functions similarly to that of the monster in *Jeepers Creepers,* in that (1) we don't yet know what this directress looks like, and (2) there are increasing hints that she is both unnatural and a threat.

Overhead and Underhead Lighting

Subjects may be lit from directly above or below. I'll call this *overhead* and *underhead* lighting, rather than overlighting or underlighting, because the latter terms may be confused with the overexposure or underexposure of film stock.

Overhead and underhead lighting, especially when the lighting is hard, and is the sole illumination (i.e., no fill lights), can cast actors in an "ominous light," distorting their faces with creepy shadows, or hiding their eyes (the windows to the soul) in darkness. Such lighting can also intensify a scene's emotional or dramatic undercurrents.

Early in *The Brood* (Canadian 1979), Dr. Raglan and Michael are sitting on a stage before a live audience, lit from above. Practicing an intense form of psychotherapy, Dr. Raglan playacts the part of Michael's abusive father, causing the young man to burst into tears. This scene's emotional intensity is reinforced by the lights' hardness, and their overhead position, thereby casting harsh attached shadows on the actors [Figure 6.8].

This lighting setup yields another aesthetic effect. After the therapy session concludes, the lights go dark. They're soon turned on again. Dr. Raglan and Michael are gone. Instead, Dr. Raglan's assistant is now on stage, bidding farewell to the audience. We never see his eyes. The overhead lights cast shadows in his eye sockets, so they appear as two black holes. This lends a sinister air to the assistant. Yet his voice is mellow, his demeanor calm. Ironically, this contrast between harsh lighting, and soothing performance, reinforces the assistant's sinister presence.

Overhead lights do not always vilify. In *Lost Souls*, Peter confronts Maya in the New Jersey school where she teaches. He demands to know why Maya's friend, a Catholic deacon, tried to kill him. Maya tells Peter that he will transform into the Antichrist on his 33rd birthday. Enraged and disbelieving, Peter advises Maya to seek psychiatric help.

This scene opens with Maya teaching children in a classroom. Out in the hallway, Peter comes up some stairs, in silhouette. He opens the classroom door and demands to speak to Maya. He takes her into the hall. In order not to be seen by the children, Maya pulls Peter farther away, into a sort of alcove or stairwell landing. Because the framing is tight, we can't be sure.

As they talk, they are lit from above, a bit off to one side. Because the lighting is almost directly overhead, their facial contours are deeply shadowed, eye sockets often lost in darkness. Because this overhead light is a bit off to one side, half their faces are often obscured in shadows. Sometimes they argue in silhouette. I say "often" and "sometimes," because

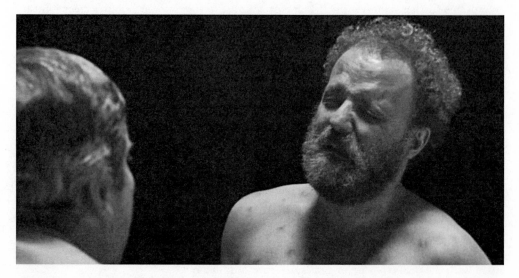

Figure 6.8 — Overhead lighting intensifies Michael's (Gary McKeehan) emotional pain in *The Brood*.

their conversation is heated, so they agitate about the confined space, at times grabbing or shoving one another. Thus, the staging of the actors reinforces this scene's dramatic and emotional intensity.

Lost Souls is a dark, brooding, fatalistic film. As with the gritty, desaturated colors of its photography and *mise-en-scène*, the low-key lighting, with its shadows and silhouettes, supports the story's conceit of Armageddon's impending doom threatening the characters and their world. Whereas the silhouettes in the asylum empower Maya and her three companions, the silhouettes in this scene's dramatic context foreshadow Earth's decent into moral darkness and turmoil.[14] Because Peter and Maya are sympathetic figures, the overhead lights do not vilify them, but rather, condemn and threaten their world (and them with it), which has sinned for millennia and will soon pay the price [Figure 6.9].

This scene's framing is mostly a series of *closeups*, intensifying the drama and drawing audiences into the characters' troubled situation. Some frames are *slightly canted*, as when Peter first hears Maya's theory. The only *extreme closeup* is on Maya's lips against Peter's ear, when he refuses to believe her and she grabs him, speaking directly into his ear. This staging and extreme closeup combine to emphasize Maya's desperation to convince Peter that he will soon transform into Satan's son.

Backlights have no monopoly on silhouettes. Overhead lights too can create silhouettes. *The Sick House* (2007) is about an abandoned London hospital, haunted by an evil spirit who belonged to "the cult of the black priest" during the plague. The film opens inside the derelict hospital, with an unseen girl whispering: "In the blood there is a sickness. There, might living creatures be seen. Visions of strange, monstrous, and frightful shapes such as dragons, snakes, serpents, and demons terrible to behold."

We then see what *might* be that young girl, skipping "hopscotch style" down a dimly lit hallway. We're not sure it's a young girl, because we see the figure from behind, wearing what resembles a hooded monk's robe. She stops beneath an overhead light. It *edge lights* her robe, casting it in silhouette. She turns around slowly ... and faces us!

Alas, despite the creepy silhouette, there's no scary payoff. It's too dark under that hood, and we cut away too quickly, to see anything definite. Although, if you pause the DVD, you'll discern the dim outlines of a deformed face.

Figure 6.9 —*Lost Souls.* Overhead lighting paints a somber, foreboding world. Peter's (Ben Chaplin) eyes are entirely lost in shadow as he confronts Maya (Winona Ryder).

The Sick House is beautifully photographed, but its ghostly thrills fall short of *The Ring* or *The Grudge*. There is violence, and gore, and gruesome images of deformed children. But the film is confusing, convoluted, derivative, and tedious. Still, its opening scene demonstrates how overhead lighting can create silhouettes.

Underhead lighting can imbue characters with menace. The Satanists in *The Seventh Victim* are portrayed as pitiable, frightened mortals who bully those weaker than themselves. Near the film's end, Dr. Judd and Jason, two good and noble men, confront a whole coven of Satanists, and easily tell them off. Jason says: "The devil worshipers. The lovers of evil. It's a joke. Pathetic little joke. You're a poor, wretched group of people who have taken the wrong turn."

Ominous music ensues. Mr. Brun, the coven's leader, arises from his chair and steps forward, closer to Jason. In so doing, Brun leaves a position where he was lit from the front, off to one side, and stops at a spot where he is lit by a hard, underhead light. With sinister shadows across his face, he calmly retorts: "Wrong? Who knows what is wrong or right? If I prefer to believe in Satanic majesty and power, who can deny me? What proof can you bring that good is superior to evil?"

Never before in this film had Satanism seemed so potent, dangerous, and *real* as at this moment. This is partially because of the sinister music, and partially because Brun approaches Jason. (In the right context, approaching someone is a threatening gesture). But it is primarily the hard, underhead lighting that momentarily transforms this small, elderly man into someone powerful and threatening [Figure 6.10].

In *Anaconda* (1997), the evil poacher, Paul Sarone, is twice shown steering the boat at

Figure 6.10—Underhead lighting empowers and vilifies the Satanic Mr. Brun (Ben Bard) in *The Seventh Victim*.

night on the Amazon river. Both times, he is harshly lit from below. Apart from casting sinister shadows across his face, the underhead lighting reinforces actor Jon Voight's performance. Not only does he scowl villainously, but he has assumed the facial expression of a snake, his eyes squinting into slits. The underhead light transforms those slits into two black holes.

As with overhead lights, underhead lights can intensify dramatic and emotional tension. In *Contamination* (aka *Alien Contamination*, Italian 1980), a Martian cyclops brainwashes humans in an attempt to conquer Earth. Near the film's end, a U.S. Air Force Colonel and her two companions infiltrate the cyclops's underground lair in South America. But the cyclops hypnotizes the colonel so that she loses her volition, and slowly approaches the cyclops — which intends to eat her.

As it happens, the colonel walks atop a metal grill, and is illuminated by the hard lights beneath the grill. Not only do these underhead lights cast stark shadows across her face, but the grill adds its own distortive shadows. These shadows (the *attached shadows* of the colonel's facial contours, and the *cast shadows* of the grill) underscore the colonel's dire situation, and heighten the dramatic tension. This aesthetic effect is reinforced by actress Louise Marleau's wide staring eyes as she approaches the cyclops, and by the intense music.

Shadows

Shadows, created by light and an aspect of *mise-en-scène*, have much aesthetic potential. A filmmaker might show only shadows of a murder, rather than the act itself, thus (1) hiding the killer's identity, (2) saving money on special effects makeup, and (3) making the film suitable for younger audiences. Bizarrely shaped shadows can suggest strange monsters offscreen (again, on a budget). Huge shadows can imply giants. Stylized shadows may enhance a film's atmosphere, as did the jagged, expressionistic shadows in *The Cabinet of Dr. Caligari* (aka *Das Cabinet des Dr. Caligari*, German 1920). Many of *Caligari*'s "shadows" were painted onto the set décor, yet real shadows can achieve similar, if not identical, expressionistic effects.

In *Aliens* (1986), an alien kills a pilot in offscreen space, whereupon blood splatters onto the windshield — the old *blood splatter from offscreen* cliché.[15] Shadows provide an equivalent cliché. In *Strange Behavior* (Australian 1981), a brainwashed teenager stabs another teenager to death. We see only shadows on a wall. The shadow of the killer, plunging the shadow of a knife, into the shadow of the victim. Same concept as blood splashing on a wall, but cheaper. Not only does this scene avoid gory makeup effects, it avoids even blood. Just shadows and the moans of a dying teen [Figure 6.11].

Because the killer soon reveals his face, these shadows were apparently used to save money, rather than to hide the killer's identity. And perhaps for poetic style; the victim plays with shadow puppets just as the killer's shadow arrives. Furthermore, we don't learn that the killer is brainwashed until much later, so revealing his identity still leaves us some surprises. He is not, after all, the ultimate villain. The mad scientist who brainwashed him is.

Showing shadows of a murder in a horror film, rather than the actual event, extends back to *The Cabinet of Dr. Caligari*. Shadows on a wall (real shadows, not painted) depict Cesare strangling a man. The aesthetic intent is not to hide Cesare's identity (we know it's him), but to depict the murder in a stylized, heightened fashion.

Figure 6.11—*Strange Behavior.* Here's a cheap way to depict a stabbing death. Just show the shadows.

In *Sleepaway Camp*, a teenager, Judy, is alone in a dimly lit cabin, curling her hair. Someone opens the door and stands in the doorway, in silhouette, resembling a teenage boy. He enters the cabin, but his face remains offscreen. Judy recognizes him and is unafraid. He punches her, knocking her out. We see his hands place a pillow over Judy's head, then pick up her curling iron. We cut to the shadows on a wall. Shadows of his hand raising the hot curling iron, then bringing it down. Shadows of Judy's arms upraised in pain. We hear her muffled screams. We cut to her corpse dumped behind the bunk, out of sight.

In this scene, offscreen space and shadows are used to (1) hide the killer's identity from viewers, and (2) save money. It's cheaper to have the actress scream and die in offscreen space, than to hire a makeup artist to cover her face with gruesome special effects burns.

In *A Name for Evil* (1973), shadows on a door suggest the presence of a ghost. John is an architect who's quit his big city job to refurbish a country house. A haunted house. The ghost is a former owner who doesn't like people moving into "his" house and changing it. So he begins the usual hauntings and mind games, seeking to evict John and his wife, Joanna.

In one scene, John and Joanna are discussing home repair plans. John sees Joanna enter another room, from where she continues talking to him. John can't see into the room, but he sees shadows on the door: a man kissing Joanna's hand. (It's a neat trick coming from a ghost, in that he haunts with *two* shadows: his own and Joanna's.)

These ghostly shadows are supported by incongruent sounds. Joanna *giggles flirtatiously*, yet continues her *bland discourse* while her "hand" is being kissed, saying to John, "The men are putting the water in downstairs in the kitchen, and I'm gonna go and help them." Disturbed by the shadows and the giggling, John warily enters the room. He finds no one there. Joanna has left for the kitchen, and there is no sign of the "man" who'd kissed his wife's hand.

In *Suspiria*, shadows flitting across a white building in an empty public square vaguely resemble witches flying on broomsticks. The definition of these shadows is just right. Not too sharp, not too fuzzy. Sharp enough to *suggest* cloaked witches on broomsticks, but fuzzy enough to leave the matter uncertain and thus avoid appearing silly. Curiously, these shadows lose their resemblance to witches when one freezes the DVD. No one shadow clearly outlines a witch; rather, this resemblance arises from the shadows *movement* across the building.

Mise-en-scène, framing, and sound support this ambiguity. An earlier shot depicts pigeons flying off the building. The eighth shot after that is a POV swooping over a blind man. The sound of a fluttering bird implies that it's a pigeon's POV. The second shot after *that* has the "witches on broomsticks" shadows. Thus, the previous shots imply that these shadows might be pigeons. Except that the shadows resemble flying witches.

Pragmatically, using only shadows rather than depicting flying witches saves money on special effects. *Aesthetically*, using only shadows (1) leaves audiences "blind" to the witches, so they emotionally identify with the blind man in the public square, and (2) avoids the potentially ridiculous sight of witches on broomsticks.

In *Bram Stoker's Dracula* (1992), Dracula's shadow dissociates from him, thus implying his supernatural nature. In this scene, he is standing before a large wall map of London, while Harker completes the legal paperwork for Dracula's purchase of Carfax Abbey. As Dracula speaks and moves, his shadow on the map roughly parallels, but does not precisely match, his movements. It's an eerie and surprising effect, one of many minor details that hint at Dracula's otherworldly nature. (Other such effects include rats scampering upside down across a ceiling beam, and perfume droplets falling upward.)

As with many of the film's special effects, the incongruent shadows were created by old-fashioned techniques. In this case, *rear projection* created the map on the "wall" (actually, a screen).[16] Then a mime behind the screen, made up to match actor Gary Oldman's costume and hairstyle, mimicked Oldman's movements, without precisely matching them.

In *Grim Prairie Tales* (1990), shadows support the characters and theme. The film is a horror omnibus set in the Old West, with four tales and a wraparound. In the third tale, a father brings his family out west to begin a new life after the devastation of the Civil War. We know he is a good man because (1) he married his wife after she was pregnant by another man, and no one else would have her, (2) he shares food with hungry neighbors when he has less, and (3) he loves and provides for his family. Yes, he is a good man.

But the daughter sees her father ride off with a lynch mob. She follows, and finds him swinging a murdered black man, hung from a burning tree. The daughter runs home, devastated by her father's evil. The mother explains that she too hates her husband's Klan activities, but she defends his good side.

The next morning, the father drives his daughter toward town in a carriage. She broods silently beside him, still hating him. The father wears a wide-brimmed hat, casting half his face in shadow, half in sunlight. The daughter sees something beside the road, and asks him to stop. She finds her bonnet in the grass, having lost it the night before. She returns to the carriage and puts on her bonnet. Now half her face is in shadow, half in sunlight. The daughter breaks down and hugs her father, saying that she loves him. They ride on into town. The End.

Much of the horror in this tale is that good and evil, and love and hate, can coexist in the same person. The father is charitable and self-sacrificing to family and neighbors, yet murderous toward blacks. It may be serendipity, but the lighting (with some assist from the hats), supports this story's characters and theme. The morally contradictory father's face is half lit, half dark. The daughter's face is wholly lit, so long as she rejects her father. Only after she puts on her bonnet, casting half her face in darkness, and thus internalizing her father's moral contradictions, does she embrace her father.

Shadows can be characters in their own right, usually some form of monster. In TV's *Dark Shadows*, the witch Angelique curses former Leviathan cult leader Jeb Hawkes by sending an evil shadow after him. Every night, the shadow looms larger in Jeb's room, and draws closer to him. Jeb keeps turning on additional lamps to outshine the shadow, terrified of the shadow touching him. (Odd, that a shadow can exist in total darkness.)

As a monster, this cursed shadow is original, creepy, and inexpensive. Angelique creates it by making a paper cutout, shaped like a ghost, then cursing it. Naturally, the shadow resembles the cutout's ghostly shape. *Aesthetically*, it's logical for the shadow to resemble its cutout origins. *Pragmatically*, it's a cheap "special effect," most likely created by placing a paper cutout in front of a stage light.

The very title, *Dark Shadows*, demonstrates the inherently spooky potential of shadows. It seems shadows are always playing a supporting role in films about vampires, slashers, ghosts, or witches. It's about time a horror show allowed a shadow to take center stage!

Another shadow monster appears in the "Shadow Boxer" episode of TV's *Friday the 13th: The Series*. Whenever Tommy wears a pair of Satanic boxing gloves, a boxer's shadow emerges from the gloves, and goes off to beat and kill someone while Tommy fights in the ring. However, this "shadow boxer" is no paper cutout, but looks to be computer generated, making it a far livelier shadow. The static shadow in *Dark Shadows* could only grow or shrink, and move across the wall, whereas the "shadow boxer" walks and jumps and fights. Yet it too is vulnerable to light. Micki hinders its attack by flashing a camera bulb at it.

It's possible that this "shadow boxer" was created by superimposition, since it's often translucent, like many "ghost effects." But it looks like a CGI effect to me, because it interacts fairly well with the set décor, ducking behind walls, jumping off a truck's rear ledge and hitting the ground. Either way, "Shadow Boxer" demonstrates that, especially as technology advances, shadows are no longer always created by light (or paint).

Hiding a Low Budget

Lighting techniques can hide a low budget. Producer Val Lewton's 1940s horror films are known both for their low budgets and low-key lighting. Of Jacques Tourneur, who directed *Cat People* (1942) for Lewton, John McCarty writes: "Faced with the combined challenge of low budgets and extremely tight shooting schedules, Tourneaur ingeniously used lighting in many of his short films, not only for atmospheric purposes but to mask his lack of elaborate sets and other productions values by inexpensively suggesting them and creating other effects with well-placed shadows and silhouettes — techniques he would employ in his Lewton films for similar reasons."[17]

In *Cat People*, Irena avoids sex with her new husband, because she believes that sexual passion will transform her into a panther. Her psychiatrist, Dr. Judd, tries to disprove her fears by seducing her with a kiss. (Of course, this breaks all doctor-patient protocol; one senses that Judd is taking advantage of Irena's fears so as to cop a feel.) They separate after kissing. We see a closeup of Irena's face. No transformation. No werewolf style dissolve. Instead, the light darkens over her face [Figure 6.12, 6.13]. We cut to Judd, who reacts in

Left: Figure 6.12 — *Cat People.* Irena (Simone Simon), having kissed Dr. Judd, is brightly lit in high-key. *Right:* Figure 6.13 — Soon lights dim over Irena's face, implying her transformation into a panther, which then occurs offscreen. In both shots, a bright but small light glistens in Simon's eyes, but its dramatic effect (intimating supernatural forces) is more pronounced after the lights dim on her face.

terror to what he sees. He whips out his sword cane. We cut to shadows on the walls. Judd's shadow struggles with a panther's shadow. (Or a shadow of a *stuffed* panther that actor Tom Conway is shaking?) And a *brief* shot of a black cat tossed onto a man.[18]

Irena's is a cheap "special effect" transformation, in that there is no transformation. Not onscreen. Rather, it's all implied with lighting and shadows. Regarding Lewton and *Cat People*, McCarty writes: "[O]n a minuscule budget of slightly more than $100,000 and a tight shooting schedule, he wasn't able to afford elaborate special effects."[19]

The Old Dark House (1932) likewise uses low-key lighting both for atmosphere, and to hide a low budget. Of the film, William K. Everson writes: "A few shots are superbly designed miniatures, and [director James] Whale wisely never gives us a really good look at the exterior of the House in daylight. Thus, even though the human menaces are explained away, the House itself, as a kind of baleful embodiment of evil, can remain undiluted in our memories."[20]

I was less impressed with the house. *The Old Dark House* has been called a haunted house film, but it isn't. There is nothing to suggest a supernatural presence, just an imprisoned man who may be a victim or psychotic murderer. The low-key lighting, with its stark contrasts of light and dark, *is* spookily atmospheric. Brightly lit candles and actors' heads float within a dark void. The set décor is lit to resemble a haunted house, but it isn't. Instead, the film has a David Lynch–like collection of eccentric characters, enlivened with James Whale's usual dark humor. *The Old Dark House* is witty rather than scary.

Star Crystal (1986) is set mostly on high-tech, futuristic space vessels. That can require expensive set décor. But what if a filmmaker can only afford cheap set décor? *The Old Dark House* solved the problem by dimly lighting its cheaper set décor. *Star Crystal* goes one step better by showing us almost *no* set décor.

Early in the film, some corporate, military, and scientific bigshots are having a tense discussion in a conference room aboard a space station. Bigshots are supposed to have a bigshot type room. This being a space station, the room should also be futuristic and high-tech. Instead, we see only a table and some actors sitting on chairs, bathed in a bright white light. The rest of the room is a pitch black void, aside from some lights blinking in the

Figure 6.14 — Darkness surrounds the hard lit table. The rest of the room might be a high-tech conference room — or the director's basement. *Star Crystal.*

background, suggesting a computer. For all we know, that dark void around the actors is hiding a soundstage, or the director's parents' basement [Figure 6.14].

The lighting is hard, shining from both overhead and underhead, highlighting the actors against the black void. The actors wear mostly light colors, further intensifying their brightness. *Aesthetically*, this lighting setup (1) focuses our attention on the characters, and (2) emotionally intensifies their anxious discussion. *Pragmatically*, this setup hides a "futuristic conference room" that the filmmaker could not afford to properly furnish.

Another low-budget lighting trick is to shoot outdoors. Sunlight is free and ensures that the filmmaker captures an image, if not always a great image. That's one reason many slasher films are set in the great outdoors. True, big studio productions stage light even the outdoors, for that perfect image. But low-budget films can usually make do with a simple aluminum reflector. (Hold the reflector steady, so light doesn't shimmer on the actor's face, and try to avoid creating noticeably bright and shiny faces, e.g., the park scene in *Silent Night, Deadly Night 4: Initiation*, 1990.)

Hiding in the Dark

A threat can hide behind (or be camouflaged amid) set décor, or offscreen, or in a blurry plane of action. Or a threat can hide in dark shadows or in bright light. The threat was always there, but unseen to us until it emerges to shock and frighten.

In *Halloween* (1978), Laurie runs screaming from a bedroom after finding three friends' corpses. She pauses in the hallway, beside an open door to another room. Or perhaps to a closet? We don't know, because it's pitch black in there. Laurie stands beside that open door, crying. Then Michael Myers's masked face appears in the doorway, as though floating in the darkness.[21] A unsettling and shocking surprise for the audience.

In *Silent Scream* (1980), a college coed, Scotty, rents a room at a secluded beachside house. She plops onto the bed, surveying her new room. We see an air duct in the ceiling. A metal grill. Behind the grill, pitch black. The camera moves toward the grill. When the grill is in closeup, a face appears behind the grill. A dark eye staring at Scotty. Startling the audience by emerging from the dark.

When I say the psycho "appears," I don't mean that we see her enter the frame. Rather, her eye is revealed through a rack focus. The camera moves up toward the grill, the grill in the foreground blurs, and the psycho in the background sharpens, simultaneous with an increased illumination, however dim.

I think that two grills were used. We see Scotty plopping down on bed, gazing up at the ceiling. Then a shot of the air duct in the ceiling, near a lamp. (This is Scotty's POV.) Then a shot of Scotty on bed, looking away from the ceiling. Then a shot moving up toward the ceiling. I'm guessing this is a shot of a *second grill* built into a *stage wall*, that we're supposed to think is the ceiling. I say this because (1) the ceiling lamp is not in this shot, (2) a rack focus suggests a camera move rather than a zoom, yet it'd be difficult to steadily raise the camera without a costly mini crane, and this film is low-budget, and (3) it's easier to place actress Barbara Steele on the floor behind a fake wall, than inside a ceiling.

In both *Halloween* and *Silent Scream*, a threat lurks in the dark. A threat that was always there, though we didn't know it. Not until it was revealed by light.

This use of lighting to *reveal a threat that was there all along* is cinema's version of a common horror literary technique. In the Ray Bradbury short story, "The October Game," children at a Halloween party sit in a dark basement, passing along a witch's "body parts," from child to child. Parents and children all assume it's just some chicken bones and innards, peeled grapes, and various other household items. A creepy but silly game. Then someone turns on the lights. *The body parts are real!*

For the characters (and the reader), part of the horror is that they're holding a dead girl's organs. But that horror is heightened from knowing that they were holding her parts *all along*, without being aware of it. Darkness created a sense of safety, which the light exposed as false.

This same technique appears in *The Haunting* (1963). Eleanor is part of a paranormal investigation team at a haunted house. One night she's lying in bed in the dark. Ghostly whispers commence, filling the darkness. Eleanor is terrified. Someone squeezes her hand. She assumes it's Theo, whose bed is beside hers. Eleanor whispers to Theo, who doesn't reply, but squeezes tighter, too afraid to talk. Then Theo turns on the light. She's in bed, *across the room*. Far from Eleanor. Eleanor shouts, "Who was holding my hand?!"

Again, the ghostly whispers in the dark were scary. But more scary was when the lights revealed that a ghost had been holding Eleanor's hand *all along*.

In *Jeepers Creepers*, Darry tumbles down a pipe into an abandoned church basement. It's the same pipe into which the redneck dumped those blood-stained sacks. Unable to climb back out through the pipe, Darry searches the basement. It's dark. Good thing he's got a flashlight.

Darry opens a sack and finds a young man, still alive. His torso is freshly stitched. He tries whispering to Darry, but soon dies. Darry is terrified. He continues searching. He finds a table laden with chemicals and cutting utensils. He stoops to retie a shoelace. In so doing, he tucks his flashlight under his arm so that it shines behind him.

The light reveals what appear to be human forms embedded into the earthen wall. The camera pans and we see more and more human forms. Darry doesn't see this, as he's tying his shoelace. Our fear increases for Darry, because we see what a dangerous place he's trapped in. Something drips onto Darry's sneaker. He looks up, scanning his flashlight across the ceiling. We see the forms more clearly now. Human corpses, embedded into the walls and ceiling. They'd been there *all along*, hovering over and around Darry. A creepy and unsettling surprise.

Darkness can suggest safety, only to have a threat enter the light. But darkness can also suggest danger, which light reveals to be a false alarm. In *The Others* (2001), ghostly whispers and footsteps convince Grace that trespassers have invaded her mansion. She searches for them, armed with a shotgun. She enters a dim room. She glances about nervously. She exits the frame, going offscreen. Behind the spot where she had stood, an eerie *pale face looms in the dark*. It is looking in the direction to where Grace has gone. Is this face a ghost? Or a trespasser?

From offscreen space, Grace opens curtains. Sunlight floods the room, revealing that the pale face is a painting. A painting of a stern man in puritanical garb. Darkness has fooled us into fearing for Grace. Light rattles us by revealing that there was nothing to fear. This time [Figures 6.15].

In *Halloween*, light exposes the threat lurking in the dark. In *The Others*, light reveals a "logical explanation" for what was a false alarm.

The Elephant Man (1980) uses the horror film technique of a "monster" emerging from darkness, not to shock and frighten, but to *prevent* shock and fear. With this film, director David Lynch faced the problem of eliciting audience sympathy for a shockingly deformed man. Lynch softened this shock for viewers by revealing John Merrick's appearance in stages, over several scenes: (1) Doctors discuss Merrick's disfigurement without him being present.

Figure 6.15 — *The Others*. When Grace goes offscreen, a pale face looms in the dark. She opens the curtains offscreen, admitting sunlight, revealing the face to be a painting.

Viewers are thus prepared for the blow. (2) We see only Merrick's outline, silhouetted against a sheet. This gives us a better idea of his deformity, without having to endure it all at once. (3) We see him in a dim bedroom, darkness obscuring his face. He quotes a Bible verse in a gentle voice. This establishes both his good heart and his gentle nature. He resembles a monster, but he isn't.

Lynch used lighting, story, and acting (John Hurt's soft voice) to prepare us for the sight of Merrick's deformity, both by warning us in advance with information, and by demonstrating Merrick's humanity while he is still comfortably unseen. Only after humanizing Merrick does Lynch reveal him in clear, bright light.

While *The Elephant Man* is not a horror film, Merrick's yearning for acceptance despite his monstrous appearance is a common horror theme. Additionally, Lynch's slow revelation of Merrick is comparable to the Frankenstein monster's slow revelation of himself to the blind woodsman's family in Mary Shelley's novel.

Darkness and its hidden threats are not only a technique, but a story idea and a theme. Or at least, an excuse for a story idea and a theme.

In *They* (2002), monsters that lurk in darkness and shun the light, target certain children. These children grow up into sexy twentysomethings. One young man figures out the nature of the monsters and their intent. He suffers from "night tremors" and carries lots of flashlights. He tries to convince a beautiful young woman of the danger they're all in. Meanwhile, the monsters pick off anyone foolish or unlucky enough to leave the light and enter the dark. This low-budget film is sparsely populated and shot outside the U.S. It's a short film, running under 75 minutes, not including end credits.

In *Darkness Falls* (2003), a monster that lurks in darkness and shuns the light, targets certain children. These children grow up into sexy twentysomethings. One young man figures out the nature of the monster and its intent. He suffers from "night tremors" and carries lots of flashlights. He tries to convince a beautiful young woman of the danger they're all in. Meanwhile, the monster picks off anyone foolish or unlucky enough to leave the light and enter the dark. This low-budget film is sparsely populated and shot outside the U.S. It's a short film, running under 75 minutes, not including end credits.

Gee, that sounds familiar...

They and *Darkness Falls* do have some variations. In *They*, the monsters are some sort of extradimensional demons. In *Darkness Falls*, it's the tooth fairy. *They* has a darker ending. Both films are smallish, supernatural horror fare, reasonably entertaining.

Darkness is a key story element in both films. The monsters lurk in darkness, and can only "get you" if you enter the dark. Naturally, characters try to stay in the light, and carry lots of flashlights and batteries. Which is good, because in both films, power failures strike at the most inopportune times. Unlike other nocturnal threats (e.g., vampires, who can survive light other than sunlight, or in some cases, UV rays), these monsters move in darkness itself. As shadows spread across a room, these monsters extend not only their domain, but their presence. Sort of like the cursed shadow that threatened *Dark Shadows*'s Jeb Hawkes, who kept turning on lamps, trying to stay in the light.

By its title, *The Dark* (1979) suggests that darkness is a key story element or theme. The film begins with a long informational scroll (as in the recently released *Star Wars*), speculating on the adaptive nature of alien life forms. Then a red fireball hurtles toward Earth. We cut to a young woman exiting a movie theater. It's night and the streets are deserted.

Was she the only patron? She's frightened and scurries up the street. She hears footsteps. Spooky voices whisper *Theeeee da-a-a-a-a-a-a-ark!* and *Theeeee da-a-a-a-a-a-a-ark — nesssss!* She quickens, runs, ducks around a corner. She sighs relief. Then an alien rips off her head. So begins *Theeeee da-a-a-a-a-a-a-ark!* I say "*Theeeee da-a-a-a-a-a-a-ark!*" because whenever it's dark and lonely, and some character is wandering about for no good reason, we hear that eerie (and eerily familiar), canned 1970s TV spooky music, mixed with nondiegetic spooky voices whispering *Theeeee da-a-a-a-a-a-a-ark!*

These voices make no sense. The atmospheric style is 1970s supernatural, but despite a clairvoyant gypsy, the story is 1950s bug-eyed-monster. The cheesy alien's hands are hairy, with long dark fingernails. He resembles Lon Chaney's werewolf more than any Gray or drooling *Alien* alien. He stumbles after our heroes in what appear to be Frankenstein monster boots. His red feline eyes shoot raygun beams. Or are they photon torpedoes?

The Dark combines all horror subgenres. Its alien behaves like a psycho and is monitored by a supernatural fortune teller. The only thing missing is anything to do with *Theeeee da-a-a-a-a-a-a-ark!*

Screenwriter Stanford Whitmore explains: "I wrote [*The Dark*] on spec as a piece that my friend, DP Bill Butler, would use to get his foot in the directing door. My script was an experiment meant to take advantage of Bill's camera, which would render the repeatedly gathering dark remindful of the score for *Jaws*. An initial deal was made with Dick Clark's company, and when that fell out, some thief stepped up to single-handedly take over the script, fire Tobe Hooper, and invent a monster shooting death rays. The upshot was the WGA bringing suit on my behalf for monies owed, whereupon said producer skipped town, putting a cherry on top."[22]

After a theatrical release, *The Dark* was released on Beta and VHS under its own title, then re-released on VHS as *The Mutilator*, making all that nondiegetic whispering of "*Theeeee da-a-a-a-a-a-a-ark!*" all the more nonsensical.[23] It's back again on DVD, under its original title.

Unlike *They* and *Darkness Falls*, *The Dark* has nothing to do with darkness as a story element or theme. Its title and incessant whispering of *Theeeee da-a-a-a-a-a-ark!* is merely an attempt to exploit audiences' primal fear of darkness. Yet you got to credit *The Dark* for trying. Its plot is a mess, its characters a parade of 1970s stereotypes, but it remains an outrageously entertaining film.

Lights as *Mise-en-Scène*

Light not only illuminates, it actively participates in a film. Its shadows and highlights affect the composition within a frame. Light can suggest emotional, dramatic, or thematic shifts in the story. Light may suggest a supernatural presence. Threats can hide in the light as easily as in the dark. Or light can be a threat in its own right.

In *Poltergeist* (1982), ghosts harass a family because their house is built on a graveyard. The ghosts manifest in various ways, such as a bright light flashing from the daughter's closet. Happily for low-budget filmmakers, this is a relatively cheap special effect. Set up a stage light and you have an instant ghost! Of course, *Poltergeist*'s impressively flashing lights incorporated expensive CGI effects, such as the giant skull monster. But that needn't concern low-budget filmmakers, who rip off what they can and ignore the rest.

The confused but far more entertaining *The Visitor* (aka *Stridulum*, Italian 1979) likewise uses bright lights to signify a supernatural force.[24] Only instead of an evil skull monster, this is a good light that releases a flock of saintly doves.

At the film's end, the evil space child, Katy, and her cohort, Raymond, invade Barbara's house to punish her for foiling their plans for Armageddon and/or world government. But soon after they begin torturing her, hurricane force winds shatter the windows. A bank of round lights shine brightly into the house. Katy's hair stands electrically on end. (I'm guessing a spaceship has landed outside, but who really knows?) Doves fly through the broken windows — to the rescue! Loud, frenetic pop music ensues. Raymond cowers in fear. A dove bites off the fishing line (or piano wire?) around Barbara's neck, saving her. Dozens of doves fly tornado-like around Katy, their white feathers darkening as they pull the sin out of Katy. One dove bites Raymond's neck, presumably killing him.

How sin-draining doves relate to an extradimensional or spiritual spacecraft (which we never see, it's only intimated by the lights, noise, shattering windows, and Katy's static hair), I don't know. In the film's final scene, the good space visitor meets Jesus among the children in a brightly lit room. We don't know whether this is on another planet, or in another dimension, but we know it's a holy place because of the bright light, made brighter by the white costumes and set décor. The film stock also appears slightly overexposed.

In *My Bloody Valentine* (1981), Sarah walks home one dark night. She is nervous. Ominous music ensues. She thinks someone is following. Tension mounts. She stops to look behind her. Is anyone there? Music rises to a fever pitch just as she turns forward — and suddenly faces a bright white light! Sarah gasps. We see her POV of the bright light. What is it? Who's there?

The light lowers. It's only a flashlight, carried by the sheriff. Sarah breathes relief.

Hidden behind the light, the sheriff appeared to be a threat, first startling the audience, then unnerving them when he was revealed as harmless. Similar to the farmer's truck in *Jeepers Creepers*, which, hidden in a blur, appeared to be a threat, only to be revealed as harmless.[25]

The Jar (1984) uses creative lighting for both style and inexpensive special effects. Paul, an office worker, brings home an old man after the two are in a car accident. Paul worries that the man is injured, but the man disappears soon after arriving at Paul's apartment. Whether he walked out, or actually dematerialized, we never learn. He's left behind a wrapped item. Paul unwraps the item in his kitchen, and finds a jar containing a blue demon thing. He examines it, puzzled, then stands up, a tranced expression on his face. He stares into a bright white light, suddenly shining from his living room. He walks into the light, silhouetted so the edges of his white shirt are aglow. When he enters the living room, the mysterious light is gone. The ceiling lamp appears too dim to have been the source. Yet Paul remains in a trance.

The blue demon thing looks cheap and rubbery, like some small toy. Yet this scene of demonic possession is mesmerizing partially because of the bright white light, assisted by Gary Wallace's acting and an eerie music soundtrack.

The Jar uses lights of different colors, but blue is most often associated with the blue demon, creating a motif that links the demon with its victims. At one point, Paul sees the old man in the mirror, lit blue from underhead, suggesting that previous to Paul, the man was possessed. At film's end, when Paul's boss knocks on his door, a quick underhead flash of blue light intimates the boss is now possessed. He enters Paul's apartment, sees the demon in the jar for the first time, and screams.

Red light also suggests demonic forces, though not specifically linked to possession by the blue demon thing. Paul awakes to rumbling one night, and sees red light shining from under his bedroom door. The walls begin to break apart, red light shining through the cracked plaster. This is one of Paul's many hallucinations as the demon's possession grows.

Like glowing red eyes, in horror, red lights often intimate evil. In the "Root of All Evil" episode of TV's *Friday the 13th: The Series*, a greedy gardener, Adrian, stuffs people into a Satanically cursed mulcher. As the mulcher masticates the screaming victims (sometimes they're still alive), it spews out money, rewarding Adrian for his evil deed. However, too much gore is expensive for a syndicated TV series, and offensive for broadcast television. So instead of seeing people torn asunder in the mulcher, we see red light flashing across Adrian's grinning face as he stares into the mulcher. Apparently, evil supernatural forces inside mulchers emit red light.

What shade of red? Hellfire Red, of course.

Red lights are an inexpensive way to suggest Hell. Six sinners die near the end of *A Day of Judgment* (1981). The Grim Reaper escorts them through a low-budget Heaven. Essentially, two white Greek columns against a blue sky, misty clouds, and bright white lights. These shots are intercut with the sinners' reaction shots. They smile blissfully, and are brightly lit in a bluish-tinged white light.[26] Heavenly music supports our locale. But the Grim Reaper shepherds on the sinners. They enter a low-budget Hell. Just a lurid red painting and a plastic skull. We hear the screams of other, unseen sinners. These shots of Hell are intercut with the six sinners' horrified expressions — red light glowing on their faces.

In *The Curse of the Cat People* (1944), a change in lighting heralds the supernatural. Amy, a little girl, is in her backyard, which is evenly lit in a high-key setup. She closes her eyes and wishes for a friend, whereupon the lighting shifts to low-key, silhouetting the trees against the sky.[27] Then a bright, hard light shines into the backyard's center, contrasting with the dark background. Amy skips merrily inside this light, thus connecting to the supernatural.

This high to low-key *lighting shift* becomes a motif, signifying the supernatural's entry into the normal world. When Amy meets Irena's ghost in the backyard, the same lighting shift occurs, and Irena enters the brightly lit area [Figures 6.16–6.19]. Still later, Amy enters the snowy backyard on Christmas Eve. Irena is already there. The lighting is relatively high-key despite her ghostly presence. Then she shows Amy a supernatural "Christmas present." The lighting turns low-key, again silhouetting the trees, followed by large patch of bright, white light that sparkles.[28]

Deadly Blessing (1981) likewise uses a *lighting shift* to suggest a supernatural presence, albeit only once, at film's end. Until then, audiences are led to believe that the sole threat is from a psycho. After that psycho is exposed and killed, Martha believes she is safe. (She never did believe all that crazy talk about an incubus.) She enters her house, the lighting relatively high-key. Her shadow on the door is diffuse, its edges blurry.

Then ominous music ensues. The room darkens. Martha glances about nervously. What's happening? A hard light slants across Martha, her face now brightly lit amid darkness.

Figure 6.16 — *The Curse of the Cat People.* Amy (Ann Carter) in her backyard. Evenly spread, high-key lighting depicts a normal world. Then...

Figure 6.17 — ...a shift to low-key lighting heralds the supernatural. Trees are silhouetted, and...

Figure 6.18—...a bright, hard light shines into the backyard, whereupon...

Figure 6.19 —...the ghost Irena (Simone Simon) enters the light.

To her shock and surprise, her husband's ghost appears. He warns Martha to beware the incubus, then fades away. The floor rumbles. An incubus breaks through the floorboards and grabs Martha. Bright red and white lights shine up from the hole in the floor. Smoke billows out of the hole, reflecting those hellfire lights. The incubus pulls Martha down the hole and into hell. (Well, we presume it's hell.) The broken floorboards replace themselves through reverse motion photography.

The room brightens again into a high-key lighting setup, signifying the departure of the supernatural. The room brightens further, brighter than when Martha entered, until the room is unnaturally bright. A rack focus blurs the background, and reveals a spider on its web in the foreground, suggesting that though the incubus has departed, this house remains its territory. It can return at any time.

In *The Ring* (2002), a *sudden shift* into high-key brightness signifies Rachel's entry into Samara's supernatural realm. Samara grabs Rachel's arm, the dim, murky, nighttime room turns *very* bright, and Rachel sees flashbacks of Samara's painful past. This sudden shift in brightness was likely achieved through a combination of lighting and post-production work.[29]

In films of every genre, sudden overhead bright lights often suggest a sudden (and often heaven-sent) revelation. It's become a satirized cliché, yet the cliché continues because it works. In *Thirst* (Australian 1979), a vampire cult locks Kate inside a room that torments and frightens her by breaking apart and tipping over. Like a rat in a maze, if Kate learns and does what the vampires want, she will be rewarded. The room will stop tormenting her. By this Pavlovian method, the vampires hope to brainwash Kate into joining their ranks.

When Kate finally drinks blood from the beer stein, the room stops shaking. Bright white light shines on Kate. Heavenly music ensues. Actress Chantal Contouri *looks up* blissfully (even though the light does not shine from any specific direction), and drinks more blood. The white light brightens further. The scene grows so bright, it appears the film stock was overexposed, either on set or in the lab.

Flickering and Strobe Lights

Lights can flicker. You've seen old fluorescent tubes flickering in many a film. As part of the set décor, they evoke a cheap, decrepit, and seedy ambiance. (Especially when covered with dead bugs.) *Strobe lights* (aka stroboscopic lamps) flicker in a constant, regular pattern. Strobes are often used in dance clubs, where their constant flickering creates the illusion of slow motion. Horror has many aesthetic uses for flickering lights.

In *Jacob's Ladder*, Jezzie dances under strobe lights at a party. As Jacob watches, he sees reptilian tentacles fondling and embracing Jezzie, a tail rising between her legs (she appears to like it), claws scratching her ass, batlike wings fluttering. A white horn or claw emerges from her mouth. At which point Jacob "freaks out," screaming and fainting.

Director Adrian Lyne explains his aesthetic intent for the strobe light by saying: "We're not sure what we're seeing."[30] That's not entirely true. We see demonic body parts. Granted, we don't see the whole, or how the parts fit together. This dance scene has a Lovecraftian quality, in that Lovecraft would describe the evil Old Ones in generalities (tentacles and such), without ever giving the reader a specific and complete description.

But apart from hiding the full nature of the demonic threat, the strobe light in *Jacob's Ladder* lends an eerie, otherworldly ambiance to the dance party. The strobe supports the film's conceit of Jacob living in a surreal world, where normalcy is always in danger of disintegrating into a nightmare. (Because, of course, the events *are* mostly his nightmare.)

In *Alien* (1979), Ripley activates the *Nostromo's* self-destruct sequence, filling the halls with hissing steam, ringing sirens, and flashing yellow emergency lights. She creeps down the halls amid all this chaotic, irrational, and entertaining *mise-en-scène*, until she reaches a spot where a white light flickers on her with strobe-like regularity. We're not sure why it's flickering, but judging by the shadows, it seems the light source is behind some moving fan blades.

Ripley peeks around a corner and sees the alien. Surprise! She pulls back, terrified. Yes, the alien is scary enough on its own. But the flickering light makes the alien even scarier by obscuring it. When we know that a threat is there, but we can't see it clearly, the threat feels all the more potent. Furthermore, the flickering light contributes a kinetic energy to this scene, thus heightening the tension.

The *Alien* series is fairly consistent in its *mise-en-scène*, lighting included. Near the end of *Alien: Resurrection* (1997), the few remaining survivors are escaping in a spaceship, only to discover an alien on board. As they battle the alien, bright white light occasionally flashes. It's not a strobe; the flashes are spaced too widely apart. Sometimes it flickers, sometimes it flashes longer than a flicker. As usual with the *Alien* series, this white light makes no sense. What's its source? And why is it flashing just now? — the spaceship's not damaged or set for automatic destruct.

Once again, it seems to be style over substance. This flashing white light heightens the tension. And yes, it looks cool. Not only because it flashes, but because of its intensity. The light is so bright, it nearly "washes out" all the colors, desaturating the image and casting the actors in a truly "new light."[31] The alien's face, when bathed in this white light, resembles a human skull, making for a startling emotional impact. It's both scary (human skulls are a horror icon), and a reminder that this alien is a human hybrid.

In *The Unseen* (1981), three TV newsgals drive to small town Solvang to do a puff piece on a folk festival. Every hotel is booked, so they stay at the home of Ernest and Virginia Keller. Unbeknown to the newsgals, husband and wife are also brother and sister. And lurking in the basement, crawling through the air ducts, is the spawn of their unholy union ... unseen!

The "unseen" is Junior Keller, who kills two of the newsgals in the film's first hour. (You know how those mutant, spawn-of-incest retards get when they see nekkid women passing by their air ducts.) Ernest locks the last newsgal, Jennifer, in his basement. Alone with Junior.

At this point, neither Jennifer nor the audience has seen Junior. When Jennifer tries to escape, shaking the bars of a basement window, she discovers the corpses of her two friends. Jennifer screams, runs, and falls onto a pile of garbage. The pile moves and grunts. Junior begins to emerge. Jennifer runs. Junior pursues and grabs her hair. In the struggle, Jennifer loosens an electrical box. (A fuse box, I suppose.)

Electrical sparks emanate from the box, flickering blue-white light. Junior is enthralled, stomps his bare feet, grunts excitedly, mimics the flickering light by shaking his head and arms. He repeatedly pounds the box, causing the flickering to stop and start up again. Jennifer is lying on the ground, screaming, hysterical.

She should be hysterical. The flickering lights have helped "the unseen" make a grand and scary entrance. If you're a threat, and you want to make a good first impression, it helps to have a flickering light.

The flickering finally stops and we get a good look at Junior. He resembles a giant baby. He's fat, wears a dirty diaper, and can't talk. And because he has Down Syndrome, his face is deformed.[32] He is ugly, aggressive, and he's killed before. Enough to scare most people.

But instead of revealing Junior too quickly — though by now the audience is anxious to finally see him — director Danny Steinmann (like Adrian Lyne nine years later) used flickering lights to obscure Junior, drawing out the moment of his entrance, heightening tension as we try to get a good look. Still partly "unseen," what we do see of Junior becomes more frightening as our imaginations fill in the blanks. Furthermore, as in *Jacob's Ladder*, the flickering lights lend their own surreal ambiance to what we do see.

The Unseen's flickering lights are reinforced by other lights and *mise-en-scène*. As Junior is scaring Jennifer, we cut to the upstairs parlor where Ernest and Virginia are listening to events in the basement. A table lamp flickers. A thunderstorm rages outside. Its blue-white, electrical lightning flickers in the window, echoing the fuse box's blue-white, electrical flickering.

In *Gothika* (2003), flickering lights suggest the presence of a ghost. Miranda practices psychiatry in a modern asylum, in an old, *Gothic* style building. (*Gothika*, get it?) Early in the film, she is working in her office. A suitable *thunderstorm flickers outside*. The lights go out. "Damn the generator," Miranda laments. "Not again."

Driving home in the rain, Miranda is stopped by a young girl in the middle of the road. Miranda goes to see if the girl needs help, touches the girl (who is really a ghost), and suddenly awakes as a patient inside her own asylum. A *fluorescent tube flickers* in her cell. Flickering lights will become a *Gothika* motif.

Rachel, the ghost, had possessed Miranda, compelling her to murder her own husband. Miranda doesn't remember any of this. Others think Miranda had just snapped.

Twenty-five minutes into the film, Miranda again awakes in her cell to a *flickering fluorescent light*. She senses a supernatural presence, which is supported by ghostly whispers and a dolly counter-zoom (a *dolly out/zoom in*, to be specific) as she watches her cell door. A modern glass door, not the kind with bars. She approaches the door. The glass fogs up. The words "Not Alone" are written in the fog. A supernatural presence is further suggested by a quick blur, and by a ghost's POV of Miranda's hair. The POV is in extreme closeup (the kind made possible by CGI effects), entering Miranda's hair, passing amid individual hairs, going around her neck, and exiting from the other side. At which point actress Halle Berry reacts, as though Miranda had felt the ghost passing by, sending shivers along her skin.

Later in *Gothika*, Rachel opens Miranda's cell door. Miranda escapes to her old office and researches recent events. She sees Rachel on her computer, via a security camera feed from the asylum's solitary confinement area. Miranda runs to meet Rachel, through hallways where the *lights are steady*. But when she enters the solitary area (where Rachel presumable is), all lights, rows of fluorescent tubes and wall units, are *flickering madly*. Miranda creeps past the cells. Suddenly, all the lights *stop flickering*. Apparently, Miranda is now where Rachel wants her to be. Miranda approaches the cell nearest her. She sees Chloe being raped. Thus has Rachel used flickering lights to guide Miranda to the right cell.

Nearly an hour into the film, Miranda is once again locked in a cell. The lights *outside* flicker. She approaches the door nervously. By now she knows that flickering lights are a sign. She hears ghostly whispers. The lights *inside* her cell flicker. Whatever was outside, is now in the cell with her. She sees Rachel. Who begins beating the crap out of Miranda, flinging her against the walls. The guards see Miranda slamming the walls on their security monitor. They don't see Rachel, so they assume Miranda is trying to kill herself. They enter the cell, giving Miranda a chance to escape. (Yet again.)

At the film's end, Miranda is in a jail cell. The lights go on, then *flicker*. She looks up expectantly. The sheriff arrives. Miranda had called for him, but the flickering lights indicate that Rachel too is interested in his arrival. As Miranda and the sheriff converse, the lights are *steady*. When the sheriff realizes that Miranda has figured out that he is partially responsible for Rachel's murder, he tries to kill Miranda. The lights begin *flickering*. This causes the sheriff to pause, giving Miranda a chance to escape. It also indicates that Rachel is here, about to exact revenge.

Nondiegetic Lights

Diegetic lights are *within the story*. *Nondiegetic* lights, though they are in the film, are *outside the story*. The words derive from *diegesis*, an ancient Greek term that refers to a story that is told by a narrator.

Horror fans are familiar with nondiegetic lights, if not with the term. In the "Father's Day" episode of *Creepshow* (1982), Aunt Bedelia is griping beside her father's grave, on a normally lit, sunny afternoon. When the father rises from the grave and attacks Bedelia, red and blue lights shine on them. These lights have no source in the story. They do not shine from Hell or from any hole in the grave. No characters are standing by the gravesite, shining red and blue lights on the revenant corpse and his screaming daughter. These lights do not exist in the story. These lights are nondiegetic.

Creepshow's *mise-en-scène* is replete with brightly colored, saturated, nondiegetic lights. When in "The Crate" episode, Fluffy attacks the student, red and blue lights shine on them. And in "They're Creeping Up on You," Richard's apartment is normally lit, until he opens the doors to Harry and Becky's revenant corpses, whereupon a greenish-blue light shines on all. This light is in the film, but not in the story. The characters don't see this greenish-blue hue. Rather, the hue creates an ambiance that comments on their situation. Harry and Becky drowned in the ocean, which is evoked by the greenish-blue light.

Aesthetically, *Creepshow*'s nondiegetic lights: (1) Evoke the visual style of a comic book. (2) Infuse the scenes with humor. Bright colors are often associated with comedy, and function as such in the context of the film's satirical tales and broad acting styles. (3) Enliven the drama and action. The colored nondiegetic lights often ensue upon some violent act.

Nondiegetic lights needn't be colored, but in horror films they often are. More than any other film, *Suspiria* popularized the "nondiegetic colored lighting style." The film is famous for its irrational, deeply saturated, primary colors (both in lighting and set décor). Irrational partially because the film's color scheme is likely to drive one mad. But irrational also because the colored lights are nondiegetic; those lights have no logical reason to be there.

Suspiria opens with Suzy exiting a pinkly lit room at the airport. Why is that room lit pink? *Is* it lit pink? Does Suzy see it, or only us viewers? The film's irrational colored lights never let up. After Pat escapes the ballet academy and seeks refuge at a friend's apartment, she looks anxiously out a window, sensing evil. The roof outside is lit blue and red. A killer breaks the window, pulls Pat through the shattered glass onto the roof, and repeatedly stabs her. Underhead blue and red lights illuminate her death throes. No colored lights line the roof *in the story*. These lights are not part of the characters' world. It is only us, the viewers, who see blue and red lights illuminating Pat.[33]

Terror (British 1978) is replete with saturated, nondiegetic colored lights. Its director, Norman J. Warren, credits *Suspiria* as his influence.[34] But though *Suspiria* popularized the style, Mario Bava's *Black Sabbath* (aka *I Tre volti della paura*, Italian 1963) did it first, and is credited with inspiring *Suspiria*'s lighting. *The House That Screamed* (aka *La residencia*, Spanish 1969), about a psychotic killer in a girl's boarding school, is regarded as the influence behind *Suspiria*'s story — and those of many slasher films a decade later, most notably *Pieces* (aka *Mil gritos tiene la noche*, Spanish 1982).

Nondiegetic colored lights are an inexpensive way to enhance a low-budget. Some of *The Jar*'s colored lights are diegetic. Paul sees and reacts to the red light shining from under his bedroom door and through the cracked walls. He responds to the bright white light shining from his living room. When Jack knocks on Paul's door, a flash of blue light on Jack implies that now he is demonically targeted. These lights are a cheap way to depict a demonic presence.

But *The Jar* also uses nondiegetic lights. As Paul drives the old man, a greenish-yellow underhead light illuminates Paul. A reddish-orange underhead light illuminates the old man. Does Paul's car have variously colored lights under the dashboard? Of course not. Nor is there any indication that these lights are an unseen demonic force within the story. Aesthetically, these nondiegetic colored lights (1) lend a surreal, supernatural atmosphere to *The Jar*, and (2) add a stylish sheen to the film's rough production values.

Nondiegetic lights should not be confused with *poorly motivated* diegetic lights. *Don't Look in the Basement* has many harsh shadows on stark white walls. It's unlikely that any light source *in the story* would cast such shadows. The source looks like a hard, bright stage light, which is not something that an asylum normally keeps around. Nevertheless, the audience is meant to believe that these lights originate from a source *within the story*. Perhaps from the sunlight streaming through a window, or from a lamp in a patient's room. Thus, these lights are diegetic.

Nondiegetic lights are unmotivated (not being in the story, nothing in the story *can* motivate them), yet they should not be confused with unmotivated diegetic lights (e.g., the "mystery light" under the capsized canoe in *Sleepaway Camp*, as discussed in the section on "Motivated Lighting").

Day for Night

When you film inside a soundstage, the time of day outside doesn't matter. A nighttime scene can be shot day or night. But when you shoot outdoors, or in a building with windows that are difficult to obscure, then night-for-night vs. day-for-night becomes a consideration.

In *night-for-night* photography, a scene is shot at night, and set at night. In *day-for-night*, a scene is shot under daylight, but set at night.

Day-for-night photography normally requires the filmmaker to: (1) Put a *blue filter* over the camera lens (unless you're filming in black and white), because viewers associate a blue tint with night. (2) Close down the lens aperture to underexpose the film. (3) Turn on lights in the *mise-en-scène* that suggest nighttime (e.g., car headlights).

Day-for-night scenes rarely fool discerning viewers. The telltale signs are easy to spot. In night-for-night, the sky is pitch black. In day-for-night, the sky is blue or violet. Sometimes you can even see bright sunlit spots on blue-tinted clouds. (Tip: When shooting day-for-night, avoid showing the sky.)

Another giveaway is that in day-for-night, everything is underexposed. Actors appear as murkily dark figures, moving under an unusually bright sky. Or past an unusually bright spot on the sidewalk. Hopefully, audiences will think those bright areas are caused, not by sunlight, but by an unusually bright moon. (Tip: When shooting day-for-night, avoid showing both sunlit and shadowed areas in the same shot. One area will be either too bright, or too dark.) Conversely, when shooting night-for-night, actors are often brightly illuminated with stage lights — we can see them! — in stark contrast to the pitch black sky above.

Why shoot day-for-night? Why shoot a night scene under sunlight? Why not just wait for night? Two main reasons. (1) It's cheaper and faster to shoot day-for-night. Filmmakers needn't rent or set up stage lights. Sunlight is free. Just bring a blue lens filter — and instant night! (2) Wide vistas, such as oceans and deserts, are almost impossible to light sufficiently at night. Or at least, prohibitively expensive, even for big studios. How do you light the ocean all the way to its horizon? Hundreds of helicopters with searchlights, hovering offscreen?

As always, CGI technology makes "lighting" vistas more feasible. You needn't light the actual ocean. You only "light" the digital ocean in your computer.

Night-for-night is almost always the better aesthetic choice for a horror film. Threats lurk in darkness. Sure, sunlight is free, but so is the night. Sunlight is a cheap way to light a location, but night is a cheap way to enhance a spooky atmosphere.

Children Shouldn't Play with Dead Things is eerily atmospheric largely because of its night-for-night photography. Early in the film, two bright lanterns, attached to the boat's mast, provide the acting troupe's only oasis against the nighttime darkness. Lanterns and street lamps pierce the blackness of the cemetery. Throughout the film, hard lighting contrasts against the night's pitch black canvas. These harsh, low-key contrasts aesthetically support the film's harsh tale of graverobbing, desperation, and panic.

The only day-for-night shot appears early in the film. The characters approach the island in a boat, night-for-night. We cut to their POV of the island. The island is silhouetted against a violet day-for-night sky. The lighting in these two shots don't match (filmmakers often intercut night-for-night and day-for-night shots), but we can forgive that. The boat carries two lanterns, so we see it despite the darkness. The island, a wide vista, would have been harder to light.

In *Anthropophagus: The Grim Reaper* (aka *Antropofago*, Italian 1980) director Aristide Massaccesi (aka Joe D'Amato) uses day-for-night photography to simulate lightning. Julie is chasing Carol through a forest during a storm, their murky forms difficult to discern within the nighttime darkness. But every so often Massaccesi opens his lens aperture *briefly* to admit more light. The impression is of lightning illuminating the landscape. But freeze frame your DVD and you'll see the "lightning" is daylight—the entire landscape is evenly lit.[35] This "nighttime" scene was shot under daylight, the film underexposed except during "lightning flashes."

Of course, Massaccesi may have achieved his "lightning effect" in a post-production lab. But I assume it was the aperture, because the "lightning" increases, then decreases, its intensity over several frames, as if someone were opening and closing the aperture Either way, the scene was shot day-for-night, the film stock underexposed.

Compare this scene to *Suspiria*'s night-for-night lightning. When Pat escapes through the forest, lightning flashes illuminate her and the trees, yet the landscape remains in darkness.

Suspiria's lightning effects (stage lights, apparently) appear more realistic, more stylized and expressionistic, and more sinister, than *Anthropophagus*'s lightning. But stage lights and lighting technicians are expensive. Massaccesi's day-for-night lightning is a thrifty alternative.

One can also shoot *night-for-day*, but that's rare and usually done by necessity. I've been on sets where a filmmaker was shooting *day-for-day*, but losing sunlight as night approached, the scene still incomplete. So more stage lights were erected, hoping to maintain the scene's daylight appearance under the darkening sky. Good luck trying to intercut those shots.

CHAPTER 7

Editing the Image

It's been said that a film is created three times. First, when the script is written. Then again when the script is filmed, because the sets and actors are often strikingly different from what the screenwriter imagined. And a third time in post-production, when colors are corrected, the sound mixed, special effects inserted, and raw footage is edited.[1] The goal of editing (except for some experimental or avant-garde films) is to eliminate extraneous footage, and connect the remaining shots into a coherent story that conveys clear and consistent themes.

Transitions

A *shot* is an uninterrupted sequence of frames. You press the camera's record button, the film or tape starts to run, exposing the film or recording onto a tape. You stop recording, and the shot is over. A shot is also an uninterrupted sequence of frames within the edited, finished film.

What if you film a table, then wait, then without moving the camera, or changing the lighting or *mise-en-scène*, film again, so the second shot follows the first with no visible break? Onscreen, the two shots appear as one. Well, I suppose they might be considered two shots, but if the viewer can't tell, they'd aesthetically function as one shot. Anyway, it's an esoteric issue for academics. It needn't worry you.

A shot should not be confused with a *scene*, which is a story event that occurs in the same locale and time frame. A scene may comprise one shot or many shots.

Shots can follow one another in several ways. In a straight *cut*, one shot ends, another begins. A cut is the least intrusive transition, relatively *invisible* in that it doesn't draw attention to itself and away from the story. It's the transition most likely to emphasize content over form.

Despite the prevalence of video recording and computer editing, connecting shots in an edit is often called *splicing*, because that's how film is edited. Film strips are physically *cut* and *spliced* (i.e., scotch-taped) together. It's also why a cut is called a *cut*. (Ever notice how people still talk of "dialing" phones that no longer have dials?)

Some "cutting" terminology: *Intercutting* splices shots within a scene. Such as two men talking in a room. *Crosscutting* splices shots between different scenes. As the men talk, we *crosscut* to the killer driving his car. An *insert shot* depicts key items in a scene's main action. As the men talk, one remembers a creepy phone message. He glances at his desk. We *intercut* to a POV *insert shot* of his message pad. A *cutaway shot* depicts something that is away from the scene's main action. As the men talk, one glances out the window. We see a POV *cutaway shot* of the killer approaching the building.

Is this cutaway shot an intercut or a crosscut? I'd say an intercut, though these terms are squishy, often used interchangeably. An insert is an aside, a cutaway is a detour, but all detours return to the main road (or scene). I suppose some cutaways detour far enough, long enough, to qualify as crosscuts. Squishy terms, but still useful. So we'll use them.

Cuts are the most common transition. But a shot can also *fade-out*, the image dimming until there is only black. We then either cut from black to the next image, or *fade-in* from black, so the next image lightens gradually until it is visible.

One usually fades in or out of black, but other colors may be used. The most common "other color" is white. But there's no reason you can't fade to orange. An appropriate color for any Halloween themed horror film. Or fade to blood red. Or slime green.

A shot can *dissolve* into the next shot, one image fading as the next image grows more distinct. Filmmakers often use dissolves for a poetic or romantic effect, or to suggest the passage of time. Horror and suspense films will more likely dissolve for the latter reason, such as when a character tensely awaits some critical news or possible threat.

A shot can *wipe* to the next shot. The new shot moves across the first shot, until entirely replacing it onscreen. Wipes are similar to *split screens*, except that in the latter case, two or more shots occupy the screen for an appreciable length of time, whereas in a wipe, the second shot quickly replaces the first.[2]

Wipes can embody graphic shapes. *Curtains* (1983) is a slasher film set in the world of theater and filmmaking. After a few opening credits of blood red letters against a black void — a blood drop hanging on the *C* in *Curtains* — a faint pattern of curtain ruffles is discernible in that void. We *wipe* to *Curtain's* opening shot, which shows an actress performing a murder scene on stage. This wipe is shaped like a theater curtain parting to reveal this actress on stage.

Several times in *Curtains*, a shot fades to black. Faint curtain ruffles appear against the blackness.[3] Then we wipe to the next shot, once again, in the shape of theater curtains parting to reveal the new scene. The film ends with "curtains" wiping over the final scene, for the first time closing rather than opening. These "theater curtain wipes" not only support *Curtains's* story and themes, but also its title. The wipes are aesthetically appropriate, if a little cute.

Filmmakers should beware of going overboard or getting "too cute" with wipes that are funky, obvious, or heavy-handed. A straight cut is usually the best transitional choice, because it doesn't draw attention to itself. The audience can better focus on the film's story, characters, and themes, rather than on all the gimmicks in the filmmaker's post-production software. Gimmicks are like spice. Best used in small pinches, lest they overpower the meal.

One can also *edit in camera*. Shots are planned and recorded in the sequence, and at the lengths, intended for the finished film. Transitions are created during the filming itself. The raw footage *is* the final cut.

In its purest form, editing in camera allows for no retakes or mistakes. Avant-garde and experimental filmmakers sometimes edit in camera for artistic reasons. Amateur, no-budget, and lazybones filmmakers may do so out of ignorance, frugality, or sloth.

Constructing Space

Editing can rearrange space and construct new physical realities. By juxtaposing shots filmed in different locations, filmmakers can set their stories in locales that are inaccessible or beyond their budget. *Island of the Dead*'s (2000) second shot is of the lower Manhattan skyline, identifiable by its Twin Towers. Several low angle shots of nondescript office buildings follow. Because these shots follow the Manhattan skyline shot, audiences believe (or willingly suspend disbelief) that the buildings are in New York. (In reality, they are in Montreal.)

In *Hell of the Living Dead* (aka *Apocalipsis caníbal, Inferno dei morti viventi, Virus,* Italian-Spanish 1980), four soldiers (or a SWAT police team, it's not clear) and two journalists trek through New Guinea, investigating an outbreak of cannibalism. The film was shot in Spain, yet the characters' journey is extensively intercut with stock film footage taken in New Guinea in 1972. This stock footage is identifiable by its inferior photographic quality. *Hell of the Living Dead* was likely shot on 35mm film, whereas the stock footage looks to have been blown up from 16mm.

Yet while *Hell of the Living Dead* has been mocked for its reliance on stock footage, the editing is impressive, effectively integrating the characters into the stock footage's space. At one point, the characters ride through a jungle in a jeep and land rover. A soldier glances *to his right.* We cut to natives running beside a river that apparently flows parallel to the jeep's path. This is a *point-of-view cut,* which helps to spatially unify the two shots. The soldier in shot 1 appears to observe the events in shot 2, thus linking the two spaces.

This *POV cut* is reinforced, and the shots' spaces further unified, in that the soldier rides in a moving jeep, and the footage of the natives was taken from a moving vehicle. The similar movements in the two shots create a nice *eyeline match,* in that the looker in shot 1 gazes from a vantage point that matches (in terms of position, angle of direction, and movement) the subject seen in shot 2.

At times, the editing is less precise. We cut to another soldier on the first soldier's *right.* Where the river should be. But we see only trees moving past the jeep. Where did the river go?

We then cut to a kangaroo rat or rabbit (I've no idea what it is) hopping in slow motion. It appears to be a small animal, yet it fills the frame, as if seen from up close. No character saw this animal; there is no POV cut. The animal is just there, in its own shot and space. It's meant to depict the surrounding terrain, but it integrates poorly into the soldiers' space. So too the monkey leaping trees in slow motion. This is because, even without POV cuts, the angle and distance of the framing of the wildlife does not match what the soldiers' POVs *should be* from the jeep. The animals are too close, or "seen" from the wrong angle. Nor would the soldiers see the animals in slow motion. For all these reasons, these shots provide poor eyeline matches.

We later cut to a shot of natives canoeing in a river that seems to flow perpendicular to the jeep's path. (Wasn't the river flowing parallel before?) We cut back to the jeep. Have the soldiers crossed a bridge over the river? We didn't see it. The parallel river was well integrated into the soldiers' space, yet this perpendicular river merely functions as depicting the terrain. We accept that it's out there somewhere near the soldiers. We're not sure where. But the film is entertaining enough so that we are forgiving.

Another lapse: the jungle *mise-en-scène* around the animals and natives don't quite match the Spanish countryside surrounding the soldiers. The greenery is different.

The intercutting grows more ambitious and admirable in the village scene. The soldiers stop outside the village. They hear drums. Sounds ominous. Lia, one of the journalists, suggests that she go ahead, because she'd spent a year with the natives and can communicate with them. She strips off her blouse and jogs ahead of the jeep. After the audience has had a good look at Lia's bouncing breasts, she tells the soldiers that they can come no farther. She must enter the village alone.

Lia's trek through the village is a masterpiece of spatial construction through editing. She enters and *observes* the village and its activities. Initially, she is framed alone, in closeups or medium closeups, and low angles, that hide her Spanish countryside surroundings. She gazes into offscreen space, creating POV cuts with stock footage of dancers, corpses, funerals, and mourners. The direction of her gaze often matches the angle of the village shots, creating many nice eyeline matches, solidifying the space between Lia's world and that of the village.

Actress Margit Evelyn Newton's performance further solidifies the space. Lia *reacts to what she sees*, wide-eyed in shock and revulsion. Her *reaction shots* are further enhanced by the Kuleshov Effect. (More about that in the following section.)

Natives too form eyeline matches into Lia's space. One shot depicts Lia staring *leftward and down*, at something on the ground. What? We cut to a corpse on the ground. Cut to several natives watching the ground. A child on a native's shoulder glances *rightward* in Lia's direction, forming an eyeline match. Cut back to Lia, still looking leftward and down [Figures 7.1–7.4].

The shot of the corpse on the ground, and the shot of the natives looking at the ground, were likely separate events. *Hell of the Living Dead* rearranges space within the stock footage itself, even as it integrates Lia into that space.

 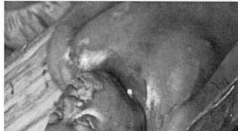

Left: Figure 7.1—*Hell of the Living Dead.* Lia (Margit Evelyn Newton) stares left (our left, not hers) and down, creating an *eyeline match* to... *Right:* Figure 7.2 —...this stock footage image of a corpse on the ground. We then cut to...

Left: Figure 7.3 —...another stock footage clip. Three natives look down, forming *eyeline matches* to the corpse in the previous shot. A child and another native look rightward, forming *eyeline matches* to... *Right:* Figure 7.4 —...Lia, thus completing the circle, and solidifying our sense of space; of where people are in relation to each other.

Later, Lia's cameraman, Max, films a mother holding a baby. The mother reaches into offscreen space, then brings her hand to her mouth, apparently taking food and eating it. What sort of food? We don't know, because the food is either offscreen, or is so small between her fingers (morsels?) that we can't identify it. But the shots of the mother eating are inter-cut with shots of fingers picking maggots from a skull. This creates the illusion that the mother is picking up and eating maggots, which Max is filming. Max's disgusted *reaction shots* further support this impression. (Again, enhanced by the Kuleshov Effect.)

After being a mere spectator, Lia more deeply enters the village's reality. This occurs by transferring *mise-en-scène* between the two spaces through a *match on action cut*. By now Lia is framed with natives and grass huts (actors and set décor). We intercut Lia with stock footage of native dancers, painted white and wearing white masks. Some are waving leaves. They approach the camera (as if this were Lia's POV of them approaching her).

Cut to a medium long shot of Lia. An actor, who is made up to *resemble the dancers* (white body paint, white mask, carrying leaves), and is *already partly in the frame*, approaches Lia, waving his leaves. This is a *match on action cut*. The actor in this shot matches the action of an approaching dancer in the previous shot.

Match on action cuts help unify space. Shot 1 depicts Joe sitting in a chair. He gets up. Cut to shot 2 which depicts Joe *completing this action*. You've seen many such cuts without noticing them. You're not supposed to. Match on action cuts usually assist in invisible edit-ing, keeping your attention on the story, not the structure.

Which is good, because while *Hell of the Living Dead*'s match on action cut is ambi-tious and impressive (matching the action of a stock footage dancer with an actor on set), it's a flawed match. The roughly matched staging of the actor can be forgiven; stock footage forces you to work with what you have. But the leaf prop is woefully inadequate. The dancers carry limp, lush, green leaves. The actor carries brown, dry leaves on a stick. Yet the film is so entertaining, the scene so rich with drama and *mise-en-scène* (e.g., the semi-nude New-ton), that few fans will notice the mismatched leaves on the first half dozen or so viewings.

Hell of the Living Dead's admirable editing is no accident. Director Bruno Mattei began his career in his father's editing studio. Mattei claims to have edited over 100 films in the 1960s and 1970s. Mark Wickum writes: "Although set in New Guinea, Mattei shot the film almost entirely on studio sets and used his experience as an editor to overcome the lack of authentic locations. 'The movie was made in Spain,' he explained, 'and as there aren't any jungles there, we bought footage from a Japanese documentary.'"[4]

Editing allows actors to simultaneously occupy several spaces in the same scene. This is helpful in stories about doppelgangers or evil twins. It also comes in handy for dream sequences. In *Psychomania* (British 1973), Abby attempts suicide with an overdose of drugs. Instead of dying, she has a nightmare. She is in a strange room. She sees a gurney wheeled in. A patient lies on the gurney, covered by a sheet. The camera moves up to reveal the gur-ney is being pushed by ... Abby! Dressed as a nurse. Nurse Abby pulls the sheet off the patient, revealing ... Abby! Lying on the gurney, apparently dead.

Actress Mary Larkin occupies three spaces in this scene: Abby as spectator, Abby as nurse, and Abby as patient. How can Larkin occupy three spaces at once? Easy. She only plays one "role" per shot. The shots are then juxtaposed to create the illusion that Abby is seeing herself wheeling herself into the room.

It's harder (and more expensive) when you want an actor to play several roles in the *same shot.* That usually involves split screens or CGI effects. Low-budget filmmakers may wish to stick to editing when creating doppelgangers, evil twins, or similar dream sequences. It's cheaper that way.

Constructing new spaces can create *continuity problems.* Filmmakers are often aware of them, but hope viewers won't notice. Some discontinuities are minor and brief. In *Night Angel* (1990), the windows in the warehouse housing Lilith's fashion magazine, as seen from outside, do not match the windows as seen from inside the offices. In *Splatter University* (1984), when Julie enters Mark's apartment building, the door contains two long, slim windows, and has two columns of frosted glass panes beside it, as seen from outside. But from inside the building, the door contains one window, wider and shorter than before, and the frosted glass panes are gone. Clearly, in both films, one building was used for exterior shots, and another for interior shots.

Generally, the less visually prominent the discontinuity, and the briefer its duration, and *the more entertaining the film*, the less likely that viewers will notice.

In *The House on Sorority Row* (1983), several sorority sisters kill their house mother. Her lunatic son (who, unknown to the sisters, lives secreted in attic), sees his mother's murder, and sets about killing the sisters during a graduation party. At one point, Jeanie runs into the kitchen after being attacked outside, and awaits Katey's return from the party in another room.[5] Someone breaks a glass pane in the back door and reaches in. Jeanie runs — not to the party where it's safe, but upstairs to the second floor. The psycho chases her. Jeanie runs into the bathroom.

I have never seen a sorority house with such a bathroom. The house looked like a normal residential house from the outside. But this bathroom has multiple toilet stalls. Multiple showers. Concrete cinder block walls. *In a residential house?* [Figure 7.5.]

This house also has a coke machine. A pay phone in the hallway. A garage so big it

Figure 7.5 — *The House on Sorority Row.* Jeanie (Robin Meloy) rushes down the upstairs hall of a normal house, then turns and runs into an institutional bathroom, complete with cinder block walls and multiple toilet stalls!

looks like a barn. A basement with an industrial sized boiler. This place looks like a cross between a suburban residential house and an institutional building. Yet *The House on Sorority Row* is so entertaining—visually stylish, with strong characters, superior writing and acting, and energetic pacing—that I didn't notice any of these oddities until after multiple viewings.

Terror (British 1978) is another film that's so entertaining, one fails to notice its gaping plot holes and glaring spatial discontinuities. Such as when Viv and Susie see blood dripping through a ceiling, and Susie climbs *two* flights of stairs to investigate the source of the blood, ignoring the middle floor, and finding the spilled paint on the third floor.[6]

Sound editing can help unify space. Consider a scene in which Joe and Mary converse. Shot 1 depicts Joe talking. Shot 2 depicts Mary listening, with Joe's dialog heard in Mary's shot. This *dialog overlap* (1) helps unify the two shots, and (2) shows us Mary's immediate emotional reaction to Joe's remarks, especially if Mary is in closeup. (If Joe's emotions are more important to the scene, or if Mary's reaction should be withheld to build suspense, the filmmaker may wish to keep the camera on Joe.)

Dialog overlap should not be confused with a *sound bridge*, though the concepts "overlap." In a sound bridge, the sound from one scene intrudes into *another scene*. Either we hear the sound from the next scene before we see the visuals, or we're still hearing the sound from the previous scene, though the next scene's visuals have already begun.

In *The Jar* (1984), Paul is sitting at home, watching TV. A documentary about ants. He absentmindedly spins a glass on his coffee table. Suddenly, he is in a bucolic playground setting. Children are riding a hand-spun carousel. We *hear children playing*. A little girl approaches Paul and extends her hand. Paul takes it. Then he is back in his living room, watching TV. Yet we *still hear children playing*. Aesthetically, this sound bridge suggests that, though Paul is in his living room, his thoughts are still at the playground.

This sound bridge also links the two scenes. Not spatially, but dramatically. Living room and playground remain separate spaces, yet Paul travels (mentally, psychically, spiritually?) between the two. *Mise-en-scène* reinforces this connection. An insert shot of the spinning glass prefigures the spinning carousel. Is this glass a catalyst for Paul's mental wanderings? Or is the glass a symbolic foreshadowing? We don't know. We probably can't know. Such ambiguity is what makes *The Jar* a horror *art* film.

Because editing can construct space, it can also *mislead* audiences by constructing a *false space*. In *Prom Night* (1980), an ax-wielding psycho chases Wendy through the deserted areas of a high school.[7] Wendy runs into a storage room. She cowers behind the door, near the hinges, away from the door's small window. We hear a *creaking noise*. Like tiptoeing footsteps. Wendy turns her head expectantly as we...

Cut to the empty hallway *on this noise*. Because the noise *overlaps* both shots, we infer that the sound source (the killer?) is near both spaces. It *sounds* like the killer is somewhere in the hallway, close to the storage room.

Cut back to Wendy in the storage room. A closeup emphasizes her fear. The *creaking noise* continues. Is the killer out there? And coming closer?

Cut to Wendy's hand reaching for the doorknob, to hold the door shut. To prevent whoever is outside from entering the storage room.

Cut to the door's other side, as seen from the hallway. Is this the killer's POV? The frame is not moving, yet it *might* be the killer's POV.

Cut back to Wendy, whimpering. Listening to the *creaking noise.*

Crosscut to the school's empty parking lot. Although this shot is brief, it implies the passage of time.[8]

Cut back to Wendy. How long has she been hiding in the storage room? A long time? Long enough for the killer, or whoever was *creaking* out in the hallway, to have left? Wendy is crying, standing near the door's hinges, away from the doorknob. She is framed in tight medium closeup. Because of this staging and framing, we only see the door's hinged side. Not the side that opens. We *hear a door opening!* Wendy *turns expectantly,* as if she sees the door opening!

Cut to a door opening *on this overlapping noise.* A tight shot that pulls out to reveal the killer entering...

Cut back to Wendy, cowering safely behind the door.

The *overlapping noise* fooled us! A hallway door opened. Not the storage room door. Wendy knew this, because she saw that her door remained shut. We didn't see this, because that side of her door was offscreen.

We heard a door open, saw Wendy's *reaction to that noise* (not a reaction to an opening door), then cut to the hallway door, the *noise overlapping* both shots. We'd assumed the storage room door was opening, admitting the psycho. This shocked and frightened us. Then unnerved us when we realized that we'd been misled. Editing, sound, framing, and staging had together created a false sense of space.

What became of Wendy? Well, the psycho in the hallway turns, about to leave. More *creaking noises* ensue. Then one of Wendy's dead friends slips off a shelf in the storage room, and hangs upside down before Wendy, in horror cliché fashion. Wendy screams and runs into the hallway — and into the killer's ax.

Those *creaking noises* had come from *inside* the storage room all along! Just a shelf straining under a corpse. Wendy's glances toward the door, and the creaking noise's *overlapping* of the hallway shots, had fooled us (and Wendy) into thinking the sound source was outside. *Island of Blood* (1982) similarly uses sound and editing to mislead audiences about space. Someone is killing the visitors to a deserted island. Lyn hides in an abandoned school's assembly hall at night. She *hears a door banging.* She turns expectantly...

Cut to a man *opening a door.* Is it the killer coming for Lyn? No, we soon see that he's in another building. But this *overlapping noise* had misled us. He seemed to be entering Lyn's space. This misinterpretation of space unnerves us for upcoming shocks: two more people are killed over the next five minutes. One outside a house. Another on the beach. Cut to...

Lyn looks expectantly toward the noise. (That's right, what's the source of *her* noise?) She investigates. It's only a *door banging* in the wind! Lyn and the audience are relieved. But our relief is short-lived. Soon after her happy discovery, Lyn is killed with a nail gun.

Something to ponder: Since the door noises in *Island of Blood* have separate sound sources (and so too, presumably, the creaking noises in *Prom Night*), these noises technically do not overlap shots. So are they *apparently overlapping noises* rather than the real thing? Creating an *apparent* (but false) space to mislead audiences?

In the best of the *Alien* ripoffs, *Galaxy of Terror* (1981), a group of astronauts explore a distant and hostile planet, hoping to learn what became of a previous spaceship and its crew. At one point, crewman Ranger searches for Trantor, the ship's pilot. He spots Trantor on one of the ship's monitors. She is approaching an airlock. This arouses Ranger's suspicions.

1. Cut to Ranger *running* through the ship's corridors, hurrying to Trantor.
2. Cut to Ranger *running* and *gazing ahead*.
3. Then a *POV cut* to his POV *moving* through the ship's corridors.
4. Cut to Ranger *running* and *gazing ahead*.
5. Then a *POV cut* to his POV *moving* toward a door, which slides open — and *out comes Ranger!*

We were fooled. Shot 5 wasn't a POV cut. It was an objective shot moving toward the door. But by *graphically resembling* shot 3 (which *was* Ranger's POV), shot 5 (an *apparent POV*) created a false sense of space, confusing us about Ranger's location. The aesthetic effect is to evoke Ranger's confusion and panic, and to unnerve us for upcoming shocks. It also works as a cute gag.

Ranger continues running. As before, we intercut shots of him running with his POV of corridors, until we have a *POV cut* to his POV *moving* toward a door, which slides open — and *out comes Trantor!*

This time it *was* Ranger's POV. We weren't sure, because the sequence of shots resemble the previous sequence that fooled us. Our disorientation (we can no longer trust whether Ranger's POV really is his POV) makes Trantor's entrance all the more shocking. Why *all the more*? Because it's Trantor's *corpse* who emerges from that door. She is burnt to a crisp!

Witchery (aka *La casa 4*, *Witchcraft*, Italian 1988) likewise spatially disorients viewers. Hoping to be rescued from a bewitched island, Gary shoots a flare into the night sky.

Cut to a car exploding. *It looks like the flare has landed on the mainland and blown up a car!* But a few shots later, we see that this explosion is merely a violent film on TV, being watched by a little girl. She glances out the window, and sees the flare in the night sky.

This brief disorientation may unnerve some viewers, but it's mostly a cute visual gag.

The Grudge (2004) demonstrates how *eyeline matches* can mislead audiences about the connection between two spaces. Late in the film, Karen returns to the haunted house. She hears a conversation from upstairs. She goes up. When she reaches the second floor landing, a pinkish-orange light glows on her. We hear tinkling noises and birds tweeting. Lighting and sound thus indicate a supernatural presence.

Karen sees Peter conversing on a cell phone. He glances in Karen's direction, but appears not to see her. We know Peter is dead, so this must be his ghost. He enters Toshio's bedroom. Toshio, the little ghost boy, is playing on the floor. He looks up at Karen (in off-screen space), creating an *eyeline match*.

Cut to a closeup of Karen, startled that Toshio apparently sees her. (Karen watches both ghosts throughout this scene, establishing her own eyeline matches with them. But we know that she sees them. The nagging question — raised by *their* eyeline matches — is do *they* see *her*?) [Figure 7.6.]

Cut to a medium shot of Peter, following Toshio's gaze, establishing his own *eyeline match* with Karen (in offscreen space). Now apparently he sees her too [Figure 7.7].

Cut to a *two shot* (so called because it frames two people) with Peter in the foreground, Karen in the background. Peter is facing Karen. This staging reinforces the previous shot's eyeline match [Figure 7.8].

Cut to a medium shot of Peter, looking away from Karen (in offscreen space). It seems

Left: Figure 7.6 — *The Grudge.* Karen (Sarah Michelle Gellar) glances down at Toshio, creating an *eyeline match* to him, who is playing near Peter's feet. We then... *Right:* Figure 7.7 —...cut to Peter (Bill Pullman), who follows Toshio's gaze and forms an *eyeline match* to Karen. We then...

Left: Figure 7.8 —...cut to a *two shot,* from behind Peter's head. He is facing Karen. This staging reinforces our sense that he sees her. We then... *Right:* Figure 7.9 —...cut to Peter, who averts his gaze, *breaking his eyeline match* to Karen. But he will later, in the same shot, turn back and reestablish the eyeline match, which he reinforces by walking toward Karen.

he doesn't see her. So what *was* he looking at? But then he looks back at Karen, creating *another eyeline match.* This is reinforced in that he walks toward Karen. *Does* he see her? [Figure 7.9.]

Cut to a medium shot of Karen, looking at Peter (in offscreen space), cringing, frightened that he apparently sees her.

Cut to a *three shot,* Karen in the foreground, Peter and Toshio in the background. Peter looks away from Karen, down at Toshio, who *continues watching* Karen.[9] Does Toshio see Karen, but Peter does not? But then Peter turns and *stares intently* at Karen. Actor Bill Pullman's performance thus reinforces his previous eyeline matches.

Cut to a closeup of Karen, glancing down at Toshio (in offscreen space).

Cut to Toshio looking up at Karen, as Peter closes the door on him. Peter looks away from Karen, breaking his eyeline match. Implying that he never saw her.

In subsequent shots, Peter enters Kayako's bedroom. Karen follows him, satisfied that he doesn't see her. Peter reads Kayako's diary. Karen kneels beside Peter, watching him. Intent to learn his secrets. A photo falls from the diary. Both Peter and Karen reach for the photo. They *bump shoulders!* Each pulls back. Apparently, they felt each other. Peter rubs his shoulder, not looking at Karen. Karen stands up.

Cut to a medium shot of Peter, glancing up, establishing an *eyeline match* with Karen (in offscreen space). Now that he's *felt* her, does he *see* her? He stands up, maintaining his eyeline match.

Cut to a medium closeup of Karen, watching Peter arise (in offscreen space).

Cut to a *two shot*, Karen in the foreground, Peter in the background. His eyes directed at her. As if he sees her.[10] Peter approaches Karen, who backs away.

Cut to Karen, watching him. Peter enters the frame, his hand raised, as if about to touch Karen. She steps aside. Peter continues past Karen, his hand reaching toward a bulletin board that was behind Karen.

Essentially, this scene establishes two overlapping spaces: Karen's contemporary reality, and a supernatural realm wherein ghosts relive the past. While Karen observes the ghosts, trying to learn the cause for the hauntings, audiences are kept wondering whether the ghosts see Karen. Do the ghosts look toward Karen because they see her? Or because they sense her presence? Or is it a coincidence? (As when Peter reaches for the bulletin board.) The evidence shifts back and forth, creating uncertainty, anxiety, suspense, and fear.

It *seems* that Toshio sees Karen, and that Peter either senses Karen, or trusts Toshio's instincts. But we're never sure. Peter's eyeline matches keep forming and breaking, unnerving audiences who think they finally understand, only to realize they were wrong again. These ambiguous eyeline matches are reinforced by the staging and performances of the actors.

Let's be clear: an *eyeline match* "matches" different shots. A character in one shot looks at something in *another* shot. (It doesn't matter which shot comes first.) The term does not refer to a character looking at something in the *same* shot.

The Kuleshov Effect

In the 1920s, Soviet filmmaker Lev Kuleshov produced an editing experiment, the result of which still bears his name. In one scene, he intercut a shot of actor Ivan Mozzhukhin looking into offscreen space, with a shot of a bowl of soup. In another scene of this same film, a shot of Mozzhukhin looking offscreen was followed by a shot of a woman in a coffin. In still another scene, a shot of Mozzhukhin looking offscreen was followed by a shot of a little girl playing.

After seeing the film, the audience marveled at Mozzhukhin's acting ability, at "the heavy pensiveness of his mood over the forgotten soup ... the deep sorrow with which he looked on the dead woman ... the light, happy smile with which he surveyed the girl at play."[11] They failed to notice that it was the *exact same shot* of Mozzhukhin. Viewers had interpreted the actor's facial expression based on what he appeared to be watching.

We saw the Kuleshov Effect at work in *Hell of the Living Dead*. Shots of Lia staring into offscreen space were intercut with shots of funerals, mourning, and disease among the villagers. This not only creates the illusion that Lia shares space with the village, but the juxtapositions of shots suggest specific interpretations of Lia's facial expressions. Lia observes death and disease, and we infer compassion, pity, and distaste in her face.

Some film theorists define the Kuleshov Effect as a demonstration of editing's ability to unify space. And it does do that. All three of Kuleshov's scenes, by juxtaposing certain shots on POV cuts, create the illusion that Muzzhukhin is, at various times, in proximity to the soup, the coffin, and the girl.

But what most impresses me is the Kuleshov Effect's ability to enhance an actor's performance. It alone cannot perfect a performance, but it can improve it. Low-budget filmmakers casting amateur actors, especially, should appreciate that. (Tip: the K.E. fills in the "emotional blanks" on an actor's face. The more an actor talks, the fewer blanks there are to fill. The K.E. can impose a wider range of emotions on a silent and subtle performance, than on a scenery-chewing blabbermouth. So if you've cast a lousy actor, less is more.)

The 180° Rule

The *180° rule* (aka *180° system*) is an editing technique that *informs the audience where everything is in relation to each other onscreen*, thus strengthening their sense of a spatial unity among the shots.

Imagine a film set. Draw a circle around it. Then draw a straight line through the circle, bisecting it into two semicircles. The line should run through the scene's main action, i.e., the event being filmed. This line is called the *180° line, center line, line of action,* or *axis of action*. The director then keeps the camera in one of the semicircles. Subsequent shots are filmed from anywhere within that semicircle, but never from the other one. The camera must not cross that line. That is the 180° rule.

How does this rule work? Imagine two actors conversing. They occupy the line of action. The camera stays on one side of that line. As a result, all shots of Joe have him looking leftward, and all shots of Mary have her looking rightward. They look in *opposite directions,* so we know where they are in relation to each other: they're *facing each other*. But if the camera crossed this line, shooting Joe from one side and Mary from the other, we'd have closeups of them looking in the *same direction*. That would be confusing, no?

Why 180° instead of some other number? Think back to geometry. A circle has 360°. A semicircle has 180°. An angle on a straight line also has 180°.

The 180° line can be repositioned during the scene. Directors may do so because things change. Actors walk about or exit the scene. New actors enter.

Traditionally, directors begin a scene with an *establishing shot* that is widely framed and depicts all actors and the entire set. This is so the audience knows where everyone is. The scene then commences along a 180° line. If the director wishes to reposition this line, this new line is often preceded by a *reestablishing shot*, so that viewers can reorient themselves to the actors' new positions.

Establishing and reestablishing shots should not be confused with *master shots*, which is when an entire scene is filmed in one uninterrupted take, usually widely framed.

Like all cinematic tools, the 180° rule is useful, but can be broken for aesthetic reasons. Sometimes it's desirable to disorient audiences. When a group of people are attacked in a horror film, breaking the 180° rule can convey the situation's chaos and the characters' panic.

Jacob's Ladder (1990) opens in the Mekong Delta during the Vietnam War. Several American soldiers are sitting in front of, or inside, an open hut. They are roughly aligned in a row, joking and complaining. They are all filmed from one side of that row. The scene thus establishes and obeys a 180° line running the length of the soldiers.

Cut to Jacob, off by himself, shitting in the brush. It's not clear where he is in relation to the other soldiers. Cut to a wider shot of Jacob, getting up.

Cut to a shot of some soldiers, *looking rightward*. One shouts, "Hey professor, how many times can you shit in an hour?" His voice overlaps the preceding shot of Jacob, which helps to spatially unify the soldiers' and Jacob's shots.

Cut to Jacob, *walking and looking leftward*. He laughs good-naturedly at the soldier's remark. By responding, he further unifies the space between his and the soldiers' shots.

Four shots follow. Two shots of soldiers, *looking rightward*, talking about and to Jacob. Intercut with two shots of Jacob, *walking and looking leftward*, first in a medium shot, then in medium closeup, suggesting that he is nearing the soldiers [Figures 7.10, 7.11].

Cut to the soldiers, *looking rightward*. Jacob enters the shot, *walking leftward*. This is

Figure 7.10—*Jacob's Ladder*. Two soldiers. The one on the left is looking rightward, creating an *eyeline match* to...

Figure 7.11—...Jacob (Tim Robbins), who is walking and looking leftward, creating his own *eyeline match* to the soldiers. The juxtaposition of these shots establishes a *180° line* from the soldiers to Jacob; we know where each is in relation to the other.

the first time Jacob and the soldiers share a frame. Yet we already knew where they were in relation to each other. The soldiers were to Jacob's right. Jacob was to the soldiers' left.

Don't get confused. Jacob was looking leftward — to the viewer's left. Which puts the soldiers to Jacob's right. Left, right. The important thing is that the viewer knows where each is in relation to the other. The scene established a 180° line extending along the row of soldiers and to Jacob in the brush, to the soldiers' left. Always, the camera stayed on one side of this line. Had it broken the line, we'd have seen Jacob walking and looking leftward in some shots, rightward in other shots. When Jacob finally entered the soldiers' frame, we'd wonder what crazy jigsaw path had brought him there.

Yes, I know Jacob was approaching the camera in a *head-on shot*. Maybe you think he was looking *forward* at the soldiers, not *leftward*? Look closer. As Jacob approaches, his body edges leftward. He glances leftward. As if to counteract the head-on shot, the staging of actor Tim Robbins reaffirms the previously established 180° line. It's that important.

POV cutting further spatially unifies these shots. The soldiers are looking rightward into offscreen space, followed by their POV shots of Jacob.

After Jacob joins the soldiers, the 180° line remains intact until the enemy attacks from the brush. Then the 180° line breaks down. The ensuing shots of the battle are taken from all directions, angles, and distances. The aesthetic intent, obviously, is to evoke the chaos of war, and the disorientation and panic felt by the soldiers.

Sometimes the 180° line is disregarded not for aesthetic reasons, but simply because it's unnecessary. We know from the scene's setup where everyone is and must remain. For instance, A and B are in a canoe, floating down a lake. B is sitting behind A. The path of the canoe would normally form the 180° line. But let's ignore all lines. Shot 1 shows A from one side of the canoe, so that A appears to be *moving left to right*. Shot 2 shows B from the other side of the canoe, so that B appears to be *moving right to left*.

Has the canoe split in half, each character going in a different direction? Of course not. It may look that way onscreen, but because we know the story and setup (the seating in canoes), we assume that both characters are still in the same canoe, heading in the same direction. We are not disoriented.

In *Kiss Daddy Goodbye* (aka *Revenge of the Zombie*, 1981), two creepy, psychic kids, Patrick and Nell, work to reanimate their father's corpse. They are interrupted by the sound of a car parking outside their house.

Cut to an *establishing shot* of a car parking off the road. A shot of the *car's left and rear*.

Cut to Patrick entering the living room, looking *leftward* out the window. We assume he's looking at the car, in offscreen space.

Cut to the car outside. Because this shot follows that of Patrick looking out the window, we assume it's a *POV cut* on Patrick's POV. The view, again, is of the *car's left and rear*.

Cut to the car, closer in, the leftward POV more pronounced. A real estate broker exits the car.

We continue crosscutting from Patrick (joined by Nell) in the living room, *looking left*, and their POV (we assume) of *car's left and rear*. But then the broker approaches the house by walking toward the *car's front*. Apparently, the car is facing the house. This means that Patrick and Nell are seeing the car's front end. So why is their "POV" of the car's rear?

Because it's not their POV. It only looks that way due to sloppy editing. Sloppy because:

(1) shots of the kids looking out the window, followed by shots of the car, implies a POV cut that isn't, and (2) the kids are filmed from one side of the 180° line extending from their living room to the car, and the car was filmed from the line's other side.

If the car were visibly facing the house, this scene might have been less disorienting. As with the canoe and its riders, we'd see where the house was in relation to the car, so we'd make allowances if the camera crossed the line. But in the *establishing shot*, when the car pulls off the road, the kids' house is hidden by trees, down a hill. We see roofs, but I wasn't sure if they were the kids' house or neighbors' roofs.

Because this "establishing shot" fails to establish the space, I relied on the POV cuts and 180° line, which mistakenly convinced me that I was seeing neighbors' roofs.

I assume the director shot from behind the car because the real estate broker would not have been visible if the camera shot him from Patrick's window. The broker would have been up the hill and behind the trees, out of view. Still, it's confusing and disorienting when the broker *approaches* Patrick's house by seemingly *walking away* from Patrick's house. A disorientation that fails to aesthetically support the film's story, characters, or themes.

Increasingly, films are *intentionally disorienting*, ignoring the 180° rule, with quick cuts and a moving camera depicting events from every conceivable angle and distance. Alleged reasons for this trend include MTV's influence, viewers' diminishing attention spans, and the notion that frenzied, haphazard editing imbues a film with energy and excitement.[12] Action and horror films are especially prone to embrace this style. Sometimes it works. Other times it's an insecure director trying to hide a mess by packaging poor substance in a slick style.

Editor and film teacher Richard D. Pepperman writes: "Over-cutting 'forms' seem to have taken hold. I find that I often comment to students that there is something seriously wrong if their projects play as a trailer tempting me to see the film, when it turns out that what I am screening is the film. It is also alarming that such methods frequently (and desperately) rely on voice-over narration and/or plenty of dialogue to keep the viewer from total bewilderment. ... the arbitrariness of this overall, and predictable, approach has led to a visibly random assembly of selected shots within individually constructed scenes.... Take a look at a scene. Take note of the selected shots and their ordered construction. Then watch it again without the audio. I think you'll start to 'see' that the images don't quite work when ambiance, dialogue, music and sound effects aren't there to assist the ongoing moments. That is, the shot selection is essentially (and mistakenly) leaning on the words to steer the choices."[13]

It's been said that a film's story should be clear even with the sound turned off. That film is visual storytelling, unlike a play or novel. This is what Pepperman means when he complains of modern films leaning too heavily on the words to make sense.

It may seem that the 180° rule is a shooting technique, having little to do with editing. *Au contraire!* While it's true that directors may plan shots with a 180° line in mind, the line itself is created in the editing room. Recall the scene in *Hell of the Living Dead*, where the native child looks *rightward*, forming an eyeline match with Lia, who looks *leftward*. The juxtaposition of these shots creates a 180° line extending from the child to Lia, so that we know where each is in relation to the other: Lia is to the child's left

This scene also demonstrates that a 180° line can be created without an establishing shot. The eyeline match alone is enough to spatially unify these shots, and create a line of action from the child to Lia. Consider that these shots were filmed thousands of miles and eight years apart, and you'll appreciate editing's power to reconstruct both space and time.

Constructing Time

Editing can *expand, contract, or rearrange time.* Story time and screen time rarely coincide. A 90 minute film rarely shows 90 consecutive minutes in a character's life.

Screen time can be *lengthened* to create suspense. In *Shadowzone* (1990), a man in a NASA funded experiment died when put into Deep Sleep Level 31 F. So that NASA won't stop their funding, the scientists attempt a coverup. Dr. Van Fleet assures Captain Hickock, the NASA inspector, that the man died from natural causes. (His head exploded, but it's not obvious, because he's been autopsied.) Hickock insists the scientists prove their project's safety by putting another man into deep sleep. The scientists agree.

While Hickock is in the sleep lab, observing the second test subject, the scientists in the control room anxiously watch both Hickock and the passing seconds. The first man died 35 to 40 seconds into deep sleep. If the scientists don't take the second man out of deep sleep before then, his head too may explode. But if they do so before Hickock is satisfied, the captain's suspicions will be aroused.

"Ten seconds," Wiley says. But my VCR's counter says it's 23 seconds since the man went into deep sleep, not 10. This temporal discrepancy continues throughout the scene, at the following inconsistent ratios: 25/61, 30/68, 40/110, 45/121. When Wiley says 45 seconds have passed in *story time* (5 to 10 seconds into the danger zone), in *screen time* 121 seconds have passed. The man's head should have exploded over a minute ago.

The aesthetic intent is to build suspense. Audiences are told that horror will strike in 35 to 40 seconds. Soon enough to *instill* suspense. Then that 40 seconds in story time is lengthened to 110 seconds onscreen, to *extend* that suspense.

Does this technique build suspense? Extending screen time in "ticking bomb" scenarios is so common, I suspect that by now many viewers feel jaded and/or cheated, thinking: "Yeah right, ten seconds. How long, really? An hour? C'mon, the guy should be dead by now."

You want to jolt an audience? Surprise them by contracting the screen time. Tell them a bomb will explode in 60 seconds. Then do it 5 seconds later.

Editing can also lengthen screen time by repeating different shots of the same event, or even by repeating the same shot. Shot 2 overlaps (i.e., repeats) the event in shot 1. Aesthetically, *overlapping edits* can (1) emphasize an event's importance, or (2) satirize through exaggeration its unimportance,[14] or (3) allow audiences to better assimilate and enjoy a quick event.

Overlapping edits of an exciting, but quick, incident is an action film cliché. A car or building explodes, and the audience is treated to repeated shots of the explosion. The filmmaker wants to make sure we enjoy every detail. Special effects explosions are expensive, so it'd be a shame not to see every bit of flying debris — and from every conceivable angle.

Overlapping edits and slow motion photography can function in aesthetically similar (if not identical) ways. Both may instill suspense by extending screen time *before* a horrific event. Both can heighten the horror by extending screen time *during* a grisly event.

Horror films usually prefer slow motion, because it lets viewers study every gory detail, some of which are missed if an incident passes too quickly. The infamous eye-gouging scene in *Zombi 2* (aka *Gli ultimi zombi*, Italian 1979) takes its own sweet time. The zombie grabs Paola's hair, and while she screams, *slowly* pulls her eye toward the wooden shard. (Whether it's slow staging or slow motion photography, the aesthetic effect is identical.) But slow motion can sap energy and dynamism from a scene, so actions films normally favor overlapping edits.

It's not either/or. In *Contamination* (aka *Alien Contamination*, Italian 1980), a biohazard team member lifts an alien egg in slow motion. When he is standing upright, the egg bursts in slow motion, spewing viral alien egg fluid. Consider this sequence:

1. Closeup shot of the egg in his hands, bursting in slow motion.
2. Cut to a medium closeup of another team member, being sprayed with egg fluid.
3. Cut to a closeup of the first team member, covering his face.
4. Cut to a *repeat* of the egg bursting, this time as a medium long shot.
5. Cut to a *repeat* of the first team member covering his face. As in shot 3, this is a closeup. But now it's a profile of his face, rather than a mostly frontal view.

Aesthetically, the overlapping action and slow motion *doubly* extend the moment of the egg spewing its fluid upon these men, causing their organs and blood vessels to burst, and their intestines to erupt from their bodies. Horror audiences enjoy seeing gory details in slow motion so much, they want second helpings.

Slow motion and overlapping edits likewise reinforce each other in *The Redeemer* (aka *Class Reunion Massacre*, 1978). Jane is running through the woods, escaping a killer. Consider this sequence:

1. Jane runs down a hill, away from the high school.
2. Cut to Jane running toward us. Slow motion ensues *during the shot* just as Jane sees something ahead. (All subsequent shots are slow motion, except shot 9.) Jane screams, still running, and *arrives at some tall grass* in the foreground.
3. A POV cut to Jane's POV of the killer, lifting his shotgun. Jane's screams *overlap* into this shot, spatially unifying it with the previous shot.
4. Cut to a *repeat* of Jane running toward the tall grass, which she *arrives at a second time*. This time she approaches the grass from a slightly different direction.
5. Cut to Jane's POV of the killer, lifting his shotgun. Shot 3 was a medium shot, but this is a closeup. Yet Jane is not closer to him, judging from shot 4. Perhaps he looms larger in Jane's POV because his menace looms larger within Jane's mind.
6. Cut to a *repeat* of Jane running toward the tall grass, which she *arrives at a third time*. The staging is similar to shot 4, but again, it's a different shot. Jane's right arm is straighter.
7. Cut to an extreme closeup of the killer's finger on the shotgun trigger.
8. Cut to a *repeat* of Jane running toward the tall grass, which she *arrives at a fourth time*. Although this time, she almost begins at the grass. She screams, as in shot 2. Storywise, we have returned to shot 2. The staging is similar so this may be a continuation of shot 2, but I think not.

9. Cut to the shotgun muzzle blasting. This is the only normal speed shot in this sequence. Slow motion was likely avoided to emphasize the energy of the blast.
10. Cut to Jane running through the grass, sinking to the ground. This seems to continue shot 8. No more overlapping action.

Aside from extending the horror of the killing, slow motion and overlapping edits lend a hauntingly surreal and tragic tone to Jane's death, in keeping with *The Redeemer*'s supernatural tale of dark angelic judgment.[15]

Screen time is often *shortened* to remove the boring parts. A common mistake of many beginner filmmakers is *overlong expository shots*. Joe is in his kitchen. He tells Mary over the phone that he will see her at work. We cut to Joe exit his house, locking the front door, walking to his car, walking, walking, walking, finally reaches the car, opens the door, gets inside, settles in, puts his briefcase and coffee here and there, buckles up, turns on the engine, backs out of the driveway, turns in the street, slowly, carefully, slowly, and finally drives off down the road.

This establishes where Joe lives, but it's boring. Boring may be aesthetically appropriate if you're doing an indie film about mundane lives. *Clockwatchers* (1997) has brilliantly comedic and informative "mundane" scenes. Of course, by finding humor in minutia, the scenes cease to be boring.

But in a horror (or most any other genre) film, a better choice is usually: Joe is in his kitchen. He tells Mary over the phone that he will see her at work. Cut to Joe opening his car door. The house is in the background, establishing where Joe lives. Cut to Joe's car driving on the road.

This is termed *elliptical editing*. That's when a cut omits story time and implied events. Such as Joe's long walk to his car. If we see him at his car, we can assume he walked there. No need to show it.

Why the term? You know what an *ellipsis* is, right? It's those three dots that denote the omission of words or sentences. Same concept. Joe's locking the front door, walking to his car, etc., have all been omitted by an ellipsis.

In *Hospital Massacre* (1982), one scene opens with the camera moving across an office to Suzy, a nurse, who is typing at her desk. The frame continues past Suzy, so that we see three doors to Suzy's right. Doors 1 and 2 are shut. Door 3, the one nearest to the back wall, is open, revealing supply shelves. The frame moves in on door 1. The door edges open. A hand emerges, wearing a rubber surgical glove. The psycho is hiding behind door 1— ready to kill Suzy!

Cut to door 4, nurse Nancy opening it and looking in. She greets Suzy.

Cut to Suzy at her desk. She greets Nancy.

Cut to Nancy, who invites Suzy for coffee.

Cut to door 1. The hand closes the door. The killer apparently prefers to strike when his victim is alone. We hear Suzy decline Nancy's invitation.

Cut to Suzy, who explains that she's busy. (Her dialog overlapping from the previous shot.) More cuts to Nancy, Suzy, and Nancy again, who leaves and shuts door 4.

Cut to Suzy, who resumes typing.

Cut to a closeup of Suzy's fingers, typing. Pay attention now. This *insert shot* functions as an *elliptical edit*.

Cut to Suzy, typing at her desk. She gets up and opens door 2. Tension mounts. Will she open door 1? The killer is behind door 1, right? But instead, Suzy goes to door 3, the one that's open. She shuts door 3 — *revealing the killer!* He's been standing against the back wall, hidden behind door 3.

How and when did he get there?

Presumably, he snuck out from behind door 1 and hid behind door 3 while Suzy was typing. Remember that closeup of Suzy's fingers? She was focused on her typing and so were we, so we didn't see the killer sneak past her. That closeup only lasted a second or two onscreen, but who's to say it didn't occupy an hour of story time? Much like that crosscut to the parking lot while Wendy was hiding in the storage room in *Prom Night*.

Hospital Massacre and *Prom Night* demonstrate how elliptical editing can fool viewers by giving a threat adequate *time* to shift locations. *Prom Night's* elliptical edit suggests the killer *had time* to leave the hallway, and so Wendy may be safe. *Hospital Massacre's* elliptical edit is a quick insert shot, so we assume the killer has *not had time* to change hiding places. But in neither case can we actually *know* how much time has elapsed during the ellipsis, making it easier for filmmakers to mislead, shock, and unnerve us.

Left unexplained: Why doesn't the killer, after emerging from behind door 1, kill Suzy right away? Why does he instead move from door 1 to door 3, wait for Suzy to find him, and then kill her? Because he's a slasher, that's why!

Apart from its elliptical editing, this scene is instructive for its spatial construction. Suzy and Nancy are never in the same shot. Also, door 4 (Nancy's door) has a different style than the three doors beside Suzy. The actresses *might* have performed days apart, on different sets. Yet the editing spatially unifies them. Nancy looks rightward, and Suzy leftward, each at an angle that's appropriate to where the other is standing or sitting. Thus, there are eyeline matches and a 180° line.

Psychomania has what may be termed an "elliptical camera move"; a moving frame that functions as an ellipsis. The police have set a trap for The Living Dead biker gang, unaware that the bikers truly are the "living dead." Abby is the bait. The bikers erroneously believe that Abby has joined their ranks by killing herself and arising from death.

The shot begins with Abby lying on a morgue table, feigning death. The camera moves up, revealing a police inspector and constable standing over Abby. Four empty shelves (used to hold corpses) are behind the inspector. The camera pans to reveal a police sergeant standing by another wall. The camera continues panning. All is silent. The camera pans past empty walls and comes full circle to the morgue shelves. Which now hold the corpses of the sergeant, constable, and inspector. The camera moves down to reveal the empty morgue table. Abby is gone.

This shot opened with the police and Abby in the morgue, awaiting The Living Dead. By the time the camera has panned the room, The Living Dead have arrived, killed the police, and taken Abby. This didn't happen *during* the pan. We never heard a struggle. Rather, the pan has omitted this incident. Seeing the dead police, and Abby gone, we can infer what happened. No need to see it.

Jump Cuts

Jump cuts compress time in a way that creates visual discontinuities. Shot 1 depicts Joe slumped in a bar. Shot 2 depicts Joe ten minutes later, similar location, framed at a similar angle and distance. Maybe he's in the same bar, but because of the time shift, he now slumps lower, drunker. Or he's facing another direction. Or he's similarly staged, in a similar yet different bar. Time has passed, so Joe or the set (location, props, lighting) have *changed*, but because of some *similarities* in location, staging, and framing, Joe appears to have "jumped" about, from shot to shot.

Although not a horror film, *Breathless* (French 1960) is often credited with popularizing jump cuts. By juxtaposing similarly framed shots of Patricia in a moving car, filmed at different times during her ride, she and the car appear to "jump" from one street to another.

Elliptical editing seeks to avoid jump cuts when contracting story time, such as with that insert shot of Suzy's typing fingers in *Hospital Massacre*. Insert shots, cutaways, crosscuts, and reestablishment shots — all of these help to achieve smooth transitions for *invisible editing* (i.e., editing that doesn't draw attention to itself) by separating shots that would otherwise "jump" if juxtaposed.

But jump cuts have aesthetic uses. They can jolt viewers, compelling them to pay closer attention. Jump cuts can energize a scene. They can imply danger, chaos, excitement, the hurried passage of time, the surreal, or the supernatural.

In *She Creature* (2001), Lily struggles for the right words to explain to Angus, her lover, that a mermaid has psychically impregnated her with child. Lily knows it sounds crazy, so she paces before a mirror, practicing her speech. She walks about, faces various directions, rubs her face, and tests multiple speeches. Because of the jump cuts, we see Lily begin a speech, then "jump" to a spot farther back, pacing, then "jump" near the mirror, talking, then "jump" to a different speech, spoken in another tone, etc. [Figures 7.12, 7.13].

Aesthetically, this incessant "jumping" conveys Lily's anxiety and frustration in finding the right words and delivery, and the extensive amount of time which she devotes to the effort.

In *The Jar*, jump cuts evoke Paul's erratic emotional state, and his weakening connection to reality. In one shot, Paul is smiling. In the next, his smile is gone. No fading smile, just a jump from one facial expression to another. The cumulative effect of *The Jar*'s jump cuts (and other elements, such as the sound fading in and out) is that of reality dissembling.

She Creature's jump cuts were likely achieved by filming actress Carla Gugino in one long take, and then removing frames to break that single take into multiple discontinuous shots. But whereas *She Creature*'s jump cuts look intentional (because the framing is unchanged), the juxtaposed shots that create *The Jar*'s jump cuts are sometimes framed from different angles, signifying a camera move between shots. This indicates that pragmatic, rather than intentional aesthetic, reasons underlie *The Jar*'s jump cuts.

Invisible editing is expensive. To ensure smooth transitions, directors may film several master shots from different angles, followed by medium shots, closeups, and insert shots of the same scene.[16] This ensures choices in the editing room. But low-budget filmmakers (at least when shooting pricey film stock, rather than cheap videotape) may try to save money by only shooting "necessary" footage. If they foresee using a closeup, they'll forgo a master shot that might have ensured a smooth transition (i.e., without unintentional jump cuts).

The Jar's jump cuts are aesthetically reinforced by subtle changes in lighting and color hues, from shot to shot. It seems that director Bruce Tuscano used different film stocks for the same scene, or filmed on different days and was unable to recreate the previous day's lighting setup.

Again, pragmatic reasons may explain these shifting hues. Big budget films normally

Figure 7.12 —*She Creature*. Standing before a mirror, Lily (Carla Gugino) rubs her head in frustration and exhaustion. We then...

Figure 7.13 —*...jump cut* to Lily already giving a speech to the mirror. She appears to have "jumped" directly from one physical stance to another.

use only one film stock per movie, for a consistent look, unless there are *aesthetic* reasons to change the graininess, contrast, color tones, etc. over the course of a film. But low-budget filmmakers are often *financially* forced to use different film stocks in the same movie. Money can be saved with *short ends* and *recans*.[17] Or by using film stock donated by studios, manufacturers, labs, cooperatives, and arts councils. Low-budget filmmakers will use film stocks of different ASAs, from different manufacturers, producing different "looks" from scene to scene, or even shot to shot.

Happily, *The Jar*'s jump cuts and changing hues support the story's surrealism. Paul is battling demonic possession and its concomitant mental breakdown. He laments to Crystal, his neighbor and nascent girlfriend, that he no longer knows what's real and what's imagined. Jump cuts and shifting hues effectively convey this deterioration in Paul's subjective reality. This is reinforced by the waxing and waning sound volume, and dramatic events displacing Paul into various in expressionistic locales.

The Jar demonstrates the power of *pragmatic aesthetics*. The jump cuts and shifting color hues may have been *pragmatically motivated* by cost considerations, but they *aesthetically serve* the story, characters, and themes.

Montages

Story time can be shortened with a *montage*, which is a series of shots that compress a story event. Certain montages have become clichés. In a romance film, two people fall in love, followed by shots of them running on the beach, shopping in an open market, a food fight in the kitchen, kissing by a fireplace, etc. In an action film, the hero accepts a mission, followed by a "training montage" of him running a military obstacle course, practicing karate, shooting at a pistol range, jogging in the rain, etc. Or before combat, we see a montage of him snapping on cartridge belts, sheathing daggers, loading guns, and simultaneously twirling *two* shotguns before holstering them.

Montages condense information and story incidents into a brief time span. In *9 Lives of Mara* (2007), a beautiful montage efficiently compresses the criminal trial of a boy who killed his stepmother, believing her to be a witch. Court documents, newspaper headlines, and tagged evidentiary exhibits dissolve upon each other. Fast motion photography shows clouds speeding across the sky over the court house, to suggest the passage of time. Especially imaginative are the attorney and expert witness, animated on a sketch pad in the style of a courtroom artist.

By abridging events, montages can also suggest a character's incomplete, impressionistic view of reality. In *Rosemary's Baby* (1968), Rosemary is half drugged and asleep when a coven of Satanists watches the devil impregnate her. A surreal montage depicts Rosemary's groggy perception: distorted memories and fears, dream images and sounds of lapping water, flashes of reality as Satanists argue over whether she is awake.

In *Silent Night, Deadly Night 4: Initiation* (1990), Kim is drugged by a coven of witches, fueling a similar montage of supernatural and surreal images; a fusion of Kim's memories, fears, and distorted views of reality.

Montage is a French word. It's been translated as "putting together" or simply "editing." But like many *cinema* terms, it sounds better *en Français, non?*

Flashbacks and Flashforwards

Flashbacks and *flashforwards* rearrange time by inserting shots of past or future events into the present story, often to inform an audience about what *has* happened or *will* happen. Or what *might* have happened or *might* yet happen. Flashbacks needn't be accurate; they can depict a character's false memories or lies. Flashforwards can depict predictions or hopes that never materialize. Inaccurate depictions of past or future events can confuse, disorient, or unnerve audiences. That's usually a good thing in horror.

In *Prom Night*, four friends (each about eleven years old) frighten Robin, a ten-year-old girl, inadvertently killing her. The proverbial slasher film "prank gone bad." We soon cut to a shot of Robin's tombstone, superimposed with "Six Years Later" and the main story begins.

The guilty children are now high school seniors, played by attractive, twentysomething actors. As they prepare for school one morning, we crosscut to a man at an undisclosed location, lurking mostly in offscreen space. We assume he's male by his voice and shadow. He has before him a list of the four guilty names: Jude, Kelly, Nick, Wendy. He phones Jude and, in a creepy voice (as if he's trying to hide his identity), he invites her to "come out and play." A rattled Jude hangs up. The man crosses her name off the list. He obviously plans revenge on Jude for killing Robin.

We know Jude is guilty because when she answers the phone, and the man says "Jude," we cut to a shot of the eleven-year-old Jude from the opening scene. This *flashback* identifies the adult Jude as one of the killers; it even inform us as to which of the children the adult Jude is.

This pattern repeats as the killer phones the other names on his list. His intended victim answers the phone, and the instant he says "Kelly" or "Wendy" we cut to a flashback shot of the young Kelly or Wendy. Thus, we know which girl is which woman. The killer also phones Nick, but Nick leaves home without answering the phone. The killer scratches Nick's name off the list with great frustration. No matter. Nick was the only boy, so this adult must be him.

It's odd that the four guilty children comprise three girls and one boy. What eleven-year-old boy plays exclusively with girls? Furthermore, they are playing a game called "killer." How many eleven-year-old girls want to play "killer"? *Prom Night* thus subordinates logic to horror's unique needs. The friends comprise three girls and one boy because, this being an exploitation film, the producers likely wanted the adult victims to be mostly beautiful young women.

Terror Train (1980) is another slasher film that opens with a "prank gone bad." At a college party, some fraternity brothers arrange for Kenny to lose his virginity. He is directed upstairs to a bedroom, where Alana, another student, awaits him. Kenny enters to find the bedroom dimly lit with flashing colored lights. A woman's silhouette is sitting in bed, obscured by bedcurtains. Alana is hiding behind the bed, encouraging Kenny to make love to her.

Kenny approaches the silhouette. "Kiss me, Kenny. Kiss me," says Alana. Kenny caresses the silhouette, which collapses, revealing itself to be a corpse. (Some of the fraternity brothers are pre-med.) Kenny "freaks out," spinning upon the bed and entangling himself, half naked, in the bedcurtains. Partygoers rush in to mock Kenny. And thus is born another vengeful, psychotic slasher.

Then begins the main story. The guilty students throw a graduation party on a chartered train. Kenny sneaks aboard, and the body count mounts. At the film's end, he reveals himself to Alana, the two of them alone in the caboose. He grabs Alana's hands, draws her close and says, "Kiss me, Alana." We cut to a flashback of Alana saying "Kiss me, Kenny," from the opening scene. "Kiss me," Kenny adds, followed by another flashback of Alana saying "Kiss me."

When they do kiss, Kenny "freaks out" again. He shrieks and stares at his hands. We cut to a flashback of him shrieking and staring at his hands after caressing the corpse. The present day and flashback shots are *graphically matched* in that actor Derek McKinnon is similarly staged in both shots. This graphic match further connects present day events with the past.[18]

Terror Train's flashbacks link Kenny's current psychosis with his previous trauma. They are informative in that they explain (or at least emphasize — for we already know) his motivation for slaughter. These flashbacks refer to previously established information.

Other slasher films spring sudden flashbacks on audiences, "out of the blue," to explain the motivations of someone who is arbitrarily revealed to be the killer. In *House of Death* (1982), a popular coach declines an invitation from some high school kids to go partying that night by the river. Midway into the film, it looks like he's killed in his garage. (We don't know; the scene is depicted in shadows and silhouettes.) At film's end, after racking up a body count, the slasher is revealed to be the coach. *Everyone is shocked! How could such a nice guy slaughter so many "slutty" teenagers?!*

Answer: We *flashback* to the coach as a boy, living in a bordello where his mother works. Well, that explains everything! Expose a child to sex, of course he'll grow up to butcher sexually active teens. This information comes as a total surprise, but it makes sense. In a slasher film logic sort of way.

Flashforwards can offer hope for the future, or a dark sense of impending doom as an inevitable fate closes in. Or they can surprise or mislead viewers when a foretold ending turns out differently. This can be done by showing future scenes that move in one direction, without revealing the outcome.

100 Tears (2009) begins with Gurdy, a murderous psycho applying clown makeup in a dimly lit room. Opening credits are superimposed. When the credits are finished, the scene goes black. A young woman's voice screams for help. A gunshot resounds. The woman screams, "He shot himself!" Who, Gurdy?

"A week earlier" is superimposed, and the main story begins.

This opening scene is a *flashforward* from that main story, which begins (a week earlier) with two tabloid reporters tracking Gurdy for a story on serial killers. By film's end, the reporters have tracked Gurdy to a warehouse massacre, where they meet the woman who was screaming for help in the opening scene. But by now we know the woman is Gurdy's psychotic daughter, and her screams for help were a trap. Nor had Gurdy shot himself.

I surmise two aesthetic intents for *100 Tears*'s flashforward. (1) To *instill suspense or pique our interest from the start.* Novels do this too. Rather than begin with a boring expository scene, you hook the reader with a bang, then go back and follow the path to that bang. (2) To surprise the audience. *The girl was not a victim. It was a trap. Surprise!*

100 Tears is an energetic gorefest, but its flashforward doesn't entirely work. It does pique our interest, but it doesn't instill suspense. Nor does it surprise viewers. Most will have forgotten the opening scene by film's end. It's not significant or impressive enough to stick in anyone's mind.

Some might suggest the opening scene is the present day, and most of the film is one long flashback. But I believe the opening functions as a flashforward, because it's brief. The reporters' investigations are the meat of the film. Their story even contains its own flashbacks, dramatizing Gurdy's origins as told by a carnival dwarf to the reporters.

Parallel Editing

Parallel editing crosscuts two or more story events that are dramatically or thematically connected. Each event has a beginning, middle, and end; otherwise it's mere crosscutting rather than parallel editing. The events are often concurrent. The classic example of parallel editing is crosscutting between a person who is under attack, and someone hurrying to the rescue. Here the events are concurrent, spatially separated, and dramatically connected. The aesthetic intent is to create suspense: Will the rescuer arrive in time?

The two reporters in *100 Tears* form a temporal core, creating a narrative timeline from which flashbacks and flashforwards emanate. Other films are temporally ambiguous, rearranging time in innovative ways. *Pulp Fiction* (1994) and *Memento* (2000) are two non-horror examples. Among horror films, *The Redeemer* is noteworthy for its temporally ambiguous parallel editing.

The Redeemer crosscuts between two related stories, which I'll call The Sermon and The Punishment. In The Sermon, Chris, a young boy who is an angel of death, emerges from a lake. His shadow flickers over a priest asleep in bed. An extra thumb appears on the priest's left hand, empowering or authorizing him to punish sinners. Chris rides a bus to church. There, the priest gives a sermon, warning of the retribution that awaits sinners. He concludes by saying: "Those who have sinned have met with the angel of the Lord's vengeance." Outside, Chris tells the priest not to worry; everything will be okay. The priest returns home to find his extra thumb gone, his hand normal. Back at the lake, Chris now has an extra thumb, indicating that he has reclaimed the powers loaned to the priest. Chris reenters the lake.

In The Punishment, the priest (in disguise) enters an abandoned high school. He cuts out six sinners' photos from a yearbook. We crosscut to the sinners at home and at work, preparing for their high school reunion. They drive to the high school. There the priest kills them, one by one.

The Redeemer begins crosscutting the stories *after* Chris empowers the priest. As Chris rides to church, we crosscut to the priest at the high school.(*When* is this? Isn't he asleep in bed or preparing for church?) During his sermon, the priest condemns various sins. We crosscut to him *still* at the high school, cutting student photos from the yearbook, then crosscut to those students as adults preparing for their class reunion.[19] (Again, *when* is this happening?)

The Redeemer's two stories can't be concurrent, because The Sermon occurs over several *hours*, whereas The Punishment happens over several *days*. Furthermore, the priest can only kill while angelically empowered. (We see his extra thumb gripping a gun.) Yet throughout his brief empowerment, he's either in bed, going to church, or in the pulpit. For that same reason, the killings can't be flashbacks or flashforwards.

Is there an explanation for *The Redeemer*'s temporal ambiguity? I can think of four. (1) God and angels are said to exist "outside of space and time." Maybe Chris enabled the priest to exit our space/time continuum, through some supernatural wormhole, and the priest punished the sinners *during* his sermon. (2) The Punishment is the priest's dream fantasy. He dreamt of Chris that morning, and continues fantasizing during his sermon. (3) The editing is intentionally vague and muddled, hoping to create a "supernatural sensibility." (4) There is no explanation other than sloppy, thoughtless editing. But *The*

Redeemer is so entertaining, memorable, and powerful, that viewers don't notice its ambiguity unless they've studied the film long and hard.

Like *Tales from the Crypt* (1972), *A Day of Judgment* (1981) is a horror anthology film that recounts how some sinners end up in hell. But whereas most anthologies begin and end their stories without interruption, in *A Day of Judgment*, the stories are interwoven, in a quasi-parallel editing structure.

The film begins by establishing all the sinners. It then relates Sinner 1's tale. But before concluding, we begin Sinner 2's tale. We then conclude Sinner 1's tale, begin Sinner 3's tale, and conclude Sinner 2's tale. And so this pattern repeats, until all tales are told. Then all sinners are gathered and taken to hell. Only to awake and discover that it was all a dream, resulting in their Scrooge-like changes of hearts.

One complaint about horror anthologies is that the stories feel unrelated, as if they were separate films. I never minded that. Horror anthologies are like a box of chocolates — you never know what you're going to get. But for the nitpicky, *A Day of Judgment* offers ways to overcome the "weakness" of unrelated stories. All the characters live in the same small town, during the Depression. They're neighbors, sharing place and time. They share a local minister, who laments his empty pews, thereby dramatically unifying the absent sinners. One night the Grim Reaper arrives in town, harvesting the sinners' souls in a quasi-parallel editing structure. All these story elements, reinforced by this editing, unify the sinners' tales spatially, temporally, dramatically, and thematically.

We began this section with a classic example of parallel editing: The race to the rescue. Parallel editing normally crosscuts "mini-stories"; brief events with a beginning, middle, and end. *The Redeemer* is more innovative and ambitious (or sloppy and confusing, depending on one's interpretation), crosscutting two long, non-concurrent stories through the entire film, in a temporally ambiguous manner. Likewise, *A Day of Judgment* parallel edits multiple stories for the entire film, juggling three tales at any one time: ending Sinner 1's tale, beginning Sinner 3's tale, ending Sinner 2's tale, etc.

Shot Duration; Tempo (aka Pace) and Rhythm

Individual shots can run for relatively brief or long periods of time. The latter is called a *long take* and should not be confused with a *long shot* (when the subject is framed from afar, as opposed to a closeup).

Shot duration affects a scene's *tempo* (aka *pace*). Generally, brief shots energize a story, while long takes instill a leisurely pace. I say "generally" because the aesthetic effect of a shot's duration, as always, depends on context. A moving frame or fast tempo music can also energize a scene, whereas a steady frame or slow music can mellow it out. These elements can support or subvert the editing.

Long takes are analogous to closeups, in that they compel viewers to closely observe a subject, whereas quick shots offer but a brief glimpse. Long takes and closeups can sometimes support — or substitute for — one another. A long take/medium shot of an actor may provide as good a look as a quicker closeup.

Action films especially have embraced a fast tempo "MTV style" of quick cuts. Yet rather than exciting or entertaining, I find many fast tempo action scenes to be annoying and confusing. The director throws too much information up onscreen; too much happens too fast to follow. I was bored during *Batman and Robin*'s (1997) climactic battle scene, my mind wandering during all the explosions and skirmishes. Occasionally, my attention returned and I'd wonder: "How did Batman get up on that ledge he's swinging from?" Then I'd zone out again. Generally, action films use quick cuts to *generate excitement*, whereas horror films use quick cuts to *frighten with a glimpse of a possible threat*. Just a peek to suggest a presence that may or may not be hideous, dangerous, or unnatural.

Apart from unnerving viewers with a peek at a possible threat, quick cuts *obscure (if not hide) cheesy monsters*. While slow motion photography and overlapping edits can extend a grisly moment, some horror filmmakers don't want audiences to get a good look at their shabby monsters. Quick cuts are a useful tool for filmmakers who can't afford impressive CGI creatures.

In *Horror Hospital* (British 1973), Dr. Storm, a mad scientist, lobotomizes hippies and turns them into robot slaves. Three escaped youths enter Storm's bedroom, discovering a mask of his face. (With latex eyes — no eyeholes!) Apparently, Storm was disfigured in a fire. *Just how hideous is he that he uses a mask?* Then his burnt arm emerges from behind bedcurtains, looking like ... mud? *1 second.* He whips a nude girl on his bed. We see her for *3 seconds* but only glimpse Storm's hand *under 1 second* per whipping. We also glimpse parts of his rump and body profile. *1 second* each.

Storm escapes. We see a *long shot* of him outdoors, *obscured* by brush, *dimly lit* by day-for-night photography. *1 second.* The youths run down Storm, decapitating him with his own car. The clearest shot of him is a zoom-in POV as the car rushes at him. *Under 1 second.* His head drops into a basket. His decapitated body sinks into a bog. *Under 1 second* each.

Abraham examines Storm's head, our longest and best view of Storm's disfigured face. *2 seconds.* It *glistens red*, like raw meat. Yet in the previous zoom-in shot, his face was *muddy-gray*.

Because Storm is always obscured and/or dimly lit while he's alive and unmasked — and all shots *1 second or less*—1970s audiences were unsure *what* they saw onscreen. Today, DVD freeze-framing reveals that Dr. Storm's "disfigurement" looks like he's covered — head to toe — in a bulky, rubbery, full-body, zip-up suit. He looks less a burn victim than a mud-pie sculpture of the Creature from the Black Lagoon.

Hence, the quick cuts. First, to conceal that Storm's red meat face differs from his mud-pie gray face. Second, so audiences will imagine something scarier than a mud-pie man. *Horror Hospital*'s quick cuts function like the strobe light in *Jacob's Ladder*. As with Jezzie, so with Storm. "We're not sure what we're seeing."[20]

In *Tower of Evil* (British 1972), some people seek archaeological treasure on a deserted island. Alas, a psycho is loose and the body count mounts. At one point, the survivors think the killer is dead. Hamp leaves Rose downstairs in the lighthouse, thinking she's safe. But Michael, the mutant psycho, kills Hamp and creeps downstairs, toward Rose.

Our first peek at Michael is of his bloody hand striking a wall. Then his profile, obscured by shadows.[21] We see only two clear shots of his face: a medium shot (*1 second*) and a closeup (*under 1 second*). Just enough to suggest his deformity. After Rose throws a lantern at Michael, setting him aflame, his face is obscured by his long hair, the fire engulfing him, and the lighting (the lens aperture seems calibrated to the fire, leaving Michael underexposed).

The aesthetic intent of revealing only glimpses of Michael is to frighten audiences by suggesting something more monstrous than is there. This doesn't always work. When I first saw *Tower of Evil* on broadcast TV, I was frustrated rather than scared, because I wasn't sure what I saw, and I *wanted* to see. Now, after freezing the DVD image, well, Michael's face isn't all that shabby. A mask, obviously, covered in blood, with one misshapen eye. It doesn't equal modern CGI effects. But it's okay.

I was similarly frustrated by only glimpsing the final victim's disfigurement (a face of molten metal) in the "Earth, Air, Fire and Water" episode of TV's *Circle of Fear*.[22] But I was less frustrated by *The Visitor* (aka *Stridulum*, Italian 1979), when Katy assumes her demonic form. Her mother, Barbara, nervously approaches Katy from behind. We see a POV of Katy's back. Her voice sounds normal. As Barbara nears, a quick cut shows Katy spinning around, facing Barbara. Cut to Barbara's shocked reaction. Cut to Katy — her "face" is a black void with holes emitting light. *What* is Katy? *It's not even a face!*

A glimpse is all we see. Henceforth, Katy's face is obscured by her hair, the staging, and the lighting. When we see her again in space heaven (or wherever), she's a normal-looking, bald little girl.

Sometimes, less is more. A glimpse of Katy's face is enough for me. It's odd, original, and surprising. Too much scrutiny may destroy its impact. Director Ed Wood's octopus in *Bride of the Monster* (1955) looks silly largely because Wood's long shots/long takes reveal too much. We clearly see actors screaming upon a lifeless dummy. But imagine Wood's octopus with tight, moving frames and fast tempo editing. Closeups, zoom-ins, and quick cuts of the octopus's head, its arms slithering across victims, their screaming mouths and bulging eyes. Better, no?

Director Sergio Martino's tight, moving frames and quick cuts effectively energized a fake alligator in *The Big Alligator River* (aka *Il fiume del grande caimano*, *The Great Alligator*, Italian 1979). The alligator still resembled a flotation device, but only some of the time.

The classic example of quick cutting for horror may be *Psycho*'s shower scene. Its fast tempo edits fooled 1960 audiences into imagining that they actually *saw* Norman's knife pierce Marion. Today we know that *Psycho* is relatively goreless.

Quick shots are as likely to frustrate as frighten. It depends on the film and viewer. I was satisfied by glimpsing Katy's black void face, but some viewers likely wanted more. I wanted a better look at Dr. Storm and Michael, but other viewers perhaps not. We react differently. That's why Hollywood test markets films.

Music videos and ever shorter TV ads have inspired a faster tempo in feature films, but "reality TV" is an opposing influence, encouraging longer takes. Director of photography Saro Varjabedian writes: "It is no surprise that the popularity of reality TV and the movement of documentaries garnering commercial success have impacted the cinematographic style of recent narrative films. That impact is reflected by the trend towards a more realistic look (e.g. less lighting) with a more 'objective' camera. The 'objective' camera stylistically acts as if the camera is there to record the unfolding of the story rather than to recreate it shot by shot. In 2006, *Children of Men* brilliantly epitomizes the use of the 'objective' camera with its *long takes* and handheld camera work bringing the horror of the future a reality that makes all the events of the film all the more horrific."[23]

The Blair Witch Project (1999) is an early "reality TV" style horror film. Its long takes and rough production values seek to impart a documentary quality, so that viewers will feel that the horrific events onscreen are real, "recorded live as they are happening," and not staged.

By *tempo* (or *pace*), I mean the duration of shots at a particular point in a film. But shots accumulate over the course of a scene or film; these shifting tempos create an overall *rhythm*.

In *The Unseen* (1981), the middle-aged Ernest Keller sits in a drunken stupor, alone in his dead father's office. He awakes and "hears" his father's voice. Not a ghost, but memories. We see only Ernest in the present time. We hear him speak to his father's *voiceover*.

The father invites Ernest to sit down for a "man to man" talk. A tense beginning to a chat that progressively darkens. We learn that Father beats his children, and that Ernest has repeatedly raped his sister and gotten her pregnant. Father threatens to castrate Ernest. So Ernest kills him.

The editing's rhythm supports these dramatic events. As in a piece of classical music, opening shots are long and languorous. An emotional storm gathers. Tension builds. Then the fight erupts. The storm breaks. The shots quicken, supporting the story's violence.

Consider this scene, paying heed to shot duration. (I abridged the dialog in the longer takes):

A shot from the hallway of the office door. A padlock hangs open. The camera slowly moves toward the padlock. An old gramophone plays from inside the room. The padlock and gramophone pique our interest. What's inside that room? This shot is *11 seconds* long.

Cut to inside the room. Closeup of a glass of liquor in Ernest's hand. *4 seconds*.

Cut to a cat on the floor, licking a shoe. *4 seconds*.

Cut to Ernest asleep in an armchair. He's woken by Father's voiceover. Gramophone music fades out. Father warmly invites Ernest to sit down. He snaps when Ernest doesn't immediately sit. Then his warmth returns. This shot begins as a *medium closeup* on Ernest, slowly moving to a *closeup* as his unease increases. That's pretty static for *56 seconds*—but it forces us to see Ernest's discomfort. Father invites Ernest to "look around," motivating a...

Cut to an old military class photo. The camera "looks around," revealing telltale *mise-en-scène* by its moving frame and racking focus. Dust and cobwebs. The cat reflected in a tarnished mirror. An old photo of Father in a military uniform. He tells Ernest there's "no need to be nervous with your daddy." *22 seconds*. He reminisces about his late wife, motivating a...

Cut to an old photo of the wife. Father laments her death. The moving camera continues exploring the room. Father says that Virginia, Ernest's sister, was crying that morning, but wouldn't say why. So Father "had to beat" the answers out of her. *43 seconds*.

Cut to a miniature cannon. This violent prop underscores Father's violent confession. The camera continues exploring the room. Father has learned that Virginia "got herself with child. Didn't think she knew about such things." He wondered what "low life piece of scum" would do "such a thing to that poor dumb child." He immediately thought of Ernest. *28 seconds*.

Cut to a closeup of Ernest. Father shouts "Did it feel good, taking your own sister?" *23 seconds*.

Cut to the cat on the floor. Father's voiceover overlaps this shot. *3 seconds*.

Cut to a closeup of Ernest. Father says that Virginia must be sent away for an abortion. He orders Ernest to stand up. "We're going to make sure this doesn't happen again. That it never happens again." This is the scene's longest shot. *62 seconds.*

Cut to the cat, for the first time glaring at Ernest, mirroring Father's anger. The cat sits on Father's mummified corpse (but we won't know it's a corpse until the scene's end). *3 seconds.*

Cut to an *extreme closeup* of Ernest's face. This emphasizes his growing terror, which is supported by actor Sydney Lassick's performance, his sweat, and the bright lights glistening on that sweat. "Pull down your trousers!" Father orders. Ernest begs not to be castrated, then resists. We *hear* a sword pulled from a scabbard, then a fight. (As with Father's voiceover, we only hear this fight from the past.) Intense music ensues. *30 seconds.*

Cut to *12 shots* totaling *13 seconds.* A scabbarded sword on a wall. The cat. Ernest's face. Parts of Father's corpse. During this unseen "fight," images are lit blue, perhaps to suggest the malignity of these memories. Images are repeated, but *framed at different distances* to energize the fight, and to begin revealing Father's corpse. We hear struggle, intense music, Father begging as Ernest overpowers him, then being killed. The last shot is of Father's corpse, medium closeup, no longer lit blue, *2 seconds.* This means the previous 11 shots *average 1 second each.*

Cut to an extreme closeup of Ernest's face. A POV cut, in that he's observing the corpse that we've just seen. (Which explains the padlock — you wouldn't want guests discovering a corpse in your house.) Lighting is softer. He barely sweats. He smiles smugly. *9 seconds.*

The Unseen varies its shot tempo, building into a rhythm that supports the story. Mostly long takes reinforce a slow rise in dramatic tension. This tension is released in a series of 12 brief shots, conveying the fight's emotional and physical violence. Then a moderate lull (not a long take, not a quick cut) as we catch our breaths.

This is a remarkable scene in an extraordinary film. This scene demonstrates how story events can motivate camera moves, photography, and editing. Father's remarks motivate cuts to his wife's photo, the miniature cannon, etc. An earlier shot depicts the stairs leading up to the office. In the foreground, a "Private" sign blocks the stairs, sharply focused. In the background, the top of the stairs is blurry. Then a rack focus blurs the sign and sharpens the top of the stairs, thus guiding our attention upstairs to Father's office. The Private sign functions similarly to the padlock, piquing our interest.

This scene also demonstrates *pragmatic aesthetics.* Time and money were likely saved by (1) not staging a fight, and (2) hiring an actor for voiceovers in a studio rather than to perform on location. (The actor playing Father *isn't even listed in the credits!*) Yet despite these pragmatic shortcuts, the scene works aesthetically as Ernest's memory; as a classily photographed and emotionally gripping substitute for a more expensive flashback scene.

Action films use quick cuts to enhance *dynamic* events. Cars speeding, guns firing, buildings exploding, etc. But *The Unseen's* "fight scene" demonstrates that quick cuts can infuse even *static* shots with energy and excitement.

In *Curtains,* a slasher stalks Tara in an empty theater. Tara hides in an air vent, peering past the grills for the slasher. When Tara thinks it's safe to come out, she is yanked *from behind* into the vent. (How did the slasher get in there? Stupid question — it's a slasher film!) After Tara disappears into the vent, we see *16 shots* inside the theater: hallways, mannequins, a previous victim's corpse, etc. We hear shrill music, the slasher's heavy breathing, and hacking sounds. *16 shots* totaling *9 seconds. Under 1 second per shot.* We don't see Tara's death, yet these offscreen sounds, the colorfully lit and eerie mannequins, and the editing's fast tempo, effectively convey Tara's violent demise.

In both *The Unseen* and *Curtains*, the victims die offscreen. We see only static objects. Furthermore, the shots themselves are static (no camera moves). Instead, to convey the stories' violence, these shots are energized through framing (changes in distance and angle) and editing (brief cuts). Music and the sounds of death further energize these scenes.

In *The Eye* (aka *Gin gwai*, Hong Kong 2002), brief cuts intensify *dynamic* shots. Mum is riding up an elevator. An old man's ghost appears. He floats toward the terrified Mum, seemingly about to touch her. The elevator doors open and Mum runs out. There follow *39 shots* totaling *54 seconds* of Mum racing to her apartment, framed from various angles, levels, and distances, from front and back, in silhouette and not, sharply focused and blurry. She rushes to "her" door and discovers that she's on the wrong floor! She runs up a stairwell and meets a boy's ghost, who leaps out a window! A shot depicts his plummeting POV. Mum runs to her apartment, enters, slams the door. *39 shots* totaling *54 seconds.*

Cut to black. *Under 1 second.*

Cut to Mum in her apartment.[24] She pants and covers her face, traumatized over seeing two ghosts. This is a long take — *32 seconds* — ending on slow violin music. *Fade to black.*

Then fade *from* black to Mum playing her violin. There begins a montage of *20 shots* that depict Mum withdrawing from life. She plays her violin, ignores her mother and sister, broods in her room, etc. Mum was blind, and now that she sees ghosts, she wants to return to blindness. Her violin music continues throughout this montage, regardless of the images, thus unifying these shots dramatically and thematically.

The montage contains *20 shots* totaling *89 seconds.*[25] A slower tempo than Mum's race to her apartment, but faster than the long take inside her apartment. But this montage's tempo is further slowed in that the 20 shots are connected by only *5 cuts* — and *14 dissolves.*

Shot *transition* affects tempo. Mum enters her apartment and we *cut to black.* A quick end to a fast tempo sequence. After a long take in her apartment, we appropriately *fade to black.* Then *fade from black* to the montage (moderate tempo shots, further slowed by many *dissolves*). This ends with a *fade to black.* We *cut* to the next scene.

In the hallways and stairwell, Mum's desperation and panic are effectively conveyed by the frantic music, erratic framing and photography, story elements (the ghost boy's suicide), and fast tempo editing. A long take inside the apartment allows both Mum and the audience to catch their breaths and assess matters. The languorously transitioning montage depicts Mum's search for tranquility.

As in *The Unseen*, the rhythm of *The Eye*'s editing evokes a music composition. A burst of quick shots (or notes), the lull of a single long note, then a series of slow but shorter notes.

This rhythm does not begin with Mum exiting the elevator, nor end with the montage. A rhythm runs through every film, and along its entire length. This rhythm can be intentional and supportive of story, characters, and themes — or haphazard and supportive of nothing. If the latter, viewers may not know what's wrong with the film, only that in some way it feels unsatisfying.

Horror films often use a fast tempo editing technique called a *staggered zoom*, usually to emphasize a shocking event or image. The image is shown in a succession of brief shots, framed ever tighter, ever closer. Sometimes as a series of *freeze frames*, but not necessarily. This image expands in size from a long shot to a closeup, in a broken, jarring fashion, rather than through a smooth zoom or dollying in on the image.

At the end of *The House That Screamed* (aka *La residencia*, Spanish 1969), Madame Fourneau, headmistress at a girls boarding school, discovers that her teenage son, Luis, has killed several students, chopped them up, and sewn together their body parts to create a girl "just like mother." After proudly displaying his work, Luis asks Mom to teach the girl to love and care for him, just as Mom does. He then locks Mom in an attic room, together with his newly-stitched girlfriend, saying gently through the door: "Talk to her, mother. Talk to her."

Cut to an *extreme long shot* of Luis sitting down by the attic door. As Mom bangs on the other side to be let out, Luis says one last time: "Talk to her."

Cut to a *long shot, same image*, punctuated by Mom screaming: "Luuuuiiiis!" Then a loud, harsh musical note.

Cut to a *medium shot, same image* (Luis is now large enough in the frame so that we see his demented smile), punctuated by Mom screaming: Luuuuiiiis!" Then a louder, harsh musical note.

Cut to an *extreme closeup, same image* (Luis's face now fills the frame), punctuated by Mom screaming: Luuuuiiiis!" Then an even louder, harsh musical note, which segues into the closing theme music. Roll credits.

The static image of Luis sitting before the door is energized by this staggered zoom, and by each cut occurring on yet another scream. This fast tempo editing contrasts with actor John Moulder-Brown's calm movements and serenely demented smile, creating an emotional dialectic that conveys Luis's insanity, his horrible handiwork, and Madame Fourneau's dreadful fate.

In horror, staggered zooms usually "zoom-in." But there's no reason they can't "zoom-out." An aesthetic function may be to reveal a shocking item, then, before the audience catches its breath, to assault them with ever more gruesome details as the frame widens from closeup to long shot. You thought that corpse was bad? See what lies just beyond it!

Staggered zooms can be created by 1. zooming closer in on the image between shots, or 2. moving the camera closer to the image between shots, or 3. increasing the image's size in post-production. Only the first technique changes the lens's focal length, which is what we normally mean by *zooming*. Even so, all three techniques create *staggered zooms*.

Graphic Similarities and Contrasts

Editing juxtaposes images that are similar or different in shape, size, color, brightness, or direction or speed of movement. One shot's composition (or sound) continues or conflicts with the next shot's composition (or sound). These graphic similarities or clashes can create an emotional or psychological effect; or support or subvert a story, character, or theme; or function as a sight gag. Or they may be haphazard, accomplishing no aesthetic effect.

Early in *Leatherface: Texas Chainsaw Massacre III* (1989), Ryan and Michelle drive past a crime scene in the desert. Police lights are flashing. It's night. Bodies are being dug out of a pit. Traffic is backed up. After some questioning, a state trooper waves on Ryan and Michelle. Ryan gets smart alecky. Michelle complains, "I just want to get this trip over with. If I drive all night, I can."

As she drives off, the camera pans to a flashing yellow emergency light. We dissolve to a closeup of the next day's sun. The round, yellow sun dissolves over the round, yellow light, their borders coextensive. Such precise compositional continuity is called a *graphic match*.

This closeup of the sun is followed by a long shot of Michelle's car, driving through the desert on this new day.

Does this graphic match serve an aesthetic purpose? (1) Matching the emergency light with the sun links the previous night to this new day. This linking visually dramatizes Michelle's remark that she plans to "drive all night," and suggests that she made good on her promise. This implies that she is exhausted. Thus, more vulnerable. And you know how much horror likes vulnerable protagonists. (2) This graphic match serves as a cute transition.

In *Final Destination 3* (2006), Ashley and Ashlyn, two teenage girls, burn to death inside their tanning beds. Cut to their funeral, the coffins graphically matching the tanning beds. Same size and rectangular shape, same position in the frame. (Not precisely, but close enough.) This graphic match underscores that the tanning beds led to the coffins. It's an obvious and heavy-handed comment, but it's also a cute transition, so we are forgiving [Figures 7.14, 7.15].

Graphic matches can support a motif. In *Hardware* (1990), the camera moves from a long shot of Jill's living room to a closeup of the droid's *round left eye*.

Cut to an extreme closeup of this *round eye*.

Cut to the droid's POV as its *round iris* opens.

Dissolve to a *round showerhead* as it releases water in the nearby bathroom.

That's three graphic matches in a row. These four circles are not coextensive, but each is centered in the frame. I'd say that's close enough for a graphic match.

These graphic matches strengthen *Hardware*'s circular motif. To learn how this motif functions in *Hardware*, see the section on "Motif vs. Cliché" in Chapter 3 (*Mise-en-Scène*).

Edits can be graphically *similar*, yet not a precise match. In *Witchery*, a family is trapped in a haunted house on a deserted island. Rose picks up a phone. The real estate broker says, "I doubt if that's working." Rose retorts, "How did you guess?" She begins to hang up the phone, but before she completes her action we...

Cut to the real estate office, where the broker's father hangs up his phone. *His staging graphically and dramatically completes Rose's action*. The father drums his fingers nervously. Was he trying to phone his son? He dismisses his secretary, glances at his watch, and we...

Cut to a closeup of Rose's watch. She glances up after checking the time. *Her staging graphically and dramatically completes the father's action*.

These graphically similar edits, juxtaposing shots whose story events mirror each other, *dramatically unify* these scenes, bringing them full circle. The folks on the island, and the father on the mainland, wonder and worry about each other. It's getting late. Is everything all right? Is help coming? Audiences see the father worrying but doing nothing. Will he do something in time? Tension rises.

Graphically similar edits can create a cute sight gag. In *Not of This Earth* (1988), an alien brings his partner to a medical office for a blood transfusion. He hooks up a *blood supply bottle*.

Cut to a restaurant, a police officer pouring *red syrup* on his pastry.

Figure 7.14—*Final Destination 3*. An overhead shot of two tanning beds on fire. Cut to...

Figure 7.15—...a *graphically matched* overhead shot of two coffins.

This juxtaposition of *mise-en-scène* produces a visual gag. A cute transition. There's no dramatic or thematic link between the *red blood* and the *red syrup*. Sometimes, filmmakers just want to have fun.

Evil Dead 2 (1987) has fun with editing. When Bobbie Joe discovers a disembodied hand gripping her, she panics and runs from the cabin. Out in the woods, demon-possessed trees attack her. Their branches drag her at breakneck speed toward a tree. A *revved up engine sound* ensues. The scene's last shot is Bobbie Joe's POV of a tree *fast approaching*...

Cut to a shot (inside the cabin) of the *Necronomicon* in a glass-fronted case *falling* onto a table. The previous scene's *engine sound* continues (creating a sound bridge) as the case *falls*, its glass shattering just when Bobbie Joe is likely hitting the tree. *The shattering glass audibly and dramatically completes Bobbie Joe's smashing into the tree.* Although we don't see Bobbie Joe's death, this breaking glass helps audiences imagine the girl's body breaking against the tree.

The *direction of movement* in these two shots are in *graphic conflict*. We see the tree racing *toward* us. Then the *Necronomicon* falling *away* from us.[26] This contrast is heightened in that, throughout the previous scene, the camera repeatedly moves *toward* both Bobbie Joe and the tree. The aesthetic effect of this conflicting movement — like much else in this film — is to *energize* events. Energy and humor are key contributors to *Evil Dead 2's* entertainment value.

Shock Cuts, aka Smash Cuts

A *shock cut* juxtaposes shots that are graphically extremely different, intending to jolt, unnerve, or shock (but not necessarily to frighten) viewers. These extreme graphical differences are often supported by extreme differences in sound. For instance, a dark, quiet, nighttime forest path, followed by an extremely bright day, city streets bustling with loud traffic.

White Noise (2005) demonstrates both the power of shock cutting, and how framing and editing can interact to support characters and story. Jonathan is trying to contact his dead wife, Anna, through the "white noise" of his TV screen. He visits a blind psychic, Mirabelle, seeking guidance. Mirabelle's home is somberly lit. Muted earth tones predominate. A quiet room. Jonathan and Mirabelle converse in low tones.

The scene opens with a closeup of Mirabelle's hands clasping Jonathan's right hand.

Five medium shots follow, intercutting between Jonathan and Mirabelle. She offers her psychic impressions. She "sees" Willow Avenue. Jonathan grows skeptical. He says there's no Willow Avenue. Mirabelle says, "Okay. It's no problem. Sometimes that happens."

Two long shots follow. These establishing shots for the first time depict the entire room. The long framing also places us farther from the characters, suggesting that Jonathan is moving away from faith in Mirabelle's abilities. She says, "Your wife. She passed over recently."

Cut to a medium shot of Jonathan, intercut with three more medium shots alternating between him and Mirabelle. Throughout this sequence, the frame *moves* very slowly closer in on the characters as Mirabelle continues making accurate observations about Anna. This editing and framing (cutting from two long shots to four ever-tightening medium shots) parallels Jonathan's growing faith in Mirabelle. She says, "I'm sorry. Just the light is way too bright."

Cut to our first closeup of Jonathan. Now he's really interested. He's been staring at TV screens, searching for Anna in the "white noise." Mirabelle's remark is dead on.

Cut to a medium shot of Mirabelle. She says, "It's like these tiny, noisy, little pinpoints. It's making it hard to see anything at all."

Cut to a medium shot of Jonathan as Mirabelle talks, his interest growing.

Cut to a closeup of Mirabelle. Silent now. Concentrating. Worried. Ominous, nondiegetic sound ensues.

Cut to a closeup of Jonathan. Eager to learn what Mirabelle "sees."

Cut to a closeup of Mirabelle. Worried [Figure 7.16].

Cut to an extreme closeup of a mouth screaming in "white noise" TV static. Sound of screaming and TV static. *This is our shock cut* [Figure 7.17].

Cut to a closeup of Mirabelle, from another angle.

Cut to an extreme closeup of her hands, pulling away from Jonathan's hand.

Figure 7.16 — *White Noise.* A silent room. Muted, pastel hues. Mirabelle (Keegan Connor Tracy) quietly ponders a psychic vision. Then a...

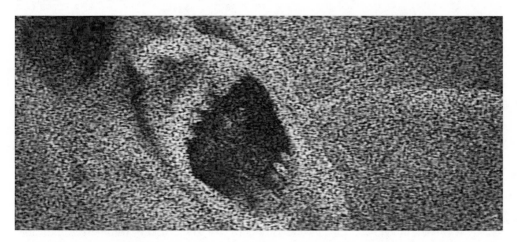

Figure 7.17 —*...shock cut* to a screaming mouth in grainy, cold hues.

Cut to a long shot with a *match on action* of Mirabelle pulling her hands away. (This *match on action cut* helps to spatially unify this shot with the previous shot.)

The scene continues. Mirabelle warns Jonathan not to meddle with EVP, because there are dangerous entities out there. Jonathan leaves, ignoring her advice.

The above shock cut is ... shocking. It jolts viewers. Shock is not the same as fear. *The Ring* (2002) frightens largely through story and atmosphere, with only an occasional shock. But it's harder and slower to frighten with a creepy story, than to shock with a corpse tumbling down and hanging upside down. Shocks do unnerve viewers, fraying their emotional defenses, making them more susceptible to fear. And one way to shock is with a shock cut.

The shock cut in *White Noise* works because of the interplay of several elements. In terms of story, lighting, sound, and *mise-en-scène*, we have a quiet, dimly lit, earth-toned scene, a slow buildup through a spooky story, nondiegetic spooky noise, a tightening frame — then a *shock cut* to a loudly screaming mouth, in extreme closeup, cold electronic colors contrasting with the previous dim earth tones.

In the surrealistic *Eraserhead* (1977), Henry is nursing a sick, mutant baby. He sets a thermometer in the baby's mouth, removes it, checks the thermometer in the light. A closeup depicts the thermometer's reading: 98°.

1. Cut to a wide shot of the baby, brightly lit. He appears healthy.
2. Cut to a medium shot of Henry, pleased. He walks toward his bed, then turns around.
3. Cut to a closeup of the baby's face. It has a grotesque rash. Discordant music resounds loudly. Dim lighting lends the baby an ominous cast.
4. Cut to Henry, exclaiming, "Oh, you are sick!"

A shock cut traditionally refers to juxtaposed shots. Yet shot 3 functions as a shock cut in relation to shot 1. In shot 1, the baby has healthy skin, widely framed, brightly lit. In shot 3, the baby is hideously ill. This sudden and unexpected dramatic turn is emphasized by the changes in framing (closer in) and lighting (dimmer), but especially by the loud, discordant music. These elements jolt viewers, having the *effect* of a shock cut despite shot 2's separation of shots 1 and 3, which technically disqualifies "cut" 1/3 as a shock cut. (I suppose some may argue that cut 2/3 is a shock cut.)

Not all shock cuts are meant to terrify, or even to shock. Sudden brightness, following a dark night scene, can evoke the sensation of a character awakening to a new day. The aesthetic effect, as always, is determined by the shock cut's context in the film.

Associational Editing

Editing can "editorialize." Juxtaposing images can "send a message" by suggesting ideas, themes, and cause-and-effect relationships. A shot of a "greedy capitalist" followed by that of a "starving worker" may imply that the former's wealth causes the latter's poverty. Even when the images are dramatically unconnected, their juxtaposition *suggests an association* between them, and often hints toward a "correct" interpretation.

Juxtaposing images can invite viewers to consider similarities or differences. Consider a shot of John Lennon giving an animated speech at a protest rally. Follow it with a shot of Hitler giving an animated speech. Both men stand behind podiums, gesticulating and shouting to large crowds. This *graphically similar* association suggests that Lennon is like Hitler. But take a shot of Lennon, sitting cross-legged among flowers, singing to children, followed by the previous shot of Hitler. This *graphically dissimilar* association now suggests that Lennon is unlike Hitler.

Associational editing was popular with the 1920s *Soviet montage* movement, which regarded editing as the key to filmmaking.[27] World War I and the ensuing Russian Civil War created a shortage of film stock, compelling filmmakers to recycle old film footage in new works. (Much like *Hell of the Living Dead*'s recycling of stock footage.) This constant recutting of old films inspired editing experiments, resulting in such discoveries as the Kuleshov Effect.

In *The Unseen*, a thematic association arises from crosscutting two death scenes. In scene 1, Junior murders Vicki. In scene 2, Virginia beheads a chicken. Crosscutting between these two scenes sends a thematic message: Vicki is slaughtered like a hapless chicken.

Without listing every shot, consider the overall sequence: Shots of an air vent grill in a bedroom floor. Vicki asleep in bed. Crosscut with shots of an ax buried in a chopping block. Chickens in a henhouse. (Message: That air vent will doom Vicki, just like that ax dooms those chickens.) Shots of Vicki awakening, screaming, trying to escape, then dragged into the vent. Crosscut with shots of Virginia entering the henhouse, sharpening the ax, grabbing a chicken, which squawks fearfully as Virginia carries it to the chopping block.

Scene 1's final shot — the *air vent grill falling down* on Vicki's head — is *graphically completed* by scene 2's shot of the *ax falling down* on the chicken's neck. The grill falls halfway, then we cut to the ax completing this movement. A metallic sound resounds when the ax hits the chopping block, just when the grill is likely striking shut in the previous shot. These shots are thus graphically *and* audibly matched, strengthening their thematic association[28] [Figures 7.18, 7.19].

In *The Visitor*, the evil space child, Katy, receives a gun at her birthday party. She gaily tosses it, "inadvertently" shooting her mother, Barbara. We then crosscut between two montage sequences. One montage depicts Barbara's medical treatments, the bullet having paralyzed her. The other montage shows Katy joyfully performing gymnastics. Aluminum bars surround both characters. A shot of Katy grabbing a parallel bar graphically resembles Barbara gripping the physical therapy bar over her hospital bed. This crosscutting contrasts the crippled Barbara with the physically sublime Katy, made more poignant in that each causes the other's pain/joy. (Katy crippled Barbara, while dutiful mom Barbara presumably pays for Katy's lessons.) The aesthetic effect of associating these images (1) emphasizes their cause-and-effect relationships, (2) evokes sympathy for Barbara, and (3) illustrates Katy's chilling cruelty.

After her montage, Katy analyzes her gymnastic performance, concluding that soon she will be "perfect." When the coach asks her about Barbara, Katy shrugs it off. "My mother's not dead. She just won't be able to walk ever again." Her remark caps the associational crosscutting. She is chillingly egocentric and cold-blooded. Horror's archetypal "bad seed."

Associational editing should not be confused with parallel editing, though the concepts overlap. Parallel editing crosscuts mini-stories that *are* dramatically or thematically connected. Associational editing *creates* a thematic connection. These crosscuts from *The Unseen* and *The Visitor* are parallel and associational. The crosscuts in *The Redeemer* and *A Day of Judgment* are parallel but not associational; the crosscuts *by themselves* do not suggest any particular themes, ideas, or messages.

While parallel editing requires crosscutting, associational edits do not. A one-time cut is sufficient to associate two images and send a message. In *The Shaft* (aka *Down*, 2001), an evil elevator stops between floors, trapping a group of pregnant women. The *heat intensifies*, power is cut, maintenance workers can't open the doors, the alarm blares incessantly. Several women go into labor, screaming, breaking water, panicking, and *sweltering*. Finally, the elevator opens its doors. The scene's last shot is of building workers gaping, horrified, at the elevator floor.

What do the workers see that so horrifies them? We don't know, because the women are offscreen. Instead of seeing their gruesome fate, we cut to a shot of chickens and eggs *broiling* on a grill. Thus begins a new scene at a diner.

This cut associates the sweltering women with the broiling food. This association is strengthened in that the edit is structured as a POV cut. The workers *stare* offscreen, fol-

Figure 7.18 — *The Unseen*. Junior drags Vicki (Lois Young) down into the air vent. Soon the grill behind Vicki's head will drop, its falling motion completed by...

Figure 7.19 —...an ax coming down on this chicken's neck, thus *associating* the savagery of Vicki's death with that of the chicken.

lowed by a shot of broiling food, as if this was what they saw on the elevator floor. (In a sense, it is. It's what the women look like to them. Hence, the association.)

Graphic matches can strengthen an association, but these concepts are separate. In *Not of This Earth*, a shot of *red blood* is followed by a shot of *red syrup*. This is a graphic match, because these images look similar. But no association is implied. The film is not suggesting that blood is like syrup.[29] By contrast, *The Shaft*'s cut is not graphically matched. The workers do not resemble broiling food. The cut is entirely associational.

Associational editing often uses *nondiegetic insert shots.* As with nondiegetic lights and sound, a nondiegetic insert depicts an image that is *outside the film's story.* A man bumps into a beautiful woman. She smiles at him, then leaves. He stares longingly after her. Romantic music swells. Cut to shots of a water fountain, a steamship blowing its horn, fireworks exploding in the sky. Cut back to the man.

The fountain, steamship, and fireworks are nondiegetic insert shots, functioning as associational edits. These images are not part of the story. No characters are sailing on that steamship. Rather, these images illustrate the man's sudden infatuation with the woman.

Nondiegetic inserts are especially popular in comedies, which rely less on story integrity than do other genres. Comedies can always suspend a story for a good joke. But horror also uses nondiegetic inserts. In *Inferno* (Italian 1980), Mark searches a building for clues to his sister's disappearance. He suffers a heart attack, staggers into the building's lobby, then collapses before some tenants. He is given "heart medicine."

Cut to Mark's blurry POV of tenants looking down at him. A wavy, rippling blur as he passes out.

Dissolve to ocean waves hitting a beach.

Dissolve to these waves superimposed over Mark, who is asleep on a sofa.

The waves dissolve away, leaving Mark asleep on the sofa. He awakes.

These ocean waves can be interpreted as Mark's dream, in which case they'd be diegetic. But I interpret them as nondiegetic and associational. Nondiegetic, because (1) the story makes no reference to dreams, much less to an actual beach, (2) the ocean waves ensue before Mark passes out and can dream, and (3) he awakes immediately alert, as if a trance were lifted.

This sequence (from the wavy dissolves, to the ocean waves, to Mark's sudden alertness) suggests a witch-induced trance. That's the associated message: the ocean waters symbolize witchcraft. *Inferno* flows with water imagery, from Rose's discovery a flooded subbasement, to the rats emerging from a Central Park lake to attack Kazanian. It seems that Mater Tenebrarum, the building's witch, rules water — a feminine element. Ocean waves are superimposed over the sleeping Mark like a magic spell. Mater Tenebrarum administered the "heart medicine," and the waves symbolize her spell's trance-like effect on Mark's psyche.

Maitland McDonagh disagrees: "This apparent dream sequence is the only one of its kind in *Inferno* ... it's profoundly out of synch with the images that surround it. In a film whose imagery is all hysterical and dreamlike, what is one to make of a perfectly straightforward shot that's bracketed in such terms (a character is about to faint — narrative — the screen ripples and fades to black — structural) that one can hardly help but read it as a conventional dream?"[30] He then spends a page spinning notions of water and Jungian archetypes, but gives up. "The problem, of course, is that this sort of dazzling interplay can easily degenerate into sophistry."[31] First, the screen does not ripple and fade to black. It "ripple dissolves" from Mark's POV of the tenants to the ocean waves. Then it "ripple dissolves" back to Mark. Never is the screen entirely black. Second, if one interprets the ocean waves as an associational nondiegetic insert shot, symbolizing the witch's trance-inducing spell, then these ocean waves are not so "out of synch" with the rest of the film.

CHAPTER 8

Putting Sound to the Image

Many amateur filmmakers treat sound as an afterthought. They'll record their actors' dialog with the camera's built-in mic (microphone), and if the words are discernible, they're satisfied. Maybe they'll add some music. Then they're done with the soundtrack. But such laziness not only yields a poor quality audio recording, it ignores sound's aesthetic potential.

The better the original on-set recording, the more aesthetic options one has. No-budget filmmakers often rely solely on a camera's *built-in mic* to record sound. More ambitious filmmakers may connect a *directional mic* held on a *boom stick*, or a *lavaliere* (a tiny mic hidden on actors), into the camera. This connection can be through a *radio transmitter* or *cable hookup*. More advanced filmmakers connect their mics into *sound recorders* that are synchronized to match the camera's speed. Sometimes they'll also use the camera's built-in mic as a supplemental sound recorder.

During post-production, filmmakers select and mix all available on-set sound recordings, adding music, sound effects, and sometimes additional dialog or voiceovers that are recorded in a studio. A soundtrack is thus built (mixed and edited) to support or subvert — dramatically, emotionally, and/or thematically — the film's visuals.

Nondiegetic Sound

As with light, sound can be *diegetic* or *nondiegetic*. Diegetic sound has its source within the story; a source that *motivates* the sound. This source can be onscreen or offscreen. Diegetic sound can be *external* (e.g., characters' dialog) or *internal* (e.g., characters' thoughts).

Music is the most common nondiegetic sound in films. We hear music, but know the musicians are not in the story. Comedies have used this audience expectation for gags. Lovers kiss on a beach. Romantic music swells. One lover turns and asks the orchestra (which the camera has panned to), to please hold down the music.

The Dark (1979) spins a spooky atmosphere by layering its eerie nondiegetic music with creepy nondiegetic whispers. Characters wander dark deserted hallways, parking lots, and streets, nervously glancing about, while we hear people whispering *Theeeee da-a-a-a-a-a-a-ark!* and *Theeeee da-a-a-a-a-a-a-ark — nesssss!* They also whisper unintelligible words that sound like some Satanic or occult language.[1]

Volume

A sound's *volume* (aka *amplitude*) can be high or low, loud or soft. Volume can convey information, or misinformation, by suggesting an object's size and distance. The unseen entity's loud bangings in *The Haunting* (1963) imply a powerful creature outside Theo's bedroom door. Its loudness not only suggests the creature's potency, but its emotional state and mental intent—it must be angry and hostile to bang so loudly and incessantly. The high volume also intimates the entity's proximity. As the noise fades, Eleanor says: "Now it's down near the other end of the hall."

Volume can *mislead* audiences. Loud ghostly bangings may suggest a threat where there is none. In *The Changeling* (1980), a house is plagued by loud bangings. The characters infer an angry ghost. Mrs. Huxley says of the house: "It doesn't want people." But eventually, John disagrees: "Whatever it is, it's trying desperately to communicate." John understands the ghost's dilemma. It's hard to communicate with mortals when almost all you can do is bang pipes.

As with visual composition, sound *directs viewer attention.* Two characters may be lost inside a crowd, near the frame's edge. Normally, such *mise-en-scène* and framing will "hide" the characters. Yet by raising their dialog's volume over the scene's other sounds, audience attention is directed to them. Volume can highlight characters or objects that audiences otherwise will not notice.

In *The Jar* (1984), Paul and Crystal converse in a restaurant, when the *crowd murmurs and Crystal's voice fade away* and *eerie noises fade up.* Paul stares at something behind Crystal. We intercut several times from Paul to his POV. Initially, he sees the restaurant's smooth wall. Then a rough stone wall, with a jar-shaped hole glowing at the edges. Crystal's voice returns (no fade up) as Paul stares, the eerie noises still present. Cut to the wall a last time (we don't hear Crystal, only the eerie noises). Cut to Paul and Crystal, her voice and crowd murmurs abruptly back (no fade up), the eerie noises abruptly gone. Crystal says "Paul" several times, adding that she hopes she's not boring him.

This *shifting volume* among the sound sources, some noises fading or abruptly replacing others, (1) focuses our attention on Paul by fading out Crystal's voice,[2] and (2) supports Paul's bizarre vision with correspondingly bizarre noises, which replace extraneous, normal noises.

Later, Paul finds himself in a desert, amid monks. One monk drags a cross in Christ-like fashion. Paul has no idea where he is or how he got there. Eerie mood music enhances the surreal atmosphere. Paul follows the monks. *Music fades* so we now hear the monk's *footsteps,* the cross *scraping the ground,* and Paul *screaming*: "Who are you?!"

Replacing the nondiegetic mood music with diegetic noises—the monks, their cross, Paul's scream—concertizes Paul's new reality, grounding him in it. This shift in volume from surreal music to concrete sound sources implies that this is not Paul's imagination—this is real. At least, that's how it seems to Paul (and to us).

Sound can *misdirect* audience attention. In *Hell Night* (1981), Marti and Jeff, a college couple trapped in a mansion with a slasher, discuss their dire predicament. Because their conversation is the scene's only sound, viewers will focus on Marti and Jeff in the frame's center-right—and initially not notice the rug slowly rising off the floor behind the couple in the frame's center-left. When the rug has risen so high that it cannot be "hidden in plain sight" much longer, spooky music cues audiences that a threat has entered the scene. Upon this ATC, many viewers will notice the rising rug (with the slasher underneath it) for the first time, and be shocked by its "sudden" appearance[3] [Figure 8.1].

This rising rug was in "plain sight," yet also "hidden" by directing viewers' attention

Figure 8.1—*Hell Night*. Jeff (Peter Barton) and Marti (Linda Blair) are brightly lit and audibly conversing, attracting the audience's attention to themselves, and away from the dimly lit and silently rising rug in the frame's center-left.

to the scene's only sound source (the conversing couple), and away from the silent threat. Lighting also helps misdirect viewer attention. The rug is dimly lit and silent, whereas Marti and Jeff are brightly lit and noisy.

Sound can link story elements. In *Fear No Evil* (1981), a high school teacher distributes corrected papers to his class. He calls on Julie to get her paper. Cut to a closeup of Julie. *Music and class noises fade into silence.* The film frame moves down to her hands TAPPING a *black marker* on her desk. All we hear is this LOUD tapping as we...

Cut to a *flashback* of a priest, years ago, having just killed Lucifer's recent incarnation.

Cut to a shot of hands TAPPING a *red marker* against a desk. It's Lucifer, reincarnated as Andrew, a student in Julie's class.

Cut to a *flashback* of Lucifer, freshly killed.

Cut to another student's hand, stopping Julie from tapping her black marker.

Cut to Andrew's hands, ceasing to tap his red marker. Normal *class sounds resume.* Frame moves up to Andrew's face.

Cut to a shot of the class. Julie accepts her paper.

In this scene, editing and sound link Julie, Andrew, and the priest. We'll later learn that Julie is an incarnation of the angel, Gabrielle, though she's unaware of it yet. The priest is an incarnation of the angel, Rafael. Their job is to kill Lucifer whenever he incarnates. Julie and Andrew tapping their pens in unison indicates their supernatural link. Increasing the volume on these tappings, while fading all other sounds into silence, emphasizes this link.

Films are becoming louder, to the point of audience discomfort. This is especially true of action films, and films influenced by action film aesthetics. (As are some horror films.) Gunfire and explosions and car crashes are supposedly more exciting when they rupture your eardrums. Ioan Allen of Dolby Laboratories blames this loudness trend on insecure directors: "Somebody said that the loudness is inversely proportional to the number of days left before the preview."[4]

Yet louder is not necessarily better. *Absolute silence* has aesthetic uses. At the end of *The Exorcist* (1973), Father Dyer revisits the house where Father Karras died the night before, having rolled down a flight of stairs beside the house. It is daytime. We hear traffic, children playing, Dyer's footsteps. But when Dyer reaches the top of the stairs *all noises fade into silence*. Cut to a closeup of Dyer gazing down the long flight of stone stairs. Cut to Dyer's POV of the stairs. Cut to the closeup of Dyer. All *noises fade back up*. Dyer turns and leaves.

This moment of silence, about 5 seconds, conveys Dyer's grief, having heard his friend's last confession and seeing him die at the bottom of those stairs. When a distressing, frightening, or joyous memory intrudes upon our thoughts, the world seems to fade, as it does now for Dyer. It's a subjective, artificial silence. The street noises are still there, but he (and we) can't hear them. The *mise-en-scène*— that the steps are of stone, devoid of pedestrians, shaded from sunlight — aesthetically supports this silence. The steps appear as forlorn as Dyer feels in his thoughts..

In *Dead Silence* (2007), Mary Shaw's ghost possesses ventriloquist dummies, using them as conduits through which to kill the descendants of those who killed her. The "silence" in *Dead Silence* has two meanings: (1) people can survive Mary's supernatural attacks, provided they don't scream, and (2), a bizarre silence falls whenever Mary's presence manifests.

Early in the film, Lisa, a young wife, is in her apartment with Billy, a ventriloquist's dummy, which was mysteriously delivered that night.

We hear *stereo music playing*. The *sound of raining* outside.

Lisa sets Billy on her bed, then gets a pillow and bedsheet from a closet, obscuring Billy. An ATC sound effect ensues. Lisa turns and sees that Billy's head has shifted, as if he's watching her. Lisa is unsettled, but dismisses it. She props up Billy with the pillow and covers him with the bedsheet, hoping to scare her husband, Jamie, when he returns.

Out in the living room, the *music slows down*, its *pitch deepening*. Hearing it, Lisa calls for Jamie, thinking he's returned. She enters the living room. Music *slows*, then *stops*. We hear the *clock ticking*. It ticks *loudly*, so it's all the more jarring as its *ticking slows down* and *stops*. The *sound of rain is gone*. A tea kettle whistles in the kitchen, *loudly*. Its *whistling slows down*, its *pitch deepening*, then *stops*.

No *ambient room sound*. Dead silence. Steam *continues blowing* from the kettle, but *no whistling*. Lisa stares fearfully at this unnatural phenomenon, uneased by the sudden silence. She hears *child's laughter* from the bedroom. Is it Billy? Lisa creeps toward the bedroom. We hear her *footsteps* and *heavy breathing* (signifying her fear), made *louder* by the silence. Lightning flashes, yet we hear no thunder. Eerie ATC music ensues. Lisa nears the bed, reaches for the sheet — it leaps up, *loudly flapping* as it engulf her.[5]

Jamie returns home to loud stereo music, raining noise, the kettle whistling. Yet though Lisa is dead, Jamie hears her voice, implying that Mary's spirit is present. An inconsistency?

Later, Jamie buries Billy in a cemetery. While he digs, Billy's mouth drops open. *Wind and ambient forest sounds fade out*, their *pitch deepening* before silence. Jamie looks up. He sees tree branches swaying, yet hears no wind. We only hear Jamie's *breathing and labors*. Jamie places Billy in a casket. Billy's head turns. It's enough to signify Mary's presence, yet the lack of ambient forest sounds contributes to the creepy, supernatural atmosphere, making the conceit of a possessed dummy more believable, thus scarier.

These recurring moments of partial silence (some noises fading, others remaining or even increasing in volume) not only bolster the atmosphere, they form a motif. Toward the end, Jamie and Detective Lipton search a derelict theater. They find a boy's corpse, made into a dummy. *Nondiegetic music and ambient noises fade out, wind down, pitch deepening, ending in silence.* "This is how it starts," Jamie warns Lipton.

Pitch

A sound's *pitch* (aka *frequency*) can be high or low. As with volume, pitch informs and directs audience attention. A *changing pitch* can suggest the speed or direction of a moving object.

In *Evil Dead 2* (1987), four people cower in a cabin, fearing the demons out in the woods. A clock on the wall stops ticking. "It's so quiet," Annie remarks. Brief silence. Then a demon, or demons, zoom about the room, left and right, up and down. We don't see them. Their presence is suggested by sound, acting, and framing. As the demons zip about, we hear the *changing pitch* of their flights about the room. In some shots, people *shift their gazes in the direction suggested by the changing pitch.* They apparently see, or at least sense, the demons' movements. Other shots depict the demons' POVs. These *POV frames' movements correspond to the noises' changing pitch.* When the frame stops moving, the noise stops.

These demonic noises are not your usual guttural screams. Rather, much of it sounds like furniture dragged across the floor, in a variety of timbre and pitches. Also, the sound of running hooves and door bangings, the frame zooming in on a stuffed deer's head and a barricaded door, respectively.

Later, Bobbie Joe is dragged through the woods by demonically possessed tree branches. They pull her ever faster toward a tree to smash her against it, her *increasing speed* implied both visually and by the *increasing pitch* of a revved up engine sound.[6]

Often in *Dead Silence*, the sounds don't just fade out (a lowering of volume). Rather, the sounds wind down, their *pitch deepening* as they slow toward silence. This *unexpected shift* from loudness to silence (not just the silence itself) contributes to the creepy atmosphere.

Comedies use pitch for gags, such as when a menacing character unexpectedly speaks in a high-pitched voice. Or a diminutive, oh-so-cute character speaks in a low-pitched voice.

Timbre

Timbre is the tonal quality (aka tonal color) of a sound. Different musical instruments (or voices, or other sound sources) "sound" different, though they may share the same volume and pitch. Tapping a book, a wooden table, or a metal door will each resound with different timbre.

Timbre is informative. In *Inferno* (Italian 1980), Mark paces his sister's apartment when a *hollow timbre* resounds under his feet, alerting him to the secret passageways beneath the floorboards. His discovery contrasts with that in *The Ring* (2002), wherein Rachel and Noah discover a water well under the cabin's floorboards because marbles form an arrow on the floor. *The Ring* uses *mise-en-scène* rather than timbre, perhaps because cabins, unlike apartments, normally have empty spaces under their floorboards.

Certain timbre are inherently spooky. In *The Leopard Man* (1943), Dr. Galbraith, an insane murderer, is haunted by his past misdeeds. He imagines seeing or hearing his dead victims everywhere. He enters his museum at night, after everyone has left. His *footsteps echo* against the stone walls. Sitting at his desk, he hears the *echo of castanets*. One of his victims, Clo-Clo, had played castanets. Is it Clo-Clo's ghost? Galbraith hears the *echo of someone else's footsteps* resounding from the shadows. A ghost? This *echo timbre* is (1) spookily atmospheric, so that it unnerves the audience, and (2) informative, confirming the museum's cold emptiness. Which is why echoes can be spooky. Galbraith is alone. Or at least, alone with whatever is echoing from the darkness.

The right timbre can empower a threat. In *Squirm* (1976), millions of flesh-eating worms arise from the soil and attack a small Georgia town. Worms flood a jail cell, diner, houses, rising like seawater. Closeup shots depict the worms spreading fangs, and emitting what sounds like a *loud, screeching horse's whinny or elephant's roar*. It's hard to describe, but it makes the worms that much scarier.

In *The Beyond* (aka *E tu vivrai nel terrore — L'aldilà*, Italian 1981), Martin, an architect, studies an old building's blueprints in a library. Startled by lightning, he falls off the ladder. He lies on the floor, alert, but apparently paralyzed. Dozens of tarantulas creep toward him, climb over him, biting his face, his tongue, his eyes. Gory closeups are enhanced by the tarantulas' *loud creaking*, at times almost *birdlike squeaking*, and the *tearing and crunching sounds* as they chew Martin's flesh.

Some timbre have become clichés. In *The Exorcist*, a demon, claiming to be the devil, speaks through Regan in a *raspy, guttural* voice. Higher-pitched than some successive film demons (e.g., *Evil Dead 2*), yet *The Exorcist* established a tradition: A demon's voice is *deep, raspy, guttural*.

For ghosts, the tradition is to *wail or moan like a wind*, or speak in *ethereal tones*, or *quavering voices*. Such clichés can work, but defying audience expectations can also have a powerful effect. Kayako, the ghost girl in *The Grudge* (2004), is memorable largely because of her innovative *creepy croaking*. When she opens her mouth, she sounds like bad plumbing. A sound reportedly made by director Takashi Shimizu.

Timbre can mislead audiences or create ambiguity. In *The Curse of the Cat People* (1944), Amy, a little girl, wanders through the snowy woods at night. She remembers the tale of the headless horseman. We hear a *voiceover* of Mrs. Farren's recounting of the tale. Amy hears *hoof beats*. She ducks beside the road. The hoof beats' volume and pitch increase, as if the horse is approaching. Then a car drives past, the hoof beats' timbre *morphing* into that of car tires.

Was it the car all along, its timbre distorted by distance and Amy's imagination? Or was it, initially, the headless horseman? As so often in Val Lewton's films, the answer is ambiguous. It was probably Amy's imagination — but it *could* have been the supernatural.

Timbre can reveal a film's budget. Low-budget films often shoot in someone's house or apartment, rather than in a *soundstage*.[7] On such locations, actors' voices may resound off hard surfaces, creating a sharp, hollow, or echoy timbre. This may be aesthetically appropriate for some scripts, but not often. Yet low-budget films rarely correct for this, eschewing pricey *sound blankets* that might cover hard surfaces to improve the acoustics. Sound blankets can also muffle camera noise. In *Carnage* (1984), hard, hollow, echoy voices and footsteps not only resound off of hard surfaces, but sometimes you hear the camera whirring.

Fidelity

Fidelity refers to a sound recording's accuracy in representing its source. High-fidelity sounds are more accurate than low-fidelity. Do worms and tarantulas really sound as they do in *Squirm* and *The Beyond*? Probably not. But high-fidelity worms and tarantulas belong to nature documentaries. Horror depicts unnatural threats. The unnatural often *sounds* unnatural.

The screams in *The Beyond* are high-fidelity, in that they sound like real screams. But are they realistic? When a seeing-eye dog attacks Emily, his blind owner, Emily screams. She keeps on screaming throughout the attack — despite the gaping hole in her throat. Wouldn't air escape, so that screaming becomes impossible? Are her vocal cords even intact? Considering all the blood, even if Emily can emit noises, wouldn't she gurgle rather than scream? No matter. While low on realism, and despite shamelessly ripping off *Suspiria*'s seeing-eye dog attack, *The Beyond* is high on entertainment value.

Fidelity is a matter of degree. Real tarantulas probably don't sound as they do in *The Beyond*, but we don't know. They might, were their noises magnified, or were they an especially nasty breed. But some sounds are so low-fidelity, they're *incongruous* (aka discordant) with the sound source. Incongruent sounds *contradict* our expectations for how the visuals should sound, creating an unsettling, or comedic, effect.

Kayako's *creepy croaking* is an unexpected timbre for a ghost, but as with the tarantulas, what do we know? Why shouldn't ghosts croak? But when Toshio, the ghost boy in *The Grudge*, opens his mouth, he *snarls like a cat*. Okay, Toshio may be a ghost, but he's still a ghost *boy*, and we do not expect boys to *meow*. That's beyond unexpected — it's incongruous.[8]

Possessed characters often have incongruous voices.[9] In *The Exorcist*, a possessed little girl, Regan, speaks in four voices other than her own: a demon, a British film director, a vagrant, and an elderly Italian woman. Regan's incongruent voices are among *The Exorcist*'s shocks. (We don't actually see Regan when she speaks with the vagrant's voice; the shot is on Father Karras's reaction — he's startled, as are we.)

In *Witchery* (aka *La casa 4*, *Witchcraft*, Italian 1988), Gary and Leslie, seeking to escape an island that's haunted by a dead witch, come upon "the lady in black" gazing out a window, her back to them. "I've been waiting for you," she says in an *old, German-accented* voice, with an *echoy timbre*. She turns around. It's Jane, a young American. The witch, possessing and speaking through Jane, explains her diabolical plans.

The witch's echoy timbre (1) makes her sound more powerful, and (2) suggests that she is partly in Jane, and partly in some supernatural realm.

The incongruity (1) establishes that Jane is possessed, and (2) frightens viewers (at least those who aren't laughing — incongruous voices often risk unintentional laughs.) Actress Linda Blair's makeup (pale skin, rings under her eyes, wild hair) and performance (stilted and jittery) further suggest her possessed state. Her makeup is not as elaborately grotesque as when she played Regan, but it works nicely for a low budget.

In *Manhattan Baby* (Italian 1982), George, an archaeologist, takes his wife and daughter, Emily and Susie, to Egypt. While he explores ancient tombs, a blind woman gives Susie an evil amulet. The family returns to New York, and are plagued by all manner of supernatural events. Susie's bedroom glows white. Susie glows blue. She offers her parents a handful of sand and a scorpion. Then she faints.

The parents call Marcato, an antiques dealer, to examine Susie. While the parents wait in the kitchen, they hear Susie scream: "Mama! Mama!" George rushes into the bedroom. His POV shows Susie in bed, eyes shut, *lips still*— yet we hear her scream: "Mama!" George's POV shifts to the floor. Marcato is convulsing, lips foaming, mouth and ears bleeding, screaming *in Susie's voice*: "Help me! Heeeelp!"

The spectacle of a young girl's voice coming from this bearded, burly, middle-aged man is both startling and creepy. Marcato's lips don't sync with Susie's voice, but that lends the scene an additional supernatural aspect. (Again, some viewers will laugh.)

Is Marcato possessed by Susie? I don't know. *Manhattan Baby* often feels incoherent and arbitrary. As Marcato explains it, the gem in the amulet: "is endowed with evil powers. A force that has seized your daughter's mind, and that is now using her as a medium for it, its own dark and wicked malefactions. The power within this gem can open the infernal gate of time and space, and work miracles of evil beyond all arcane dimensions." Okay. Whatever.

Spirit mediums too speak incongruently. In *Night of the Demon* (aka *Curse of the Demon*, British 1957), Julian sends a demon to kill Harrington in an apparent accident. Julian then sends the demon after John. Harrington's niece, Joanna, drags John to a séance, hoping to learn how to lift the curse. Also attending are two older women, and the medium, Mr. Meek.

Lights are dimmed. The two women unexpectedly sing "Cherry Ripe." Mrs. Karswell explains: "The spirits like it." Their high-pitched singing of this frivolous song, in the context of this spooky atmosphere, is both funny and creepy. One senses these people are weird, and weird things may happen tonight. They cease singing when Meek begins convulsing.

Meek slumps, now still. He sits up straight, stern-faced, *bellowing in a guttural foreign language* as he channels Crimson Eagle, a "red Indian chief." He stops. Relaxes, grins hugely, saying in a *thick Scottish accent*: "Well, a kindly good evening to you friends. Bonnie weather we're having." He continues speaking as Mr. MacGregor. Then he assumes a *distressed little girl's voice*: "Mummy, oh mummy, oh mummy. I can't find, I can't find Frederica." Finally, he assumes *Harrington's voice*: "Joanna, Joanna, are you there Joanna?" Harrington warns John not to fight Julian. He ends by *screaming*, reliving the moment of his death.

Actor Reginald Beckwith (as Meek) changes his posture and facial expression with each spirit. But the creepy part are the voices, each one increasingly incongruous, "topping" the previous one. Crimson Eagle's voice sounds like Beckwith. But MacGregor's voice is clearly not Beckwith. It's another actor's voice dubbed in. Despite MacGregor's friendly tones, it's unsettling to see Meek speak in a different voice from the one we expect (Beckwith's voice). Then comes the little girl's voice, even more incongruous than MacGregor's. And then Harrington's voice.

Horror and comedy both aim to intensify events as the story progresses. The scares must get scarier, the jokes funnier. Comedians try to "top" each joke with a funnier one. Harrington's voice is not as discordant as the little girl's, yet he "tops" the little girl because, as Joanna's dead uncle, he's more important to the main characters and to the story. Just like audiences are startled by MacGregor, then again by the little girl, they are startled by Harrington. His voice convinces Joanna, and probably some viewers, that Meek is no fraud. (An unknown man's voice, after the little girl's, would have been a "let down" rather than a "top.")

In *The Legend of Hell House* (1973), four people investigate the reputedly haunted Hell House for evidence of an afterlife. They hold a séance in a vast, dim room. A fire burns in the fireplace. Florence, a medium, says a prayer, then, eyes shut, she gives her psychic impressions: "This is evil house. Place of sickness. Evil." While she continues, we hear eerie, ethereal noises, implying the presence of supernatural entities. From these noises emerge what sounds like a voice saying: "Laura, Laura."[10]

Florence says: "There is a young man. Very young. Says he must speak. Must speak." Then: "I don't know you people." On this line *Florence's voice morphs into Belasco's voice.* Its timbre is that of a *young man's voice, electronically warped.* Florence says in this voice: "Why are you here? Does no good. Nothing changes. Nothing."

Cut to a closeup of Florence's profile, silhouetted by the firelight: "Get out or I'll hurt you. I can't help myself. Goddamn you, you filthy sons of bitches! Goddamn you!"

Cut to a reaction shot of Ann.

Cut to an extreme closeup of Florence's lips, silhouetted by the firelight: "I don't want to hurt you. But I must, I must. Get out of this house before I kill you all!"

Actress Pamela Franklin's voice was apparently morphed in post-production to create the voice of Belasco. Meek's spirit voices *manifest immediately*, so their incongruity is all the more startling. Florence's voice *morphs* into Belasco's, so the incongruity is less startling, but perhaps more believable. Hence, less likely to spark unintentional laughs.

Franklin's voice might have been morphed into something more natural-sounding, but Belasco's *electronically distorted timbre* has an extradimensional quality. Like the witch's echoy timbre in *Witchery*, Belasco's timbre suggests a voice from another realm.

Florence's incongruent voice is enhanced by editing, framing, lighting, photography, and *mise-en-scène.* Seeing this young, religious woman cursing in a discordant voice is unsettling enough. But as Belasco grows angrier, his words harsher, the vocal incongruity is intensified by cutting from a closeup of Florence, to a tighter closeup of her profile, (then a quick intercut to Ann), to an extreme closeup of Florence's lips. The firelight silhouettes her, emphasizing her moving lips. The fire also casts Florence in an orange glow, as if she were amid hellfire. (Well, she *is* in Hell House.) A telephoto lens blurs the fire behind Florence, emphasizing her sharply focused lips in the foreground [Figures 8.2–8.4].

Curiously, the timbre of Belasco's voice resembles that of Andrew in *Fear No Evil*, when Andrew assumes Lucifer's discordant voice. Perhaps actor Stefan Arngrim and Franklin had their voices distorted in a similar manner?

Incongruous sounds are not limited to inappropriate voices. In *House by the Cemetery* (aka *Quella villa accanto al cimitero*, Italian 1981), a young boy, Bob, waits in a car for his parents. A closeup of Bob. We hear a young girl's voice: "Bob. Bob." Ominous music ensues.[11] Because of her vocal timbre, we assume the girl is next to Bob, offscreen. We suspect she's a ghost. Bob looks up, but doesn't turn to see who's beside him, if anyone. The girl's voice: "I'm here. Behind you." Bob turns. "On the other side of the street," she says. Bob looks out the rear window. A rack focus reveals the girl outside, across the street.

An unsettling trick. The ghost girl's timbre had sounded as if she were inside the car. Of course, being a ghost, she can manifest her voice in one spot, and her appearance elsewhere. Ghosts don't usually do that, and there's no reason for her to do so now — other than that it's a neat trick on the audience.

Incongruent sounds can be funny. In *Evil Dead 2*, a demon possesses Ash's hand. The

Figure 8.2 — *The Legend of Hell House*. Speaking in Belasco's ghostly voice, Florence (Pamela Franklin) is framed in closeup. We intercut to Ann's reaction shot, and then cut to...

Figure 8.3 —...a closer shot of Florence. A shallow depth of field blurs the orange fire behind her, which edge lights her profile. Cut to...

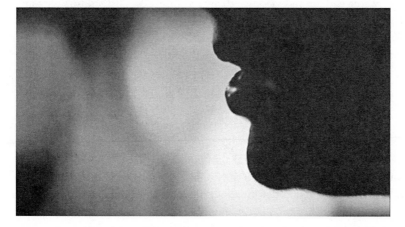

Figure 8.4 —...an extreme closeup of Florence's silhouetted lips. The lens's depth of field seems shallower; the fire is so blurred as to be unrecognizable. Cutting to ever closer shots on Florence's lips reinforces the voice's intensifying threats and anger.

hand flaps about, pulls Ash's hair, and breaks dishes on his head. It mutters in a squeaky, high-pitched, chirpy timbre. It's often unintelligible, but we can discern "Up yours, you son of a bitch!" when Ash (after chainsawing off his hand) laughs at it for stepping on a mouse trap. Later, a stuffed deer's head laughs hysterically, as does a desk lamp, books, and other inanimate objects in the cabin.

The deer's head laughs with its mouth. But the desk lamp, the hand, the books, they have no mouths. Nor does the hand have eyes, yet some shots depict its POV as it crawls on the floor. But because *Evil Dead 2* weaves much satire into its horror, its story requires even less "sense" than a typical horror film. The personification of these objects (relying heavily on incongruent voices) adds a comedic, light-hearted tone to this gorefest.

Dubbing Voices

Dubbing is the copying of recorded material. One *dubs* a videotape when copying its contents to another tape. One *uploads* content to a computer or the internet, and one *burns* a CD or DVD, but it's all the same thing. Whether you call it dubbing, uploading, burning, or copying, you're transferring recorded material from A to B.

Dubbing is also the adding, or replacing, of specific sounds on a soundtrack. In foreign language films, a new cast of actors' voices are often dubbed onto the soundtrack, replacing the original cast's voices, so audiences can understand the dialog. Foreign language dubbing is done for marketing reasons, but it has aesthetic ramifications.

Cineastes insist that films can only be truly appreciated with the original actors' voices. Cineastes are high-brow film fans (naturally, they use a French word to describe themselves), but they have a point. Acting is both physical and vocal. Imagine a Sylvester Stallone or Clint Eastwood film without their unique voices. It wouldn't really be them. *Hercules in New York* (1970) features a pre-stardom Arnold Schwarzenegger, his voice dubbed by an accentless American. Seeing Schwarzenegger perform without his now famous Austrian accent is a jarring experience.[12]

Cineastes prefer their foreign films *subtitled* rather than dubbed. Exploitation fans would rather watch the sex and violence than read subtitles. Distributors try to please everyone. High-brow art films are usually subtitled, whereas kung-fu, horror, and other exploitation films are often dubbed. Atypically, recent Asian horror imports have been subtitled (e.g., *Ringu*, 1998; *Gin gwai* 2002; and Japan's *Tomie* series). Possibly, distributors believe these films appeal to a higher-brow horror audience. Or maybe they figured the market was too small to justify the higher expense of dubbing.

Continental European films often cast from multiple countries, each actor performing in his own language. Especially if it's an exploitation film, the actors expect to be dubbed. Even so, they aren't always happy about it. English actress Mary Maude traveled to Spain to appear in *The House That Screamed* (aka *La residencia*, Spanish 1969). She performed in English, but her voice didn't even make the English language version. Explains Maude: "Both Spain and Italy have — or did at that time — a different attitude toward dubbing than ours. It was considered not only necessary, but, possibly, an advantage, as opposed to a necessary evil. Unfortunately, I did not dub my own voice, as I was working on something else at the time. I regret this, as I feel that only half the performance is mine. It is my understanding that the English dub was not very good. But, then again, the Spanish one wasn't much either."[13]

I think Maude is being too hard on the film. Both she and the actress who dubbed her voice perform well. But Maude has a point about hers being "only half the performance." Dubbing grafts a second interpretation onto the first, especially if the original director is absent during the dubbing session, resulting in two directors guiding two casts.

Despite the disdain of cineastes, *voiceover actors* insist that dubbing is its own art form. Yet while celebrities have long been "taking over" other areas of voiceover work (e.g., audio books, radio and TV commercials, cartoons), they've ignored foreign film dubbing. Celebrities will provide voices for cartoon characters, but they won't share a performance with a flesh-and-blood actor.

Maybe it's me, but I sometimes have difficulty telling apart European actors when their voices are dubbed. At times, I'd confused Mike and Vincent (portrayed by actors José Gras and Selan Karay) in *Hell of the Living Dead* (aka *Apocalipsis caníbal, Inferno dei morti viventi, Virus,* Italian-Spanish 1980). Delete an actor's voice, and you dilute his uniqueness. Especially since voiceover actors tend to sound alike. Always so bland and clearly enunciated. Even their gasps and laughter are clearly enunciated — and often satirized for it. Maybe it's their training, but something pounds all the individuality and character out of their voices. Unlike celebrities, who retain their distinctive timbre.

What may be termed "low-fidelity dubbing" (when a dubbed voice ill fits the actor) can be unintentionally funny. For some inexplicable reason, European boys are often dubbed with annoyingly whiny, high-pitched voices. When Dr. Freudstein's shambling corpse menaces Bob in *House by the Cemetery,* Bob's dubbed crying and shouting for help is morbidly hilarious.[14] In *Extra Terrestrial Visitors* (aka *Los nuevos extraterrestres* Spanish-French 1983), Tommy is likewise dubbed with an annoyingly whiny, high-pitched voice—another reason the film is among *Mystery Science Theater 3000's* most popular satirical targets.

Avant-garde and underground films use low-fidelity dubbing, to the point of incongruity, for social satire and political statements. Lisa Hammer's *Period Piece* (2004) dubs the soundtrack from a 1971 educational video (in which a family teaches a retarded girl about sanitary pads), onto newly filmed visuals featuring actors who lip sync (barely) the old soundtrack. Thus, the caring and respectful voices in the 1971 soundtrack are spoken by a retarded girl who smokes cigarettes, sticks sanitary pads to her face, and sniffs her sister's bloodied pads; by a lewd older sister who swoons and crawls on the bathroom floor (is she on drugs?) and smacks her retarded sister; and by a creepy dad who looks like a pedophile. This resulting incongruity is both jarring (compelling viewers to consider American cultural attitudes toward menstruation) and hilarious.

This incongruity is supported by jump cuts, which, by shattering visual continuity, lend a schizophrenic sensibility to the twisted proceedings.

Damon Packard's *Reflections of Evil* (2002) follows the travails of an irate, obese man as he peddles watches in Los Angeles. Visuals are sped up (so the actors move in a jittery fashion), and dubbed with sound effects and voices. The voices are often low-fidelity. One woman has a chipmunk cartoon voice. Other voices are sped up, so that people shout, threaten, and curse in high-pitched squeals. Harsh noises of police helicopters, car crashes, people tripping and falling, barking dogs, and gunfire resound throughout the film. Some of these noises are also low-fidelity (particularly the trips and falls). These incongruent voices and noises contribute to an impression of Los Angeles as a city in a state of disintegration.

Packard heightens this impression through associational editing. He peppers his film with 1970s film trailers, TV commercials, and ABC TV promos, because he considers the 1970s and early 1980s as a more innocent time.[15] These sweetly nostalgic cultural images contrast sharply with his discordant vision of contemporary L.A.

Apart from any *aesthetic* effect, incongruent dubbing has a *pragmatic* benefit: it can hide poor acting. Both Hammer and Packard star in their respective films. Are they skilled thespians? We can't judge from these films. Both filmmakers give broad, hammy performances that are appropriate to their roles, but also easy to pull off. Neither role is vocally challenging. Packard's voice is often distorted and poorly synced, while the adult Hammer (playing the retarded child) badly lip syncs another actress's voice (from the 1971 soundtrack).

Ambient Sound and MOS

Every location, indoors or out, has an *ambient sound*, that is, a background noise. Every room has a unique ambient sound, called a *room tone*. Professional filmmakers, upon finishing with a location, will record its ambient sound. This way, if a filmmaker wants to dub new dialog or sound effects into a scene during post-production, the room tone can be mixed under the new dialog to maintain audio continuity. Otherwise, the dialog recorded on location, and the dialog recorded in the sound studio, will sound as if they were spoken in different rooms.

Continuity can also be strengthened by using the same *wild sounds* in a scene, which are *unsynchronized background noises*, such as crowd murmurs or forest noises.

Dead Silence demonstrates the emotional power of ambient sound (apart from its serving continuity), and how its sudden loss can unsettle or terrify audiences.[16]

Some films are shot *MOS* (without synchronized sound). The term is thought to have originated from one of Golden Age Hollywood's many German emigre directors, who referred to scenes shot "mit out sound." His crews mimicked his accent, and the acronym gained acceptance.[17]

Filmmakers normally shoot MOS when a scene has *no dialog*, because it saves on labor and equipment — no sound crew! Wild sounds, voiceover narration, and nondiegetic music can be added during post-production.

Low-budget filmmakers sometimes shoot *dialog scenes* MOS. Later, the actors perform their lines in a recording studio, viewing the film while trying to sync their voices to their lips on screen. This seems to be the case with *Easy Kill* (1989), a noir crime thriller. Although actress Jane Badler's lips are grossly out of sync at one point, the cast does a mostly decent job of it. The giveaway is the lack of ambient sound, creating an empty, disembodied timbre. It doesn't matter if the location is inside a moving car, or in an alley, or in a house — much of the dialog has that clearly enunciated, bland quality, unaffected by surroundings.

Zero-budget filmmakers, who can't even afford to rent a recording studio, might record dialog with an unsynchronized sound recorder. This is how *The Jar* was made. Says actor Gary Wallace: "[Director Bruce Tuscano] didn't use the 60 hz signal to sync the sound and movie. He and [production manager] Cameron McCloud ended up cutting the vocal tape into little pieces and splicing them together to make the sound track."[18]

Perhaps because Tuscano lacked synchronized recording equipment, his script contains limited dialog. Many scenes depict only Paul or his visions. Because he is often alone, we hear his voiceovers (which need not be synced) rather than dialog. Limiting the dialog *pragmatically* limits the number of poorly synced scenes, but it also *aesthetically* supports *The Jar*'s conceit by presenting Paul's mental breakdown as a subjective experience. His internal voiceover thoughts predominate over external contact with other characters. Hence, pragmatic aesthetics.

The Jar also lacks ambient sound. Some scenes use wild sounds (e.g., restaurant murmur) or surreal mood music, but many scenes lack any background noise, so the dialog or voiceovers resound against a disembodied timbre. It's as if we hear the characters at high altitude, our ears congested. The dubbed voices are poorly enough synchronized so that, against this disembodied timbre, they support the story of Paul's growing disassociation from reality. His conversations with Crystal and Jack evoke Pink Floyd: "Your lips move but I cannot hear what you're saying." Paul hears what they're saying, but the vocal desynchronization creates an impression that the fabric of his universe is disintegrating. This desynchronization is not recognized by Paul, but it lies within the film's subtext, however aesthetically unintentional. Once again, Tuscano's pragmatic shortcuts aesthetically enhance the film.

In *Carnival of Souls* (1962), shot largely MOS, Mary's soul is disconnecting from reality. Although film critic Jeff Hillegass considered actress Candace Hilligoss's detached performance appropriate to her role of a lost soul trapped between life and death, he also wrote that: "Much of the audio had to be post-dubbed, which led to unfortunate difficulties in sync which remain in the final film."[19]

I agree with Hillegass's assessment of Hilligoss's performance, yet I also believe that the imprecise synchronization *enhances* the film for the same reason. It reinforces the impression of a soul trapped in an imprecise twilight world, one in which material reality is ever ready to slip away. Unfortunately, it's the initial scene, wherein Mary is still alive, that is most poorly synced.

If you must shoot a dialog scene MOS, it's a good idea to (1) obscure the actors' mouths, or (2) frame them in a long shot, or (3) dimly light them. Anything to make their lips difficult to discern. Tuscano occasionally blocks one actor's mouth with another actor's head.

Lemora: A Child's Tale of the Supernatural (1973) opts for dim lighting. Late in the film, the vampire Lemora addresses Lila in a dark room. We don't see Lemora, only her burning torch. Her voice emanates from pitch blackness. Because we don't see her lips (or anything of her), the scene was shot MOS. Actress Lesley Gilb, who played Lemora, wasn't even present. A crew member held the torch. Gilb's lines were recorded on another day, then dubbed into the scene.[20]

The torch fire floating in darkness creates a surreal image, appropriate to a child's bizarre, sexually charged nightmare, which is one possible interpretation of the film. Filming MOS saved money, while supporting *Lemora*'s dramatic premise. More pragmatic aesthetics.

Yet something about *Lemora* invites misinterpretation and confusion. The film has been described as "leavened with a fierce anti–Catholicism."[21] Barry Kaufman writes "the entire plot of the film reeks of anti–Catholicism"[22] and recounts Lemora "shedding Lilah [sic] of her Catholic inhibitions."[23] Yet Lila's guardian is a Protestant minister. Lila refers to herself as a Baptist. Both Hardy and Kaufman claim the Catholic Film Board condemned *Lemora*, but a CFB condemnation does not alter the story, converting Baptist characters into Catholics. Silver and Ursini further obfuscate matters, writing that Lila wishes "to escape the sexual advances of the minister."[24] But the minister makes no advances. Lila embraces him, while he recoils in guilt. Silver and Ursini also write that *Lemora* was condemned by the Catholic Legion of Decency, rather than the Catholic Film Board.

Reflections of Evil, while aesthetically befitting from its low-fidelity dubbing, also saved money by shooting MOS. Packard admits that many of his creative decisions (such as his heavy use of old film trailers, and TV promos and ads) are motivated by financial restraints.[25]

Today, in this age of DV video, zero-budget producers rarely shoot MOS. Instead, they'll use the built-in mic on their camcorders. Bigger-budgeted filmmakers, who use sound recorders, still regard MOS as an option for scenes without dialog.

Threats Unseen Yet Heard

Cinema is often called a visual medium, yet sometimes the storytelling burden is carried primarily by sound. Many things are "heard but not seen." In a romantic comedy, it may be noisy lovers fumbling in the dark. In horror films, it's often a noisy threat. Because the threat is offscreen or in the dark — heard but not seen — audiences must fill in the blanks, interpreting the sounds with their own unnerved imaginations.

In *The Haunting*, Theo and Eleanor huddle fearfully in Theo's bedroom while an unseen entity haunts the hallway outside. Loud bangs alternate with softer bangs, light tappings, what sounds like something dragged across the floor, a scraping on the door, animalistic breathing, children laughing (softly and loudly), and stark silence. The loud bangs resound intermittently, allowing for softer interludes. These tense silences allow Theo and Eleanor (and the audience) to tremble at the prospect of the next volley of bangs. Like the proverbial horror "rollercoaster," the women fret during the silences as they await the next plunge.

We never see any ghosts in *The Haunting*, only their handiwork: chalk on a wall, a door pressed from the other side, etc. Rather than showing themselves, these ghosts (or whatever they are), frighten Hill House's residents mostly through sounds of every volume, pitch, timbre, and apparent sound source (adult and child, animal and mineral). Even the *sight* of the door pressing inward is made creepier by the *sound* of its creaking wood. This creaking is underscored by the scene being otherwise mostly silent.

Likewise in *The Blair Witch Project* (1999), sounds conjure uneasy images in audiences' minds. While shooting a documentary about a witch, Heather, Josh, and Mike get lost in the woods. One night they're awakened by *crackling echoes*. Heather and Josh leave their tent to investigate. Because of night-for-night photography, Heather is surrounded by pitch blackness, lit only with a single hard light. She says of the noise: "It's all around us. That is fucking weird."

Left to the audience's imagination: *What* is all around them?

The following night, the *crackling echoes* resume. Amid darkness, the three filmmakers discuss the weird sounds, planting suggestions in viewers' minds. At first, Mike proposes that it's a deer. Heather says, "It sounds like footsteps." Mike replies, "I know, that's a fucking person."

Next morning, three piles of rocks are outside their tent. That was no deer.

That night, the filmmakers are awakened by sounds of *children laughing* and *human speech*, muffled and indistinct, like some of the ghostly voices in *The Haunting*. Audience anxiety rises because we strain to hear, yet can't discern what's being said. The three filmmakers cower in their tent, flashlights on. Then a *rushing sound*, conjuring images of a crowd of people running past the tent. "Go fucking go!" the filmmakers scream, exiting the tent. (Why? Because it's scarier to *not know* what's outside?) Heather runs within pitch blackness, lit only by a single hard light. She points into offscreen space, screaming "Oh my God, what the fuck is that?! What the fuck is that?!"

What Heather sees, and the source of those sounds, are left to our imaginations. Heather never tries to describe what she saw. Maybe she can't?

In the morning the filmmakers return to their disheveled campsite. Josh's belongings are strewn about and covered with "slime." That night, no noises.

Next morning, Josh is gone. That night, Heather and Mike hear *tortured screams* in the dark — forcing audiences to imagine the bizarre cruelties being inflicted on Josh.

Next day, Heather and Mike find a bundle of sticks, containing a rag, containing *bloody teeth!* Conjuring new images of Josh's suffering.

In *The Blair Witch Project*, the threat remains unseen, its true nature (a witch's ghost? a backwoods lunatic?) suggested solely by its noises and handiwork (the pile of rocks, the bloody teeth). But with other films, audiences *glimpse* a threat before the lights go out — seeing enough to conjure a ghastly image, but leaving much to their imaginations as they struggle to interpret the noises in the dark.

In *The Resurrected* (1992), Charles Ward conducts scientific experiments to resurrect the dead, creating monsters along the way.[26] John, Lonnie, and Claire — a detective, his assistant, and Ward's wife — discover Ward's dungeon laboratory, a subterranean complex of stone walls and archways. Open pits contain Ward's failed experiments: misshapen humanoid freaks with exposed organs and snarling mouths. Monsters both ugly and unfriendly.

Amid pitch blackness, John, Lonnie, and Claire have only a lantern, a broken flashlight, and a matchbook to light their way. They're armed with a shotgun and pistol. Their light reveals a monster. *It's escaped from its pit!* Lonnie drops his lantern to raise his shotgun. The lantern shatters, bringing complete darkness. We *see* nothing. We *hear* panicked voices: "Don't move." "Lonnie, Lonnie." "I'm looking." "Where are you?" "Where the fuck are they?"

Left to our imagination: *Where is that monster now?* We don't hear it. We only hear the people.

Lonnie lights a match. A feeble glow. We glimpse all three people — *and the monster!* It's maybe ten feet away. Both men fire their guns. The match goes out. Pitch blackness. We hear the monster's growl. Or is it a subterranean wind? We hear voices: "John?" "Where are you?" "Over here." (As if anyone can see where "over here" is.) "Lonnie, Lonnie your matches."

Lonnie lights another match. Feebly lighting him, amid blackness. "This way." Claire's voice. Lonnie turns. Claire's face is dimly visible in the distance. "What your step." John's voice. Lonnie walks — *and falls into a pit!* Claire picks up the matchbook, the match still burning. John tries to pull Lonnie out. Claire assists. Another monster in the pit grabs Lonnie and pulls him in! The match goes out. Total darkness. *What's happening to Lonnie?!*

John urges Claire to light another match. She does and — the first monster is *right beside them!* They leap away, hitting the floor. Match goes out. Total darkness. John gets the flashlight working. He sees Claire on the ground. The monster roars from *somewhere* in that blackness. *Is it near?!* John sweeps his flashlight — and *spots the monster!*

Much of this scene occurs in pitch blackness. We hear mostly voices and a subterranean wind. Sometimes intense mood music and the monster's roar. More often, only silence, broken by the voices and wind. It's a tense silence, because when the monster is quiet, we can't judge its proximity. As *The Haunting* demonstrated, volume suggests a sound source's proximity, and *The Resurrected*'s silence refuses to suggest anything. All is quiet before Claire lights her match, making the monster's presence beside her and John a shocking surprise.

Apart from its use of sound to conjure scary images in our imaginations, this scene is also admirable for its low-key, motivated lighting. The ever-changing lights in the story include a lantern, gunshot flares, matches, and a flashlight. Yet the stage lights, if any are used, are not noticeable. The scene's illumination always appears motivated by the *mise-en-scène*.

Similarly in *Suspiria* (Italian 1977), we see only a silhouette of the ballet academy's directress behind some bedsheets. Yet her snoring's hideous timbre, alternately wheezing and roaring, conjures hideous images in our minds [Figure 6.7].[27]

Low-Budget Sound

Horror films use sound to suggest an *unseen threat*. Low-budget horror films use sound to suggest *anything* that's too expensive to show. In *Bride of the Monster* (1955), two cops are in a diner. Actually, just two actors standing by a wall. To create the illusion of a diner, director Ed Wood adds a few props (coffee, table, phone), and the *sounds of people murmuring*. We don't see these customers, but we hear them, so we accept that they exist. Thus, Wood saves money on both location rental and extras. In *Plan 9 from Outer Space* (1959), Wood depicts an accident by showing actor Bela Lugosi walking offscreen, then the *sounds of screeching tires and a scream*. We never see this accident, but, though the screams sound silly, we accept that Lugosi has been hit by a car. No need to hire a stuntman, rent a car, or buy a film permit to stage an accident on a city street.

In *Stage Fright* (aka *Nightmares*, Australian 1980), somebody is killing the cast and crew of a "play about death." This low-budget film suggests a crowded theater by intercutting stock footage of theater crowds, supported by *wild sounds of crowd murmurs, applause, and laughter* mixed with *original dialog of unseen theatergoers*. During the play's intermission, we cut to the stock footage and crowd murmurs, and hear comments like: "A little obscure, don't you know." and "She may be pretty, but she's got a sour mouth." Naturally, nobody in the stock footage is visibly mouthing these comments.

Sound can save money on a film by "telling, not showing." If you can't afford to *show* a man transforming into a werewolf, a character can *tell* us about having seen it. *Voiceovers* are another popular way to save on a budget.

In *Fear No Evil*, an unsuspecting couple have their baby son baptized. But because the baby is an incarnation of Lucifer, the baptism turns bloody. The parents rush from the church. Cut to a shot of their house. Over the next 50 seconds, three *dissolves* transition to three other shots of the same house, looking increasingly dilapidated. The parents' *voiceovers* bicker about their son, in increasingly bitter tones. Superimposed over the final shot of the house: *Eighteen Years Later*. Cut to the mother inside the house, preparing her son's 18th year birthday cake.

These changing images of the house, and the voiceovers, intimate the son's corrosive effect on his parents' marriage over time, in a relatively inexpensive manner. One could have instead shot several scenes of the parents arguing, wearing different costumes and progressively "aged" makeup, set amid different room furnishings. But money is saved by filming the house four times, from the same position (no new camera setups, just a progressively unkempt lawn, etc.), and recording the actors' dialog in a sound studio.

In the horror anthology film, *Gallery of Horrors* (1967), stock footage and voiceovers are pushed to a shamelessly penny-pinching extreme. In the tale, "Monster Raid," Dr. Spalding's wife and assistant (Helen and Dr. Sevard) have an affair. They steal Spalding's medical research and bury him alive — but only after he's taken his rejuvenation formula! Desmond, a servant, frees Spalding from his crypt and drives him, in a horse-drawn coach, to his castle, to take revenge on Helen and Sevard.

The story is told in flashbacks and voiceovers. It *begins* with Desmond freeing Spalding from the crypt, which is when Spalding's voiceover begins relating events. Cut to stock footage (apparently from another horror film) of horses pulling a coach. Spalding's voiceover continues telling his tale. Cut to a flashback scene, to before Spalding apparently died and was resurrected by his formula. We continue crosscutting between these flashbacks and the *same exact stock footage*, "enhanced" by Spalding's voiceovers.

"Monster Raid" contains 10 minutes, 36 seconds of original footage, and 5 minutes, 10 seconds — nearly *a third* of the story — of the *same brief shots* of horses pulling a coach (long shots, closeups, and the ocean beside the coach), with Spalding's voiceovers. His voiceovers tell us everything that *has* happened. Then in the original flashback footage, the actors *again* tell us what *will* happen. In case the audience is still confused, Spalding's voiceovers *again* recount everything that *has* happened so far, and *will* happen. And so on, throughout the crosscuts.

Even after we're acquainted with every minutia, late in the story, we again crosscut to yet another 55 seconds of stock footage of horses pulling a coach, during which Spalding's voiceover says: "Yes, they buried me. My faithful wife dressed in black. Her lack of tears hidden by a heavy veil. And my good friend, Dr. Sevard, who conveniently signed my death certificate, standing by the side in deep sympathy. They did not realize that the highly concentrated injection of my formula had placed me in a state of suspended animation, and had preserved my brain, heart, and lungs long after the exterior of my body had begun to rot and decay and yield to the elements. But faithful Desmond came for me, as I knew he would. I wonder if dear Helen will recognize me? Muhahaha!"

"Monster Raid" is a traditional *Tales from the Crypt*–type revenant corpse revenge tale. Spalding returns to his castle and kills both Helen and Sevard. All those flashbacks and stock footage lead to an ending so quick, you'll miss it if you blink. Luckily, *Gallery of Horrors* is "so bad it's good." Adding to the fun factor are actors John Carradine and Lon Chaney Jr., and a bevy of bloopers and inconsistencies. Spalding's voice in the flashback scenes (when he's portrayed by actor Ron Doyle) sounds *nothing* like his voiceovers (when he's portrayed as a mummified corpse — and *why* was this 19th century scientist mummified? — because the producers couldn't afford even Ron Doyle for an extra day of shooting?).

Using *Gallery of Horrors*'s technique, one could do a low-budget remake of *Titanic* by running thirty seconds of historical *Titanic* film footage in a loop, along with a three hour voiceover recounting the entire story: "Then the ship broke. Its mighty stern rose high. My lover told me to hold on. I saw people drowning below. A woman's heart is an ocean of mystery."

Does *Gallery of Horror*'s low-budget sound work? Not aesthetically, but the film got distribution, so it "worked" financially. Of course, crappy horror films were easier to sell in the 1960s, since few people could afford to shoot a film on 35mm stock, or even 16mm. Today, so much amateurish horror is being shot on DV tape, crappy horror is harder to sell.

Zaat (aka *Attack of the Swamp Creatures, Hydra*, 1975) is another low-budget horror film that relies heavily on voiceovers. Dr. Leopold transforms himself into a catfish monster, so he can kill all his scientist colleagues who scoffed at his brilliant plan of creating a super race of catfish people. Because he has no one to talk to, and because he *can't* talk after he turns into a giant, walking, killer catfish (just like Spalding couldn't talk beneath his mummy wrappings), Leopold explains his plans through lengthy voiceovers, often played over stock footage of fish. Actor Marshall Grauer's listless performance starkly contrasts with the voiceover's exuberantly delivered, purple prose. I suspect that, as with Doyle, Grauer did not perform his character's voiceovers.

Voiceovers

Voiceovers are words that are spoken over a film's visuals, without any of the characters in the scene speaking them aloud. Voiceovers can depict a character's thoughts or memories, or narration of events. In *The Unseen* (1981), Ernest sits in his father's office, remembering a past conversation. We hear his memories as a *voiceover* dialog between himself and his dad, which functions as an *audio flashback*. Which is cheaper than filming an audio*visual* flashback.[28]

The Unseen's voiceover is *diegetic*. Voiceovers can also be *nondiegetic*. In *The Age of Innocence* (1993), an unseen and unidentified narrator comments upon everyone and everything throughout the length of the film. In *Evil Dead 2*, a similarly "invisible" narrator opens the film by recounting a brief history of the *Necronomicon*. Both voiceover narrations, spoken by people outside the films' stories, are nondiegetic.

Nondiegetic voiceover narrations can create an omniscient, omnipresent, "voice of God" sensation; because the narrator is outside the story, yet sees and knows all, she speaks with objective authority. Narrators can use this authority (and word choice, and tone of voice) to influence viewers on how story events and characters should be judged. In *The Age of Innocence*, the narrator speaks with wry amusement, affectionately mocking New York's high society of the 1870s. In *Evil Dead 2*, the narrator's stern, ominous tone intimates the dreadful power of the *Necronomicon*.

The Turn of the Screw (English 1992), an updating of Henry James's novel, uses *diegetic* voiceover narration. The film opens amid a psychiatric group therapy session, in which a patient relates the true story of a haunted governess, set in the 1960s. Most of the film depicts the governess's travails, supplemented by the patient's voiceover narration. Occasionally, we return to the therapy session, reminding us of the present day situation, and that the governess's story occurs in the past. The photography further segregates present and past. Until the very end, all present day scenes are in black and white, while the past is in vivid color.

Narrating from the future can impart a fatalistic tone. By seeing the dreary, grim, black and white, present day (the governess's future?), and by seeing our haggard narrator undergoing therapy among gloomy patients, we may infer that the governess's tale will not end happily.

Some voiceover narrations, spoken by characters who are reminiscing from the future, are ambiguous as to *who* is being addressed — other characters in the story (diegetic), or solely the audience (arguably, nondiegetic)? To whom are the characters in *Goodfellas* (1990), *Casino* (1995), *Clockwatchers* (1997), and *Girl, Interrupted* (1999) reminiscing? The narrator in *Sunset Boulevard* (1950) is already dead. Who's he talking to? From where?

Diegetic voiceovers can convey a character's past memories (Ernest in *The Unseen*), or contemporaneous thoughts. In *Mermaids* (1990), we hear the voiceover thoughts of the teenage Charlotte as she struggles to grow up. Sometimes her thoughts are directed to herself, sometimes to God, sometimes to us, the audience. Not being omniscient or omnipresent, nor reminiscing with 20/20 hindsight from the future, Charlotte isn't always accurate in her observations. Her misconceptions are embarrassing for her, and amusing for viewers.

Mermaids ends with Charlotte's voiceover observations from a year later, to which the story fast-forwards. She recounts how everything turned out for everyone, with apparent 20/20 hindsight. She allays all suspense and fatalism by assuring us that everyone lived happily ever after. An appropriately upbeat ending for a gentle, coming-of-age comedy.

Horror and mainstream films mostly shun feature-length voiceover narrations. They're considered a lazy device used by inept screenwriters who can't master the "show, don't tell" rule of writing. Lengthy voiceovers are also presumed to be unpopular with ticket-buyers. But many indie art films, films noir, and Hollywood films aiming for an Oscar, favor voiceover narrators, because they infuse a film with a strong, personal voice.

Although not strictly a voiceover, radio DJs (or some equivalent) in a film can perform similar functions. DJs can comment on events, with less risk of violating the "show, don't tell" rule because their diegetic broadcasts are part of the story. In *Vanishing Point* (1971), DJ Super Soul broadcasts moral support and advice to Kowalski, an outlaw driver, while also interpreting the "meaning" of Kowalski to his radio listeners and the film's audience. But while Super Soul sees the bigger picture, he remains within the story (rednecks attack his radio station), and falls short of *The Age of Innocence*'s omniscient "voice of God" narrator. Angry Bob, the DJ in *Hardware* (1990), is more godlike because we never see him. He's in the story, but doesn't participate. His broadcasts bookend *Hardware* with wry, cynical commentary on the piss-poor state of his post-apocalyptic world.

Music

Music in a film can be diegetic or nondiegetic. In *Island of Blood* (1982), someone is killing cast and crew members in a low-budget film. The killer plays a tape cassette of a rock song before, during, or after the murders, the song's lyrics describing the victim's death (e.g., "Boil me, boil me" or "Spear me, spear me" or "Burn me, burn me").[29] It's a typical 1980s slasher film, in that young people die in a series of gory deaths. And like many typical slasher films, *Island of Blood* attempts a unique twist. Here, the song is that twist. Not a brilliant twist, but a nice example of how diegetic music can enhance a horror film.

Most film music is nondiegetic, establishing mood and atmosphere, and supporting the story's historical era, setting, characters, and themes. *Rocky*'s opening score captures the joyous exuberance of a hard-won victory. *Dr. Zhivago*'s balalaika music evokes a romanticized, rural Russian folk culture, swept away by revolution. *The Godfather*'s music likewise evokes a fading and romanticized Old World Sicilian culture, pushed aside by a less honorable, new generation of gangsters. *The Good, the Bad and the Ugly*'s overblown and maniacal orchestral score reflects the film's violent and avaricious criminal characters. The ponderous *Jaws* theme music suggests a shark pushing inexorably forward, then speeding toward its prey. Similarly, *Zombi 2*'s ponderous beat conveys the zombies' inexorable advance, while also establishing an atmosphere of nihilistic despair. *Psycho*'s high-pitched string instruments evoke a lunatic's fragile mind. The sumptuous classical music in *Blood and Roses*, supported by the film's impressionistic framing and *mise-en-scène*, enhances this tale of vampiric romance among Old World aristocrats. *Suspiria* opens with what sounds like a music box's tinkling, foreshadowing the film's fairy tale story structure of an ingénue entering a dark forest, and happening upon a lair of witches.

Music can shift between diegetic and nondiegetic. The songs in *American Graffiti* (1973) and *Saturday Night Fever* (1977) sometimes resound diegetically from the radio or disco floor, and sometimes play nondiegetically. These songs establish (1) time periods and locales, and (2) the characters' shifting moods and fortunes. In *Saturday Night Fever*, the Bee Gees's selections are intense on the disco floor, but more softly romantic when Tony courts Stephanie.

Like *mise-en-scène* (clothing, makeup, props), music helps create characters; so much so that music can even sustain a character across a series. Although many actors have played James Bond, audiences accept that it's still Bond up on screen, partially because of Monty Norman's "James Bond theme." Likewise, theme music from *The Pink Panther*, *Dragnet*, *The Godfather*, *Rocky*, *Psycho*, *Jaws*, and *Halloween* have helped characters migrate from film to film, and even from TV to film.

As with associational editing, music can link disparate elements. Specific music can, in the minds of audiences, become associated with, and therefore can evoke, specific characters, series, time periods, settings, genres, or formats. Music that becomes associated with a character or a series can provide nostalgic and ritualistic pleasures. John Carpenter's *Halloween* score has become associated with Michael Myers. Whenever *Halloween* fans hear that familiar theme music playing in a sequel or remake, they feel chills of excitement as they anticipate a recurrence of past pleasures. Similarly, Bond fans thrill to the opening "gun barrel" logo and theme music that precede most 007 films.

Through its associational powers, music can help merge genres or formats into hybrid shows. I refer to that practice where a TV series sets its characters in another genre for one "special" episode. For instance, a sitcom's characters will find themselves in a 1940s noir setting (perhaps in one character's dreams or fantasies), supported by appropriate jazz saxophone music. Or characters may enter a 1930s horror film, either literally (e.g., the "Bride of the Wolfman" episode of *Love and Curses*[30]) or stylistically (e.g., "The Post-Modern Prometheus" episode of *The X-Files*). Naturally, their sojourn includes the usual mad scientist *mise-en-scène*, black and white photography, purple dialog, and dramatic music. Similarly, the "Badge of Honor" episode of *Friday the 13th: The Series* stylistically mimics *Miami Vice*. To retrieve a cursed sheriff's badge from a vigilante cop hunting a crime lord, Micki and Ryan enter an underworld milieu of flashy guns, snazzy fashion, and Moog synthesizer music.

Absence of music is itself an aesthetic choice. Some documentaries use nondiegetic music to comment on events (e.g., sinister music when a "bad guy" is onscreen), but TV's *Cops* avoids music to enhance the realism of its police ride-alongs. This absence of nondiegetic music also assists in merging *Cops* with *The X-Files*.

The "X-Cops" episode of *The X-Files* opens as an episode of *Cops*, with the familiar "Bad Boys" theme song. Then a prologue has a documentary camera crew following a cop, who runs terrified from a monster. Cut to *The X-Files*'s opening credits and eerie theme music. Then, unlike typical *X-Files* episodes, no more music. "X-Cops" mimics *Cops* in that it's shot on video, documentary style, without mood music. The camera crew, and their police hosts, stumble upon Mulder and Scully, and the FBI team are swept up into what appears to be an episode of *Cops*. We only see of Mulder and Scully what the *Cops* camera crew sees.

A shift in music, or cessation of music, can imply a plot twist. In *House by the Cemetery*, a family discovers Dr. Freudstein, a blood-drinking, living corpse in their basement. *Tense mood music plays* as he kills Norman (the father), leaving Lucy and Bob (mother and son). Then he backs away from Norman's corpse — and away from Lucy and Bob. Is there hope for them yet? Lucy spots an opening above some previously unseen stairs. Abruptly, *music ceases*. Lucy urges Bob to the stairs.

Music had accompanied Freudstein's attack, so this cessation of music raises audience expectations of a new plot direction. Atop the stairs, Lucy tries to widen the opening so she and Bob can squeeze through. (The opening is a fissure in a gravestone.) Then we hear *Freudstein's footsteps*. The frame closes in on Lucy, as though it were Freudstein's POV, the corpse drawing nearer. *Music resumes*. Its previous cessation had misled us, just as its recommencement signals that Lucy and Bob are not safe after all.

Absence of music can also establish mood and atmosphere. William K. Everson writes: "Unlike *Dracula*, and so many other early horror films, *The Old Dark House* [1932] does not suffer from a lack of music. Apart from a few notes of highly evocative music in the main titles, there is no music, but the constant sounds of wind, rain, thunder, flapping shutters, billowing curtains, forms its own kind of symphony. Moreover, the film is so tightly paced (it runs a little less than 70 minutes) that there are none of those awkward pauses where one becomes aware of the absence of music."[31]

The Old Dark House is a rare example of a music-free horror film that does not mimic a documentary (e.g., "X-Cops" or *The Blair Witch Project*). Most dramatic films use nondiegetic music to establish mood and atmosphere. In horror films, that usually means music that "feels" spooky, creepy, haunting, eerie, suspenseful, or evocative of some similar emotion. Music is the most emotive of art forms, and thus has much to offer horror, an emotive genre. Composer Billy Goldenberg's spooky tunes were among the chief strengths of the 1972 TV series, *Ghost Story* (aka *Circle of Fear*).

Spooky mood music unsettles an audience, establishing an emotional foundation for upcoming shocks and scares. Early in *The Grudge*, Yoko nurses an elderly woman. Eerie music creates a sinister, supernatural atmosphere, "creeping out" audiences, warning us that something is "not right" in that house. Yoko goes upstairs to clean. She hears rumbling from a room. She enters to investigate. Rumbling from the attic. She opens a closet to access the attic. Throughout her search, the music darkens, emotionally fraying the audience's nerves. As Yoko peers into the attic, the music grows even more ominous.

Horror film music needn't always be spooky. It's an obvious choice, often a good choice. But many musical styles can serve horror, depending on the desired aesthetic effect. In *Dèmoni* (aka *Demons*, Italian 1985), demons possess and slaughter a whole theaterful of people. No eerie mood music for them. They kill to the accompaniment of hard rock music from artists like Billy Idol, Mötley Crüe, Rick Springfield, and Claudio Simoneti of Goblin. Their music enlivens this fast-paced gorefest.

In *Island of the Dead* (2000), an evil billionaire, The Rupert, greets the mayor and city officials at a ferry dock, on their way to an island photo op. Hip hop music plays while slow motion photography shows The Rupert, the mayor, and their retinues, emerging from black limos, approaching each other and shaking hands. As they glad-hand each other, a truck carrying caskets full of paupers arrives, forcing these power brokers to step aside. They scowl upon being inconvenienced.

Hip hop music often comments on "haves" from the perspective of "have nots." Here the slow motion photography and hip hop music underscore the power and disdain of these movers and shakers, as seen by the homeless dead, whose island these men hope to exploit.

A secondary aesthetic intent for the hip hop music may have been to "update" *Island of the Dead*'s classic spook tale. To remind audiences that they are watching a story set in current times. However, because music can become associated with specific eras, "current" music can date an otherwise timeless film. Which may or may not be aesthetically desirable.

The psychedelic string composition in *The Velvet Vampire* (1971), resembling sitar music and evocative of The Doors's "The End," anchors the film in its hippie era. This doesn't hurt the film, but enhances it. Forty years later, *The Velvet Vampire* continues to draw strength from its haunting score.[32] Plus, in being rooted to a specific era, the film serves as a curious cultural artifact. By contrast, *The Haunting* is a relatively timeless ghost story, partially because of its traditionally spooky mood music. I say relatively, because every film inevitably becomes dated to some extent.

When selecting music, filmmakers should consider if they wish to risk dating their films. Which musical scores or styles are likely to become classics, which will fade into obscurity (deserved and undeserved), and which will become the butt of jokes? Music that "speaks to a new generation" can age very quickly. TV's *Beavis and Butthead* successfully mocked singers and songs that only a few years previous were considered hot, hip, and cutting edge. Yesterday's groovy is tomorrow's ridiculous. Hippie slang, 1970s fashion, and 1980s Valley Girls inspire laughs today. Yet 1940s noir exhibits remarkable resiliency, continually reemerging in retro and neo-noir expressions (e.g., *Blade Runner*, 1982; TV's *Werewolf,* 1987; *The Resurrected*; *In the Mouth of Madness*, 1995; and *The Matrix* 1999).

Audio Threat Cues

Music contributes to a film's mood and atmosphere. But snippets of music can also alert audiences to specific threats. The story events onscreen appear normal and safe, when suddenly, we hear ominous nondiegetic music or sound effects. (It can be difficult to distinguish the two; the musical snippet may lack melody, or the sound effect is created by musical instruments.) These ominous nondiegetic noises cover a vast array of eerie sounds; they can be loud or soft, their tempo fast or slow. Their only consistency is an aesthetic *intent* to instill fear and anxiety in the audience; to signal that a threat is either onscreen or lurking nearby, soon to pounce.

I'll call this ominous nondiegetic noise (be it music or sound effect) an *audio threat cue* (ATC), because it cues a present or impending threat. ATCs unnerve audiences, darkening the mood and atmosphere in a scene, helping to create that Lovecraftian "atmosphere of breathless and unexplainable dread of outer, unknown forces"[33] that is fundamental to horror.

In *The Grudge*, Karen, a caregiver for an old woman, goes upstairs to clean the house. She hears rumbling from a bedroom. As with Yoko before, spooky mood music establishes that something is "not right" in the house. Karen enters the bedroom. She sees a closet, sealed with tape. Music intensifies, corresponding to more rumbling from the closet. Karen begins to leave. A cat meows from inside the closet, changing Karen's mind.

Karen removes the tape in a series of jump cuts that quicken her frantic efforts. The jump cuts, Sarah Michelle Gellar's performance, and the mood music together convey Karen's anxious desire to open the closet. And because Karen is anxious, the audience becomes anxious.

Karen opens the closet and finds a book. A cat leaps past her, creating an *audio shock*.[34] Cut to a closeup of Karen, gawking at something inside the closet. Then a *POV cut* to a closeup of the cat in someone's hands. Whose? Cut to a *profile* of Karen, so that what she sees inside the closet is offscreen. The camera moves past Karen until we see a boy inside the closet, holding the cat. He's looking down at the cat, so we don't see his eyes.

By beginning the shot on Karen's profile, *then* moving the frame to show the boy, the shot extends the moment and builds suspense, because we must wait to see what Karen sees. When we finally do see the boy, the *music intensifies as a rising crescendo*. Karen backs away, hyperventilating. Her breath is heavy, coarse, and loud. She trips over backward, still gawking at the boy. The boy looks up at Karen. We see his eyes for the first time. The *music's crescendo peaks*. This crescendo, which begins when we first see the boy, and peaks when he looks up, functions as an ATC, signaling that this boy is a threat.

Consider this scene without music. Karen is an adult who discovers a small boy and a cat sealed inside a closet. Does she feel pity? Or outrage over a case of child abuse? No, she backs away from the child, hyperventilating, terrified. Why? No rational reason. Normal, sane people do not panic upon seeing little boys. Yet we accept that Karen has good reason to fear, largely because of the music.

Play this scene without mood music or ATC/crescendo, and Karen will appear neurotic, perhaps even insane. This scene rests on a delicate balance of elements (including music and ATC) that create an eerie atmosphere, without which the dramatic incidents border on satire.

This scene also demonstrates how *volume* can highlight pertinent elements. Most scenes offer the potential for many different sounds, as characters walk about, open doors or drawers, breathe, drink, and do all manner of busywork. Yet not every sound should be recorded or mixed at its "realistic" volume. High volume should emphasize those sounds, and sound sources, that aesthetically serve the story or themes. In this scene, actress Gellar's hyperventilation is heavy, coarse, and *loud*, effectively conveying Karen's fear. Her loud breathing, supported by the ATC, helps convince audiences that Karen has *reason* to fear.

High volume can emotionally assault an audience, forcing them to pay attention to the sound source. Karen's hyperventilation is too loud to ignore. Less dramatically or thematically pertinent sounds are often mixed at lower volumes, existing primarily for realism. We hear Karen's comparatively low volume tearing of the tape only because tearing tape makes noise. Unlike Karen's loud hyperventilation, the tearing tape noise serves no aesthetic purpose other than realism.

This is not to say that low volume is always less emotionally intrusive. If a sound source is dramatically interesting, low volume can highlight and draw attention to the sound source by compelling audiences to strain to hear it.

The Grudge's soundtrack is remarkable for its long stretches of silence and mood music, punctuated by ATCs, audio shocks, and creepy or incongruent noises. Silence, eerie music, and creepy noises (Kayako's croaking) help make these ghosts frightening. They prefer to manifest in silence and isolation. When a throng of detectives search the house, we feel they're safe. When one detective returns alone, we fear for him. As Karen says to Doug, "I didn't want to be alone."

In *The Woman in Black* (British TVM 1989), Arthur, a solicitor, visits Marsh Island to settle a deceased old woman's estate. He is alone on the island, amid stark vistas and gray skies. He visits its cemetery, wanders among the graves. He suddenly stops. Why? An ATC of creepy music ensues. He grabs the back of his neck, as if he'd felt something. He spins around, stepping aside to reveal a "woman in black" behind him, in the distance. Her dark form is silhouetted against the barren vista. How did she get there? Since the vista *is* barren, she'd have been seen walking to that spot behind Arthur. It seems she just "appeared." (Well, of course. She's a ghost.)

Arthur had stopped walking because he suddenly felt creeped out. The audience accepts this — and also feels creeped out — because of the ATC music.

Silent Scream (1980) also uses ATCs to alert us to a dangerous character. Nearly an hour into the film, the camera enters and explores an attic. Ominous mood music establishes a creepy atmosphere. Mrs. Engels is sleeping in a chair. The camera moves toward a door and we dissolve into the next room. We see Victoria, sitting at a dresser, facing a "mirror" that is entirely covered with a photograph of a beautiful, young woman. Victoria turns, looking at something behind her in offscreen space. She turns back to her "mirror."

Cut to a *closeup of her face*. Music intensifies briefly, functioning as an ATC, signaling us that Victoria is a threat. She studies herself in the "mirror," playing with her hair, lifting it to reveal a *lobotomy scar*. A second ATC of more intense music supports this revelation.[35] Victoria turns around again, looking offscreen.

Cut to a *corpse* in Victoria's closet. A third ATC ensues, the music still more intense.

In this scene, sounds and visuals create a mutually supportive tempo. The first two ATCs, cuing the closeup and lobotomy scar, respectively, alert us that Victoria is a threat. The third ATC, cuing the corpse, confirms this. Each ATC corresponds to the revelation of some new visual information.

ATCs can function without prior establishing mood music. In *The Eye 2* (aka *Gin gwai*

2, Hong Kong 2004), after leaving a birthing class for expectant mothers, Joey sees Mrs. Chow crying, sitting with her husband in the locker room. No mood music. Only the building's ambient noise. Joey comforts the tearful Mrs. Chow.

Mrs. Chow weeps that her husband is leaving her. Joey responds, "You should talk it over, be patient." But Mrs. Chow is inconsolable. Joey says to the husband, "Maybe you should take your wife home now. Talk it over when she calms down."

Mrs. Chow glances at her husband (in offscreen space), then at Joey. Mrs. Chow asks, "Who are you talking to?" *Eerie music commences, functioning as an ATC—signaling us that something is "not right."*

Joey points to the man (in offscreen space) and asks, "Isn't he your husband?"

Camera swings to where the man had been sitting. He's gone! *A heavy beat punctuates the ATC music.*

Mrs. Chow looks nervously to the empty spot where Joey is pointing, then says, "Don't scare me. I don't see anyone here" [Figures 8.5–8.8].

Joey looks at the "empty spot." The man is there again! Staring at Joey. *The heavy beats continue, rising in volume.* "Who are you?" Joey demands.

Mrs. Chow screams. Blood trickles down Joey's leg.

Although the scene ends, the music doesn't. The ATC continues as a *sound bridge* into the next scene, making a dramatic cause-and-effect connection between Joey's bleeding and her arrival at the hospital.

This scene is admirable for its creepy supernatural shock, surprising the audience by revealing that the man sitting near Mrs. Chow is a ghost. The ATC contributes to this shock—but staging, framing, and editing also help.

Audiences first see Mrs. Chow and the ghost in a *two shot*. This is the *only shot where they share a frame*. It's also the *only shot that is Joey's POV*. Mrs. Chow and the ghost share no *objective* frames. They only share that one *subjective* frame of Joey's POV. Only Joey sees both worlds, the natural and the supernatural.

Aesthetically, this framing places Joey into overlapping worlds: Mrs. Chow's natural world, and the ghost's supernatural world. Sometimes Joey is framed in one, sometimes in the other. She never shares the frame with *both* Mrs. Chow and the ghost. But because *mise-en-scène*, lighting, and photography never change, viewers are unaware of Joey's straddling two worlds until the ATC music alerts us to something "not right."

Later, Joey dines at a restaurant with Mrs. Chow. No eerie mood music. They enjoy their meal and their conversation. Then the ATC music ensues. Joey's expression shifts from happy to uneasy. Actress Qi Shu's performance and the ATC signal us that something is "not right." And sure enough, Joey soon discovers that pesky ghost hiding under the table.

When horror audiences hear an ATC, they expect an impending threat. But ATCs can also *mislead* audiences by using their expectations to unnerve them with a false alarm.

Early in *Hospital Massacre* (1982), Susan, a little girl, leaves her friend in the living room while she enters the kitchen for cake. Susan opens a drawer and removes a big knife. An ATC of ominous music ensues, cuing us that Susan is dangerous. Will she kill her friend? Susan stares coldly as she approaches the cake with the knife. Actress Elizabeth Hoy's performance and the ATC thus reinforce one another, each imbuing Susan with menace.

Then Susan cuts the cake. Her expression softens. The ATC music ends. Susan is not evil! The scene fooled the audience. Unnerving them. Preparing them for...

 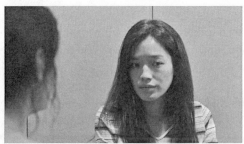

Left: Figure 8.5 — *The Eye 2.* Joey's POV (a *subjective* frame) of a man sitting with Mrs. Chow (Ren Yuan Yuan). *Right:* Figure 8.6 — Joey (Qi Shu) shares several *two shots* with Mrs. Chow. Here Joey creates an *eyeline match* to the man sitting across from her, whom she presumes to be Mr. Chow, but is actually a ghost.

Left: Figure 8.7 — The ghost (Chuwong Earsakul) shares several *two shots* with Joey, staring silently at her. (He does not create an eyeline match, because Joey is in the frame.) *Right:* Figure 8.8 — After Joey asks Mrs. Chow "Isn't he your husband?," the camera swings to an empty spot where the ghost had been. Cut to this *two shot* of Mrs. Chow ("I don't see anyone here.") with Joey pointing to the ghost. She *still* sees him. But he won't share an *objective* frame with Mrs. Chow, only with Joey.

Susan enters the living room with cake for her friend — and discovers that her friend has been killed!

In *Tower of Evil* (British 1972), after several murders on a deserted island, the survivors instruct Hamp to take Rose inside the empty lighthouse tower. He does so. An ATC of ominous music ensues, suggesting that Hamp — now alone with Rose and creeping up behind her! — is dangerous. Rose finds a photograph on a desk. Hamp stares at the photo. He approaches Rose. ATC music swells louder.

Hamp isn't doing anything clearly menacing. Rose knows he's behind her, so he's not sneaking up. And while we know he has secrets, he's not shown himself to be a killer. Yet the ATC, and actor Jack Watson's staring eyes, suggest that Hamp is a threat — especially now that Rose may have found an incriminating photo.

But as in *Hospital Massacre*, this ATC is a trick. The music stops when Hamp reaches Rose. They discuss the family photo. Hamp's eyes have softened; his voice is compassionate. Once again, the ATC misled the audience. Unnerving them. Preparing them for...

Hamp goes upstairs. He soon staggers back downstairs — freshly stabbed!

The ATCs in *Hospital Massacre* and *Tower of Evil* unnerve viewers with false alarms, emotionally fraying them for immediate followup shocks. But not all misleading ATCs have followup shocks. Some ATCs unnerve viewers for the longterm, functioning almost as part of the mood music by contributing to the atmosphere. Like many cinematic tricks that unnerve, shock, or frighten, ATCs are scarier if unpredictable.

In *1408* (2007), Mike Enslin, a cynical author who writes about ghosts, though he doesn't believe in them, visits the Dolphin Hotel to investigate its reputedly haunted room 1408. He exits the elevator on the 14th floor (really, the 13th floor). The vaguely creepy *Muzak ends.* Ominous *mood music ensues.* Enslin saunters through the hall, skimming a file containing morbid photos of the deaths in room 1408. Subtle cinematic touches create a spooky atmosphere. Low-key lighting. Dull red, gold, and brown set décor. Banal chatter and laugher muffled behind closed doors. A *minor* dolly counter-zoom (*dolly out/zoom in*). Sometimes the frame swoons, canting *slightly*, as if the hotel were at sea. Or it's at low height, implying an unseen entity's POV. The editing intercuts from the morbid photos to Enslin passing doors, turning corners, passing corridors. These intercuts disorient us; like Enslin, we're not watching where we're going.

A minute later, the *ominous music peaks* and *ends*, the elevator *rings*, its *doors open* and *muzak* replaces mood music. Enslin looks up, surprised to find himself where he'd begun. While there's a rational explanation — he was so absorbed in the photos, he wasn't paying attention and missed or passed room 1408 — it still feels eerie.

Low mood music recommences. Enslin walks again, paying attention, determined not to bypass room 1408. He passes a half-eaten dinner, left outside a room, flies *buzzing*. A mother pushes a baby carriage into another room. Enslin finds room 1408. *Ominous music swells.*

Enslin *knocks* on the door. (Who might be inside?) He inserts the key. Cut to the lock's interior as the key opens it. (Similar to the sliding doors' interior in *Suspiria*). He opens the door. Cut to the door opening, as seen from inside the room —*from a ghost's POV?!* All is dark, except for the bright doorway silhouetting Enslin. *Music swells — what lurks in that darkness?!* Enslin turns on two light switches. Cut to his POV, surveying the room. Cut to a medium closeup of him, studying the room. *Music swells in a crescendo —* an ATC suggesting an imminent threat. And then ... *Music ends.*

"This is it?" sneers Enslin. "You gotta be kidding me." A dull room. *Street noises from outside* waft in, comforting in their familiarity. That creepy atmospheric buildup, peaking in an ATC crescendo, has led to nothing much. Although unnerved, viewers sigh relief. Enslin shuts the door — punctuated by an *ominous musical beat* that promises shocks to come. But not right away. For now, no ominous music. No ATCs. Only normal, banal sounds.

This scene demonstrates how mood music, an ATC, and other cinematic tools can work together to create a creepy, disorienting atmosphere. Of horror's many threats, ghosts especially require atmosphere. Not that there's necessarily a ghost in room 1408. The hotel manager has a simpler explanation: "It's an evil, fucking room."

Audio Shocks

As with visuals, sound can be edited for tempo and rhythm. In horror films, a common tempo is a period of silence or low volume, followed by a sudden loud noise. This silence may feel tense or safe. A *tense silence* uneases viewers so they anticipate danger.[36] A *serene silence* lulls viewers into a false sense of security. Either way, a sudden loud noise will startle viewers, unnerving them so that they are emotionally more receptive to upcoming shocks or frights.

Let's call this sudden loud noise an *audio shock* (AS).

Almost every horror film uses audio shocks. In *Night School* (1981), Eleanor is walking down a deserted street, late one night. A creep seems to be following her. Eleanor pauses by a fence to glance back. A savage dog, previously unseen, *suddenly barks* from behind the fence. Eleanor and the audience are duly shocked and unnerved.

In *Jeepers Creepers* (2001), a panicked Trish and Darry enter a diner, saying they need the police. A waitress goes for help. Trish and Darry huddle *beside a pay phone*. (Do you see it coming?) Each admits they are terrified. The latter half of their conversation — 21 seconds — is quietly tense. The *pay phone rings!*— jolting Trish, Darry, and the audience.

Framing, photography, and lighting assist this AS. The pay phone is in the foreground, ready to "pounce," but is framed to the extreme right; the composition favors Darry, in the center-right. The phone is blurred and dimly lit (by subtle edge lighting). We see the phone, but all cinematic tools direct our attention to Darry, so we don't really notice the phone until its AS ring surprises and shocks us [Figure 8.9].

Ringing phones are among the most clichéd and satirized audio shocks in horror. They can be done on a low budget, and they work. Dropping or knocking over items is also popular, for the same reasons.

In *Alien* (1979), Ripley, Dallas, and Ash enter the infirmary, seeking the alien. It had been on Kane's face, now it's gone. *Tense silence*. The three astronauts *speak softly* and thread lightly. Spaceship *hums electronically*. Kane's ventilator *hisses softly*. Then — BANG!— Dallas knocks over a metal cabinet. Ripley SCREAMS. As does the audience.

"Sorry," says Dallas. Silence resumes. More searching. An alien tail drops behind Ripley. The alien falls onto Ripley's shoulder. She SCREAMS. But the alien is already dead.

Figure 8.9 —*Jeepers Creepers*. This composition directs our attention to Darry (Justin Long), who is sharply focused and centrally framed, and away from the pay phone, which is blurry and framed at the edge.

Two shocks, both false alarms, in one scene. First, the AS of the non-threatening cabinet. Its noise unnerves us for the apparently threatening second shock of the dead alien. Much like a musical composition in which the second beat carries us higher than the first.

The dead alien is a shock, but it's not an AS, because we *see* the alien — and thus expect Ripley to scream — before it slips silently onto her shoulders. *Mise-en-scène* (such as this alien) often works with sound to startle viewers. Unlike ATCs, audio shocks are usually diegetic, and are motivated by a sound source within the story.

In *Aliens* (1986), a group of space marines enter a deserted mining colony, and discover a room full of glass tanks containing aliens. Most are dead. Burke approaches a tank, peers in ... an alien BUMPS the glass — jolting Burke and the audience. As with Ripley's dead alien, this shock arises primarily from the *mise-en-scène* rather than the BUMP noise, because we *see* the threat before it makes a sound.

Then the marines' radar detects an alien in the halls. The marines creep forward, quietly. *Tense silence. Radar beeping.* Then — BANG! — Lt. Gorman knocks over a metal canister. We didn't see that coming, so we are duly startled. But apart from startling us, this AS also serves a secondary aesthetic purpose: it reinforces Gorman's character as an inept officer.

In *The Eye* (aka *Gin gwai*, Hong Kong 2002), Mum studies Chinese calligraphy in a teacher's studio. After instructing Mum, the teacher goes off to hang papers on a wall, leaving Mum to practice at a desk. She feels happy and safe. After 25 seconds of *serene silence*, a woman's voice asks, "Why are you sitting in my chair?"

Mum looks up. A woman is standing in the corner, dimly lit. Ghostly sound effects (an ATC) inform us that this woman is a ghost. Mum turns to the teacher. He doesn't respond to the woman. When Mum looks back, the woman is gone. Until recently blind, Mum is confused. Is it normal for women to appear and vanish?

Mum resumes her work, glancing about uneasily. Eerie, nondiegetic noises for *23 tense seconds*. Then LOUDER: "Why are you sitting in my chair?!" The ghost is back. More brightly lit, face now distorted (dark rings under her eyes), supported by LOUDER music. She leaps at Mum, flies toward her, *fast tempo music rising in a crescendo*. Then she evaporates.

This ghost's creepy visage contributes to the shock. But because the music and her voice are *sudden and loud*, this second manifestation also functions as an AS. Her first manifestation is not an AS, because the volume is low. Rather, it's a dramatic shock (i.e., rooted in the story), and supported by makeup, ATC, etc. Her second manifestation tops the first one (brighter lighting, louder sounds, scarier makeup which is heightened by a CGI morph as she attacks Mum), and also functions as an AS.

Horror sequels usually try to repeat the original film's strong points, while topping them. *The Eye 2* repeats the above rhythm from *The Eye*, then "tops it" with additional scares.

Joey is waiting at a bus stop when a voice asks: "Ma'am, what time is it?" Joey looks up. She sees only one woman, also waiting, but too distant to have asked the question. Joey resumes counting her change.

After *14 seconds*, the voice repeats: "What time is it?" An ATC of spooky music ensues. Joey is startled and drops a coin. She looks at the woman, whose face is hidden by long black hair. ATC intensifies. Joey strives for a better look, waiting for the woman to turn and reveal her face. After *25 tense seconds*, the women turns. She *looks* normal. Her normalcy is confirmed by the nondiegetic ATC music fading, replaced by diegetic pop music, presumably emanating from the woman's earbud. (Though we see no wires.) Joey breathes relief.

The Eye's rhythm has repeated itself. A ghost twice asks the same question, the second time louder and supported by an ATC. But unlike in *The Eye*, the ghost in *The Eye 2* remains unseen.

Joey resumes counting her change. *Safe silence* for *25 seconds*. Joey enters the street to retrieve the coin she'd dropped. A boy's body THUDS onto the street, having fallen from an above window. Joey screams. Then *5 seconds* later, a woman's body THUDS onto the street, beside the boy. Joey screams again. The boy (splattered on the sidewalk) says to Joey, "Miss, don't tell her the time. Don't tell her." The mother (similarly splattered) says, "Where is your dad? Why hasn't he come home yet? It's so late! Why isn't he home yet?"

The Eye 2 tops an unseen ghost's first question with a second question. Then tops both questions with the ghost boy splattering onto the street. Then tops that with the ghost mother splattering beside him. Then tops that by having both ghosts speak in normal tones, despite half their bodies squashed upon the street. These "toppings" startle and unnerve viewers. It's like the horror cliché of someone waking from a nightmare to a "real" horror, then waking a second time (e.g., *An American Werewolf in London*, 1981; *Headhunter*, 1989; *She Creature*, 2001).

Audio shocks require silence to be heard, but they don't always follow a long period of silence. Some audio shocks follow a cacophony, startling audiences because they'd thought the din was finally over.

In *Gothika* (2003), a ghost helps Miranda escape from a psychiatric hospital, late one night. She speeds away in a car. During a harrowing *two minute* sequence, we hear *fast tempo mood music*, an *eerie ATC* when the ghost appears in the rearview mirror, Miranda *shrieks*, the car's *engine revs* faster, *pitch rising*, as the ghost assumes control, tires *screeching*, the *blare* of an approaching tanker truck, *shattering metal* as the car brushes past the truck, Miranda *laughs maniacally* at surviving the near accident, then *screams* as "road closed" cones *slam into the car*, which *screeches* to a halt.

Miranda *screams* to the ghost, "What do you want from me?!"

Near silence. Just a rumbling car engine. The audience's frayed nerves being to calm. All of *9 seconds* pass.

The car radio BLASTS MUSIC, startling Miranda — she SCREAMS!— and viewers. This AS is reinforced by the car's tail lights and headlights simultaneously lighting up. All of which unnerve us for...

Cut from the car's rear to its front, whereupon the camera pulls back and we see that the car has stopped at the edge of a sinkhole. Miranda had almost plummeted to her death! Camera rises in a crane shot. Radio music fades. Mist wafts past the car's headlights, heightening the spooky atmosphere.

Consider this scene as a musical composition. A loud, frenetic tempo, culminating in a single instrument as Miranda screams her question, then a sudden lull, a final burst, and then it fades away.

CHAPTER 9

The Appeals of Horror

Every Halloween, and on every promotional junket for a horror book or film, journalists, radio DJs, and TV talking heads ask their horror guests the same question: Why do people enjoy horror? Why do they enjoy "being scared"?

A valid question, but usually asked and answered in a lazy, rote fashion, without thought on either end. A quickie interview to fill airtime or print space during a promotional event. A shallow puff piece to pad out a DVD's special features. A cursory ritual, the question asked, answered, and ignored, to be asked again next Halloween.

What *is* the appeal of horror? I don't think there's one answer. It's a personal question. Everyone enjoys horror for their own unique blend of reasons. Even so, most of these reasons probably fall within one of four broad categories.

Horror as Catharsis

According to this theory, we all suffer from repressed anxieties, which are released when we watch a horror film. This release makes us feel good, purging or exorcising those anxieties.

This is the most popular boilerplate answer. Every Halloween, horror actors, authors, critics, and filmmakers fill the airwaves and print media with buzzwords like "catharsis" and "rollercoaster ride." Asked about horror's appeal, Screamfest film festival co-founder Rachel Belofsky said: "Horror films are just a release. We love to be scared, because we're exorcising our inner demons with them.... You have a bad day, and go to see something like *Freddy vs. Jason*, where there's blood and arms flying everywhere. It's like being on a fun rollercoaster ride in a safe environment."[1]

This theory, and its allied buzzwords, are given so mechanically, seemingly by everyone in every interview, that I wonder how many advocates of this theory have actually *considered* it?

I have a theory about this theory.

This whole "horror as catharsis" idea apparently originated from Sigmund Freud's 1919 essay, "The Uncanny" (aka, "Das Unheimliche").[2] *My theory* is that some academics, perhaps bored or unhappy with their daily grind, wanted to "research" horror movies, popular music, or other fun stuff. But they had to justify this with some high-brow rationale. So, citing Freud, they imposed a psychoanalytic interpretation upon horror. "You see, dear colleagues, I'm doing some pretty brainy stuff here. You study quantum mechanics and organic chemistry, whereas I watch *The Horror of Party Beach*. Same thing." (Much like *The Haunting*'s Dr. Markway, who studied anthropology as a respectable way of researching his real love, the supernatural.)

Not that there's anything wrong with studying horror. I do it. You're doing it now.

The problem arises when academics impose incoherent jargon and baseless interpretations onto the genre. Deeming horror unworthy of study for its own sake, on its own terms, academics burden horror films with their personal politics and deconstructionist paradigms, then study those rather than the genre itself.

An article in New York's *Village Voice* observed that university professors, when writing about film these days, generally ignore aesthetics in favor of socio-political analyses.[3] Apparently, professors, tenure committees, and university presses consider aesthetics too trivial a topic when discussing an art form.

Yes, some horror films have socio-political themes. But when they do, the themes are obvious. They *should* be obvious if the film is well made. *Deathdream* critiques the Vietnam War—duh! At most, a horror film should require a little intelligent thought, but no special university training on how to "read" a film before one can understand it.[4]

Academia has imposed too much jargon, deconstructionism, personal politics, and Freud onto film studies. This Freudian "horror as a catharsis" theory then trickled down from academia to the horror industry, which has parroted it ever since.

Why would the industry, its filmmakers, actors, writers, critics, journalists, et al, embrace the "horror as catharsis" theory? I think because (1) it makes horror sound respectable, and (2) they never really gave it much thought. Artists create horror from their hearts, and souls, and guts, rather than over-analyze why they do it. If someone asks, well, everyone says it's about catharsis, so they pass it along. Sounds like a high-brow, brainy answer.

Does the horror industry need or crave respectability? Says Belofsky: "[H]orror seemed to be the bastard child of the industry. So we decided to do a horror film festival that would give those filmmakers a platform to further their careers."[5] Explaining why she founded the Shriekfest film festival, Denise Gossett says: "I was talking to the producers [of *Chain of Souls*], and they were saying there weren't any horror film festivals around. I was like, oh my gosh. Why don't I start this? It's a great genre that should have the attention that it deserves."[6]

"Lack of respect" is a common complaint among horror professionals, but it's groundless. To quote Bobbi Flekman in *This Is Spinal Tap*: "Money talks and bullshit walks." Horror is big business. Halloween is second only to Christmas as the largest revenue-generating holiday in the U.S.[7] Hollywood's major studios welcome horror projects. That's been true for most of the past century. Yes, horror is largely ignored by Oscar, but that's no big deal. Oscar also snubs comedies, fantasies, thrillers, sf and action films. But these are the genres, horror included, that keep Hollywood financially afloat. These genres also earn big bucks for those successful in it—and that's 99 percent of the respect the matters.

Horror doesn't need film festivals, or awards, or any kind of promotion. Horror has been around for millennia. People don't promote horror. Rather, horror promotes people who are lucky enough to grab onto its coattails. Did you read this book because of me, or the genre?

Is horror cathartic? I suppose it might be, sometimes. I usually feel better after watching a horror film. But the theory is over-promoted and under-analyzed. At least by the horror industry people who promote it, if not by academics.

Does the theory account for horror's appeal? Less so than its reputation would have you believe.

Metaphysical Transcendence

Horror's appeal is personal. For some it may mostly be catharsis. But the better horror films unnerve, and even fascinate, audiences in deeper ways. Watching a horror film is like standing at a cliff's edge. One feels fear, but also a *sense of wonder* and *awe*.

In 1997, *Horror* magazine published a debate on the question: *Are the old monsters dead?* Have true-life human horrors (rape, child molestation, serial killers, genocide, etc.) jaded readers and filmgoers to the point that they're no longer frightened by traditional monsters, like vampires, ghosts, etc. David Niall Wilson argued *Yes!* Stephen Mark Rainey argued *No!* Rainey wrote:

> Remember, if you will, the story from a century or so back, of the Navajo Indian, who, while seeking shelter from a violent thunderstorm, happens upon the fossilized skeleton of a pteranodon. Having no knowledge of dinosaurs, nor of the fossilization process, he believes the skeleton to be of some horrific creature — one that must surely exist in his own time, perhaps nearby. Imagine the *sense of wonder* he must have experienced, the *awe of finding something with implications that transcended himself — or any man, for that matter.*
>
> Now, imagine that same Indian, instead of finding a dinosaur, encountering a hostile brave from another tribe. Perhaps he might feel fear; he might even die from the encounter. Yet, it is highly unlikely that our Indian would have known a *moment of awe;* of having been *brushed by the wings of something grand and humbling.* More than likely, the familiar emotion of anger and the instinct for self-preservation would have carried him into a battle for survival; in his day, a situation perhaps all too familiar.[8]

Rainey's two scenarios distinguish *unnatural* from *natural* threats.[9] *Unnatural threats* do more than frighten; they fascinate. Unnatural threats evoke a different *quality* of fear compared to natural threats. To face the unnatural is to glimpse divinity. Biblical prophets trembled in the presence of God and his angels, much like Rainey's Indian feels before the dinosaur skeleton. To quote Rogan from TV's *Werewolf:* "When the world isn't the same as our minds believe, then we are in a nightmare." Which is whenever we face, as Lovecraft put it: "a malign and particular suspension or defeat of the fixed laws of Nature."[10]

Consider the changing *quality* of fear in *Jeepers Creepers* (2001). The film opens with Trish and Darry driving on a deserted country road. A redneck tries to run them off the road. We feel fear. Trish and Darry find the redneck's lair, filled with mutilated corpses. "That's one crazy motherfucker!" we think. This redneck is *dangerous.* Our fear increases. The redneck kills two cops. He jumps over a speeding car. He is *strong.* Perhaps some inbred freak. Maybe even an uberpsycho. Our fear increases. An hour into the film, Trish drives over the redneck. Several times. He appears dead in the road. Then...

He sprouts wings!

At that instant, our fear not only increases, its *quality* changes. Until now we'd thought we were fighting a human threat. An inbred, mutant hillbilly, or some other uberpsycho, but still, human.[11] But when that wing appears, suddenly, "the world isn't the same as our minds believe." We feel the Navajo's awe at seeing something that transcends him ... something grand and humbling.

There is more than catharsis here. There is fascination. Attraction as well as repulsion. Freud said we're attracted to death because we have a death wish, but I'm not big on Freud. I don't think people are fascinated by *Jeepers Creepers*'s monster (what *is* it?) because of any subconscious death wish, but because we're fascinated by any glimpse at the transcendent, the supernatural, the divine.

Clive Barker has often acknowledged a connection between horror and spirituality:

> I write religious fiction, though the phrase causes people to pale around the gills. Clearly fantasy and horror are often about the fundamental problems of existence. Horror itself is very often religious in its roots. Where else can you credibly deal with the absolutes of good and evil or probe life beyond the grave? Where else can characters converse with the dead? Those are the same tools of the metaphysician...[12]

Kirk J. Schneider writes:

> I am sitting in a dark theater watching David Cronenberg's *The Fly*. Suddenly, I am struck by my fascination. How could I, a relatively temperate individual, be so fixated on the grisly events before me? ... because there are elements of the sacred in what we witness. There is an intersection here between horror and the holy! Creation, destruction, the monstrous — each of these touch on the extraordinary as well as on the pathological.[13]

Without endorsing Barker's or Schneider's specific views on religion, or on horror, I think we're all groping in the same direction. Horror enables us to taste metaphysical transcendence.

Whenever I visit a World Horror Convention art show, I am fascinated and struck by the beauty of the grotesqueries. Each October, I admire the Halloween props and decorations found on lawn displays and in haunted houses. I don't think it's catharsis. I don't fear the glowing Jack O'Lanterns or skeletons or ghosts. I delight in them. I'm not confronting inner demons. I'm facing something dark, yet alluring. Even comforting. Nostalgia for boyhood Halloweens, to a degree. But also something more, I think.

As a child, I occasionally shivered to TV's *Creature Features* and *Circle of Fear*, but nothing terrified me so much as those documentaries about UFOs and ancient astronauts.[14] My Catholic worldview could accommodate vampires and witches — they were of Satan — but where did gray aliens fit into God's universe? The Grays were the ultimate Other, creatures neither of God nor Satan. Vampires were human, once. They could relate to us and our morality. But the Grays were wholly alien.

No horror fiction scared me so much as Erich von Daniken's "non-fiction" *Chariots of the Gods*, which suggests that Biblical miracles are the high-tech handiworks of alien astronauts. That God revealed only his back to Moses to hide his alien face.[15] That the God I worshiped was so *hideously alien* that he must turn aside, lest Moses run off screaming. We were not children of a loving God, made in his image. We were lab rats for the ultimate Other. As a child, I could deal with demons and ghosts, but supplanting God with alien astronauts was the utmost "the world isn't the same as our minds believe."

A Gray is terrifying because it is metaphysically transcendent. Powerful beyond human scope, awesome in its historical and cosmological implications in that it upturns our fundamental understanding of the universe. *Fire in the Sky* (1993) and TV's *The X-Files* gave me some of my creepiest moments watching horror. By then, I no longer considered ancient astronauts or Grays to be plausible. But these horror works are brilliant enough to allow me to suspend my disbelief, and tap into my childhood fears.

Watching *The X-Files* is not catharsis. I shudder before the Grays much like the Navajo trembled upon seeing the dinosaur skeleton. With awe and a sense of wonder.

If horror fans were divided into theists and atheists, between those who believe in a supernatural realm, and those who believe "this is all there is," would we find that these two camps, broadly speaking, fear different things? Are theists more affected by (and more likely to "enjoy") horror films about *unnatural threats*, whereas materialists find that *naturalistic psycho gorefests* strike the deeper chord? Do theists find Samara frightening yet fascinating, but Jigsaw merely sordid and vicious? Are atheists more likely unnerved by Jigsaw, but merely annoyed by Samara?[16]

The gorier the horror film, the more it requires humor—or metaphysical transcendence—to leaven it, or else it sinks into ugly, mean-spirited sadism. *Don't Go in the House* (1980) and *Make Them Die Slowly* (aka *Cannibal ferox*, Italian-Spanish 1981) exemplify sordid, mean-spirited splatterporn.[17] But *Zombi 2*'s nihilism is apocalyptic in scope, attaining a transcendence that redeems the film's visceral gore.

Like science fiction, the best horror conveys a *sense of wonder*. Somebody once said that either other intelligent life exists in our universe (*Fire in the Sky*), or we are alone (*Zombi 2*)—and that either prospect is mind-boggling.[18] And terrifying.

Sympathy for the Other

Monsters (by which I mean any traditional horror threat icon) aren't always *perceived* as villains or threats. Rather than feeling fear or catharsis, sometimes viewers sympathize with the monster, or even empathize with it, essentially identifying with the Other. This may or may not be the filmmaker's intent, but viewers are the final arbiters of how they interpret a film, and what they enjoy about it.

People sympathize with monsters for all sorts of personal reasons. At times, this affection is understandable. Some monsters are just plain *nice*; cute and cuddly, or warm and friendly, or funny, or sexy, or hip. Nice monsters include TV's *The Munsters*, the Franken Berry and Count Chocula cereal characters, and TV horror hostess Elvira.

Social outcasts and misfits (e.g., nerds), and viewers belonging to marginal subcultures (e.g., goths and punks), are probably among those most likely to sympathize, or identify with, monsters, perhaps because that's how (they feel) "normal society" already treats them. Many horror filmmakers likely felt *themselves* to be misfits when young. This helps explain all those horror films and TV shows that depict nice monsters helping lonely, artistic, sensitive children.

In "The Boy Who Cried Werewolf" episode of TV's *Werewolf*, a sensitive young boy, Davey, prefers his stuffed monsters over more manly pursuits. Bobby, an abusive redneck, dates Davey's single mom, and mocks Davey for "playing with dolls." Then Davey discovers Eric, an actual werewolf, and hides him from Rogan, the bounty hunter. Davey doesn't fear Eric. Davey trusts monsters. His trust is well-placed. When Eric transforms into his werewolf form, he stops Bobby from brutalizing both Davey and his mom.

In the "Mr. Swlabr" episode of TV's *Monsters*, a sensitive young boy, Roy, is bullied by his vain and selfish mother and sister. Like Davey, Roy is imaginative and likes to play indoors. He constructs model train sets. Then Roy finds a toy in his cereal box, which, when dipped in liquid, grows into a huge, talking, dinosaur-like creature. His name is Mr. Swlabr. He befriends Roy, and halts the mother's and sister's bullying of Roy.

Both Davey's and Roy's fathers are dead. It's implied that the fathers would have appreciated their sons' artistic natures, and protected them. The monsters, far from threatening the boys, intervene as surrogate dads.

In *The Curse of the Cat People* (1944), a sensitive young girl, Amy, is a dreamer and a loner who doesn't make friends easily with other children. She lives in her own fantasy world. Her parents love her, but worry that her poor social skills will cause problems as she gets older. Luckily, a benevolent ghost, Irena, intervenes to set Amy on a happier path.

Some monsters are too nice to qualify a film or TV episode as horror. "The Boy Who Cried Werewolf" is horror, because Eric suffers from his werewolf condition, and we're supposed to believe that he is a *potential* threat to Davey and his mom. Eric worries that someday he won't be able to maintain control during his werewolf transformations. But Mr. Swlabr and Irena are not a serious threat to anyone. Mr. Swlabr scares Roy's mother and sister into being nice to Roy, but he doesn't hurt them. Irena doesn't even scare anyone. These works are closer to comedy and fantasy, respectively, than to horror.

But sympathy for monsters can sink to darker levels. Sometimes, rather than a nice monster helping a nerd, the nerd *becomes* the monster — and brutally retaliates against his or her tormentors (often, stereotypically, jocks and cheerleaders, and frat boys and sorority queens).

In *Horror High* (aka *Twisted Brain*, 1974), a scrawny high school nerd, Vernon, avoids gym class (where the jocks bully him), so he can spend more time in biology lab. There he develops a formula that transforms him into a Dr. Jekyll type fiend, enabling him to kill his tormentors, teachers and students alike. In *Carrie* (1976), *The Spell* (TVM 1977), and *The Initiation of Sarah* (TMV 1978), nerdy girls use telekinesis and/or the supernatural to punish their bullying classmates. In *The Craft* (1996) and *Cheerbleeders* (2008), high school goths use witchcraft to punish their tormentors.

These films thread the edge of horror. As with many a *Tales from the Crypt* episode, audiences are expected to sympathize with an unnatural threat, one that punishes evil, yet ordinary, people. These are horror films to the extent that good nerds suffer from their unnatural powers, plus the extent to which they injure the innocent, or go overboard in injuring the guilty.

In *Horror High*, Vernon attacks a nice girl toward film's end. In the next three examples, Carrie's, Rita's, and Sarah's powers likewise harm the innocent. Although in Sarah's case, it isn't her fault; she doesn't know her own strength. In *The Craft*, the goth girls' own witchcraft turns against them. In *Cheerbleeders* (a short film), the goth boy uses witchcraft not to punish the cheerleaders, but to become their new boyfriend, thus abandoning the goth girl. "I thought he was hardcore!" she laments. So she turns on him, killing him and destroying the unnatural.

Audience sympathy for monsters can get darker still. While many horror filmmakers and fans are among the gentlest people on earth, horror does attract its share of creeps and sadists. That's unavoidable. Whatever a film depicts (car chases, sex, murder, torture) it's inevitable that *some* people will enjoy seeing it for its own sake, ignoring themes, characters, and dramatic context. *Some* people will sympathize with the slasher, and believe that "the bitch deserved it."

In TV's *Tales from the Crypt*, the bitch (or bastard), usually *does* deserve to suffer and die, because she's vain, or greedy, or an adulteress, or murderess, or simply mean to poor people, small children, and puppies. Even so, the Cryptkeeper leavens his brutal, Old Testament "eye for an eye" retributions with dark humor. With a pun and a cackle, he implies that we shouldn't take his message too seriously, much less literally.

But *some* horror fans enjoy seeing *innocent* people tortured and killed—and in a sordid, clinical fashion, the sadism undiluted with humor (e.g., *Don't Go in the House*). In a scathing critique of slasher films, Janet Maslin wrote: "To say that these films aren't very frightening is not to say that they don't have a profound effect on those who watch them. Go see one, and you'll have empirical proof that a film like this makes audiences mean."[19] She doesn't mention what specific instances of meanness she saw in the audience, if any.

Maslin then likens the appeal of slasher films to pornography:

> The oldest argument on behalf of the horror genre is that it produces catharsis. By putting us in contact with our deepest fears, it provides some relief.... Horror films used to fulfill this function, and the best of them still do. But the stripped-down, impersonal bloodbath movies to which I've been referring do nothing of the kind, any more than sexual pornography fulfills a viewer's romantic longings. This latest kind of pornography—violent pornography—doesn't even begin to allow its audience the catharsis of the traditional horror story. ... the extreme gore works against any possibility of release, since it deadens the audience and creates a feeling of utter hopelessness. These films aim simply at shocking and numbing their audiences, and perhaps the only good thing to be said about them is that their future isn't bright.[20]

Maslin was wrong about the future popularity of slasher films, though the post–*Scream* neo-slasher cycle *is* aesthetically inferior to the post–*Halloween* slasher cycle. I also disagree that slasher films lack merit, or are invariably inferior to other horror subgenres. But Maslin unearths a nugget of truth. *Some* people do doubtless watch horror films because they "get off" on graphic violence, just as some people "get off" on graphic sex. Such fans—seeking cheap thrills rather than catharsis or a sense of wonder—are equally satisfied by unnatural threats, naturalistic psycho gorefests, straight sadism (e.g., *Daughter of Rape*), and snuff films, just so long as the violence is graphic.[21]

Murderers claim to have been inspired by horror films. Richard Boyer blamed an LSD flashback of *Halloween 2* for his 1982 stabbing murders of Francis and Aileen Harbitz.[22] After the 1999 Columbine massacre, victims' families accused the film, *The Basketball Diaries*, and the video games Doom, Duke Nukem, and Redneck Rampage for partially inspiring Eric Harris and Dylan Klebold in their school shootings.[23] The youths were apparently fans of these works. *The Basketball Diaries*, the video games Quake, Doom, and Castle Wolfenstein, and porn websites were also blamed for a 1997 school shooting spree by Michael Carneal.[24] It may be a lawyer's excuse ("A horror film/video game made me do it!"), but regardless of the argument's legal or factual merits, it's noteworthy that violent films count actual killers among their fans.[25]

It's a vast moral plunge from children who love Franken Berry and Mr. Swlabr, to nerds who cheer Carrie's carnage, to misogynists who are excited by the sadism in *Don't Go in the House* and *Daughter of Rape*, to actual murderers who emulate film slashers. But a common thread runs through these folk. Horror is not always a catharsis. Some viewers do not see the monster as a threat to be feared, but as a friend, a protector, an avenger, or even a role model.

Ideological Palette

Writers have long used fantastique imagery to convey philosophical and political views. In TV's *Werewolf*, Rogan observes that the talking flower in *Alice in Wonderland* would elicit terror in the real world. Yet Lewis Carroll's intent, at least partially, was to satirize Victorian personages and customs.[26] Likewise, the anthropomorphized creatures in Aesop's fables and *Animal Farm* are not meant to frighten, but to instruct. Even *Animal Farm*'s pigs are scary not because of their unnaturalness in being a talking pig, but because of their Stalinist policies.

Some authors express their opinions explicitly, in naturalistic novels. But fantastique imagery has advantages. (1) Fantastique creatures provide shorthand metaphors for complex ideas or character traits. Lions are courageous and regal. Foxes are clever and deceitful. Monsters are ugly and evil. Vampires are parasites. Authors may also convey lasting impressions by subverting these metaphors. *The Wizard of Oz*'s lion is cowardly. *Frankenstein*'s monster is well-intentioned, doing evil only because he is hated for being ugly. (2) Fantastique characters are usually more colorful, thus more memorable, than their naturalistic counterparts. *The Grapes of Wrath*'s Tom Joad and *Animal Farm*'s Boxer both embody the long-suffering workingman, yet I believe Boxer leaves the greater impression in more readers' minds. (3) Fantastique images can camouflage an author's message, slipping it past state censors or publishers, in hopes that readers will "get it." Thus, fantastique metaphors can be both memorable, yet subtle. High-impact, yet covert.

Horror abounds in fantastique, unnatural imagery, providing filmmakers and authors with an ideological palette for any message or theme. In *Society* (1989), wealthy WASP bluebloods are depicted as a monstrous species, feeding on the working class. In my own novel, *Vampire Nation*, Communist Party officials are portrayed as vampires, feeding on the working class.

Because all films arguably convey themes, if only by default, let's call it a *message movie* when the message is blatant and intentional, and call it a *theme* when the message is more subtle, and perhaps even unintentional.

Using fantastique metaphors to send a message is one of horror's appeals for filmmakers, if not always for viewers. Message movies are not necessarily bad, but they annoy some horror fans. They came to be frightened, perhaps feel a sense of wonder, and instead were preached to. This is especially annoying if one disagrees with the message.

Themes enrich a story, and, being subtler than a message, can be fun to search for and discover. Viewers enjoy discussing, analyzing, and interpreting films with friends. But doing so presents a problem: *To what extent do we interpret the film, as opposed to imposing our own ideologies or insecurities onto it?* Do we see a message because it's *there* on screen, or because we *want* to see that message, or because we're *hypersensitive* about that message?

Some viewers perceive a blatant message where others don't even see a subtle theme. About *The Seventh Sign* (1988), *The Overlook Film Encyclopedia Horror* says:

> Opening with the suggestion that God and Ronald Reagan have the same foreign policy as the first signs of the Apocalypse involve smiting Haiti, the PLO and the Sandinistas, this fails to live up to the spectacular possibilities of the material.... Despite its immortal priestly villain and ambiguous Christ, the film embodies a return to the reactionary fundamentalism of the Devil Movie cycle inaugurated by *The Exorcist* (1973). Aside from God's apparent political sympathies, the film comes out against sex, incest, religious unorthodoxy and any kind of

moral complexity. The heroine's baby, unlike Rosemary's, is a holy innocent who restores Christ's faith in humanity.[27]

I don't get that. *The Seventh Sign* is a thought-provoking and original take on the Biblical End Times. I see no Reaganesque politics in the film. Christ surveys the killing fields of war-torn Central America, lamenting the carnage. How is that Reaganesque? Because Christ does not explicitly blame the Contras and cheer the Sandinistas? How is the film anti-sex? Because a retarded child of incest murders his parents, and is executed for it?

Yet this demonstrates how viewers of different political and religious sensitivities can interpret the same film in wholly different ways. The *Overlook* perceives a "reactionary fundamentalism" in *The Seventh Sign*, whereas I perceive a "politically correct" bias in many of the *Overlook*'s reviews. Rather than judge a film on its own terms, the *Overlook* often judges by whether it approves of the film's perceived message. An ambiguous Christ, villainous priest, and "moral complexity" (i.e., casting Christian morals into doubt) are good; reaffirming Christianity is "reactionary" and bad.

The *Overlook* also gets it wrong. The baby does not restore Christ's faith in humanity. It's the mother — her love for her baby, and her willingness to die for him — who restores Christ's faith in humanity's potential for goodness.

Even viewers who agree with a message may find its presentation so blatant that it ruins the film for them. Then again, for some people the message is the primary attraction. Some Ayn Rand fans claim to have read her lengthy (over 1,100 pages), politically didactic novel, *Atlas Shrugged*, dozens of times. Obviously, not for any surprise ending. Likewise, I once overheard an NYU film student praising director Don Siegal's "anti–McCarthy" message in *Invasion of the Body Snatchers* (1956). I interposed that Siegel insisted that he'd put no political messages into the film. The student appeared crestfallen. As if I'd taken something away from the film, making it less enjoyable for him.

Some people require that a film affirm their political or religious opinions before they can give themselves permission to enjoy it. At the very least, they must know that the film does not oppose their views. Other viewers are more forgiving. If a film is sufficiently entertaining, they'll enjoy it even if they dislike the message.

While blatant messages are often annoying, too much subtlety risks defeating the filmmaker's intent. Some messages are so cleverly camouflaged that viewers don't see it. For several years, *Starship Troopers* (1997) was perceived as celebrating fascism. It took a while before viewers realized that the film was satirizing fascism. Screenwriter Ed Neumeier thinks this subtlety made for a better film, despite the problem of some initial misunderstanding. Neumeier explains:

> While we may have suffered when *Starship Troopers* was initially released because we were not willing to underline for the audience and critics that this was a movie about the dangers of fascism, it was our feeling then, as it is now, that such a satirical (and, in hindsight, subtle) approach was more interesting, more honest, and more thought-provoking, whereas the latter and common approach would render a movie that was little more than preaching to the choir. I believe that one reason *Starship* endures so successfully in its afterlife, finding a growing and loyal audience along with many re-appreciations by the critical community, is for precisely this reason.[28]

Critics continue to debate whether horror more easily accommodates certain views over others. Is horror inherently conservative or subversive? Does horror reinforce the *sta-*

tus quo by demonizing the Other? Or does horror promote the Other? Are teen campers punished for having sex? Is the Last Girl a feminist icon because she's a strong woman who defeats the slasher? Or is she a Christian icon because she draws strength from her virginity?

I believe neither. Horror does not inherently support any particular ideology. Part of horror's enduring strength is that it's elastic enough to express all views. *The Devonsville Terror* (1983) and *A Day of Judgment* (1981) are both low-budget indie horror films, shot in the early 1980s, in small rural towns. (In Wisconsin and North Carolina, respectively.) Their stories are similar. Supernatural beings arrive in town to punish evildoers. Yet ideologically, these films are polar opposites.

In *The Devonsville Terror*, the town fathers torture and execute three nice witches in 1683. The witches reincarnate and return to Devonsville, 300 years later, seeking vengeance on the town's male chauvinists. In their spare time, they preach women's liberation to housewife radio listeners, and that "God is a woman" to local schoolchildren.

In *A Day of Judgment*, the Grim Reaper arrives in town to slay sinners who've broken God's Commandments, and escort their souls to Hell. After which, the sinners awake to discover that it was all a nightmare. "Born again," they mend their evil ways and become regular churchgoers.

Both films have rough production values, crude special effects, some subpar acting, and a slow pace. Some viewers may enjoy one over the other, depending on their political or religious views, but I found each film entertaining on its own terms. That two so similar films can effectively convey opposing worldviews demonstrates horror's thematic elasticity.

This was also demonstrated in an *American Film* article in the 1980s. The writer interpreted *Them* (1954), *The Thing from Another World* (1951), *The Day the Earth Stood Still* (1951), and *Invasion of the Body Snatchers* as being liberal, conservative, radical left, and radical right, respectively.[29]

The writer argued that *Them* and *The Thing* both affirm the legitimacy and competence of the establishment, which successfully defeats giant ants and a space alien, respectively. In *Them*, scientists outperform the military's attempts to defeat the giant ants, hence the film leans left. In *The Thing*, it's the reverse. Soldiers outdo science in defeating the alien. The scientist mistakenly wants to communicate with the alien. The soldiers wisely kill it. Thus, *The Thing* leans right. But in both films, soldiers and scientists cooperate, sharing a common cause to maintain the *status quo*. Thus, the films are liberal and conservative, rather than radical left or right.

In *The Day the Earth Stood Still* and *Invasion of the Body Snatchers*, a few individuals fight the majority and the establishment, hence these films are politically radical. In the former, an individual opposes the military establishment, and succeeds in forcing a collectivist regime and world peace onto the majority. In the latter, an individual fights collectivist rule, though it would bring world peace. Radical left and right, respectively.

Is *Invasion of the Body Snatchers* a radical right film? Danny Peary thinks that an anti–Communist interpretation is feasible: "In *Invasion of the Body Snatchers*, that there are aliens in our midst taking over all phases of our lives and brainwashing our children is shown to be fact, not paranoia ... the space aliens of *Body Snatchers* fit the mold that American schoolteachers describe as being characteristic of Russians: ice cold, outwardly peaceful but very authoritarian, emotionless."[30] Yet Peary adds that an anti–McCarthy interpretation is also reasonable:

> In *Body Snatchers*, the pod people, who, like McCarthy and the other red-baiters, look like typical, fine, upstanding Americans, search out rebels like Miles who refuse to conform to what has been newly defined as the "American Way"—just as McCarthy and HUAC destroyed the lives of those who refused to knuckle under to their directives. The mob hysteria, the sense of paranoia, the fascist police, the witch hunt atmosphere of the picture certainly mirror the ills of McCarthy America.[31]

Then again, E. Michael Jones believes that Jack Finney's novel *The Body Snatchers* is a metaphor for the destructiveness of sexual liberation and divorce. Jones writes:

> The two young divorcees find each other sexually attractive, and the more the attraction grows, the more the pods proliferate. In the inchoate manner typical of the horror genre, there is a causal connection here that never is expressed causally.... The root of the uncanny in this story is Mile's ambivalence about sexual morality.... He wants something that he knows is impossible — sexual liberation — but he also wants the tight-knit social fabric that can only be based on the inviolability of the marriage bond.... The sudden realization that marriage is a possibility for both of them fills Miles with a new sense of purpose in life and a strengthened resolve to defeat the pod creatures.... If divorce had created the monsters, then marriage would defeat them.[32]

Jones thinks that horror reflects social anxieties, a popular belief among academics and critics.[33] Well, naturally. If horror is a catharsis that exorcises our psyches of anxieties, then the question logically follows: *What are those anxieties?*

But I think the Freudian Rollercoaster is given too much credit. Horror films are not organically grown pods, absorbing society's collective mind, then projecting those anxieties on screen. Horror films reflect a filmmaker's personal creative vision, constrained by marketing and budgetary concerns. Slasher films are produced not so much because of teen viewers' anxieties about sex, but because it's relatively cheap to film young, unknown actors running and screaming in the woods.

Yes, some filmmakers get ideas from current news events. But do 1950s monster movies reflect social anxieties about The Bomb? Or did filmmakers simply use radioactivity as a readily available excuse for a really funky monster? Just how much catharsis can be had from a silly rubber suit creature?

Yes, some horror films strike a psychological cord with audiences. Catharsis and social anxieties may explain some box office successes. But too often, academics don't interpret a film's messages or themes, much less any social anxieties the film supposedly mirrors, as impose their own ideologies and insecurities onto the film. Some interpretations reveal more about the critic, or faculty politics, than about the film.

My own interpretive method: Let the film speak for itself. Accept what's on screen at face value absent a strong reason to do otherwise. A cigar is almost always a cigar. Don't look for hidden symbols. As with Occam's razor, the simplest (and most explicit) meaning is usually the best. Yes, it's fun to get creative and read all sorts of themes into a film. But know when you're making an interpretive stretch, rather than interpreting what's on screen.

Horror's appeal is personal. My attraction for horror falls, to greater or lesser degrees, under all four categories. I usually feel better after seeing a horror film (my drug and therapy of choice), so maybe there's some catharsis. I love *The Ring* and *The Grudge* and *The*

X-Files for their sense of wonder. I sympathize with Vernon and Carrie and Sarah, and enjoy their bullies' comeuppance. I created a nation of Communist vampires as a metaphor for Communism in my novel, *Vampire Nation*.

These four categories should cover it for everyone. But I could be wrong. Perhaps you have your own reasons for loving horror, not covered by any of the above?

Chapter Notes

Chapter 1

1. My italics. *Supernatural Horror in Literature*, by Howard Phillips Lovecraft, Dover Publications, New York, 1973, p. 15.

2. *The Philosophy of Horror or Paradoxes of the Heart*, by Noël Carroll, Routledge, New York, 1990, p. 12.

3. Frank Lupo's pithy teleplay for *Werewolf*'s TV pilot is replete with sharp observations.

4. *The Philosophy of Horror, op. cit.*, p. 28.

5. *The Monster Show: A Cultural History of Horror*, by David J. Skal, W.W. Norton, New York, 1993, p. 344.

6. *Ibid.*, p. 145. Stephen King, too, singles out these three novels for special attention in *Dance Macabre*, Everest House, New York, 1981, pp. 60–88.

7. Although Wiccans may wish to own the word "witch" and disassociate it from Satanism, Satanists themselves embrace the term (e.g., *The Satanic Witch*, by Anton Szandor LaVey).

8. See *Victor Frankenstein* (aka *Terror of Frankenstein*, Swedish-Irish 1977) for a faithful film adaptation of Shelley's novel.

9. *Androids, Humanoids, and Other Science Fiction Monsters: Science and Soul in Science Fiction Films*, by Per Schelde, New York University Press, New York, 1993, p. 2.

10. *Them or Us: Archetypal Interpretations of Fifties Alien Invasion Films*, by Patrick Lucanio, Indiana University Press, Bloomington, 1987, pp. 15–16.

11. *Ibid.*, p. 16.

12. *Ibid.*, p. 2.

13. *Ibid.*, p. 17.

14. *Ibid.*, p. 4.

15. *Ibid.*, p. 19.

16. *Ibid.*, p. 7.

17. *Ibid.*, p. 133, n. 20.

18. *Ibid.*, pp. 10–11.

19. *Ibid.*, p. 9.

20. *Ibid.*, p. 6.

21. *The Bulletin of the Science Fiction and Fantasy Writers of America*, Fall 1996, p. 25.

22. *Ibid.*, p. 25.

23. *Supernatural Horror in Literature*, p. 42.

24. *X-Files Confidential: The Unauthorized X-Philes Compendium*, by Ted Edwards, Little, Brown & Co., Boston, 1996, 1997, p. 6.

25. *The X-Files Declassified*, by Frank Lovece, Citadel, Secaucus, 1996, p. 4.

26. This is why *I Confess* (1953) is suspense. Although the murder occurs early in the film, this is no mystery; we already know whodunit. (Not a psycho; just a regular killer.)

27. I differentiate suspense stories from thrillers in that the hero's victory is assured in the latter, as in the James Bond spy thrillers. However, screenwriter Ross LaManna informs his UCLA class that he regards films featuring a "skilled professional," such as Bond or Rambo, to be action films, whereas thrillers involve an "everyman" caught up in events (e.g., *Enemy of the State, The Fugitive*).

28. *Psycho* (1960) begins as a suspense film about an embezzler. It broaches horror in that the murders are sudden and graphic, the killer's identity unknown. *Psycho* is no mystery because this identity is discovered rather than solved. The sequels are more clearly suspense than horror, because we know it's Norman and that he is no uberpsycho.

29. Yes, *The Terminator* (1984), an action film borrowing sf icons, did it first.

30. A project earlier attempted in *The House That Screamed* (aka *La residencia*, Spanish 1969).

31. *Official Splatter Movie Guide Vol. 2*, by John McCarty, St. Martin's Press, New York, 1992, p. viii.

32. *Ibid.*, viii–ix.

33. *Ibid.*, p. ix.

34. *Ibid.*, p. viii.

35. My italics. *The Philosophy of Horror, op. cit.*, p. 28.

36. *Official Splatter Movie Guide Vol. 2, op. cit.*, pp. vii–viii, 165.

37. A mutant killer does appear at the very end of *Mother's Day*, but she arrives too late to qualify *Mother's Day* as an unnatural threat horror film.

38. *The Philosophy of Horror, op. cit.*, p. 17.

39. *Pulp Fiction*'s copycats tried to replicate its formula of (1) A large ensemble cast of sleazy, bizarre, and criminal types, (2) Several interrelated criminal vignettes, rather than a single story, (3) Rambling dialog of non-sequiturs, intended as witty and incongruent philosophizing by lowlifes, (4) Outside-the-mainstream sexual fetishes, (5) Gory violence, often casually dispatched, (6) *Faux* sentimentality. Lacking originality, many copycats tried to compensate by upping the violence and/or bizarreness. Some copycats include *Flypaper* (1997), *Lock, Stock and Two Smoking Barrels* (British 1998), and *Spanish Judges* (1999).

40. *Official Splatter Movie Guide Vol. 2, op. cit.*, p. 55.

41. *The Philosophy of Horror, op. cit.*, p. 17.

42. *Laughing Screaming: Modern Hollywood Horror & Comedy*, by William Paul, Columbia University Press, New York, 1994, p. 20.

43. E. Michael Jones interprets the entire horror genre, from Mary Shelley's novel onward, as the moral order's reassertion of natural law against its transgressors. *Monsters from the Id: The Rise of Horror in Fiction and Film*, by Jones, Spence Publishing, Dallas, 2000.

44. *Cronenberg on Cronenberg*, edited by Chris Rodley, Faber and Faber, London, 1992, p. xvii.

45. "The Visceral Mind: The Major Films of David Cronenberg," by William Beard, appearing in *The Shape of Rage: The Films of David Cronenberg*, edited by Piers Handling, New York Zoetrope, 1983, p. 4.

46. *Terror and Everyday Life: Singular Moments in the History of the Horror Film*, by Jonathan Lake Crane, Sage Publications, Thousand Oaks, 1994, p. vi.

47. *Ibid.*, p. 40, n. 9.

48. *Immoral Tales: Sex & Horror Cinema in Europe 1956–1984*, by Cathal Tohill & Pete Tombs, Primitive Press, London, 1994, p. 5.

49. *Vampyres: A Tribute to the Ultimate in Erotic Horror Cinema*, compiled by Tim Greaves, Draculina Publishing, Glen Carbon, 1996, p. 33.

50. *Sex, Shocks and Sadism! An A–Z Guide to Erotic and Unusual Horror Films Available on Video!*, by Todd Tjersland, Threat Theatre International, Olympia, 1996, p. 23.

Chapter 2

1. *The Zombies That Ate Pittsburgh: The Films of George A. Romero*, by Paul R. Gagne, Dodd, Mead, New York, 1987, pp. 21, 23.

2. *Ibid.*, p. 21.

Chapter 3

1. CGI stands for computer-generated imagery.

2. Or to cite James Bond's epitaph in Ian Fleming's novel, *You Only Live Twice*: "I shall not waste my days in trying to prolong them. I shall use my time."

3. *Bram Stoker's Dracula: The Film and the Legend* by Francis Ford Coppola and James V. Hart, Newmarket Press, New York, 1992, p. 98.

4. *Ibid.*, p. 127. This quote is not sourced. It may have been written by the book's editor, Diana Landau.

5. *Ibid.*, p. 18.

6. *Ibid.*, pp. 126–127.

7. *Ibid.*, p. 18.

8. I was an extra in the film, and privy to crew gossip. Among other roles, I portrayed a monk in the scene where Dracula weeps over Elizabeta's corpse — Gary Oldman's first scene in "the beetle suit."

9. Although on those rare occasions when actress Grayson Hall does "lose it," she can chew scenery with all the gusto of *Star Trek*'s William Shatner.

10. A shaved head might have been even more snakelike than slicked-back hair, but that's not to complain.

11. I was an extra in that scene and saw Oldman's impressive performance firsthand. No actress was present for him to react to; not even a dummy to "stand in" for the corpse.

12. And why are American direct-to-video exploitation films dominated by scrawny starlets? Top-heavy women on chicken legs, as opposed to fully fleshed, Eurotrash scream queens, such as Erika Blanc in *The Devil's Nightmare* (aka, *La Plus Longue nuit du diable*, Belgian-Italian 1974).

13. If you freeze frame, you'll see that at least some of the blackened "doves" are pigeons. I guess it's easier, and cheaper, to cast pigeons in the role of "darkened doves" than it is to cast doves and color their feathers. Especially since *The Visitor* is pre–CGI era.

14. Email from Norman J. Warren, February 20, 2004.

15. Chapter 5 (Photographing the Image) has more on how focal length supports *Hardware*'s themes.

16. The film also has an impressive shot of Carmilla reflected in a door's glass panel. Her reflection is barely visible in the glass when it faces the wallpaper, but when Leopoldo moves behind the glass (replacing the background wallpaper with his darker suit), Carmilla's reflection turns strikingly vivid (as if her heart "comes to life" at the sight of Leopoldo).

17. *The Hidden* (1987) and *The Hidden II: The Spawning* (1994).

18. They carry boxes to the roof of a building in downtown Atlanta, line up for inspection by the space visitor, set up rows of opaque screens, and then run their hands across the screens. This set décor has no discernible story purpose; the screens exist only because they look weird and "alien."

19. Inviting two types of bloopers into a single scene: (1) some thunderclaps coincide with lightning flashes, instead of following them, and (2) some thunderclaps have no lightning flashes at all.

20. Expressionism is a style conceived by German painters in the early 1900s, wherein the artist shuns visual accuracy, instead distorting objective reality through a subjective prism. Reality as seen from an emotional or psychological perspective. *Caligari* is set in a lunatic's visually bizarre fantasies. Because his vision is presented as unnatural and threatening, as compared to the normal world in which he lives, *Caligari* is horror rather than dark fantasy.

21. In the original script, the murders were not "all a dream." This more explicitly supported the theme of evil authority figures. *The Monster Show: A Cultural History of Horror*, by David J. Skal, W.W. Norton, New York, 1993, p. 43.

22. Spaceship crews complaining about cheap bosses would become a horror/sci-fi cliché, going strong two decades after *Alien* (e.g., *Alien Cargo*, TVM 1999).

23. "I'm genetically engineering a cure for cancer," says the biochemistry professor. "What about you?" The cinema studies professor replies, "I watched some horror movies. Uh, what I mean is, I examined cinematic extrapolations of psycho-sexual, socio-political, class dynamics in postmodern Western culture."

24. The better ones include *Cherry 2000* (1987), *Circuitry Man* (1990), and *Neon City* (1991).

25. A Lamborghini Countach, provided by Executive Coachcraft, Torrance, CA. This was likely a product placement deal. *Product placement* is when a company provides a product to be used visibly in a film as a form of free advertising. It's a great way to get free stuff and sometimes also money. Big studio films are full of product placements. Low-budget films have a greater need for free props and cash but, ironically, have a harder time securing such deals because companies rarely provide product placements until a film has secured a distribution deal.

26. A voodoo woman arranges the deal, but I presume she's merely a broker for Satan.

27. *The Films of Roger Corman: Brilliance on a Budget*, by Ed Naha, Arco Publishing, New York, 1982, p. 16.

28. *Cinematic Hauntings*, edited by Gary J. and Susan Svehla, Midnight Marquee Press, Baltimore, 1996, p. 23.

29. Curiously, the killers in all three of these slasher films are female (sort of). Nor is there a Last Girl in *Stage Fright* or *Sleepaway Camp*, mostly because the Last Girl *is* the killer. Other slasher films with no Last Girl include *Hide and Go Shriek* (1988), *Splatter University* (1984), and *House of Death* (1981). Apparently, the Last Girl, though a slasher film cliché, is less ubiquitous than some believe.

30. Even foreign producers think so. Ironically, *Contamination* and *Zombi 2*, both Italian productions, filmed more in New York City (using it for both location and lo-

cale) than do many American films that are shot in Canadian or European cities meant to substitute for New York.

31. The film bureaus of every city, state, province, and nation claim, in Hollywood trade paper ads, that their locations can convincingly substitute for every other locale on the planet. But it just ain't so.

32. With a "surprise twist ending" identical to that in *The Number 23* (2007). In both films, the hero is schizophrenic and a killer, without knowing it. Like those protagonists who turn out to be ghosts, or already dead, without knowing it, in *The Sixth Sense, The Others*, and *Jacob's Ladder*.

33. I know, having worked as an extra on over 60 productions.

34. Film heroes and heroines possess mystical abilities to survive horrors that destroy lesser characters. In *Arachnid* (2001), heroine Mercer falls partway into a hole, whereupon a (presumably) giant spider grabs her leg. Mercer struggles, and is pulled free with nary a nick. Later, a giant spider grabs hero Valentine's head in its jaws. Amazing, Valentine pulls his head free, with nary a nick. As one may expect, other characters prove easier pickings for the giant spiders.

35. *Inferno* DVD, Special Features, "Interview with Dario Argento," Blue Underground edition.

36. Yes, I suppose one can read that into the scene, or that the surreal skyline portends the coming of the Antichrist. But *Bless the Child*'s CGI skylines are rare, whereas *Lost Soul*'s desaturated colors and "mistimed shutter" are present throughout the film, hence, more explicitly portend the Antichrist's arrival; see the chapter on Photography, the sections on "Contrast" and "Shutter Speed."

37. Mad scientists are always either trying to *advance* humanity, or *return* humanity to its "purer form." In *Island of the Fishmen* (aka *L'Isola degli uomini pesce, Screamers*; Italian 1979) a mad scientist tried to genetically and surgically transform men into amphibious "gill men." So that when the Earth became overpopulated and without food, man could return to the waters from which he evolved, and farm the ocean floor. (Well, it made sense to him.)

38. *Terror* is so engrossing and enjoyable, I watched the film several times before I noticed that Susie climbs *two* flights of stairs to seek the blood's source, never investigating if the blood originates from the interim floor. (She's right, it doesn't.) Director Norman J. Warren says that most people never notice it. Email to the author, February 18, 2004.

39. One critic called it a manikin, and wondered what manikins were doing in a hospital. But I'll be generous and assume it's supposed to be a medical school dummy.

40. The *rack focus* technique is covered in the Chapter 5 (Photographing the Image).

41. Critics have described Neo's long coat as evoking a Jesuit priest, so it's appropriate that *Lost Souls* "return" the favor by evoking Neo. However, though *Lost Souls* was released after *The Matrix* (2000 and 1999, respectively), *Lost Souls* was shot in 1997. So this scene can't be accused of "ripping off" *The Matrix*'s look.

Chapter 4

1. *Dark Romance: Sexuality in the Horror Film*, by David J. Hogan, McFarland, Jefferson, NC, 1986, p.155.

2. Early 1980s American music videos borrowed from European aesthetic styles, such as German expressionism and Soviet montage, because music videos were not anchored by a story, and were thus free to be surreal or abstract. Post–MTV American mainstream cinema has since "loosened up" stylistically, catching up to pre–MTV horror.

3. It's no surprise that crime films also appreciate canted frames (e.g., *Kiss Me Deadly*, 1955).

4. For more on the aesthetic similarities of comics and films, see "What Comics Can Teach You About Movies," by Steve Gerber, *Film Maker's Guide to Super-8*, compiled by the editors of *Super-8 Filmaker Magazine* (sic), Sheptow Publishing, New York, 1980, p. 83. Also see "Want to Write a Screenplay or Make a Movie?: Read Comics!" by David Kaminski, *Student Filmmakers*, December 2008, p. 22.

5. *Solarization* is when an image's color tones (or black and white tones) are reversed, wholly or partially. Solarization is one way to create an unnatural POV, one which depicts a world not as normal people see it.

6. This is the emotional effect, even if we intellectually believe that Donald is insane and only imagines the corpses' voices, and perhaps even their POVs.

7. Email from Gary Wallace, September 8, 2008.

8. *The Jar* is only available in out-of-print VHS editions, in fullscreen. I don't think I'm missing anything in offscreen space. This imaginative horror art film cries for a restored, widescreen DVD edition.

9. *Bram Stoker's Dracula: The Film and the Legend*, by Francis Ford Coppola and James V. Hart, Newmarket Press, New York, 1992, p. 86.

10. *Ibid.*, p. 52.

11. "The Devil Made Flesh," by Christopher Probst, *American Cinematography*, December, 1999.

12. Conversation with Erasmo P. Romero III, Santa Monica, CA, October 9, 2008.

13. Director Andrew Wiest says he is influenced by such high-energy filmmakers as Sam Raimi and Richard Rodriguez. Email interview with Wiest, September 21, 2007.

14. Email from Andrew Wiest, September 21, 2009.

15. *Broken Mirrors/Broken Minds: The Dark Dreams of Dario Argento*, by Maitland McDonagh, Citadel Press, New York, 1991, 1994, p. 151.

Chapter 5

1. *Soft* and *hard* light is explained in Chapter 6 (Lighting the Image).

2. The Video Communications Inc. VHS tape edition of *The Redeemer* plays brighter than the Eastwood-DVD.com DVD edition. The overexposed "angelic light" is in both editions, but the actors are less dim on the tape. Both editions are full screen, and the DVD itself appears struck from a tape, as it carries tape glitches. Both editions are unknown generations away from the original film print, with an unknown number of poor transfers from generation to generation. It's therefore hard to determine the film print's true exposure and image details, and thus its original aesthetic intent and effect.

3. While these superimposed words imply that this boy, Chris, is "the Redeemer," the end title credits list the priest as "The Redeemer."

4. I saw the film as *The Redeemer* at the Midway Theater, in Queens, NY, in fall 1979. That's the title on my Video Communications Inc. VHS tape box. The DVD

title is *Class Reunion Massacre*, which I suspect was meant to connect the film to the post–*Halloween* slasher cycle and its emphases on high school and college settings, themes, and victims.

5. *Broken Mirrors/Broken Minds: The Dark Dreams of Dario Argento*, by Maitland McDonagh, Citadel Press, New York, 1991, 1994, p. 144.

6. http://en.wikipedia.org/wiki/Suspiria.

7. Email from Norman J. Warren, February 20, 2004.

8. Email interview with C.J. Johnson, June 24, 2008.

9. "The Devil Made Flesh," by Christopher Probst, *American Cinematography*, December 1999.

10. *Ibid.*

11. *Ibid.*

12. *Ibid.*

13. See Chapter 2 (Pragmatic Aesthetics).

14. TV news crews normally use faster film stocks than do Hollywood studios, because reporters can't always predict or control the available lighting on location.

15. Greg Langille posting at http://www.deadmedia.org/notes/35/357.html and quoting http://www.beyond 2000.co.uk/umbrella/ which is described as "a curatorial agency funded by the Arts Council of London."

16. The similar hues assist the staging and editing to mislead audiences into thinking that Peter's ghost exists in Karen's world, rather than his being a flashback. For details about this scene, see the section on "Constructing Space" in Chapter 7 (Editing the Image).

17. See the section on "The Moving Frame" in Chapter 4 (Framing the Image).

18. "Silent Film Speed," by James Card, http://www.cinemaweb.com/silentfilm/bookshelf/18_car_1.htm.

19. "Building Jacob's Ladder," a documentary on the Special Edition DVD of *Jacob's Ladder*.

20. This demonstrates *Nightstalker*'s disregard for facts. The film opens by stating the year is 1985 (Ramirez was caught on August 31, 1985), yet the Bhopal chemical plant leak occurred on December 3, 1984. Not good enough for a fact-based, true crime film but close enough for an impressionistic, horror film vision of Ramirez's Los Angeles.

21. When Elliot turns vigilante cop and demands that Martinez kill Ramirez, Elliot's head shakes, implying that Old Testament "eye for an eye" retribution is Evil. Ramirez also demands that Martinez kill him. But she refuses, because, she says, "I'm not like you." Her moral compass is accurate.

22. The fast shutter speed may have been in addition to, or instead of, the fast motion film. Shutter speeds are covered in greater detail later in this chapter.

23. *The Redeemer* has mistakenly been classified as part of horror's slasher cycle, but it isn't. (1) The film's year of release has variously been listed as 1976, 1977, and 1978, indicating that it was shot before *Halloween*'s 1978 release. Thus, *The Redeemer* was not influenced by the subgenre's founding film. (2) *The Redeemer*'s killer uses a shotgun. Slashers are called such for a reason. They may drown or burn a victim in a pinch, but no guns allowed. (3) *The Redeemer* is a supernatural film, whereas true *uberpsychos* are enigmatic, defying explanation. Several *Halloween* sequels were weakened by their lame, after-the-fact, Celtic magic "explanations."

24. Not surprising, since *The Omen* is one of *The Visitor*'s many "influences."

25. Or rather, strikes a wall. This special effect "fall" was achieved by spinning actress Lee Remick on a turntable, as it moved along a track toward a wall, that was dressed up (with rug, broken glass, and goldfish) to resemble the floor. No goldfish were killed in making *The*

Omen. They were dead, painted sardines. (See commentary by director Richard Donner on *The Omen* Special Edition DVD.) *Jeepers Creepers* may have copied this trick of "falling" onto a wall in slow motion. When Darry strikes the church basement's "ground," the shaken soil falls toward Darry's feet, not back onto the "ground."

26. Much like a zoom-in, but this appears to be a "blow-up" of the image done in a post-production lab, hence, no change in focal length or perspective.

27. Some previous shots might also contain brief instances of forward motion, amid mostly reverse motion. Voices are always distorted, but when Miranda confronts her husband, she sounds like she's saying "Hello" in forward motion, albeit at the "wrong" speed.

28. *Bram Stoker's Dracula: The Film and the Legend*, by Francis Ford Coppola and James V. Hart, Newmarket Press, New York, 1992, p. 89.

29. *Ibid.*, p. 89.

30. Email from Miguel Gallego, August 16, 2008.

31. MySpace message from Daniel Zubiate, August 14, 2008.

32. Email from Joe Fontano, August 14, 2008.

33. Many low-end consumer video cameras only have automatic exposure, which doesn't allow one to control the shutter speed. However, with Super-8 film cameras, even if it only has automatic exposure, the shutter does stay open longer at 18 fps than at 24 fps (33⅓ percent longer — do that math). Not as nice as full manual shutter control, but if you need every bit of available light, at least you have the option of shooting at 18 fps.

34. Email interviews with Bill Whirity, October 8, 2006, and August 8, 2008.

35. Email from Jose Zambrano Cassella, September 15, 2008.

36. "The Devil Made Flesh," *op. cit.*

37. *Ibid.*

38. My Sankyo Super-8 camera does dissolves "in camera." While filming, you press the "dissolve" button when you wish to do so. The camera begins closing its lens aperture, admitting ever less light, increasingly underexposing the film until the aperture is closed and the camera stops. Then the camera rewinds the film to the point where you pressed the "dissolve" button, and waits. When you begin filming again, the lens aperture begins opening, initially underexposing the film, but opening until you're filming at the correct exposure setting. Thus have you filmed one shot partially atop another, dissolving between the two shots.

39. See the section on "Day for Night" in Chapter 6 (Lighting the Image).

40. http://www.tiffen.com/fog_filters.htm. The Tiffen Company is a leading manufacturer of lens filters. Their website contains much useful information about a vast variety of filters.

41. The 2-disc DVD edition of *The Others* has a special feature entitled "Visual Effects Piece" which provides detailed analysis of how its digital fog was created.

42. Email interview with Miguel Gallego, June 18, 2008.

43. Email interview with Christopher Alan Broadstone, June 18, 2008.

Chapter 6

1. A *scrim* is a wire mesh placed in front of a stage light to decrease its intensity. As with a lens aperture, a

scrim's ability to reduce light is measured in *f/stops*. *Barn-doors* are flaps that partly block stage lights. Consult a technical manual to learn about stage lighting tools in greater detail.

2. A *dry* thunderstorm. Plenty of spooky lightning flashes and loud thunder, but no rain to soak actress Pamela Franklin in her nightgown. This *is* broadcast television. Although, *Anthropophagus: The Grim Reaper* and *Pieces* were feature films, yet they too had dry thunderstorms. Saves money on the water bill, I suppose.

3. Well, not every stage light is immobile. When Elizabeth enters the classroom building, a stage light follows her journey through the lobby, at least partway. This is likely because the lobby presented a wide expanse, so it was easy for a lighting technician to move a stage light as Pamela Franklin moved. Less easily done from the narrow confines of hallways.

4. Nor is this a *nondiegetic* light. It's *diegetic* because it's in the story. Kenny sees it by it. Nondiegetic lights will be discussed later in this chapter.

5. *The Amazing Herschell Gordon Lewis and His World of Exploitation Films*, by Daniel Krogh with John McCarty, FantaCo Enterprises, Albany, 1983, pp. 6–11.

6. It's possible there was no separate stage light to backlight actor Danny Aiello, but rather, that either the stage light that created the "sunlight" streaming from the window, or the examination light (part of the *mise-en-scène*), created the backlit halo effect — an example of one light serving two functions.

7. This shot's composition is discussed in detail in the section on "Composition" in Chapter 3 (*Mise-en-Scène*).

8. Arguably, their silhouettes function like director Hal Hartley's deadpan acting style, which likewise strips the drama of nonessential elements. See the section on "Acting" in Chapter (*Mise-en-Scène*).

9. Judging by Adara's floor-length skirt, she's not on a pedestal. There is no reason for Jon to look up at her. Nor is the direction of his gaze consistent.

10. More about *day-for-night* later in this chapter.

11. While the camera is mostly with Mary, we do cut once to Mrs. Redi's side of the curtain. But we don't see Mrs. Redi, thus maintaining her silhouette's power. Instead, we see Mary from Mrs. Redi's POV (i.e., blurry behind the shower curtain).

12. This red glow seems to have been done with stage lights rather than in a post-production lab because the female students aren't uniformly lit in red. Also, we once see the teacher's side of the sheets, which is lit blue.

13. Although *Suspiria*'s irrational colors unnerve us throughout the film, the students never remark on the colors, accepting them as normal. As would anyone in a nightmare.

14. The asylum silhouettes are discussed in detail in the section on "Composition" in Chapter (*Mise-en-Scène*).

15. This scene in *Aliens* is discussed in the section on "Hidden or Unseen Threats" in the chapter on *Mise-en-Scène*.

16. In *rear projection*, actors perform *in front of* a screen while images are projected onto its *rear*. In *Terror* (British 1978), a sword flies through the air (the sword suspended before a screen, images of a speeding room projected onto its rear), impales Ann, carries her through the room (actress Carolyn Courage standing before images of the speeding room, a wind machine blowing her hair), then pins her to a wall. It's a beautiful effect. See *Ten Years of Terror: British Horror Films of the 1970s*, edited by Harvey Fenton & David Flint, FAB Press, Surrey, England, 2001, p. 304.

17. *The Fearmakers: The Screen's Directorial Masters of Suspense and Terror*, by John McCarty, St. Martin's Press, New York, 1994, p.41.

18. The cat's owner? This scene also demonstrates how brief shots can help hide cheesy monsters (or harmless pussycats), a topic covered in the section on "Shot Duration" in Chapter 7 (Editing the Image).

19. *The Fearmakers: The Screen's Directorial Masters of Suspense and Terror*, op. cit. p. 42.

20. *Classics of the Horror Film*, by William K. Everson, Citadel Press, Secaucus, 1974, pp. 82–83.

21. Here's a fun thing to observe. As Laurie stands in the hallway, a "moonbeam" shines upon her. When Michael's face appears, it is conveniently level with the moonbeam, so we all see him clearly. Even more conveniently, as his face lowers, as if he were crouching before sneaking up on Laurie, the "moonbeam" helpfully moves down the frame with him, keeping him illuminated. Obviously, this "moonbeam" is a stage light — and no, I did not notice the "moving moonbeam" the first half dozen times I watched *Halloween*.

22. Email from Stanford Whitmore, August 13, 2004.

23. Not to be confused with the 1985 slasher film, *The Mutilator*, aka *Fall Break*.

24. Or maybe it's an extradimensional force? Or a spaceship?

25. For details on this scene, see the section on "Long Focal Length, aka Telephoto Lens" in Chapter 5 (Photographing the Image).

26. Oddly, some of them also appear to have some pinkish-violet underhead lighting. I don't know if it's the lighting or just shadows, due to a poor VHS edition. I wonder what a digitally remastered blu-ray DVD edition would look like?

27. Or rather, against a soundstage made up to resemble a sky.

28. It looks to be some sort of optical house special effect.

29. This scene is discussed more fully in the section on "Contrast" in Chapter 5 (Photographing the Image).

30. "Building Jacob's Ladder," a special features documentary on the Special Edition DVD of *Jacob's Ladder*, Artisan Entertainment.

31. Because of the desaturation, I considered the possibility that this "bright white light" effect was not created by a stage light, but perhaps by some film developing process or CGI effect. Yet I detect faint attached shadows on the actors when bathed in this whiteness, indicating a stage light.

32. Well, it's someone's idea of Down Syndrome. See the "Interview With Make Up Supervisor Craig Reardon" on Disc Two of the Code Red DVD edition of *The Unseen*. Also see the "Interview with Tom Burton." The factors influencing Junior's eventual makeup included the director, multiple makeup artists, and a potential lawsuit over one makeup artist's past work.

33. The aesthetic effects of *Suspiria*'s nondiegetic colors are discussed more fully in the section on "Contrast" in Chapter 5 (Photographing the Image).

34. Email from Norman J. Warren, February 20, 2004. The aesthetic effects of *Terror*'s colors are discussed in the section on "Contrast" in Chapter 5 (Photographing the Image).

35. Two more anomalies: (1) There is no rain; it's a dry storm. (2) The thunderclaps resound simultaneously with the "lightning," rather than afterwards. Even so, the film is so enjoyable, few will notice or care.

Chapter 7

1. Some film theorists suggest that films are created a fourth and final time by audiences, because each viewer "sees" a different film from what the filmmaker intended — enjoying, hating, or focusing on different elements, or rooting for different characters, or inferring different themes and messages.

2. For more on *split screens*, see the section on "Split Frames, aka Split Screens" in Chapter 4 (Framing the Image).

3. I think I discern curtain ruffles against the blackness, but it's faint. Mine is an old, much-viewed Beta copy of *Curtains*. The film is unavailable on DVD in the U.S. I'm pretty sure the curtain patterns would be clearly visible on a digitally remastered, blu-ray DVD edition. But who knows?

4. Bruno Mattei Bio, Extras, *Hell of the Living Dead* DVD, Anchor Bay Entertainment, 2002.

5. Some shots depict a crowded party, with music. Yet we hear nothing in the kitchen. This film has both sound and spatial discontinuities.

6. This scene is discussed in the section on "Sight Gags" in the Chapter 3 (*Mise-en-Scène*). Also read about *Terror* in the section on "Contrast" in Chapter 5 (Photographing the Image).

7. As in *The House on Sorority Row*, surprisingly vast areas of the building are deserted, despite a large party nearby. In horror films, there's never a spillover crowd when you need help.

8. An example of *elliptical editing*, discussed in the section on "Constructing Time."

9. This is staging, not an eyeline match, because Karen and Toshio are in the same shot.

10. Staging, not an eyeline match. See previous footnote.

11. Vsevolod Pudovkin, "Naturshchik vmesto aktera," in Sobranie sochinenii, volume I, Moscow: 1974, p.184. As cited at http://en.wikipedia.org/wiki/Kuleshov_Effect.

12. While MTV has been influential, its originality is overstated. Many 1980s music videos borrow from 1920s European cinematic movements, such as expressionism, impressionism, surrealism, and Soviet montage.

13. "Editing Structure: Avoid Over-Cutting," by Richard D. Pepperman, *Student Filmmakers*, July 2008, pp. 38–39.

14. Much like a low angle frame can either lionize or satirize a subject.

15. For more about this scene, and the above scene from *Contamination*, see the section on "Speed of Motion" in Chapter 5 (Photographing the Image).

16. Tip: When some filmmakers shoot only one actor in a scene (usually in closeup), they have the actor *perform alone to the camera, without the other actors present*. This may save money, but such shots can appear to be from an unlikely vantage point, creating a rough edit. For smoother transitions, film even closeups with all of the key actors performing (even if offscreen), changing only the camera position and/or focal length for closeups. This helps maintain the scene's staging and eyelines. Also, actors find it easier to remain "in character" and maintain the rhythm of their dialog when performing with other actors, rather than performing to empty space. (Low-budget films are less likely to film a master shot, less likely to shoot closeups with the other actors performing offscreen, and less likely to hire skilled actors who can better perform to empty space. This is why low-budget films are plagued with roughly edited, stiffly acted, closeups.)

17. *Short ends* are unexposed leftover film stock that are sold to film dealers (at about 25% of retail value) then resold to filmmakers (at about 50% retail value). *Recans* are film stock that has been opened and loaded into a magazine (the camera's film container) but then recanned, unused. Recans are usually of full or nearly full magazine length because the roll has not been shot. Short ends are leftover pieces from rolls that have been partly shot, thus short ends occupy less than a full magazine.

18. *Graphic matching* is explained in the below section on that topic.

19. *Prom Night*'s flashbacks juxtapose shots of high school seniors with shots of them as kids. Similarly, *The Redeemer* crosscuts shots of the priest listing sins, with shots of the person (in the yearbook photo and as an adult) guilty of that particular sin.

20. Quoting *Jacob's Ladder* director Adrian Lyne from the section on "Flickering and Strobe Lights" in Chapter 6 (Lighting the Image).

21. Michael's emergence from the shadows recalls the section on "Hiding in the Dark" in Chapter 6 (Lighting the Image).

22. This series debuted in 1972 as *Ghost Story*. Its midseason title change did not save it from cancellation in 1973.

23. My italics. "Modern Cinematography: Recent Stylistic Trends in the Industry," by Saro Varjabedian, *Student Filmmakers*, May 2008, p. 8.

24. At least, Mum *appears* to have just entered. Yet sunlight seems to be shining through curtained windows behind her, though outside it was night. Still, these "windows" are in the background, heavily blurred, so maybe they're … curtained wall lights?

25. I'm not counting the blackouts that bookend the *montage*, and I'm counting the dissolve of Mum's mother within one shot as two shots. Recall a similar "same shot dissolve" in *9 Lives of Mara*, in the section on "Superimposition and Dissolve" in Chapter 5 (Photographing the Image).

26. Both shots are POVs, the falling *Necronomicon* being the POV of the people in the cabin, the approaching tree being Bobby Joe's POV. As with mirror opposites, the similarities in these shots reinforce their polarities.

27. The *Soviet montage* movement should not be confused with *montage* sequences. Yes, it's the same French word.

28. It's odd that the ax resounds *metallically*, because the chopping block is *wood*. Nor could the *grill* resound metallically, because it hits Vicki's *head*. Nevertheless, this metallic sound, however illogical, thematically links these shots. (However, this metallic sound does not overlap the scenes — it resounds only in the second shot — and thus is not a sound bridge, unlike the engine rev in *Evil Dead 2*.)

29. Some may argue that *Not of This Earth*'s cut is associational, because blood is food for aliens, just like syrup is for us. But an associational edit should "editorialize," offering an opinion or commentary. "Red liquid food is like red liquid food" is not an insight, but a visual gag.

30. *Broken Mirrors/Broken Minds: The Dark Dreams of Dario Argento*, by Maitland McDonagh, Citadel Press, New York, 1991, 1994, p. 149–150.

31. *Ibid.*, p. 151.

Chapter 8

1. For details on how *The Dark*'s nondiegetic whispers function in the context of the film, see the section on "Hiding in the Dark" in Chapter 6 (Lighting the Image).

2. This shifting of audience attention to Paul is reinforced by framing actor Gary Wallace from his front, and actress Karin Sjöberg from behind, and by Wallace's acting. His staring eyes intrigue us. What's he seeing?

3. This spooky music is an ATC: *audio threat cue*. ATCs are discussed further below.

4. Ioan Allen, quoted in "Beyond the Ear-Death Experience: Tech Experts Blame Helmers for Current Loudness Syndrome," by Neil S. Yonover. *Daily Variety*, August 21, 1997, p. 13.

5. This loud flapping functions as an *audio shock*. More on audio shocks and *ambient sounds* (and yes, ATCs) later in this chapter.

6. For more on this scene, see the section on "Graphic Similarities and Contrasts" in Chapter 7 (Editing the Image).

7. They're called *sound*stages for a reason: their walls are insulated to muffle noises from outside and to provide good, easily controlled acoustics inside. By *acoustics*, I mean how a room or area affects the sounds produced therein.

8. Toshio's voice is inspired by a Japanese myth of a servant who defeats a king at chess and is thus executed, along with his wife, child, and the child's cat. The spirits of child and cat fuse into a demon, which roams the land seeking an unattainable revenge. Stephen Susco, "The Myth of the Ju-On," *The Grudge* DVD, Columbia Tristar, 2005.

9. I say *often* because sometimes the possessor wants to keep its presence a secret. In TV's *Dark Shadows*, Count Petofi didn't want anyone to know that he'd switched bodies with the unwilling Quentin Collins. Naturally, while inside Quentin's body, he spoke in Quentin's voice.

10. The characters seem not to hear these noises or the voice. I'm not even sure if it is a voice, or if I'm seeing Elvis in my toast. There is no "Laura" in the film.

11. Functioning as an ATC: *audio threat cue*.

12. The Lion's Gate DVD edition can be played with either Schwarzenegger's original voice or the dubbed voice. Compare the difference for yourself.

13. "An Interview with Actress Mary Maude," by Michael Orlando Yaccarino, *Filmfax*, No. 75–76, Oct/Jan 2000, p. 53.

14. Jacklove1986 posted on the Internet Movie Database: "OMG that kid has got to have to most annoying voice ever! his big fish lips! and the scene where he is crying, enuf sed!" http://www.imdb.com/title/tt0082966/board/nest/21201642.

15. Conversation with Damon Packard, Culver City, CA, September 15, 2008.

16. This aspect of *Dead Silence* is discussed in detail in the section on "Volume."

17. *The Film Encyclopedia*, by Ephraim Katz, Crowell, New York, 1979, p. 835.

18. Email from Gary Wallace, September 8, 2008.

19. *Cinematic Hauntings*, edited by Gary J. and Susan Svehla, Midnight Marquee Press, Baltimore, 1996, p. 26.

20. Director Richard Blackburn and actress Lesley Gilb, Audio Commentary, *Lemora: A Child's Tale of the Supernatural* DVD, Synapse Films.

21. *The Overlook Film Encyclopedia Horror*, edited by Phil Hardy, Overlook Press, Woodstock, 1994, p. 279.

22. *Demonique #4*, FantaCo Enterprises, Albany, 1983, p. 3.

23. *Ibid.*, p. 4.

24. *The Vampire Film: From Nosferatu to Bram Stoker's Dracula*, by Alain Silver and James Ursini, Limelight, New York, 1993, p. 194.

25. Conversation with Damon Packard, Culver City, CA, September 15, 2008.

26. The film is based on H.P. Lovecraft's "The Case of Charles Dexter Ward."

27. For more on this scene, see the section on "Silhouettes and *Mise-en-Scène*" in Chapter 6 (Lighting the Image).

28. Read more about this scene in the section on "Shot Duration" in Chapter 8 (Editing the Image).

29. Yes, the killer is inconsistent as to when he plays his tape. *Island of Blood* is a horror film, not a mystery, so naturally, the killer has a sloppy M.O.

30. *Love and Curses* began life as *She-Wolf of London*, but the show changed its name when it moved from London to Los Angeles in mid-season. This failed to save it from cancellation in 1991, after one season.

31. *Classics of the Horror Film*, by William K. Everson, Citadel Press, Secaucus, 1974, p. 82.

32. When I say *The Velvet Vampire*'s sitar score is "haunting," I don't mean that it's spooky, but rather, "haunting" in that psychedelically spiritual, Jim Morrison sense. The Doors's music and Morrison's performances have often been called "haunting."

33. *Supernatural Horror in Literature*, by Howard Phillips Lovecraft, Dover Publications, New York, 1973, p. 15.

34. *Audio shocks* are covered later in this chapter.

35. Observant viewers see part of the scar before Victoria lifts her hair. Less observant viewers don't notice the scar until the hair is raised, the ATC functioning as an exclamation point—*Look! You see that? A lobotomy scar!*

36. Silence can be made tense through mood music, an ATC, or a story incident (e.g., Joe says something that indicates he may be the slasher), among other techniques.

Chapter 9

1. "Rachel Belofsky: Slashing and Screaming for the Love of Horror," by Daniel Schweiger, *Venice*, October 2006, p. 32.

2. *Terror and Everyday Life: Singular Moments in the History of the Horror Film*, by Jonathan Lake Crane, Sage Publications, Thousand Oaks, CA, 1994, p. 24.

3. I'm relying on memory. I *think* the article appeared in the summer of 2005. If not, then some other mid–2000s summer.

4. "Reading" a film is academic jargon, best translated as "interpreting" a film. It's okay if you don't understand. You're not supposed to. I didn't understand much of my assigned readings at film school. I still got A's and B's.

5. *Venice*, *op. cit.*, p. 32.

6. Conversation with Denise Gossett, Hollywood, CA, September 20, 2003.

7. *Death Makes a Holiday: A Cultural History of Halloween*, by David J. Skal, Bloomsbury, New York, 2002, p. 56.

8. My italics. "Monsters—Antedeluvian Horrors," by Stephen Mark Rainey, *Horror*, Dark Regions Press, issue no. 9, 1997, p. 41.

9. See the sections on "Horror as an Unnatural Threat" and "Horror as a Naturalistic Psycho Gorefest" in Chapter 1 (Defining the Genre).

10. *Supernatural Horror in Literature*, by Howard Phillips Lovecraft, Dover Publications, New York, 1973, p. 15.

11. Yes, uberpsychos are unnatural, but winged

demons even more so. For more on this scene, see the section on "Backlights: Halos and Silhouettes" in Chapter 6 (Lighting the Image).

12. www.clivebarker.info/religion.html, citing "Horror's Roots — Writer Clive Barker on Good and Evil in the Modern World," by Sid Smith, *Chicago Tribune*, May 23, 1993. Many of Barker's comments on the topic of horror and spirituality, drawn from many sources, are collected on this webpage.

13. *Horror and the Holy: Wisdom-Teachings of the Monster Tale*, by Kirk J. Schneider, Open Court, Chicago, 1993, p. xi.

14. *In Search of Ancient Astronauts* (1973), *UFOs: Past, Present, and Future* (1974), *In Search of Ancient Mysteries* (1975), *The Outer Space Connection* (1975), *UFOs: It Has Begun* (1976), all narrated by Rod Serling. The first is a reedited version of *Chariots of the Gods* (1970), which is less scary without Serling's eerie voiceover.

15. Exodus 33:20–23. Well, that's what I inferred from von Daniken's book, though there's a more benevolent interpretation. This alien only wants to protect Moses from too much radioactivity. (Moses' face *does* glow after seeing the alien/God's back. Exodus 34:29–34.)

16. I am of course referring to the demon girl from *The Ring* and the serial killer from *Saw*.

17. See the section on "Erotic Horror vs. Splatterporn" in Chapter 1 (Defining the Genre).

18. I *think* it was Arthur C. Clarke or Carl Sagan.

19. "Bloodbaths Debase Movies and Audiences," by Janet Maslin, *The New York Times*, November 21, 1982.

20. Ibid. As examples, Maslin cites *The Burning, Maniac, The Slumber Party Massacre, Humongous, Friday the 13th, Halloween, Halloween III*, and *Carrie*, though it's unclear from the context if she equates *Carrie* with those other films.

21. See the description of *Daughter of Rape* in the section on "Erotic Horror vs. Splatterporn" in Chapter 1 (Defining the Genre).

22. *Death Makes a Holiday: A Cultural History of Halloween, op. cit.*, pp. 168–170.

23. "Columbine lawsuit against makers of video games, movies thrown out," Associated Press, March 5, 2002, reprinted at: http://www.freedomforum.org/templates/document.asp?documentID=15820.

24. "Federal appeals panel upholds dismissal of lawsuit against movie, video game makers," Associated Press, August, 14, 2002, reprinted at: http://www.freedomforum.org/templates/document.asp?documentID=16730.

25. Advertisers spend billions a year, thinking their 30 second ads influence behavior. Activists present media awards for positive plugs. Minority groups monitor the media to discourage negative portrayals. *Everyone* believes that *media influences behavior*, so let's not pretend otherwise. Horror media is no exception. However, a free society allows free expression *even when that expression has a harmful influence*. Individuals bear the sole responsibility to control their behavior, regardless of any media's (or artist's) influence on people.

26. "Bill the Lizard may be a play on the name of Benjamin Disraeli." http://en.wikipedia.org/wiki/Alice's_Adventures_in_Wonderland.

27. *The Overlook Film Encyclopedia Horror*, edited by Phil Hardy, Overlook Press, Woodstock, 1994, p. 440.

28. Email from Ed Neumeier, February 9, 2003.

29. Again, I rely on memory. My stack of *American Film* magazines is long since gone.

30. *Cult Movies*, by Danny Peary, Delacorte Press, New York, 1981, p. 157.

31. *Ibid.*, pp. 157–158.

32. *Monsters from the Id: The Rise of Horror in Fiction and Film*, by E. Michael Jones, Spence Publishing, Dallas, 2000, pp 196, 200.

33. Skal writes at great length about how various horror film cycles reflect this or that period's social anxieties. Sometimes he makes sense. Other times he overreaches, imposing his message rather than interpreting what's on screen. *The Monster Show: A Cultural History of Horror*, by David J. Skal, W.W. Norton, New York, 1993.

Bibliography

Books

Balum, Chas. *Lucio Fulci: Beyond the Gates*. San Leandro, CA: Blackest Heart Books, 1996. A short book (80 pages), but informative, readable, and filled with photos.

Bordwell, David, and Kristin Thompson. *Film Art: An Introduction*. New York: McGraw Hill, 2008. An excellent introduction to film aesthetics. The first edition (1979), published by Addison-Wesley, inspired me in film school. My copy of the 8th edition has "2008" printed inside it, but Amazon.com lists the 8th edition as being released in 2006.

Carroll, Noël. *The Philosophy of Horror or Paradoxes of the Heart*. New York: Routledge, 1990.

Coppola, Francis Ford, and James V. Hart. *Bram Stoker's Dracula: The Film and the Legend*. New York: Newmarket Press, 1992. A publication of Hart's screenplay, full of photos, production sketches, notes, sidebars, and comments from many of the film's participants. I appear in the photo on page 87, uncredited, standing just above Anthony Hopkins. Although the cover credits Coppola and Hart as the book's authors, inside the book, Diana Landau is credited as editor.

Crane, Jonathan Lake. *Terror and Everyday Life: Singular Moments in the History of the Horror Film*. Thousand Oaks, CA: Sage Publications, 1994.

Dawidziak, Mark. *The Night Stalker Companion: A 25th Anniversary Tribute*. Beverly Hill, CA: Pomegranate Press, 1997. An excellent history of the Carl Kolchak phenomenon, from unpublished novel, to TV movies, TV series, novelizations, original novels, and comics. The coverage of the show's production and legal troubles offers insight into how Hollywood mistreats writers and outsiders.

Diehl, Digby. *Tales from the Crypt: The Official Archives*. New York: St. Martin's Press, 1996. An excellent history of this horror phenomenon, from 1950s comic book, to its films, TV series, and merchandising.

Edwards, Ted. *X-Files Confidential: The Unauthorized X-Philes Compendium*. Boston: Little, Brown, 1996, 1997.

Everson, William K. *Classics of the Horror Film*. Secaucus, NJ: Citadel Press, 1974. By my late horror film teacher at NYU.

Fenton, Harvey, and David Flint (eds.). *Ten Years of Terror: British Horror Films of the 1970s*. Surrey, England: FAB Press, 2001. The 1970s was a great decade for indie horror films, in the U.S. and in Britain. This is an excellent overview of Britain's post–Hammer horror film scene.

Film Maker's Guide to Super-8. New York: Sheptow Publishing, 1980. This book has no attribution other than "Compiled by the Editors of *Super-8 Filmaker* [sic] *Magazine*." An anthology of articles by various authors, reprinted from the 1970s magazine. *Super-8 Filmaker* changed its name to *Moving Image* in the early 1980s, hoping to please both the declining super–8 film market and the rising number of Beta and VHS videomakers. Super-8 filmmakers felt abandoned, and videomakers preferred magazines devoted exclusively to video. *Moving Image* folded within a year.

Gagne, Paul R. *The Zombies That Ate Pittsburgh: The Films of George A. Romero*. New York: Dodd, Mead, 1987.

Greaves, Tim. *Vampyres: A Tribute to the Ultimate in Erotic Horror Cinema*. Glen Carbon, IL: Draculina Publishing, 1996.

Handling, Piers (ed.). *The Shape of Rage: The Films of David Cronenberg*. New York: New York Zoetrope, 1983.

Hardy, Phil (ed.). *The Overlook Film Encyclopedia Horror*. Woodstock, NY: Overlook Press, 1986, 1993, 1994. Does a good job covering foreign language horror feature films, but it ignores horror TV movies, even American-made ones.

Hogan, David J. *Dark Romance: Sexuality in the Horror Film*. Jefferson, NC: McFarland, 1986.

Jones, Michael E. *Monsters from the Id: The Rise of Horror in Fiction and Film*. Dallas: Spence Publishing, 2000. Jones bucks mainstream academic thought, interpreting horror from a traditionalist Catholic perspective.

Katz, Ephraim. *The Film Encyclopedia*. New York: Crowell, 1979. I only own the 1st edition (1979). They're apparently up to a 6th edition (2008) from Collins Reference. The book is still credited to Katz, though he died in 1992.

King, Stephen. *Dance Macabre*. New York: Everest House, 1981. In this engaging non-fiction book, the best-selling horror novelist analyzes all things horror.

Krogh, Daniel, with John McCarty. *The Amazing Herschell Gordon Lewis and His World of Exploitation Films.* Albany, NY: FantaCo Enterprises, 1983.

Lovece, Frank. *The X-Files Declassified.* Secaucus, NJ: Citadel, 1996.

Lovecraft, Howard Phillips. *Supernatural Horror in Literature.* New York: Dover Publications, 1973. Highly influential work by an American horror master.

Lowry, Brian. *The Truth Is Out There: The Official Guide to the X-Files.* New York: HarperPrism, 1995. This first volume of *The Official Guide to the X-Files* covers seasons 1 and 2 of the TV series. Subsequent volumes cover one season each: *Trust No One* (vol. 2, season 3, also by Lowry, 1996), *I Want to Believe* (vol. 3, season 4, by Andy Meisler, 1998), *Resist or Serve* (vol. 4, season 5, by Meisler, 1999), *The End and the Beginning* (vol. 5, season 6, by Meisler, 2000), and *All Things* (vol. 6, season 7, by Marc Shapiro, 2001). Vols. 2 and 3 are also from HarperPrism; vol. 4 from HarperEntertainment; vol. 5 from HarperPerennial; vol. 6 from HarperCollins. Despite the changes in imprint, the books are similar in binding and appearance.

Lucanio, Patrick. *Them or Us: Archetypal Interpretations of Fifties Alien Invasion Films.* Bloomington: Indiana University Press, 1987. Lucanio argues that 1950s alien invasion films are science fiction, not horror. I disagree.

McCarty, John. *The Fearmakers: The Screen's Directorial Masters of Suspense and Terror.* New York: St. Martin's Press, 1994.

_____. *Splatter Movies.* Albany, NY: FantaCo Enterprises, 1981. McCarty has been credited with popularizing the term "splatter movie." St. Martin's Press released an expanded edition of *Splatter Movies* in 1984.

_____. *Official Splatter Movie Guide Volumes 1 and 2.* New York: St. Martin's Press, 1989 (Vol. 1) and 1992 (Vol. 2).

McDonagh, Maitland. *Broken Mirrors/Broken Minds: The Dark Dreams of Dario Argento.* New York: Citadel Press, 1991, 1994. Despite pre-dating *Mother of Tears* (2007), which completes Argento's "three sisters" film trilogy, McDonagh's book remains the best critical analysis of Argento's work that I know of. Intelligent and readable. I especially admire McDonagh's analysis of *Suspiria* as a fairy tale.

Muir, John Kenneth. *Horror Films of the 1970s.* Jefferson, NC: McFarland, 2002. America's answer to Fenton's *Ten Years of Terror: British Horror Films of the 1970s* (see above).

Naha, Ed. *The Films of Roger Corman: Brilliance on a Budget.* New York: Arco Publishing, 1982.

Paul, William. *Laughing Screaming: Modern Hollywood Horror & Comedy*, New York: Columbia University Press, 1994. Paul argues that the "gross out" is a film genre. I disagree.

Peary, Danny. *Cult Movies.* New York: Delacorte Press, 1981. Peary later wrote *Cult Movies 2* (1983) and *3* (1988), and *Cult Movie Stars* (1991). His clear prose (intelligent yet accessible) demonstrates how film criticism should read.

Rockoff, Adam. *Going to Pieces: The Rise and Fall of the Slasher Film, 1978 to 1986.* Jefferson, NC: McFarland, 2002. When I saw the execrable *April Fool's Day* in 1986, I knew that *now* the slasher film cycle was dead. Others had prematurely declared its death, but Rockoff correctly notes the cycle's end year — *and* that 1978 (the year of *Halloween*) was the cycle's start. Some people mistakenly think that *Friday the 13th* (1980) began the cycle. In short, Rockoff knows his subject.

Rodley, Chris (ed.), and David Cronenberg. *Cronenberg on Cronenberg.* London: Faber and Faber, 1992.

Schelde, Per. *Androids, Humanoids, and Other Science Fiction Monsters: Science and Soul in Science Fiction Films.* New York: New York University Press, 1993.

Schneider, Kirk J. *Horror and the Holy: Wisdom-Teachings of the Monster Tale.* Chicago: Open Court, 1993. Schneider bucks academic trends, focusing not on horror as a Freudian catharsis, or as socio-political commentary, but as metaphysical transcendence. Schneider is on to something.

Scott, Kathryn Leigh. *My Scrapbook Memories of Dark Shadows.* Los Angeles: Pomegranate Press, 1986. Former *Dark Shadows* actress Scott founded Pomegranate Press to publish this book. Through Pomegranate, she later published other *Dark Shadows* historical works, including *The Dark Shadows Companion: 25th Anniversary Collection* (1990), *Dark Shadows Almanac: 30th Anniversary Tribute* (1995), and *The Dark Shadows Movie Book* (1998). She's received cooperation from former cast and crew members, making Pomegranate the definitive *DS* history publisher.

Silver, Alain, and James Ursini. *The Vampire Film: From Nosferatu to Bram Stoker's Dracula.* New York: Limelight, 1993.

Skal, David J. *Death Makes a Holiday: A Cultural History of Halloween.* New York: Bloomsbury, 2002.

_____. *The Monster Show: A Cultural History of Horror.* New York: W.W. Norton, 1993. A great introduction to horror for people who don't "get" horror.

Stephenson, Ralph, and Jean R. Debrix. *The Cinema as Art.* London: Penguin, 1969, 1974, 1976. This book on film aesthetics makes some good observations on the nature and purpose of art, whatever the medium. Penguin published a revised edition in 1990, by Ralph Stephenson and Guy Phelps.

Svehla, Gary J., and Susan Svehla (eds.) *Cinematic Hauntings.* Baltimore: Midnight Marquee Press, 1996. Essays mostly on ghost films.

Tjersland, Todd. *Sex, Shocks and Sadism! An A–Z Guide to Erotic and Unusual Horror Films Available on Video!* Olympia, WA: Threat Theatre International, 1996. More a catalog than a book. Very un–PC, yet it provides insight into what fans of "violent underground films" are watching.

Tohill, Cathal, and Pete Tombs. *Immoral Tales: Sex & Horror Cinema in Europe 1956–1984.* London: Primitive Press, 1994. An American edition was published by St. Martin's Griffin imprint (New York) in 1995.

Articles

Kaminski, David. "Want to Write a Screenplay or Make a Movie?: Read Comics!" *Student Filmmakers* December (2008).

Maslin, Janet. "Bloodbaths Debase Movies and Audiences." *The New York Times* (November 21, 1982). Maslin's slam on 1980s slasher films.

Pepperman, Richard D. "Editing Structure: Avoid Over-Cutting." *Student Filmmakers* July (2008).

Probst, Christopher. "The Devil Made Flesh." *American Cinematography* December (1999). An excellent overview of the technical and aesthetic aspects of *Lost Souls*'s (2000) cinematography. I found this article online. I assume it's also available on paper.

Rainey, Stephen Mark. "Monsters — Antedeluvian Horrors." *Horror* 9 (1997). Rainey argues that slashers and serial killers will not displace older, supernatural monsters in the public's imagination. The now defunct *Horror* magazine was published by Dark Regions Press.

Schweiger, Daniel. "Rachel Belofsky: Slashing and Screaming for the Love of Horror." *Venice* (October 2006). Screamfest L.A. film festival founder Belofsky discusses the appeal of horror.

Smith, Sid. "Horror's Roots — Writer Clive Barker on Good and Evil in the Modern World." *Chicago Tribune.* (May 23, 1993). I found this article cited at www.clivebarker.info/religion.html. You'll find much Barker information at that site.

Varjabedian, Saro. "Modern Cinematography: Recent Stylistic Trends in the Industry." *Student Filmmakers* May (2008).

Yaccarino, Michael Orlando. "An Interview with Actress Mary Maude." *Filmfax* 75–76 (Oct/Jan 2000). My favorite obscure English horror actress discusses her work in *The House That Screamed* (aka *La residencia,* Spanish 1969). Her brief horror career includes the hilariously bizarre *Crucible of Terror* (British 1971), the impossible to find *La muerte incierta* (aka *La morte incerta,* Spanish-Italian 1973), and a small role in Norman J. Warren's entertainingly gonzo *Terror* (British 1978).

Yonover, Neil S. "Beyond the Ear-Death Experience: Tech Experts Blame Helmers for Current Loudness Syndrome." *Daily Variety* (August 21, 1997). Things haven't improved since 1997. Film theaters are *too damn loud!* At a Shriekfest film festival screening in 2009, I was covering my ears, pining for ear plugs.

Index

Numbers in **_bold italics_** indicate pages with photographs.